The Story of the Royal Military Police

HRH The Duke of Gloucester at Inkerman Barracks, Woking on 23 July, 1947 after the 'Royal Prefix' Parade.

STANDING (*from left to right*): Lieut-Colonel C. Wortley, *DPM British Troops Austria*; Lieut-Colonel W. T. J. Rumsey, *DMP Northern Command*; Lieut-Colonel J. Taylor, *DPM Central Mediterranean Force*; Lieut-Colonel J. Innes, *DPM Western Command*; Lieut-Colonel C. D. M. Hutchins, *DPM Scottish Command*; Lieut-Colonel E. Fitzgerald, *DPM Northern Ireland District*; Major G. J. Clarke, *APM Northern Command Depot RMP*; Lieut-Colonel H. Purslow, *DPM HQ SIB*; Lieut-Colonel A. R. Forbes, *Commandant Depot & Training Establishment RMP*; Lieut-Colonel T. H. H. Grayson, *DPM London District*.

SEATED Brigadier R. A. Leeson, *Provost Marshal FARELF*; Major-General H. Murray, *Director of Personal Services, War Office*; General Sir Richard O'Connor, *Adjutant-General*; General HRH the Duke of Gloucester; Major-General I. D. Erskine, *Provost Marshal*; Colonel P. Godfrey-Faussett, *DPM PM's HQ*, *War Office*; Colonel H. V. McNally, *Provost Marshal BAOR*.

THE STORY OF THE

ROYAL MILITARY POLICE

Exemplo ducemus

BY

MAJOR A. V. LOVELL-KNIGHT

LEO COOPER · LONDON

First published in 1977 by
LEO COOPER LTD
196 Shaftesbury Avenue, London WC2H 8JL

ISBN 0 85052 222 6

Set in 11 pt Imprint type
Printed in Great Britain
by Ebenezer Baylis and Son Ltd
The Trinity Press, Worcester, and London

CONTENTS

PART III · OCCUPATION AND RECONSTRUCTION

PART IV · IMPERIAL POLICING

PART V · SPECIALIST ARMS AND FORMATIONS

PART VI · WINGS AND BRANCHES, DEPOTS AND CORPS ORGANIZATION

APPENDICES

MAPS

ILLUSTRATIONS

ACKNOWLEDGEMENTS

The photographs are reproduced with acknowledgement to—Gale and Polden Ltd: the Frontispiece; The Imperial War Museum: 2, 3, 4, 5, 6, 7, 8, 11, 12, 13, 17, 18, 19, 20, 21, 22, 23, 24, 28, 29, 30 and 40; R. Cossins: 10, 37 and 39; A. L. Mowforth: 14; The War Office: 34 and 41; Brigadier A. R. Forbes: 15; Major R. S. Warman: 42; Major D. F. G. Pringuer RMP: 55 and 56.

ALLIANCES

Royal Australian Corps of Military Police
Royal New Zealand Provost Corps
Corps of Military Police (Pakistan)
The Sri Lanka Corps of Military Police
Malaysian Military Police

FOREWORD

by General Sir Cecil Blacker
GCB, OBE, MC, ADC, GEN

To tell the story of the Corps of Royal Military Police it is necessary to cover the history of the British Army itself, for in all its campaigns, particularly in this century, the Military Policeman has been an indispensable and familiar figure. The task of bringing the Corps history up to date since the Second World War is thus a formidable one; worldwide commitments ranging from low-key Imperial Policing to full-scale war in Korea, often with several theatres operating simultaneously, have had to be covered in one consecutive narrative. This the author has achieved with marked success.

The history is a tribute to past and present RMP officers and men—and women, for the WRAC Provost has played an increasingly important part in recent years. The rôle of the Corps has always been demanding, and often as dangerous, though less newsworthy, as that of the fighting units, but it took the Northern Ireland emergency to make this fact more generally realized—and acknowledged by an impressive list of honours and awards.

The same qualities of—above all—professionalism, combined with alertness, good temper, bravery and selfless devotion to duty, which past members have displayed so magnificently in earlier campaigns and emergencies have laid the foundations of the Corps' performance in Northern Ireland, where at the time of writing a third of the RMP serve.

Here, working long hours under conditions of strain and often danger its members—some very young—continue to set the example to the rest of the Army which has throughout its history been the Corps' pride, and which is so well described in this book.

General
Colonel Commandant
Corps of Royal Military Police

PREFACE

The first attempt at compiling a history of the Military Police was by myself during the Second World War: published in 1943—*The History of the Office of the Provost Marshal and the Corps of Military Police*. The first part of that book was culled from the researches of Brigadier H. Bullock. The second part was abstracted from Corps Order Books and Records which were just about to be sent for salvage (now, fortunately, preserved in the RMP Museum) and enabled a factual account of the Corps history from 1855 to 1940 to be recorded.

In 1951 the late Major S. F. Crozier, a Provost officer in the Second World War and a well known and respected journalist of his day, then wrote *The History of the Corps of Royal Military Police*. This book opened with a condensed form of the 1943 publication leading into a very full account of RMP in all theatres and aspects of the Second World War, a very great task indeed.

In its turn, due to the limitations of space, that book has been condensed and now forms the earlier chapters, in point of time to 1945, of this present history, the primary object of which is to continue the story over the last thirty years. The emphasis is, therefore, on continuity. A detailed record of this most ancient service, whose origins extend back to the 14th century and beyond, would indeed take many volumes.

In the preface to his book Major Crozier referred to the work of many contributors and mentioned that to reduce their literary efforts to a common flatness would remove much of its essential character. Moreover, it is true that the words of a participant make much more interesting reading than those of an author concerned with style and grammatical perfection.

I have therefore endeavoured to follow Major Crozier's lead. I hope he would have approved of the result as, undoubtedly, had he been here, the task would have been his, not mine.

One, perhaps justifiable, criticism of the manuscript was the paucity of names mentioned. Rightly or wrongly, I have regarded the Corps history as a collective achievement. While one has a full appreciation of the direction of the staff officer, the leadership of the company commander, the drive of the warrant officer, and the fortitude of the NCO, they cannot all be mentioned. Moreover, such qualities were often displayed in circumstances that did not come to notice and many did not have the opportunity. At least I have avoided invidious comparison by silence. Names have been mentioned only where they directly contribute to the narrative.

Throughout the three books above mentioned there have been many contributors, too many to mention individually. I am grateful to them and trust they will find their reward in self-recognition.

Major Crozier did make specific acknowledgment to Brigadier Bassett F. G. Wilson who contributed much of the story of 21 Army Group from Normandy to the Elbe, and, in addition, revised his manuscript with meticulous care; and to Lieut-Colonel F. H. Elliott. To those I would add the names of Major (later Brigadier) R. Davenport from whose report the chapter on Korea is taken, Lieut-Colonel (later Brigadier) L. F. Richards for his account of Suez, and Major A. H. Bushell who specially prepared the chapter on Northern Ireland.

A direct link between the two books is to be found in the then Colonel, now the Reverend, Peter Godfrey-Faussett. To Major Crozier he was the Deputy Provost Marshal, War Office, who made his book possible. To me, he is the doyen of the Corps to whom I am indebted for advice and guidance.

Finally, it must be recorded that, in addition to writing the chapter on Regimental Headquarters and the RMP Association and all the appendices, in the selection of maps and illustrations and the final revision and checking of the manuscript and proofs, Major R. J. R. Whistler has borne the brunt of the whole administrative and business burden that alone has made this publication possible.

Grateful acknowledgment is made to the Imperial War Museum for their assistance in selecting, and permission to publish, many of the photographs used in this history.

L-K,
Ambergarth,
Milford, Surrey.
June, 1976.

INTRODUCTION

'You cannot have a good Army without a good police force within'
—NAPOLEON.

This book, being virtually a continuation of an earlier history, recounts the Second World War period and before only in condensed form. While operational training continues in Germany with NATO forces, the emphasis on military police duties, at least in so far as they appear in the public image, is their rôle in support of the civil power in Northern Ireland.

Therefore it may not be amiss to reflect upon the military policeman of 1940–1945 in order to appreciate his rôle in the 'Order-of-Battle' of the Second World War.

At its wartime peak the Corps of Military Police, in all its wings and branches, mustered some 36,000 men. On mobilization in 1939: barely 3,500. Why this vast expansion?

Not unnaturally the 'maintenance of discipline' rôle of the military police was not appreciated in all quarters. The 'Bloody Redcap' was still an object of abuse among certain sections of the soldiery. To put the matter in its proper perspective, it may be as well to point out that in 1940–41, at the time the nation stood alone facing imminent invasion, the number of soldiers struck off unit strength as absentees and deserters was 22,103. This represented 0·088 of the Army strength at that time.

This figure in itself speaks highly of the discipline of the Army as a whole and the loyal and conscientious attitude of the individual soldier. But, in fairness to the vast majority that stood to their posts and to the problems facing General Officers Commanding with long coastlines to defend, needing every man, to have something of the order of two divisions absent was a most serious matter. Provost were performing an essential duty.

As a point of interest, not necessarily attributable to CMP, the total number of court martial convictions from 1 September, 1939, to 31 August, 1945, was 210,029 (all offences at home and overseas). And the primary concern of military police is the prevention of crime.

In war, mobility is vital both in forward areas and on the lines of communication, not only to ensure that supplies and reinforcements keep coming forward but that redeployment, often involving vast cross-traffic flows across congested forward routes, is a calculated and immediate possibility. The military police task is to ensure the success of the plan by making it possible for the right troops to arrive at the right place at the right time in the right order and, moreover, in a fit condition to fight.

Perhaps the importance of military police control on the ground in battle can best be illustrated by quoting two examples from the experience of the enemy. In the *Rommel Papers* edited by Sir Basil Liddell Hart, Field-Marshal Rommel, recounting the withdrawal from El Alamein under the threat of the British follow-up and encirclement, describes

> '. . . the wild confusion on the coast road between Fuka and Mersa Matruh' and '. . . a vast column of vehicles, thirty to forty miles long, was jammed up this side of the Halfaya and Sollum passes, and the retreat over the hills which lay under continual RAF low-flying and bomber attack, was probably going to take a week. It was very unlikely that the enemy would grant us all that grace so I gave orders for movement through the passes to be speeded-up by co-opting large numbers of officers for traffic control duties'.

Elsewhere it has been recorded that, in fact, some seven hundred officers of field rank had to be used to bring some sort of order out of the chaos and to enforce traffic discipline.

Even then, it appeared the enemy still had not learnt the lesson for in the 'Battle of the Bulge', his last great effort in the Ardennes, the counter-offensive had fallen short by 18 December, 1944. After 11th Panzer Division had achieved its spectacular success across the Ourthe river Hitler made available to Field-Marshal von Rundstedt two divisions from the General Reserve for exploitation.

von Dietrich, commanding 6th Panzer Army, who had driven the wedge into the American lines with Colonel Peiper's SS Panzer Group (responsible for the Malmedy massacre), had four roads open to him for the advance westward: to the retaking of Antwerp and the cutting-off of 21 Army Group.

von Dietrich tried to push three other SS Panzer Groups through the gap in an area allotted to 5th Panzer Army. The whole attacking force became hopelessly bogged down. At one point Field-Marshal von Model personally helped direct traffic near St Vith and found General von

Manteuffel doing the same thing. (On the allied side of the line Brigadier-General Bruce C. Clarke was doing likewise.) So critical was the jam that Field-Marshal von Rundstedt on 21 December ordered two of von Dietrich's SS Panzer Groups to 5th Panzer Army to the south. The push had lost momentum. This failure to organize traffic control in very large part contributed to the frustration of von Manteuffel's dash to the Meuse and enabled the counter-offensive to be contained.

After the end of hostilities the next two decades of unsettled years saw the British Army involved in four major commitments. The rehabilitation of liberated countries, the occupation of enemy territory, the garrisoning of the Empire during the transition period in preparation for self-government and the minor wars that were to follow in the struggle to spread spheres of political and economic influence by confronting ideologies.

During this period it may perhaps be said that the Army 'had greatness thrust upon it' in tackling many most unenviable tasks, especially as at this time it was mainly composed of short service and National Service officers, non-commissioned officers and men. The Royal Military Police had their fair share of both the tasks and the personnel and certainly had many burdens, as well as a measure of greatness, thrust upon it.

The first and shortest phase was concerned with the immediate reconstitution of the liberated countries, in which RMP played an important part in the transitionary stages of re-establishing law and order and re-equipping and training indigenous police forces. During this phase the tasks that fell to all wings and branches of the Corps included the rehabilitation of refugees, the vast problem of displaced persons and the widespread crime that centred on the flourishing black market to which were attracted not only the natural indigenous criminal but large numbers of deserters from the allied armies whose stores were in great demand.

The occupation of enemy territory followed a similar pattern but was to last much longer though with, at first, a different attitude. Commencing with the rôle of victor, with imposed Military Government and non-fraternization, it gradually relaxed into friendly help, and finally in Germany, into allied co-operation.

In the occupied countries progress was one of relaxation and co-operation. Unfortunately, in Empire territory, the garrisons often found the reverse process. A welcome-back slowly but steadily turned into violent and treacherous opposition as the patience needed for self-determination was worn down by extremists and power-seekers. However, this was not always the case and much good was done in training local forces to take over responsibility for their own protection. Whichever way ran the course of events RMP wrote a praiseworthy chapter into their history as imperial policing terminated with independence for the many new countries which emerged in their own right.

Of the minor wars the most important was that in Korea.

Lest it be thought that in proportion to the scale of the respective wars the chapter on Korea seems long and details sections instead of strategic bounds, excuse is tendered that it was a unique war in modern history, comparable to the Protestant League against Catholic Spain, Europe against Napoleon. A war of West versus East, a war of ideologies. It was the first war to be waged under the United Nations banner and the first war in which the nations were not only united but, as far as the British Commonwealth was concerned, integrated. This unity and integration was to reach its fullness in the formation of 1st Commonwealth Division Provost Company on 28 July, 1951, as part of a United Nations force.

The period astride 1950 saw the Corps spread world-wide. On the South American Guiana coast, in Honduras and the Caribbean, across the Atlantic to Gibraltar, in France, Belgium, Holland, Germany and Berlin, Austria, Trieste, Malta, Cyprus, the Canal Zone of Egypt, West and East Africa, Aden, across Asia to Malaya, Singapore, Hong Kong, Korea and Japan. The gaps in between filled by Asian and African military police inheriting the RMPs' legacy in their own countries: virtually a 'White Belt round the world'.

The Regular Army was augmented by National Service and, in reserve, Territorial Army units composed of volunteers and ex-active list National Servicemen, 'Z' reservists, later to become the Supplementary Reserve, and then the Army Emergency Reserve. In the various reserve categories all the wartime wings and branches other than Traffic Control were kept alive; Airborne, Beach Provost, Vulnerable Points, SIB, Ports and, in the Regular Army, Dogs and Military Mounted Police, to which was to be added Signals as part of normal company strength.

The decade that followed was to see the rundown of the Army as a whole, including RMP.

As this history concludes, however, as undesirable as the circumstances giving rise to the necessity may be, an expansion of the Corps once again took place.

In Northern Ireland the RMP story is much the same as this history records in Alexandria, in Cyprus, in Aden and Singapore and in many other places. A familiar feature of terrorist campaigns, wherever Security Forces have had to support law and order, has been the intimidation—even liquidation—of witnesses, thus frustrating the rules of evidence and undermining the proper procedures by which the Courts enable justice being seen to be done.

In riots the professional agitator throws his brick or fires his shot from behind the screen of the incited mob—often composed of children against whom retaliation is impossible. The answer to this is the infantry 'Snatch Squad'. The soldiers making the arrest may be a continent distant by the time the trial comes to court. The military police 'Arrest Teams' provide an answer to this problem by taking into custody the 'snatched' prisoner, taking on-the-spot statements supported by eye-witness accounts and photographic records of the incident. The Courts can then depend on reliable evidence and qualified testimony presented in a professional manner. Acquittals, through lack of evidence, become replaced by convictions.

Equally valuable are WRAC Provost to deal with women and children who may well be carrying the terrorists' weapons.

As the rôle changes, so do methods and techniques, but the tasks and targets are the same as are the hazards and the qualities needed to perform the duties.

Though the organization may have changed—sections and companies becoming regiments, it is still, basically, a pair of NCOs patrolling friendly and 'no-go' areas alike to help, advise, control, to observe and report. To maintain order. Their most effective weapon—'Example'.

'The test of a good police force is the absence of disorder: not the visible means of its repression' (Charles Reith, *Police principles and the problem of war*).

PART I

From the Curia Regis to 1939

CHAPTER I

Origins and Development to 1914

DURING the reigns of the Norman and Angevin kings the country was governed by the Royal Court, the Curia Regis, composed of feudal Tenants-in-Chief, the Barons. One of the Inner Courts was the Court of Chivalry presided over by two officers of the Household, The Lord High Constable and the Earl Marshal.

The Earl Marshal's duties were to marshal the Army and to ensure that the Barons fulfilled their obligations to the King in times of war, issuing writs of Summons to ensure attendance at Court and enforcing the King's Peace within military assemblies and discipline in the field.

This particular side of his duties was carried out by one of his executive officers, the Provost Marshal. The Provost Marshal was concerned to check doubtful loyalties and prevent internal quarrels between the Barons likely to prejudice the Royal interest and authority; therefore he had to be of known allegiance and was appointed personally by the King.

The office and duties were in existence in the twelfth and thirteenth centuries, and in the fourteenth it became apparent that such an officer was on the customary establishment of field forces and is known to have exercised his duties in the first expeditionary force of King Edward III. It is evident that he functioned at Crécy and Agincourt and in the fifteenth century had under him a form of camp police referred to as Tipstaves and Under-Provosts as is born out by references to an already existing organization in the first decade of the sixteenth century when we hear of Provost Marshals claiming on point of precedence their entitlements to personal status and personnel for their provost companies.

The Lord High Constable (now Master of the Horse) and the Earl Marshal no longer having a military function, the Provost Marshal is now the most ancient military officer under the Crown and his 'Under Provosts' the forebears of the Royal Military Police.

In the port of Plymouth in May, 1511, there mustered an expedition against the Moors of Barbary under command of Lord Darcie, the King's Captain-General. Among his subordinate officers was a Provost Marshal, Henry Guylford, 'a lusty young man and well-beloved of the King'.

He was a busy official and had plenty of work from the moment the expedition arrived in port, for the soldiers, we are told,

> 'fell to drinking hote wynes and were scarce masters of them selfes. Some ran to the stewes, some broke hegges, and spoyled orchardes and wyneyardes and orynges before they were ripe and did many other outragious dedes; wherefore the chefe of the tourne of Caleys* came to complaine to the Lord Darcie in hys shippe, whiche sent forth his Provost Marshal which scarcelie with payne refrayned the yomen archers, they were so hote and wilfull, yet by commaundement and policie, they were all brought on borde their shippes.'

Guylford was not the first Provost Marshal but he is the first of whom any personal record has been found.

In 1547 the Provost Marshal was Sir James Wylford, who is recorded as setting up a gallows in the market-place in Newcastle for the hanging of a soldier for quarrelling and fighting.

Two years later Sir Anthony Kingston was appointed Provost Marshal to deal with the West Country rebels. His grim humour was in keeping with the nature of his work. There is a story of a miller who, having been out with the rebels, feared reprisals and persuaded a servant to take his place and name. This man was arrested by the Provost Marshal. 'Are you the miller?' asked Kingston.

'If you please, yes,' was the reply.

'Up with him,' said the Provost Marshal to his assistants. 'He is a busy knave, hang him up.'

The unfortunate man protested in vain that he was no miller but an honest servant.

'Then thou art a double false knave,' said the Provost Marshal, 'to be false in two tales; therefore hang him up'.

The Mayor of Bodmin was associated with the rebels but, unlike the miller, he did not fear reprisals, relying upon the influence of friends and a bold face. Kingston visited Bodmin and sent the Mayor a notice that he would dine with him, adding that he had a man to hang, too, and a stout gallows should be made ready. The dinner was eaten and the gallows afterwards inspected.

* Cadiz.

'Think you,' said Kingston, 'is it stout enough?'

'Yes, sir,' replied the Mayor, 'it is of a surety.'

'Well, then,' replied the Provost Marshal, 'get you up, for it is for you.' The Mayor protested.

'Sir,' said Kingston, 'there is no remedy. You have been a busy rebel and this is appointed for your reward.' And so, 'without respite or stay', the Mayor was hanged.

The ruthless Kingston was succeeded by men of milder temperament. Barnaby Googe, who was appointed Provost Marshal in Ireland in 1582, was only paid £40 a year, exclusive of rations, perquisites and free quarters but, in keeping with the custom of the times, he had other perquisites such as charge of the Marshal's gaol, worth some £20 a year, and the custody of hostages, usually the sons of Irish chieftains, surrendered as a surety for their fathers' good behaviour. From them he hoped to secure about £100 a year but he was disappointed for, as he himself records, he drew not a penny. Poor Googe also complained that the Queen had, contrary to all precedent, failed to provide him with any regular soldiers to accompany him and that he therefore had to employ a local bodyguard for his protection.

'These,' he reported, 'are commonly more given to extortion than the Englishman is. Neither can I, since they serve without pay, use whatever means I can, restrain them of their evil demeanour: besides, serving altogether with such kind of companions I am always in danger to have my throat cut amongst them.' As a result of these complaints he seems to have been allowed at least a dozen horsemen. Finally, thoroughly disillusioned, Googe applied in 1585 to be allowed to dispose of the patent of his office to a 'gentleman of good discretion' having five and twenty horsemen from Connaught under his command. The 'gentleman of good discretion' offered Googe £100 for the office.

The year of the Armada was a busy one for the Provost Marshal, Captain Peter Crisp. The Queen's orders, issued to the Lord Lieutenants of the counties in 1588, contained instructions not unlike those issued to the police in England in 1940 when invasion was expected:

> '. . . and because in such doubtful times it falleth out commonly that divers false rumours are given forth and spread abroad, which do distract the minds of the people and breed confusion, it is thought very requisite that a care should be had thereof, and that the authors of such rumours and tales should be diligently and speedily punished.'

Crisp, and subordinate Provost Marshals appointed in each county, were charged with the duty of punishing the rumour-mongers.

Henry VIII is said to have been the first person to lay down specific duties for his Provost Marshal. These rules, contained in the Articles of

War, bear a remarkable resemblance to the duties of a provost officer in the field today. The Provost Marshal's duties included: laying out the boundaries and divisions of the camp; marking a market place and streets and setting a place of honour in the Field for the Lieutenant-General; seeing that no tent was pitched within 20 feet of the camp perimeter; posting all sentries himself, giving them their orders and the watchword, inspecting them two or three times in a night; and ensuring that all the men in the camp were quiet.

To assist him he had a company of tipstaves, to keep good order, prevent brawling and fighting and to arrest offenders who were punished at his discretion.

A reference to the grimmer side of the Provost Marshal's duties is contained in *A Pathway to Military Practice* by Barnaby Rich, published in 1587:

> 'The Provost Marshal is to have charge of the Marshalsea; he must be provided of fetters, gyves, handlocks and all manner of irons for the safe keepings of such prisoners as shall be committed to his keeping. He is to see due execution of all malefactors having received sentence of death, and to apprehend the authors of any disorders.'

A detailed description of the Provost Marshal, and especially his more grim activities is given by Francis Markham in his *Five Decades of Epistles of Warre* published in 1622. This included:

> 'For the nature of his office he is first the greatest and principal gaoler of the Army, having power to detain and keep prisoner whosoever shall be committed unto him by lawful authority, and though some contemptuously have called him the Hangman or Executioner of the Army, yet it is not so but as our Sheriff's of Counties are bound to find slaves for such needful uses; so he by his place is obliged to find men and other implements for all such occasions and to that end hath allowance for many attendants to dispatch any execution how suddenly soever commanded and to that end it is not lawful for the Under-Provosts to go at any time without halters, withs, or strangling cords of match, ever about them.
>
> 'The Provost Marshal hath the charge of all manner of tortures, as gyves, shackles, bolts, chains, belbowes, manacles, whips and the like and may by his ministers use them, either in the case of judgment or commandments from a Martial Court or otherwise upon unruliness at his own discretion; he is by his officers to see all places of execution prepared and furnished with engines fitting to the judgment, whether it be gallows, gibets, scaffolds, pillories, stocks or strappadoes, or any other engine which is set up for terror and affright to such as behold it.'

The first Provost Marshal of the Army, as distinct from the Provost Marshal who was an officer of State, was appointed in 1643 to the Royalist Army (the commission read 'Provost Martial General of all the Forces in England'). The post became permanent in 1685. Although at this date Provost Marshals became Army officers, they were still appointed personally by the Sovereign.

Deputy Provost Marshals were appointed from 1663 onwards and Assistant Provost Marshals are first mentioned in 1809. During the early stages of the Peninsular War, police duties within the Army were carried out by Provost Marshals, helped by their Assistant Provost Marshals. These were non-commissioned and this custom seems to have survived into the eighteen-eighties.

The Army in the Peninsula was notoriously ill-disciplined and the Provost Marshal's staff was hopelessly inadequate to cope with the situation.

Moreover, recent changes in military law had considerably reduced the summary powers of Commanding Officers, had reduced the severity of punishments and introduced a new constitution of and for Courts Martial bringing them into line with the Rules of Evidence established in the civil Criminal Courts of Justice.

Wellington, both frustrated and exasperated, wrote in bitter terms to Viscount Castlereagh from Abrantes on 17 June, 1809: complaining of the behaviour of the soldiers and suggesting an expansion of provost numbers and powers:

> 'There ought to be in the British Army a regular provost establishment of which a proportion should be attached to every army sent abroad.
>
> 'The authority and duties of the provost ought, in some manner, to be recognized by law. By the custom of British Armies, the provost has been in the habit of punishing on the spot (even with death, under the orders of the Commander-in-Chief) soldiers found in the act of disobedience of orders, of plunder or of outrage. There is no authority for this practice excepting custom, which I conceive would hardly warrant it; and yet I declare that I do not know in what manner the army is to be commanded at all, unless the practice is not only continued but an additional number of provosts appointed.'

The letter had some effect, at least as far as Provost were concerned for Wellington made a considerable increase in his provost establishment and in April, 1810 he drew up the following orders for his Provost Marshals:

> 'The Commander of the Forces is concerned to observe that the power of the Assistants of the Provost Marshal of the Army had, in more than one instance, been abused; and that officers have thought themselves authorized to send orders to the Assistant Provosts, under which abuses have been committed, contrary to the established usages and rules of the service, and the intentions and orders of the Commander of the Forces

'The Office of the Provost Marshal has existed in all British Armies in the Field. His particular duties are to take charge of the prisoners confined for offences of a general description; to preserve good order and discipline; to prevent breaches of both by the soldiers and followers of the Army, by his presence at those places in which either are likely to be committed; and if necessary he has, by constant usage in all Armies, the power to punish those whom he may find in the act of committing breaches of order and discipline.

'The authority of the Provost Marshal to punish must be limited by the necessity of the case; and whatever may be the crime of which a soldier may be guilty, the Provost Marshal has not the power of inflicting summary punishment unless he should see him in the act of doing it. If he should not see the soldier in the act of committing the offence of which he may have been found guilty, a report must be made to the Commander-in-Chief of the Army, who would give such orders as might be deemed expedient, either for further enquiry, for the trial of the soldier or for infliction of summary punishment according to the nature of the case, the degree of evidence of the soldier's guilt and the existing necessity for an immediate example.

'The Commander of the Forces desires that it may be clearly understood that no officer whatever has a right to order the Provost Marshal or his assistants to exercise the authority entrusted to them; nor can the Provost Marshal or his assistants inflict corporal punishment on any man excepting they should see him in the act of committing a Breach of Orders and Discipline. Their duty is, by vigilance and activity, to prevent those breaches which the Commander of the Force is sorry to observe are too common and to punish those they catch in the Act.'

The Duke's exhortations, however, proved of little avail and desertion and crime continued on a scale beyond the control of the Assistant Provosts.

A scheme to combat this state of affairs was suggested in January, 1813, in a letter from the Duke of York, Commander-in-Chief, to the Secretary of War. A new establishment was to be found without delay and at the same time the problem of finding orderlies (normally found by taking men from the cavalry regiments) was to be eased by combining this duty with the work of the new unit. Four troops were to be formed, two in the United Kingdom and two in the Peninsula.

The Secretary of State for War had sent a copy of the Duke of York's letter to the Duke of Wellington in Spain stating that this police corps should be charged with the duties which were understood to be executed in the French Army by their *Maréchaussée*. Following a letter from the Prince Regent in March, 1813, the Staff Corps of Cavalry was raised in April, 1813, by the General Orders of 13 March and 21 April. The Commandant was Colonel Sir George Scovell. At the end of the

Peninsular campaign the Corps was disbanded on 25 September, 1814, but the return of Napoleon saw the Corps being re-raised; commissions being dated 10 August, 1815, once again under Sir George Scovell, the original commander. The two new troops ranked in precedence between the cavalry and the foot guards and served at Waterloo. In January, 1816, the establishment was increased to four troops and they appear to have been engaged in the occupation of France. The final disbandment is dated 24 December, 1818.

After the Napoleonic wars the Provost Marshal played no outstanding part in military affairs. The appointment became that of a junior or semi-retired officer, but during the remainder of the nineteenth century several important changes took place, including the abolition in 1829 of the office of the Provost Marshal General. The senior provost officer was then the Provost Marshal and those provost officers attached to garrisons and field formations were known as 'Assistant Provosts', though non-commissioned.

Queen's Regulations for 1844 recognized the status of the Provost Marshal and laid down that 'the officer appointed to act as Provost Marshal of the Army is to rank as Captain in the Army' and emphasized that 'the appointment is one of great responsibility and requires the utmost vigilance and activity'.

Section 74 of the Army Act of 1879 expressly forbad any Provost Marshal to inflict any punishment on his own authority and from that date Provost Marshals lost their powers of summary punishment.

One fallacy connected with the origin of the Corps of Military Police is that it was born in 1877 and that there was no military police force in the Army between the Napoleonic wars and this date. This presumably arose out of the fact that military police were not shown in the Army List, but this was because military policemen were shown on the muster rolls of the regiments to which they had originally belonged and the name of the Corps did not appear in their pay books.

During these years men from various units who volunteered for police duty were sent to the Provost Marshal at Aldershot for instruction and to be equipped. The force, however, was a small one and insufficient to police the whole Army. Aldershot itself was always policed by these qualified military policemen but at the other stations discipline was maintained by garrison police, reinforced by regimental picquets. If occasion so demanded, a posse of military police would be detached from Aldershot.

This small force also found the staff for detention barracks but the men employed on this service became specialized and gradually broke away so that they eventually became a military prison staff. They are now known as the Military Provost Staff Corps and they still perform that part of the Provost Marshal's traditional duties as 'chief gaoler in the Army'.

In 1855 the Provost Marshal, in putting forward his recommendations for additional men, said he wanted good 'policemen'. This term was unknown in military circles and gave the impression that it was proposed to start a new service rather than augment and reorganize an existing one, and the War Office, in a letter to officers commanding cavalry regiments, referred to the formation of a Corps of Mounted Police for the Cantonment of Aldershot and asked for a return of NCOs and men for this duty. They were to be men of not less than five years' service, if of ten so much the better, of sober habits, intelligent, active and capable of exercising a sound discretion. This development was the beginning of the existing organization of the Corps of Military Police.

Further correspondence at about this time between the War Office and the General at Aldershot showed that reliable NCOs and men were being transferred in increasing numbers to the Military Police. It was then, too, that corps pay—1s 6d for sergeants and 1s for privates—was first granted.

It had been customary for some years for sergeants of the provost service to be appointed Assistant Provost Marshals, and in 1855 there transferred to the Military Police a cavalry NCO, Troop Sergeant-Major T. Trout. In 1861 he was commissioned (an exceptional case) as Provost Marshal. Although the appointment was to be an 'exceptional case' it seems to have acted as a precedent as the four next Provost Marshals, Captain W. Silk (1881), Major C. Broackes (1885), Major J. L. Emerson (1894) and Major J. W. M. Wood (1898) all appear to have risen from the ranks of the military police to be Provost Marshal and Commandant of the Corps. It was Major Broackes' wife who it is said, selected the red cap-cover subsequently worn by all military police.

The Military Mounted Police became established as a distinct Corps for service at home and abroad on 1 August, 1877 with the establishment of one sergeant-major, seven sergeants, thirteen corporals, fifty-four privates and seventy-one horses. From this date the Corps maintained its own muster and pay rolls and all promotions were within the Corps. By this time Military Police were again serving on detachment in garrisons at home and with formations overseas and on 16 September, 1877, one sergeant, one corporal and six lance-corporals were dispatched to Portsmouth and one corporal and five lance-corporals to Shorncliffe, Dover, to form permanent detachments for duty in those garrisons.

Military Police were permanently stationed in Cairo after 14 September, 1882. They accompanied Sir Garnet Wolseley's expedition which landed at Alexandria on 15 August, 1882. In the RMP Museum at Chichester, together with other similar medals awarded to members of the corps, is a medal for the Egyptian Campaign, dated 1882, awarded to No. 1300 A. Gould, Military Mounted Police, with bars for Tel-el-Kebir (13 September, 1882), Suakin 1884 and El-Teb (29 February, 1884); and in the casualty record it is noted that No. 75 Cpl J. Howie was wounded in action in the Battle of El-Teb. No. 113 Sergeant-Major J. L. Burke took a detachment to accompany the Nile Expeditionary Force in September, 1884.

It was during the Egyptian War of 1882 and for service in Egypt that the Corps of Military Foot Police (MFP) was raised. It was formed on 1 August of that year from NCOs and men recalled to the Colours who had served with the London Metropolitan Police during their period of reserve service. They did not, however, become a permanent corps or serve at home for another three years.

In 1885 the Corps of Military Police began to expand. It now became divided into the Military Mounted Police (MMP) and the Military Foot Police (MFP) each with their own promotion rosters but in other respects one corps consisting of 263 NCOs. Detachments of MFP were stationed at Aldershot, Colchester, Dover, Shorncliffe, Chatham, Woolwich, Portsmouth, Gosport and Devonport.

Up to this time there has been no mention of officers within the Corps, other than the Provost Marshal. In 1889 the question was raised with the War Office by Mr. J. L. Emerson, a future Provost Marshal, but at that time just appointed Quartermaster and acting as Assistant Provost Marshal at the Curragh who asked: '. . . I would be much obliged if you will inform me if I am to consider myself an officer of the M.M. Police or as a Quartermaster in the Army belonging to no specific Corps.'

The War Office replied that 'Quartermaster and Hon. Lieutenant J. L. Emerson is to consider himself as a Quartermaster in the Army, his pay being provided for as such, and not as an officer of the Military Mounted Police.'

Emerson put up a vigorous fight and eventually the War Office agreed that 'Quartermaster Emerson was gazetted a Quartermaster in the Army, but it has been decided that he shall be considered as belonging to the Military Mounted Police and he will be so shown in future in the Official Army List.'

So was set the precedent for Quartermasters of the CMP to be the only officers commissioned within the Corps, a situation which lasted until 15 May, 1954, as far as Regular officers were concerned.

In June, 1892, the War Office ordered that all promotions to and above the rank of sergeant in both MMP and MFP should be made in future within the Corps and the Provost Marshal, as the Officer Commanding, was instructed to prepare and maintain seniority rolls of each Corps.

On the outbreak of the South African War in October, 1899 the military police were posted as follows: twelve MMP and twelve MFP to GHQ, twelve MMP to cavalry divisions, twenty MFP to infantry divisions, and detachments of about sixteen MFP on lines of communication.

In 1900 the APM and all the military police in Egypt were drafted to South Africa. Three provost NCOs were awarded Distinguished Conduct Medals and QM and Hon. Captain C. Burroughs MMP and six NCOs were Mentioned in Despatches for their services between 1899 and 1902 in South Africa. The three DCMs were the first awarded to members of the Corps (Corporal F. Jones MFP, Corporal A. H. Northeast MMP and Colour Sergeant G. S. Gale MFP).

From the earliest times the Provost Marshal and his assistants had been maintaining discipline in the King's forces. When regiments which claim to be among the oldest units in the Army were not born, before indeed there was any standing army at all, the coming of the Provost Marshal and his troop behind him was feared by the law-breaker, the deserter and the drunkard, and respected by the good soldier.

In the Napoleonic wars, in South Africa and in campaigns elsewhere the military police had shown that they could maintain the proud traditions of the oldest service in the Army in war as well as in peace; but war of a new kind was on the way, war which would develop and expand the police service of the Army, thrust new duties upon it and pave the way for the transformation of tasks, personnel, equipment and organization of the Corps in the twentieth century.

CHAPTER II

The First World War, 1914–1918 and Post-War, 1918–1939

THE FIRST WORLD WAR

At the outbreak of war the strength of the Corps of Military Police, mounted and foot, was three officers, a Provost Marshal (Commandant) at Aldershot, Assistant Provost Marshals (APMs) at the Curragh and Tidworth and 508 warrant officers, NCOs and men available for duty in the United Kingdom and overseas garrisons.

On mobilization the strength of the Corps was increased by 253 reservists, many of whom had been civil policemen, making a total of 761. To meet the urgent need for recruits the Corps was thrown open to direct enlistment and many old soldiers enlisted. But the expansion of the Corps could not keep pace with the rate at which the Army was growing and it was necessary to transfer certain units *en bloc* to the Military Police.

During the First World War military police served in France and Flanders, Gallipoli, Mesopotamia, Macedonia, Palestine, Egypt, Italy, North Russia, North-West Persia and Afghanistan. Formations proceeding overseas had an APM and small establishments of military police at the HQ of corps and divisions. These were looked upon as useful for security duties at HQ of the formation and in some cases were made available for duties as orderlies or grooms. No consideration had been given before the war to the duties involved in the new kind of operations, nor did any manual of regulations furnish a guide to provost duties in the field. Officers who suddenly found themselves saddled with the appointment of APM had to rely on their wits and do what they felt to be right—often in the face of strenuous opposition and orders countermanded by staff officers who wished to use the police as orderlies.

On landing in France the duty on which there was general agreement was the necessity for providing security patrols at formation headquarters and this was given to provost. Unfortunately, a precedent was established which was to die hard; and, as every military policeman knows today, this improper use of police is a problem to every provost staff officer and military police unit.

One of the first legitimate tasks that fell to the lot of provost to perform was the control of stragglers, which presented itself during the retreat from Mons. The military police, reinforced by cavalry as required, collected and brought in many hundreds of exhausted men who would have fallen into the hands of the advancing Germans. It was remarkable how these men responded to the encouragement of the police, who adopted various methods; in some cases an emergency ration, in others a few minutes' drill or singing; in a few extreme cases, threats.

It soon became recognized that wastage of manpower, arms and ammunition, could be prevented by the military police manning stragglers' posts, collecting stations and what in those days were called 'battle-stops' immediately behind the front line. The wounded were directed to first-aid posts, their weapons and ammunition being retained and, at intervals, returned to forward units. Stragglers might be either genuinely lost men or men in a state of temporary fright but not intentional deserters. These were collected into groups, fed, rearmed if necessary and sent back. In this way units received a constant supply of manpower and ammunition, which on more than one occasion just tipped the balance in necessary strength at a vital moment.

During one enemy attack military police manning stragglers' posts held, defeated, captured and disarmed over 800 Germans who had overrun our front line.

Several NCOs at the battle-stops were decorated for their valuable work. In one instance the front line gave way but the NCOs organized their stragglers into defensive positions and held on. This enabled the front line troops to use the posts as rallying points and reorganize with the result that the line was held.

The need for control of traffic and clearance of roads had become apparent during the early days of the retreat when thousands of refugees had to be turned off the roads daily to enable the troops to march. Many a heart-rending situation had to be dealt with by the police, who could show no sympathy for the frightened civil population. But planned traffic control was hardly appreciated in those early days and the police in every brigade were expected to clear a way for their own formation.

The control of one-way traffic during the retreat proved simple compared with the difficulties which arose when the advance began and the Battles of the Marne and Aisne were fought, when arrangements had to be made for forward and rearward movement, for supply and ammunition lorries and for the evacuation of the wounded as well as the tactical movement of troops. Strict police control was essential as nearly every commander, however small his unit, was convinced that he should be given priority.

As static warfare developed after the Battle of the Aisne so traffic control difficulties increased, and the early days of the first Battle of Ypres presented an entirely new problem.

This was solved partly through the introduction of traffic circuits by Colonel Marker, a senior staff officer who was killed a few weeks later, and partly by trained military police supervision.

Night after night military police, reinforced by other troops where necessary were on duty in rear of the trenches at road junctions, frequently under shell-fire, sorting and directing traffic not only of different formations but of different nationalities. Without the efficient performance of this duty, relief of troops, provision of supplies and ammunition and the evacuation of sick and wounded could not have been completed during the hours of darkness.

Traffic control was gradually becoming one of the most important duties of the military police and during 1915 was brought to a high pitch of efficiency. It proved invaluable when any special attack was launched. The first time that traffic control by military police was employed to any extent in the battlefield was at Neuve Chapelle in 1915. Ammunition and supply circuits were worked out which resulted in lorries doing the distance in forty minutes less time than before. Posts were put out and all civilian traffic stopped at 3 am, which ensured a clear run for transport and avoided the ditching of lorries in attempting to pass farm wagons. This was also the first occasion on which organized stragglers' posts were maintained with supplies of food and facilities for returning stragglers.

It was soon recognized by Commanders and their staffs how largely the success of any operation depended upon freedom of movement in rear of the actual fighting, and from that time the importance of the work of the military police was more generally appreciated and traffic control companies were organized.

During the struggle for the Somme in 1918 traffic control personnel manned the bridges over the Somme for thirty-six hours under continuous heavy shell-fire and not one man left his post until all the fighting troops were across. They then fell back and were the last over. In one case a man was blown over the bridge into the river twice in a few hours by shell-fire but climbed back to carry on with his duty of getting the traffic through. These men were later called upon to fill a breach in the line.

The duties of the provost service in the British Expeditionary Force (BEF) in France and Flanders were many and varied. Besides stragglers' posts and the ever-increasing traffic control duties they embraced: detection of crime and the arrest of offenders, custody of POWs; control of civilians and their protection against violence by soldiers or camp followers; the shooting of dogs found unattended near the forward lines and search of the bodies for messages; seizure of carrier pigeons.

Brigadier-General H. S. Rogers, who started his war service as a division APM and became Provost Marshal BEF, left on record an account of the activities of the Provost Marshal in the First World War, which he introduced with a quotation from Napoleon. 'You cannot have a good army without a good police force within.' He recommended that 'every high Commander should insist on seeing his senior provost officer frequently, because on him depends to a very large extent the prevention of crime and the prevention of disease which go a long way to keeping an army fit for action.'

But the military police also had their front-line duties and the following account of a day in the life of an APM and his division provost company can be regarded as typical:

In an attack it was necessary for provost to be well up in order that they should be the first to get hold of civilians in captured villages and round up hidden enemy agents. During the Battle of Hermies, at dawn of the day of attack, the APM with twelve military police, took up his position behind a hill. As the attack was put in they moved in with the fighting troops and were actually in the village before the assaulting troops had finally captured it.

The police immediately set to work on a house-to-house comb-out for civilians and hidden agents, then took over all POWs, thus saving the necessity of escorts. They made the prisoners carry back our wounded and consequently by 8 am the battlefield was entirely cleared of prisoners and wounded. The returning escort was able to guide reinforcements and thus avoid a German machine-gun which they had located, and was then able to send back and direct the wagons of the Royal Engineers which had come up for bridging and other services.

They picqueted wells which, according to Intelligence officers, had been poisoned.

The APM was back almost immediately after the battle, reporting in person to the GOC what had happened, the number of prisoners taken, etc. For this he was awarded the DSO.

375 men from the Corps of Military Police lost their lives during the

War, 144 from the Military Mounted Police and 231 from the Military Foot Police and 13 Distinguished Service Orders, 8 Military Crosses, 65 Distinguished Conduct Medals, 260 Military Medals, 26 Meritorious Service Medals and 105 Mentions in Despatches were awarded to members of the Corps, including provost officers, between 1914 and 1918. The Adjutant-General, BEF, wrote this letter to the Provost Marshal in 1918:

> 'The Field-Marshal Commander-in-Chief has expressed his satisfaction with the work of the Corps of Military Police . . . He congratulates you on the efficiency of your organization and wishes you to convey to your PMs and APMs and those serving under them, his appreciation of the manner in which they have discharged their duties and stood to their posts. The orderliness which has prevailed behind the front is directly attributed to their efficiency and devotion.'

The Commander-in-Chief in his final despatch said this of the Corps:

> 'In the battle zone, where frequently they had to do duty in exposed positions under heavy fire and suffered severe casualties, the military police solved an important part of the problem of traffic control by preventing the unavoidable congestion of troops and transport on roads in the vicinity of active operations from degenerating into confusion. In back areas their vigilance and zeal have largely contributed to the good relations maintained between our troops and the civilian population.'

POST-WAR: 1918–1939

On 1 December, 1918, British troops marched into Germany. The 1st Cavalry Division entered the Rhine Province near Malmédy, accompanied by their normal complement of MMP. A military policeman was actually the first British soldier to cross the Rhine, motor-cycling across the *Hohenzollernbrücke* and talking to the German sentry on the farther side.

The difficulties of the military police at once began. Precautions against treachery on the part of the enemy inhabitants had to be taken and the inhabitants themselves as well as their property had to be protected against the natural desire for reprisal which was felt by every British soldier who had marched through devastated Belgium.

The immediate difficulty encountered on crossing the frontier was the lack of interpreters but the posting-up of proclamations to the inhabitants by the first provost officer to enter each village greatly eased the subsequent work of the military police.

The actual strength of provost in the Field at the cessation of hostilities on 11 November, 1918 was 5,000 all ranks.

However, there were still many tasks for the military police after the Armistice, and they served in the North Russian Campaign of 1918–19 involving a heterogeneous force of allies supporting White Russians against the Bolsheviks; Constantinople; and between 1919 and 1922 in Ireland, where their work was onerous, exacting and unpleasant. Much of the Army at home was sent to the Irish Command in connection with what Sein Fein called 'war' and the British Government 'disorder'. They remained until 15 January, 1922 when the Irish Free State came into being.

On 27 February, 1926, the Military Mounted Police and the Military Foot Police were merged into one corps, under the title of the 'Corps of Military Police' with the establishment (after the disbandment of the British Army of the Rhine) of 508 all ranks, conforming to the pre-war strength in August, 1914.

In 1927 the first self-contained and self-administered provost company for a specific purpose overseas was formed to accompany the Shanghai Defence Force.

No very great interest was shown in the Corps for a decade following the post-war run-down until, in 1931, the annual Army manœuvres showed up the effect of mechanization and it became apparent that the speed of movement required the co-ordination of provost into field Formations and under an officer's direction. As a result eighteen officers were selected to attend a course on traffic control in February, 1933 and in the manœuvres of the following year a movement exercise was carried out and given great prominence. The selected officers practised their rôle successfully, were ear-marked for provost duties on mobilization and returned to their units.

As a result of a War Office review, in 1935 the Corps was organized into companies and sections and mechanized with a total strength of 500 Other Ranks, sixty-seven horses (riding) plus three horses for officers. Permanent Military Police Stations then became:

United Kingdom (including Depot and School of Instruction)	346 Other Ranks;
and overseas in Egypt (Cairo, Abbassia, Moascar and Alexandria)	three companies

and sections in Malta, Gibraltar and China (Shanghai) and companies in Hong Kong and Singapore with a total strength of 154 Other Ranks.

(See Appendices 6 and 7 for details.)

As the Second World War approached in February, 1939, a provost company was allotted to each Territorial Army division which then gave an overall strength for the Corps of:

1 King George V with the Prince of Wales talking to a Military Policeman at Béthune on 11 August, 1916.

2 The Battle of the Ancre: prisoners being brought in near Mailly by Military Mounted Police on 22 November, 1916.

3 *The Dom Hotel Cologne, Headquarters of the APM, 1919. A Military Policeman on duty outside.*

4 *Major R. W. Maude, APM Cologne and formerly APM Amiens, with his RSM and NCOs in Cologne on 6 March, 1919.*

5 Three DAPMs lunching in Schlebusch on 30 April, 1919.

6 The Commander-in-Chief, Army of the Rhine, inspecting the Cologne Military Mounted Police on 7 June, 1919.

7 The Commander-in-Chief, Army of the Rhine, inspecting the Cologne Military Foot Police on 7 June, 1919.

8 Military Police in Cologne leaving their quarters in 1919 to go on a raid.

Regular Army	769
'A', 'B' and 'D' Reservists	500
Supplementary Reservists (Automobile Association patrols)	850
Territorial Army	1,002
Guards Reservists	500
Civil Police and Ex-CMP Reservists	500
	4,121

This provided an effective strength on mobilization of approximately 3,000. The Corps was about to demonstrate both the vital nature of their work in the new form of mechanized warfare and their ability to adapt rapidly and flexibly to changing and demanding conditions.

PART II

The Second World War 1939–1945

CHAPTER III

The British Expeditionary Force (BEF)

THE provost component of the first contingent of the field force, which formed on the outbreak of war and later went to France as part of the BEF, consisted of Nos 1, 2, 5, 6 and 7 Provost Companies and No 8 HQ Provost Company, mobilized at the Depot, and Nos 3 and 4 Provost Companies mobilized at Bulford and London respectively.

Field formation companies were allotted to army, corps, division and lines of communication and were, at that time, and with the exception of the latter, on a standard establishment consisting of a company headquarters and six sections, all fully mechanized.

On arrival in France the military police were immediately confronted with much vaster problems of traffic control than ever before. The road movement forward from the disembarkation ports was the largest ever undertaken with motor transport by the British Army. The late E. A. Montague, correspondent of the *Manchester Guardian*, described in a despatch on October, 1939, the part the military police played in it:

'Visitors to the Aldershot Tattoo may hardly have noticed the military policemen who have shepherded them so efficiently round the right corner and into the right car park. These same men have carried out equally unobtrusively in the last few weeks a far bigger traffic job with brilliant success. They have steered and signalled the British Army across France.

'In cold figures, some 720 men of the Corps of Military Police have brought 25,000 vehicles many miles across country which they themselves had never seen until the day before the operation began and they did so without any block or hold-up or serious inconvenience to the normal French traffic. Never at any time did the driver of a vehicle have to open a map; his way had been marked for him by signs and military police at cross-roads.

'To each section of police was allotted a stretch of about fifty miles of road, to which it went on the day before the march began, explored its ground, stuck up its signs and posted its human traffic controls. With the aid of its *gendarmes* it had to make itself known to the local French authorities and arrange common problems with them. In other words, it had to act for itself, and if it had acted wrongly no amount of good organization higher up would have saved the general movement of the Army from being blocked, perhaps seriously.'

During the period of inactivity of the BEF in France and Flanders, police duties were similar to those at home with the additional responsibility of maintaining cordial relations with the French civilians—relations liable to be frayed by bad behaviour on the part of British troops. Brothels also had to be kept under surveillance. Liaison with the French police was quickly established and the CMP became the symbol of fair play to the British soldier and French citizen alike.

Pilfering of stores at the ports in France and in transit reached such alarming proportions that in December, 1939, the Home Office sent a Scotland Yard Chief Inspector to France to investigate and he recommended that the military police should be augmented and given a CID of its own. The first detachment of the Special Investigation Branch (SIB) arrived in France on 29 February, 1940.

Towards the end of March, at the Provost Marshal's request, Colonel J. Seymour Mellor, Chief Constable of the War Department Constabulary (WDC) visited France to make recommendations for the policing of docks, entrance-guarding, passes, etc. Colonel Mellor recommended an increase in the numbers of SIB sections.

With the opening of the enemy offensive on 10 May the BEF moved forward to the River Dyle.

The 12th Lancers crossed the frontier on their dash to the Dyle; and following them, and some six hours ahead of the main body, came the military police. They had to find and sign the routes and lay down a system of traffic control and the main body was able to move forward over a routing system signed right through to their positions.

Then down these routes broke a tide of refugees in farm wagons and high-speed cars, on cycles and on foot, converging on the main routes from every junction and track, and making them useless for military movements.

Almost before the military police had completed their task of freeing the roads of refugees they were called upon to undertake an even more exacting task—the evacuation of the British Army from the Continent.

Everywhere in France and Belgium policemen were standing unrelieved at cross-roads while the armies rushed back to escape the closing German pincers. When the last vehicles had passed him the 'Redcap' would discard his white traffic sleeves, take a rifle and join the infantry covering the retirement. At Arras, for example, a section under command of Corporal Lucas, armed with Bren guns and anti-tank rifles, helped to man the defences in front of the town, Corporal Lucas recalls:

> 'By this time I had managed to get all my men armed, mostly with rifles, for which there seemed to be a scarcity of ammunition. However, by stripping the dead and picking up odd stuff lying about each man soon had a hundred rounds or so.
>
> 'We were actively engaged from about 1330 to 2000 hours, mostly with enemy motor cyclists, light tanks and infantry. Enemy planes, of course, were over all the time. About 1400 hours a group of tanks came forward, but a CSM of an infantry unit who was with us scored two direct hits with an anti-tank rifle on the leading one. Our gunners then got direct on the target, knocked out two, and the others withdrew.
>
> 'This sort of thing, interspersed with infantry attacks, kept on spasmodically up to about 7 pm, by which time I had lost five of my men. Then a lone motor-cycle combination approached. I waited until it got within 200 yards and then let go a magazine out of the Bren. It must have killed all three Jerries outright but the machine kept turning round and round in the road before it went into the ditch.'

At Dunkirk the British Army was assembling to embark for England. Weary, hungry, constantly harried by German fighters, the exhausted troops gained confidence from the unmoved 'Redcaps' directing traffic and men in Dunkirk and on the beach. One corporal, after five NCOs of his section had been killed, removed the white sleeves from his dead predecessor and, still wearing his service dress cap and red cap-cover, maintained a vital post at a cross-roads for twelve hours until all the British troops had passed through. The city around him was burning. He was the last soldier to leave it. As he did so he collected his traffic signs so that they should not act as pointers to the enemy.

On the beaches the military police achieved their highest peak of service and self-sacrifice. One after another, as divisions arrived at the beach, their own provost companies saw them embark and then fell out, staying back to assist others. They acted as marshals to the waiting queues, recovered thousands of pounds' worth of arms and equipment, organized the evacuation of wounded, and acted as messengers. As a last duty they carried the wounded on board before sailing for England.

The last boat to leave the beaches before General Alexander's final inspection about midnight on Sunday, 2 June, contained many military police, but many there were whose bodies marked the site of their duty.

Military policemen also accompanied the Calais force. Towards the end their main function was as anti-fifth-column patrols. In twos and threes, armed only with revolvers, they undertook a complete search of the city, rounding up and disposing of the legion of snipers who were shooting at British troops from the rear. Many an unseen fight to the death took place in garret and cellar in Calais between an MP and a sniper.

Finally, after all communications were cut, two volunteers were called for to carry a message from the encircled city to Dunkirk. Two CMP corporals undertook the duty. One was killed, but the other, Corporal Illingsworth, completed his task. When he last saw the remainder of his comrades they were forming themselves into an infantry platoon to reinforce the Rifle Brigade in the line.

The provost service gained much in experience during the short campaign in France and Belgium. Two things were clear. One was that military police could no longer be regarded as base troops who would never be in contact with the enemy and the other that traffic control in a modern war demanded more men than the existing provost service could supply.

CHAPTER IV

At Home

BY the end of June, 1940 the soldiers of the British Expeditionary Force were back in the United Kingdom but practically all transport, equipment, ammunition and stores were lost. Holland, Belgium and France had capitulated; Russia and the United States were neutral; Britain stood alone.

In the United Kingdom were a certain number of mobilized divisions and corps and many new ones forming; thousands of men were passing through infantry and other training centres; military camps and new HQs were springing up everywhere and there was activity in planning and preparing coastal and inland defences against the expected invasion. But in June, 1940, we were practically defenceless against invasion.

The lightning German campaign through Holland, Belgium and France had illustrated the appalling dangers of the refugee problem. In France we had seen thousands of refugees driven ahead of the German forces to mask thc fire of the defending armies. We had also seen vast French armies virtually immobilized by roads blocked by the civilian refugees. In Britain the possibility of a repetition produced a military traffic control problem of the first importance; in addition all road signs and place names in the United Kingdom had been removed for security reasons. This added to the difficulties of controlling and organizing our own military traffic routes. The need to solve these problems was to lead to the formation of the CMP Traffic Control Wing in July, 1940.

The Army as a whole did not, at this stage of the war, appreciate either the difficulties or scope of the operational rôle which traffic control in modern mechanized warfare was to cast upon the provost service. This lack of understanding was to prove an obstruction to the operational development of the use of military police in the early days. Further it was to lead to misuse of the military police on duties for which they were not designed, a habit which took a long time to eradicate.

For a long period during the war the status of most provost officers was below that of officers of other important services, which put provost officers at a disadvantage in conference as it caused a loss of weight in argument.

From the start it was clear that manpower was to be a difficult problem. It was soon found that too many 'A' category men were employed guarding depots, dumps, installations, HQs, etc. The double need to release all fit men from these duties and to enable them to be carried out with fewer men was to lead to the formation of the CMP Vulnerable Points (VP) Wing in February, 1941.

The arrival in Southern Command of Dominion troops and, later in 1942, of American forces, at first increased the burden for provost until the respective Dominion and Allied provost contingents became operative. Friction occasionally resulted and the duty of the military police was to prevent incidents and endeavour to keep relationships as amicable as possible.

The London 'Redcap' undeniably had a more interesting job than many of his less fortunate comrades hidden away in comparative backwaters. Just as the London 'Bobby' has rightfully earned for himself a reputation for reliability, so did the London military policeman come to be regarded as a fair if firm disciplinarian on the London streets.

From a 1939 establishment of three officers and 116 other ranks the London District Provost Company increased steadily until, in June, 1945, its complement was 598 other ranks controlled by a DPM, 5 APMs, 2 DAPMs, 1 APM (VP) and 1 DAPM (VP). The following extract from a letter written by a retired colonel to the Editor of *The Times* is a tribute to the London 'Redcap':

'There must be many ex-officers like myself who served in their Regular Army as far back as forty years ago and who have observed wth great pleasure the remarkable improvement in the conduct of the troops, especially in such places as railway stations, trains, restaurants, cafés and public houses, etc, where large numbers congregate from time to time.

'I should like to pay tribute to a particular branch of the services which I feel has played a most important part in helping to maintain this remarkable display of general good conduct. It is one of which little is heard and is known as the Corps of Military Police. The Provost Marshal and his assistants have without doubt inculcated a remarkable spirit of 'first-aid' in the military police. There is a striking resemblance in this corps to the London 'Bobby', who has a reputation of being, first and foremost, always helpful. I have watched the military police carrying out their duties in railway stations and other places. They appear to be imbued with the spirit of helpfulness and advice rather than seeking for offenders. I recently watched two of them examining leave passes at one of the London railway stations and could not help but notice the friendly spirit in which they stopped troops for the inspection of their passes and in returning the passes to them often gave advice regarding such matters as the buttoning up of coats or the wearing of hats at the correct angle, etc. A smile on both sides and the soldier buttoned up his coat and walked off. I am sure there must be many others who have observed the work of the military police and who can testify to the same effect. The absence of military offences in the Army today is due to many reasons, but the Corps of Military Police can certainly be credited with their share of minimizing offences outside barracks and camps.'

During the defence period there was the greatest activity in Northern Ireland, for not only had precautions to be taken against IRA activity but a field force had to be mounted to advance into Eire in case of a landing there by the Germans. In this plan the military police played an important part. On receipt of information that the Germans were about to invade Eire the Border between Southern and Northern Ireland was to be closed and the Army concentrated upon it before advancing upon the Germans, with the possible approval and assistance of the Eire Army.

The military police forces in Northern Ireland at this time were comparatively larger than those in the rest of the United Kingdom. Corps and each of the three divisions had their own provost company. In addition there was a Command provost company in Belfast and an Army company at HQ British Troops Northern Ireland.

The provost resources at the DPM's disposal were increased by one of the newly-formed Traffic Control (TC) Groups (three companies) which was sent over to Ireland to assist in the movement of the British forces south if invasion took place. The IRA gave no serious trouble but from time to time their activities were a problem to the traffic control companies. When controlling an exercise or other road movement the traffic control patrols would put out signs and arrows, but within an hour the signs would either be turned round or would be missing altogether. The culprits were never caught but the traffic companies had to change their method of signing. A red powder dye was produced by a local chemist and placed in small paper bags. A truck would be loaded with these bags and to indicate a direction round a corner an NCO would throw out one or two bags which left a red streak in the direction required. This successfully foiled the IRA's activities. On the whole the IRA had a healthy respect for the military policeman and although shots were quite often exchanged with members of the Royal Ulster Constabulary, the 'Redcap' patrols remained unmolested.

As the new armies were formed commanders were apprehensive that the colossal intake of civilian recruits little amenable to Army discipline would cause a major problem. On the whole their fears were not realized, as men who were called up to the colours joined up with a sense of urgency and defiance of the enemy and readily accepted military dress, routine and discipline.

During this early period military exercises were usually defensive, often rehearsing the withdrawal from a prepared defensive position to a switchline or vice versa.

The police of at least one division provost company were the only troops a commander could call on to defend his HQ in the event of an attack by parachutists. An NCO of one of these companies has described those early days:

'We were a mixed lot of NCOs, racing motor-cyclists and ex-civil policemen, mostly, with a few regulars. Some of us knew all there was to know about how to get the best out of our motor-cycles and others all about the laws of evidence and the Larceny Act, but I can't say that many of us had much idea of military discipline. Between the Company we had four red cap-covers. These were allotted to the men on the division HQ gate. Town patrols just did without. Soon after Dunkirk when the invasion scare was at its height we were issued with revolvers and six rounds of ammunition. There weren't any holsters and we went around with our pistols, old-fashioned 45s, stuck in our belts like pirates. Most days, sometimes several times a day, we were called out to defend division HQ from imaginary parachutists.'

Towards the end of 1940, owing to shortage of officers, DAPMs (captains) were struck off the War Establishment of corps HQ and APMs corps (majors) were left to cope alone. This was, operationally, a retrograde step; especially as the new CMP TC Wing, having just been formed, the chances of the provost service asserting their influence and attaining full executive responsibility for the employment of this wing became even more remote. Moreover, in February, 1941, the second big addition to CMP strength was made by the formation of the Vulnerable Points Wing.

Brigadier Sir Percy Laurie, upon his appointment as Provost Marshal, had the task of organizing and expanding the SIB, the TC and VP Wings and throughout his three years of office the whole provost service grew rapidly from a total provost strength of 194 officers and 8,350 other ranks on 17 July, 1940 to 553 officers and 32,000 other ranks on his retirement on 25 July, 1943.

On 22 June, 1941, the Germans invaded Russia; on 7 December, after the attack by Japan at Pearl Harbor the United States entered the war as our active ally. Within a short time American troops in vast numbers began to pour into Northern Ireland on their way to various areas in Great Britain for training and formation. The first contingents of US troops were accompanied by MP companies, some of which had received little police training.

In Londonderry disorders between US marines and British sailors were frequent—too often British soldiers joined in to support their naval comrades. Eventually a picked detachment of military police under the command of a staff lieutenant, all of them big men and ex-civil policemen, was sent to Londonderry. In a few weeks' time, with the help of the Royal Ulster Constabulary and other Service police, they had suppressed the worst disorders and arrested the trouble-makers, but it was not until the arrival of the United States Marines Shore Patrol that really effective measures were taken against the obstreperous US troops. Within a short time an effective system of combined patrols (one British and one US military policeman) was introduced throughout the United Kingdom.

The Provost Marshal, War Office, was granted the local rank of major-general in 1942. This was a step in the right direction, followed in May by the upgrading to APMs (major) of DAPMs in divisions.

In preparation for operations against the Axis forces, 'Exercise Tiger' was staged in South-Eastern Command by Lieutenant-General B. L. Montgomery. It was of great interest to the provost service. 12 Corps and Canadian Corps were fighting. 12 Corps, which was the first to attack, carried out a large dumping programme, followed by a precipitous fighting advance, in the middle of which they were suddenly and unexpectedly ordered by the Director to withdraw. The rôles were immediately reversed, and 12 Corps had to conduct a fighting retirement at high speed, relentlessly pursued by Canadian Corps.

The exercise strained and tested to the full the traffic control arrangements of the corps and divisions. It was the first time that traffic control companies were employed in an exercise of this kind, one company being allotted to the APM of each of the competing corps.

The provost part of the report on 'Tiger' recognized that in modern warfare a corps could not function without the addition of a traffic control company to its normal military police resources and recommended the setting-up of a central corps traffic control plan, coordinated by APM corps, with firm links between corps and division areas of responsibility.

A Traffic Control Group consisting of six picked traffic control companies under command of Major Hart was detailed in 1942 for special training for the forthcoming operations with 1st Army in French North Africa. Each company was equipped with jeeps, which were to become part of the normal transport of all provost and traffic control companies.

Their task was one of great responsibility. Immediately after the first landings upon the beaches successive waves of craft would continue to arrive carrying troops, vehicles and stores. The task of the military police beach detachments was to get ashore in the early stages, organize and control the traffic routes for wheeled and tracked vehicles and walking personnel from the beaches into their respective transit areas, and thence on to the various assembly areas. These routes followed a key plan which was prepared from aerial photographs and other forms of reconnaissance.

There was also the important task of signing and controlling traffic circuits covering the ammunition and supply dumps, vehicle parks, field dressing stations, prisoner-of-war cages and other installations. Experience was to show that two military police sections without an officer were inadequate for this difficult task.

The build-up and preparation for the provost resources of 1st Army were completed by the end of the autumn, when the force embarked and left the United Kingdom. On 23 October the battle of El Alamein began and the 8th Army started to advance. On 8 November the Allied Forces, including 1st Army, landed in French North Africa at Casablanca, Oran and Algiers.

From the end of 1942 the preparation of the Second Front forces became the principal task to which everything else was subordinated. In the early stages the only guides to intelligent anticipation were that the forthcoming invasion involved an assault landing upon a number of beaches, the capture of a port or ports, two Ls of C each 250 miles long and an Order of Battle consisting of GHQ, two armies and a large L of C organization.

GHQ, Home Forces, was charged with the formation of the Order of Battle and raising, equipping and training the forces and units which it comprised. In February, 1943, a DPM, Home Forces was appointed to cover the provost side, which had hitherto had no direct representative.

The development of the military police machine had to be moulded upon a just mixture of lessons drawn partly from provost reports from overseas (particularly from 8th Army and 1st Army) and partly from large-scale assault and invasion exercises in the United Kingdom.

A continental assault was a fairly safe assumption; hence planning proceeded on the assumption of a landing and subsequent campaign in an enclosed country with all the complex traffic problems which a network of main roads, lanes, rivers, bridges, towns and villages would provide.

The preparation of the Second Front provost force was attended by many difficulties. Bids for officers and men had to be sustained against an ever-growing manpower problem and the natural reluctance of COs to part with good officers or NCOs, while bids for essential transport and equipment were made against the conflicting claims of other arms out of a pool insufficient to satisfy the needs of all.

Provost staff officers were still out-ranked by their opposite numbers in other services and consequently their voices in conference and biddings continued to suffer.

The first fortnight of March, 1943, was taken up with a great exercise called 'Spartan'. Two armies were in conflict. A British invading force, under the command of Lieutenant-General McNaughton, with a Canadian Army staff reinforced by some British staff officers, including a British 'Q' (Movements) staff, composed of British and Canadian troops who functioned along an L of C from Southampton to a line north of the Thames. This tested the operational and administrative traffic problems which arise from the capture of a port and swift penetration into an enclosed country. The other Army was based in the Eastern counties and represented the forces of an invaded enemy country.

The importance to the provost service of 'Spartan' cannot be over-emphasized. The confusion on the roads in the rear of the fighting formations showed the fundamental weaknesses of the existing traffic control system; but this time the lessons were learned and the sequel defined the practical and proper relationship between staff and military police and put the provost service in a position to carry out, on their own responsibility, the taxing operational rôle for which the development of modern mechanical warfare had cast them.

The important operation of marshalling and embarking the expeditionary force was one of great complexity for the military police. It involved the transport of troops and vehicles from all parts of the United Kingdom, their concentration in special areas where they could be finally briefed, the waterproofing of their vehicles and other final preparations. Then they had to be marshalled into boatloads, taken down to ports and 'hards' and embarked in small parties at short successive intervals.

The scheme was first considered and put into preliminary shape during the winter of 1942–43; its improvements and final perfecting remained a commitment of the first importance to DPMs, Command. One further step forward was now obtained by the reappointment of DAPMs on the staff of APMs corps.

On 22 July, 1943, 21 Army Group was formed and Lieut-Colonel Bassett F. G. Wilson, who had been DPM Home Forces, became Provost Marshal, 21 Army Group, with the rank of colonel; Major F. A. Stanley, his APM in Home Forces, became his DPM in 21 Army Group with the rank of lieut-colonel. Lieut-Colonel F. C. Drake was already DPM 2nd Army and Lieut-Colonel G. Ball had been appointed DPM 1st Canadian Army.

In July, 1943, shortly after 21 Army Group was formed, a big scale invasion exercise, 'Jantzen', took place in South Wales; the purpose was to test the whole assault machinery for a landing in force from the sea and the building-up and exploitation of a bridge-head and beach maintenance areas and sub-beach areas. It was, in fact, a full dress-rehearsal for the provost beach units.

In January, 1944, General Sir Bernard Montgomery took over command of 21 Army Group from General Paget and during the summer of 1944, as the invasion date approached, military police were responsible for sealing both marshalling camps in which the invasion troops were briefed and the hospitals to which casualties who had been briefed were sent.

As General Montgomery and his staff were in charge of the joint planning for both 21 Army Group and the American forces under General Bradley, American staff officers were attached to their opposite numbers in 21 Army Group to ensure proper co-ordination between British and American forces. Two American military police representatives, Lieut-Colonel Rudolph and Lieut-Colonel Phillips were accordingly attached to the staff of Provost Marshal, 21 Army Group, until shortly before the beginning of hostilities in June, 1944, they returned to their own armies.

All troops who were to take part in the initial assault were put through an intensive training upon prepared territory of the dimensions and containing as far as possible similar features of the area in which they would be operating after the assault. Nothing now remained to be done except to wait for D-Day and to hope that no vital steps had been missed out either in training or equipment.

In the latter days of May and the early days of June, 21 Army Group was fully mobilized and duly concentrated and assembled for embarkation. The provost and traffic control arrangements worked without a hitch.

An officer of a traffic control company responsible for the control of D-Day traffic wrote this account:

> 'Came D-Day and the vehicles, the tanks, jeeps, trucks, bulldozers, cranes, SP guns, all the assorted engines of war, moved forward to their embarkation points. The columns moved endlessly. The nights were filled with the grinding roar of tanks, the squeal of their tracks, the grumble of their engines. The darkness was punctured with the blue flames of their exhaust.
>
> 'At all critical points were the traffic control police and their auxiliaries, working all hours, leading convoys, pointing the way, marshalling vehicles, splitting up units into unit craft parties, building up unit craft parties into

craft serials, timing them, setting them on their way, calming the agitated, stimulating the laggard, always alert, always present.

'One can see them now, the sergeant with his clip of orders from Movement Control, working in the vehicle parks; the corporal at the telephone in his traffic post, counting the vehicles in each craft serial as it passes his point, endlessly and tirelessly; the officer in charge of marshalling in the embarkation area, ushering the serials into their boxes, holding back the thruster, chasing the laggard, calling each serial forward as the landing craft were made available; the DR on his motor-cycle, taking orders to a craft serial commander, rounding up a straggler, taking over point duty at a temporarily busy road junction.

'Not a vehicle was lost, not a serial was late, there was never a hold-up nor a delay which could be attributed to the fault of traffic control. By the end of July nearly 30,000 vehicles had passed through the marshalling area. Traffic control had handled them all.'

So ended the staff planning, organization and troop training for the invasion. For some eighteen months the task of forming and training this vast Expeditionary Force had been carried out with determination and despite the problems, there remained a conviction that elasticity had been preserved and that the mainsprings of this great fighting machine were so well tempered and tightly compressed that, once released, they would carry the British liberating armies irresistibly forward.

CHAPTER V

North Africa

WHILE preparations for the invasion of North West Europe were being made extensive fighting had been taking place in North Africa and the Mediterranean theatre. Before September, 1939, there was approximately one full regular provost company in Palestine and less than that in Egypt; there was no depot, all the administration being centred in Bab-el-Hadid Barracks in Cairo; there were few facilities for training men: in short, there was practically nothing.

At the outbreak of war little change occurred in CMP in the Middle East. Locally-based units provided a few volunteers, a few more trickled out from the United Kingdom and a few more officers joined the Corps.

Before the New Year, 1st Cavalry Division arrived in the Middle East without any military police and a company was formed for the division. Soon after this 4th Indian Division arrived. It was believed that the division was completely equipped as far as provost was concerned; a rude awakening took place on their arrival when it was found that practically all the personnel were untrained. So the British military police got down to it again, found some space somewhere in Bab-el-Hadid and instituted a series of training courses in all that a military policeman should know.

It was obvious that Italy would soon enter the war and that the aim of the Axis would be the capture of the Suez Canal, so provost were instructed to earmark personnel for a Western Desert Force. By this time a few reinforcements had arrived from home, a cadre was formed and went into preparatory training at Bab-el-Hadid.

Lieut-Colonel F. C. Bryant was promoted colonel soon after his arrival in 1940 and appointed the first Provost Marshal Middle East Forces (MEF). Then came reinforcements of officers and NCOs; but, in spite of this, for the first three years of the war Middle East provost

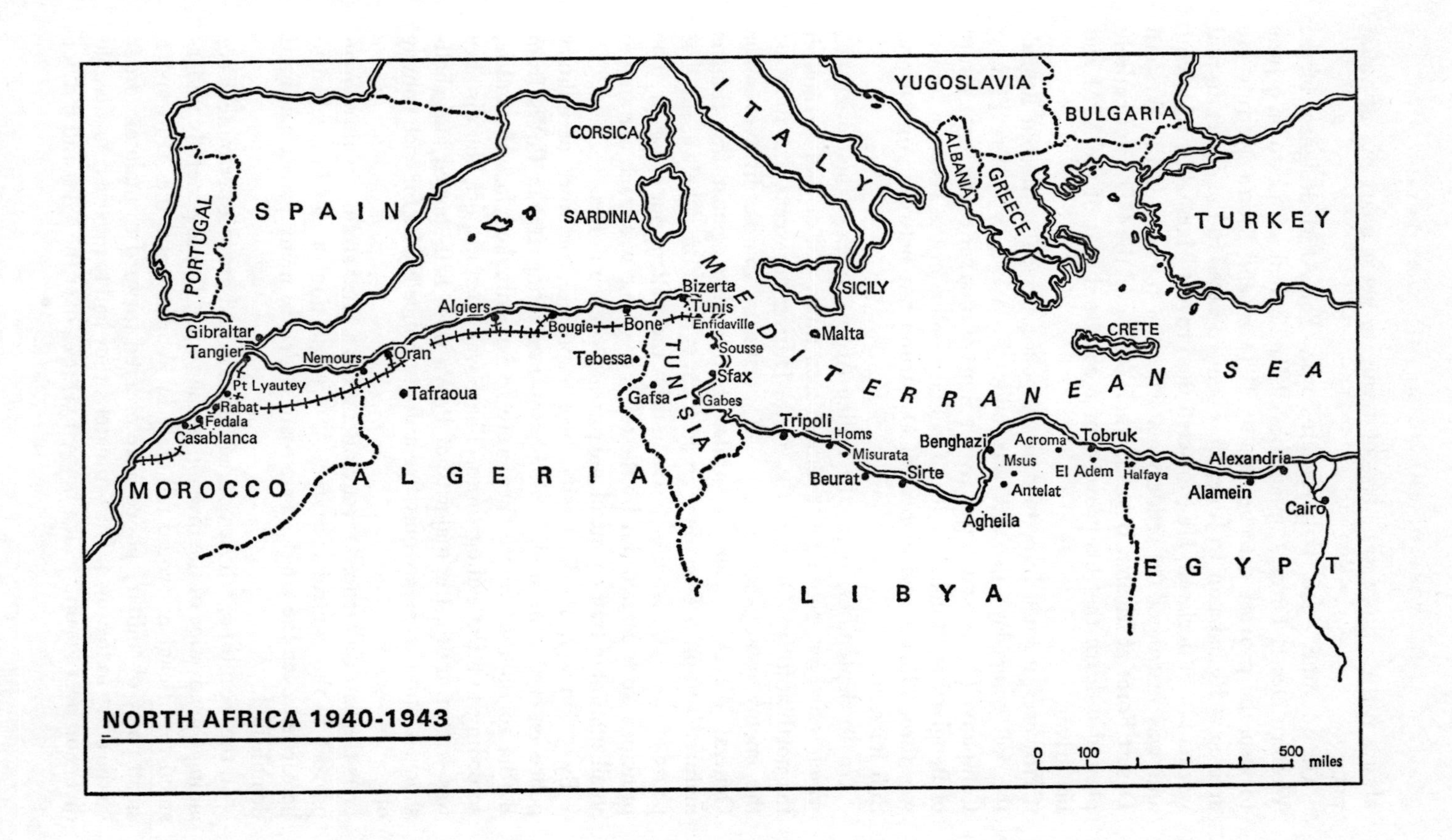

NORTH AFRICA 1940-1943

always had the impossible task of trying to get a quart out of a pint pot.

On 10 June, 1940, Italy declared war. The APM designate of the Western Desert Force, Captain Lovell-Payne, had left Cairo on 9 June to visit the provost detachments at El Daba and Mersa Matruh. He arrived at El Daba on 10 June, after being delayed in the desert, to find war had been declared. He contacted the Provost Marshal by telephone and was instructed to rendezvous with the nucleus of the Western Desert Force at Maaten Bagush, where he found the GOC not entirely pleased to learn that his provost force consisted only of the APM and his driver.

However, a small force of military police arrived at Maaten Bagush the following day; on this was built the Western Desert Provost Company. The company was always short of men: after the first capture of Benghazi the total strength of military police in the Western Desert was three officers and eighty NCOs strung out between Antelat and Sidi Barrani.

On 10 September, 1940, the Italian Army launched their offensive, which, however, petered out some fifteen miles east of Sidi Barrani in the north and Sidi Omar in the south. During the weeks that followed the enemy established a series of perimeter camps. In November General Wavell's plans for a British offensive against the Italians matured and on 9 December an attack was made on Nibeiwa, the first phase of the operation which was to drive the Italians out of Egypt. The principal work carried out by the military police was track marking, a small amount of traffic control and prisoners of war duties.

By 5 January, Bardia having been captured, the work of military police entered a most difficult phase—evacuating Italian PoWs from Bardia to Sollum, where they were to be embarked for Alexandria, according to strict sailing times. There was no transport, the distance was sixteen miles, the majority of PoWs were half-starved and shell-shocked, and there were only five military police NCOs for each convoy of 500 prisoners.

As the battle advanced towards Benghazi a great strain was thrown on provost in the control of traffic. A large portion of the forces had to be carried over the single coast road, which in many places had been demolished.

In the meantime, 7th Armoured Division and provost personnel were aiding the advance of the division in the south. It was generally understood that Benghazi would fall early in February and the APM and a small party of military police were ordered forward to maintain order on the entry to the town. Unfortunately, they had to make a considerable diversion over ground which bogged vehicles over the axles and did not arrive until the day after the capture of Benghazi, to find the usual state of chaos.

At this period no form of military control, such as Civil Affairs, existed and the APM was entrusted by the Sub-Area Commander with reorganizing the entire police system in Benghazi. Members of the *Carabinieri*, national police, Italian African police and municipal police were welded into a composite force which functioned fairly satisfactorily. Provost shared with the civil police the responsibility for running the fire brigade.

By drastic measures reasonable order was restored in the town and looting and drunkenness restricted, though on at least one occasion by unorthodox methods: the entire stock of a Benghazi brewery was removed and consumed one night by the guard unit responsible for the security of the premises and contents.

HQ, Western Desert Force, was at Maaten Bagush, divided into two parts about a mile apart. Rear HQ lived and worked in tents dug down in silvery sand and chalk close to a small bay. The APM was located here. Main HQ lived in tents on higher ground but worked in a network of underground offices free from sand-storms.

Towards the end of August, 1941, an army HQ, soon to be named 8th Army, was formed in Cairo, and in September, 1941, 8th Army HQ assumed command in the desert with Advanced HQ near railhead at Mischeifa. For the first few weeks, while 8th Army was still waiting for a provost company to be allotted, the DPM's task was difficult.

Railhead Sub-Area Commander had only a provost officer and one section, which was inadequate for the many duties, two of which had to take priority over all others, namely track marking and signing. Important duties at water points and prevention of pilfering had to be neglected.

Sand-storms meant additional work for provost and signal line maintenance parties between railhead and corps. In their anxiety to keep to the tracks in bad visibility, drivers used to go far too close to track signs and signal poles, usually with unfortunate results.

With the advent of the first offensive by 8th Army, railhead gradually became a hive of activity. Enemy air attack increased but the dummy railhead a short distance west of the real one came in for most attention. The dispersal of vehicles was an important function of provost at railhead forward maintenance centres and all HQs. Normally the plan was 'one bomb one vehicle' but when space was limited vehicles were parked in twos.

The advance of 8th Army was held up soon after crossing the frontier into Libya and provost detachments at the various gaps in the frontier wire and minefields had a very busy time. It was also necessary to institute forward provost patrols to prevent wanton pilfering of scarce and valuable instruments and fittings from knocked-out armoured fighting vehicles and crashed planes.

With the relief of Tobruk the town became the responsibility of 105 Provost Company. A strong detachment was located in one of the few remaining buildings intact overlooking the harbour, where because of the hazards of sunken ships, nearly all off-loading had to be done by lighter.

This handling of stores gave added opportunities for pilferers, but a rigorous security system helped to prevent losses, although it was not made easy by the frequent bombing raids. Traffic always presented a problem in Tobruk and vehicles frequently broke down on the twisting gradient above the harbour.

Plans were made for a further advance westwards and these included extending the railhead to Mechili and marking a track across the desert from El Adem to Msus. The task of marking this route was given to the DAPM Army, Captain Cashen, an officer with an almost uncanny knack of finding his way about in the 'blue'. The day after completing this task he set out over the route and found his way with little difficulty to HQ 13 Corps, a trip of some 250 miles over every conceivable type of desert. A few days later the German *Afrika Korps* started an offensive and advanced along this very route which Captain Cashen had so painstakingly marked the previous week.

By the end of January it was clear that the *Afrika Korps* attack had gained considerable impetus. Main Army HQ was at that time at Tmimi and, with the evacuation of Benghazi and then of Derna, orders were given at short notice for Main Army to move back once more to Tobruk. The move out of Benghazi by provost was well planned and they left their HQ scrupulously clean and tidy. Captain D. W. L. Melville, the DAPM, left a note in German on his desk saying that CMP had left their accommodation clean and would expect to find it left clean by the Germans when they returned.

The first few miles were very difficult indeed, the road narrow, gradients steep and corners sharp. When a vehicle caused an obstruction CMP put it over the side.

Another small detachment of 105 Provost Company, assisted by a few NCOs of a traffic section detached from the traffic organization in Cairo, had been controlling the exceedingly steep and hazardous Derna Pass. Some drivers could not face the descent and their vehicles were driven down by military police NCOs.

While all this was going on to the west, provost were fully employed along the L of C. Pilfering from trains and at railhead was a problem requiring continuous attention. At Christmas a lorry load of whisky, valued at several hundred pounds, had vanished. The DPM, therefore, issued instructions for a series of simultaneous raids to be carried out at selected points on receipt of a coded message. Large quantities of NAAFI and other stores were recovered after many hours of search and digging. One rubbish dump at railhead concealed wines, spirits, sweets, canned goods and even tooth-brushes.

It was hoped that once the *Afrika Korps* had been halted west of Tobruk it would be possible to launch another offensive. Towards the end of May, 1942, 8th Army was once more prepared to attack the *Afrika Korps* and the morale of the men was high. The Army Commander's plan was to let General Rommel attack and then fight him on ground of his own choosing. The tank battles which took place in the first week of June, however, resulted in heavy casualties for 8th Army's armour, which received rough handling from exceedingly well-concealed 88-mm guns. When it appeared that the battle was going badly, preparations were made to bring into operation a plan for further retirement. 105 Provost Company, already widely dispersed, was split up into fourteen detachments to control the coming rearward move. It was, however, watched, sorted out and controlled efficiently. After the Battle of Acroma the forward elements of 13 Corps began to retire via the bottle-neck between the Tobruk defences and Knightsbridge, the centre of the battle. APM, 13 Corps had no time to concentrate any large number of military police to control this narrow defile and progress through it was slow.

There was enough work for at least six provost companies but only the army company and two corps companies were available.

The stream of traffic along the Alexandria–Mena road seemed never-ending and every now and again a thoughtless driver would turn back in the face of on-coming traffic, with disastrous results as the sand on either side of this road was for the main part the soft, silvery kind in which a vehicle soon gets stuck. When possible the offending driver was ordered to drive into the sand where he ceased to be a nuisance to others for many hours.

Once the El Alamein line had been consolidated the situation became more static; Rommel had shot his bolt. By the end of the first week in July it was possible to set up an effective provost plan which worked with great efficiency until the final preparations for a further offensive made a change necessary.

A check post was set up at El Deir on the coast road about mid-way between El Alamein and Amiriya. Every vehicle was checked and personnel travelling eastwards had to satisfy the military police as to the authority for their journey. The police were ordered to shoot anybody failing to halt when challenged. An officer who deliberately forced his way through received a bullet in the shoulder.

One morning an Arab came to 105 Provost Company and indicated that there were some enemy soldiers hiding in an old tumbled-down house about a mile away. Only Captain Mandy, RSM Sims, a driver, one cook and a clerk were available. Captain Mandy and his driver set off with the Arab and found themselves facing twelve Italians armed with tommy-guns and grenades. After a staring match of some seconds, followed by a few words in Italian from Captain Mandy, the Italian party put down their arms and filed out into the open just as the RSM, company clerk, and cook arrived. The Italian officer said afterwards that the most frightening part of the whole operation was the drive to 105 Provost Company HQ with Captain Mandy at the wheel!

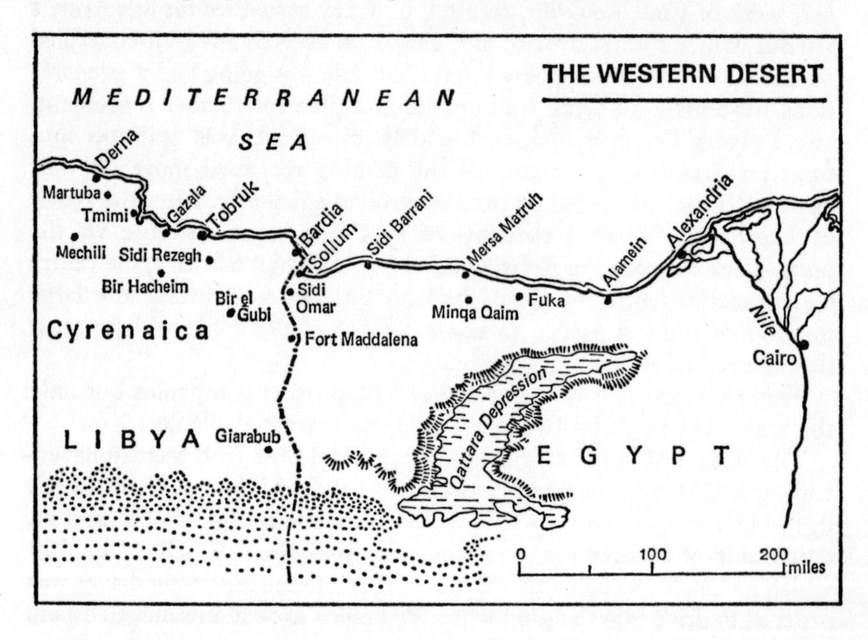

Throughout the first phase in the desert war, the military police had indertaken new rôles; they had worked side by side with combatant troops and by their efficient traffic control and discipline helped to produce an orderly retirement to the line of El Alamein. Fighting troops came to take a new and good view of the 'Redcaps'. Stragglers' posts and information posts were established, manned by two or three military policemen and the survivors, ranging from single stragglers to brigade columns, passed back to comparative rest and safety behind the wire. Practically all the men who had escaped from Gazala, west of the mine-field, many of them wounded, all of them exhausted and without water for days on end, were put on their way by the 'Redcaps' manning stragglers' posts.

9 A Military Policeman on traffic duty in Cherbourg, 1940.

10 A US Indian motor-cycle built for the French Army and diverted to the United Kingdom after Dunkirk. The rider is Lance-Corporal R. Cossins CMP near Lisburn in 1942; he later landed in Normandy on D-Day.

11 North Africa, 1942: a Military Policeman offering a German prisoner a cigarette. The other three prisoners are Italians—note the state of their clothing.

12 North Africa, 1943: Military Police NCOs preparing temporary road notice boards.

13 Military Police NCOs negotiating rough parts of the Western Desert in 1943.

14 Western Desert, 1943: CSM A. L. Mowforth, 151 Independent Brigade Group Provost Company, interrogating Italian prisoners.

15 Lance-Corporal Brown, 105 Provost Company at Tobruk using as his platform part of an Italian MTB.

16 Traffic control in Italy in 1945.

17 Sergeant Wilson CMP passing harmlessly through the trap which would normally cause severe injuries to the rider and has been known to decapitate its victims.

18 A CMP NCO removes German signs from a post near Aunay-sur-Odon after the British advance to the River Orne in 1944.

19 Manning this Information Post are Lance-Corporals F. Heward and G. Thompson at Villers Bocage, Normandy, 1944.

20 A lone Military Policeman on a motor-cycle takes some 400 prisoners back to a prisoner-of-war cage near Abbeville in 1944.

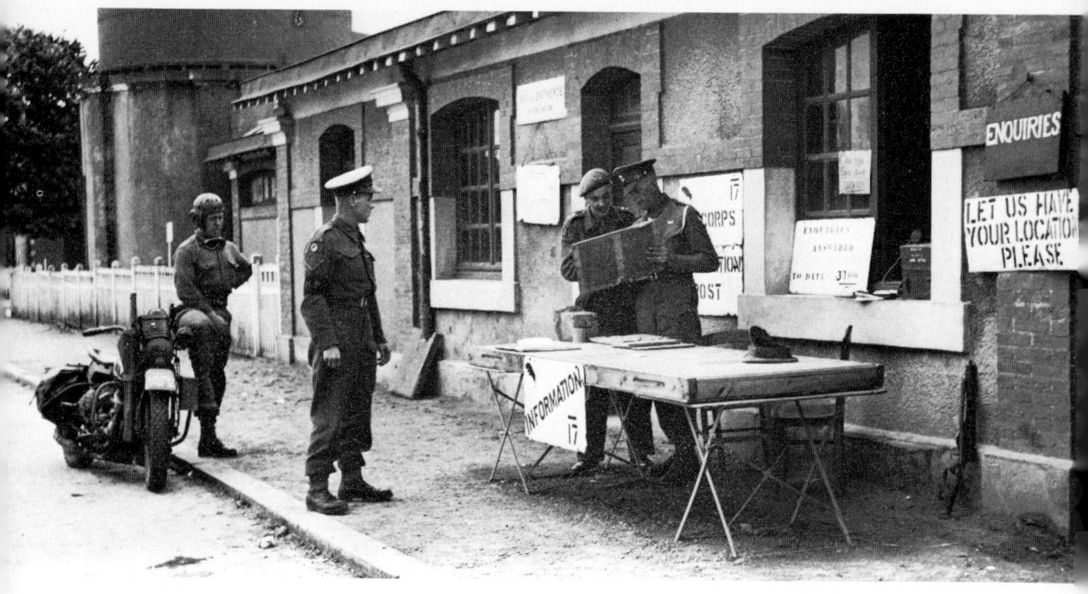

21 Lance-Corporal F. Everard and Corporal A. Thomson manning an Information Post, 113 Provost Company, France, 1944.

22 British and American Military Policemen meet at Tinchbray crossroads in France, 1944. The British NCOs are Lance-Corporals Hornsby and Baker.

23 Colonel Bassett F. G. Wilson PM BLA speaking to Sergeant J. Lindridge BEM during an inspection in France, 1944.

24 'There's many a slip . . .' and this one at Brighton Bridge on the Belgium-Eindhoven road held up hundreds of military vehicles. The horse slipped on the bridge incline and it took twenty minutes to get him on his feet again.

25 *Antwerp Signs Factory, 73 Company TC CMP, 1945. Sergeant Tillar CMP with civilian painters produced 5,900 signs in five months. On the right is Major J. G. Wilby APM Antwerp.*

26 *CMP route signing in BAOR in 1945.*

27 CMP route signing: 2nd Army, 1945.

28 A group of 2nd Army Military Police and Pioneers who erected the British Zone Germany 1945 Frontier Sign.

29 Lt-General Horrocks, GOC 30 Corps, receives the surrender of German forces in Northern Germany on 5 May, 1945.

As long as troops came in, so the posts were kept manned, in places for more than a week and, as there were no reliefs available, the same men stayed there, living on bully beef, biscuits and water.

On 13 August, 1942, Lieut-General B. L. Montgomery took command of 8th Army and all thought of further retirement was dismissed.

In September, 1942, Lieut-Colonel T. C. Irvine was appointed DPM 8th Army, to replace Lieut-Colonel A. R. Forbes. For the actual preparation and preliminaries of training for the Battle of El Alamein the following account has been given by Lieut-Colonel Irvine:

'On reporting to 8th Army I found them in the process of re-equipping and it was no secret that we were about to go into battle on a large scale.

'I found my police developed into a force of seventy-three provost officers and two thousand and forty-seven rank and file.

'At this time the allied forces had been driven back to a position around El Alamein. In front of them was the narrow waste known as the Qattara Gap, bounded on the south side by an impassable escarpment and on the north by the sea.

'At a very early stage it became evident that the "easing" of the 8th Army fighting troops, their armour and their "soft" vehicles through this gap was going to be a great task. It also became obvious that a large proportion of the task before the General Staff was a traffic problem and that therefore the opening stages were to be in the nature of a trial for provost and, in the words of the Army Commander, "Day One would make or mar the name of provost for ever".

'We felt confident that with the large provost personnel at our disposal the task would not be beyond our capabilities.

'A general plan was formed for provost, in conjunction with the Chief Engineer's and Chief Signal Officer's organizations, to operate the movement through the Qattara Gap up to and through our minefields and eventually through the German minefields. Provost were to control traffic by diverse means, the Sappers were to grade tracks and clear minefields and Signals were to provide special communication facilities.

'The enemy, aware that attack was due, was ignorant of the direction from which it was to come and of the forces and strength of armour against them. It was not possible, therefore, to mark and grade tracks by means of "graders", which would be obvious to air reconnaissance. On the other hand, our task was to bring forward on the night of 23 and 24 October, through an area twenty-six miles in length and four miles in width, the New Zealand Division, the 9th Armoured Brigade and the 1st and 10th British Armoured Divisions.

'Before this for five days between D+5 and D+1, provost handled through the Qattara Gap, mostly by night without lights, 51st (H) Division, 4th Indian Division, 10 Corps Artillery, 30 Corps Artillery, 'B' Echelon, rations, petrol and ammunition vehicles.

'Arrangements for D and D+1 were planned as follows:—It was decided to provide six clearly defined tracks, in addition to the main coastal road, through the corridor of the Qattara Gap. These were christened: Sun, Moon and Star; Bottle, Boat and Hat. The general direction was marked by means of cairns of stones painted white on the approach side. In these cairns were placed iron bars surmounted by the silhouette of the insignia of the track name. The average length of these tracks proved to be twenty-six miles. The ensuing movements were to be carried out during the full moon period, so the white-faced cairns with their silhouetted sign-tokens were easily visible even to the drivers of tanks. In order, however, that no mistake could possibly be caused through loss of direction, each of these lines of entry was equipped, at regular intervals, with petrol tins containing hurricane lamps, the pattern being stamped out in the tin to display the appropriate insignia. These improvised lamps were manufactured by police NCOs. In addition two sections of provost were allotted to each track for point duty, general control and lamp maintenance.

'From Springbok Road, which incidentally was well up in the 25-pounder artillery barrage, division provost took over. At twilight they lit their appropriate lamps, up to and through gaps in our own minefields; during the barrage they advanced across no-man's-land with their attendant sappers and signalmen, marking and lighting their passage, the signalmen laying their communication lines. On arrival at the enemy minefield the sappers, in conjunction with our NCOs, selected a suitable location for penetration and commenced to sweep for mines, the policemen and signallers following in their wake. All this time a barrage, the density of which is now well known, was being operated. The enemy reply was largely directed on no-man's land and included machine-gun and mortar nests within their own minefield. The mortar nests were unsuspected and although the barrage to some extent nullified their activities, the "minefield force" was suddenly called upon to give battle. In no cases were these developments allowed to hinder the "gap makers".'

One of the 'gap-makers', L/Cpl J. Eeles of 10th Armoured Division was the military police candidate recommanded for immediate reward. He received the Distinguished Conduct Medal. When all his policeman comrades had been either killed or wounded he and two sappers, whose help he enlisted on his own initiative, completed their gap under heavy fire, thus providing the passage for the armour to advance.

On the morning of 5 November, *Exchange Telegraph* reported to London newspapers:

'In one of the recent attacks by General Montgomery's Forces against Rommel's weakening African Army, tanks of a British Armoured Division were led into battle by highly-trained specialists of the Royal Engineers, Royal Corps of Signals and by "Redcaps" of the Corps of Military Police. This complete reversal of the previously accepted order of battle in which specialists were given a certain amount of protection by combatants in front is inevitable in the type of warfare in which British armour has been engaged.

'In an attack on a position strongly organized for defence against tanks it is essential for the sappers to clear gaps through the enemy minefields. Signallers must be there to establish communications from the front to the rear at the earliest possible moment. "Redcaps" must be there to mark routes as they are made and control the immense volume of traffic being rushed through gaps in the minefields.

'So brilliantly have these three arms worked in face of fierce enemy fire that the officer commanding the Armoured Division gave them high praise in a special order of the day. "They marked routes", he said, "with the same precision and efficiency as in training schemes in the rear areas". At intervals along the route "Redcaps" quickly established inquiry posts where information could be obtained. At every cross-road or bad patch of sand policemen were on duty adeptly controlling traffic. It is the first time "Redcaps" have been front-line troops in desert warfare—and they did a grand job.'

The two divisions were passed through the tracks in roughly six hours, well ahead of time, with few incidents and excellent unit discipline.

Practically speaking, every desert track was laid and marked by provost throughout the campaign. Seven signs to the mile was the average and every one was manufactured out of whatever was available (the 4-gallon tin was available in large numbers) with the track sign or number cut in silhouette in the side.

As the advance continued, so traffic control on the coast road became more important. The road was practically free from air interference by the enemy, so the deviation tracks (all reconnoitred and marked by military police) had rarely to be used. Transport drivers had been well trained in Coast Road Regulations, a code of traffic rules worked out by provost officers. The first and most important rule was 'Do not stop on the road'. This was enforced with vigour and if a vehicle broke down the driver had to stop following or approaching vehicles and have the break-down either towed or pushed off the road.

105 Provost Company HQ and a number of the sections were encamped in the desert near Wadi Zemzem some hundreds of kilometres south-east of Tripoli. One morning the DPM sent for the OC 105 Company, Captain A. G. Joslin, and told him that the move towards Tripoli was imminent.

The DPM's parting words were: 'If you do get there before I do, lose no time in establishing a police station and Town patrols, this is vital'. How true those words were. The troops of 8th Army had had their sights on the fleshpots of Tripoli for some time. This was the first large sophisticated town of any significance since El Alamein and it was of the utmost importance that strong military police measures be instituted without delay. Bounds and vice control were high on the priority list and it was rumoured that there were millions of gallons of Chianti in vats, stores and factories scattered in and around the town. This rumour proved to be substantially true.

The advanced elements of 51st Highland Division pushed along the coast road, hotly pursued by 105 Provost Company, through Misurata and Homs, where quick appreciations were made and small detachments dropped off to look after these small towns. Finally in the early hours of 23 January, 1943, to quote the words of OC 105 Provost Company,

> 'We found ourselves on a slight rise looking down on the dark and brooding town of Tripoli. It was strangely silent at this moment.
>
> 'Even the tanks which were grouping around us for the final leg were still, and the groups of Highlanders who were later to mount the tanks and be borne in triumph through the streets of Tripoli, seemed unusually quiet. We were all enthralled in the spectacle of Tripoli which lay before us, the town which had eluded the 8th Army for so long and which would be occupied before the sun was up. Soon the spell was rudely shattered and we were sweeping down the road towards the town. I had left the bulk of the company by the roadside to await calling forward and with the RSM beside me in my vehicle we entered the last phase of the race to get to Tripoli. It was still dark and we had been travelling for some time on our own when the RSM, who had been peering rather anxiously out of the window, said, "We passed this spot a short time ago". In fact we had been going round the ring road and had completed the circuit twice! However, it was dark and we were, to say the least, somewhat excited. Soon we were speeding towards the centre of the town and the main Government building.
>
> 'Choosing the most imposing doorway it was not long before we had persuaded a rather bedraggled Italian official to rouse none other than the Governor himself and acquaint him of our requirements, i.e., one large barracks suitable for use as a police station and centrally situated. The Governor was persuaded to escort us personally and, arming himself with three nervous looking officials and a small torch, he led the way through the dark and deserted streets to the main *Carabinieri* barracks. It too was deserted and in rather a shambles but after a tour round with the aid of the Governor's torch my R.SM and I decided it would be most suitable. The Governor formally handed the building over on the spot.
>
> 'Our "Governor" of the early morning was in fact the Italian General who, in a ceremony later, formally handed over the keys of Tripoli to General Montgomery.'

Ten weeks earlier, British and American troops under General Eisenhower had invaded North Africa and assaulting troops of British 1st Army landed, together with some L of C troops, to open the port of Algiers.

78th Division and 6th Armoured Division with their provost companies pushed forward along the coastal road to secure the main objectives of Tunis and Bizerta. Traffic control duties were carried out by provost units both in the forward area and on the L of C under extremely difficult conditions, as the number of good roads in the country was limited.

Maintenance of supplies in the forward area entailed constant forethought and improvisation because of the state of the roads and restricted railway facilities. The problem was made more difficult by the fact that the enemy then had air superiority and vehicle road movement had to be confined mainly to the hours of darkness.

The potency of the local wine which the troops thought they could drink like their native beer caused a great deal of drunkenness and disorderliness. To these were added the temptations of the Casbah of Algiers and the less desirable quarters of other base towns, such as Bône, Bougie, Sétif and Constantine. This created a problem which taxed to the limit the resources of the restricted number of military police.

As the troops became acclimatized and control of cafés, restaurants and undesirable establishments was tightened up, conditions became easier. 227 and 230 Provost Companies, although hard-worked, profited by their experience which stood them in good stead later in the campaign.

The initial landings were unopposed but a good deal of disorganization occurred and useful experience was gained for the planning and executing of the later invasions of Sicily and Italy. It was found that much of the signing equipment could be dispensed with—the maximum use being made of local resources.

During the advance of 78th Division Provost Company it was found that when crossing country it was impossible for motor-cyclists to keep up with their sections. An establishment of three jeeps, two 15 cwt trucks and five motor-cycles per section was introduced, motor-cycle combinations were discarded and it was found that radio trucks were essential to control the movement of large columns of transport.

Towards the end of February, 8th Army, which had captured Tripoli on 23 January and had been advancing north-west in the face of a series of Axis rearguard positions, made contact with the enemy on the outposts of the Mareth Line. HQ 18 Army Group was now formed under General Alexander to co-ordinate the action of both 1st and 8th Armies. No representative of the provost service served on the staff of HQ 18 Army Group—Lieut-Colonel Sykes, who some time earlier had been appointed DPM Allied Force HQ, with Lieut-Colonel Paton-Walsh, his successor as DPM 1st Army, controlling the operation of provost units in the field.

Provost continued to sign, patrol and control 8th Army, which had developed into a great mechanical war machine. Dusty tracks, bad roads, the constant overpowering smell of oil and petrol; eyes full of grit, lungs full of sand and choking white dust; the ever-present risk of being crushed under a tank or a five-tonner, a bulldozer, or guns; all this had become part and parcel of the military policeman's life. Night and day troops and vehicles moved incessantly on through Gabes to Sfax and Sousse, nearer and nearer to Tunis, the town coveted by the Army in the east as much as by the Army in the west.

On 22 April the final assault began; by 7 May, 1st and 8th Armies had broken through to Tunis and Bizerta had fallen to the Americans; on 12 May Field-Marshal von Arnim surrendered and the Axis lost their last remaining foothold in Africa.

Not only was the North African campaign the turning point of the war it was also the turning point in the employment of military police.

The BEF campaign in Belgium and at Dunkirk had already shown that the 'Redcaps' could no longer be regarded as 'base troops'. El Alamein and the subsequent operations in North Africa confirmed this claim. The message from Cairo to London newspapers after El Alamein had reported: 'The Redcaps are front-line soldiers now'. And front-line soldiers they were to remain.

CHAPTER VI

Italy

On the night of 9 July, 1943, the airborne operation against Sicily was launched, prelude to the first invasion of the homeland of an Axis member. The Sicily operation came to its climax with the entry of British and American forces into devastated Messina on 17 August. It was during this campaign that 8th Army provost had its first taste of blown-up passes, blown bridges and the urgent necessity of finding and policing diversions.

Towns such as Syracuse and Augusta, Catania, Acireale, Taormina and Messina, all had permanent detachments of military police drawn from one or more of the following units: Army, 13 Corps, 30 Corps, 505 and 501 Provost Companies.

The assault on the Italian mainland was made in the early hours of 3 September, 1943. Resistance was negligible and the main hindrance to the advance proved to be extensive demolitions on all roads. 5th Division advanced up the main west coast road while the Canadian Division took to the hills, crossed the toe and reached the coast on the east side. During this period the main provost problem was moving large numbers of vehicles over roads where many bridges had been blown.

It was not long before the Army provost companies were fully deployed on the road behind 13 Corps and by 15 September Army Provost were deployed from Reggio to Belvedere on the west coast road and across to Nicastra via Catanzaro to Crotone on the east coast. Apart from two days' rain in the hills above Reggio which hindered the Canadian Division the weather was good and the diversions through river-beds held firm. By this time 2nd Parachute Brigade had landed in the Taranto area and arrangements were made for 78th Division to cross from Sicily to Reggio, move by road to Crotone and then by LCT to Taranto, as it was thought that the route Crotone–Taranto would not be available for large-scale moves for some time.

This plan was cancelled and it was decided that 78th Division should go the whole way by road. It therefore became necessary for 105 Provost Company to be switched from the west coast road behind 13 Corps to cover the Crotone–Taranto stretch, thus relieving 78th Division Provost Company of any commitments behind their forward division concentration area. The gap behind 13 Corps on the west coast road was not filled. By this time supplies were reaching Corps through LCT to Sapri, thus the L of C was quiet with practically no maintenance traffic and Corps had completed its move up.

505 Provost Company was sent to Bari from Crotone and the detachment of 181 Ports Company to Taranto, a very busy port. 505 Provost Company arrived at Bari on 26 September well ahead of the main influx of troops, which did not take place until some days later. One section was sent to Brindisi, which was to open shortly as a port.

On 24 September, 8th Indian Division and HQ 5 Corps disembarked at Taranto. 101 (5 Corps) Provost Company was only three sections strong; the remaining six sections were not to arrive for some weeks. While in this area 101 Provost Company, 8th Indian Division Provost Company and 2nd Parachute Brigade Provost Company assisted with police duties in Taranto, which was full of troops of all nationalities. There was considerable trouble in the early stages of occupation as large numbers of unemployed Italian naval ratings wandered round the town all day.

By 24 October 8th Indian Division had moved north to Foggia and concentrated in the Ururi area. The APM had only three sections of British police in a six-section company and the quality of those three sections was not good. They consisted chiefly of transfers from British troops in the division and had undergone a short course at the CMP Depot, Almaza. 8th Indian Division axis presented great difficulties through breaking weather. A section of 105 Provost Company was sent to assist temporarily. This section operated with 8th Indian Division for a period of about ten days until the balance of 5 Corps Provost Company arrived. During this move in appalling weather on a breaking road the APM was killed when the jeep in which he was patrolling slid over a precipice.

The arrival of 230 L of C Provost Company for No 2 District enabled 509 Provost Company to move forward and take over behind 13 Corps on the Campobasso road and release 34 Beach Brick Provost Unit from Brindisi. This latter unit was dispatched to Termoli to assist 5 Corps until the Termoli area became the Army roadhead, where the unit would be in a position to take over roadhead duties.

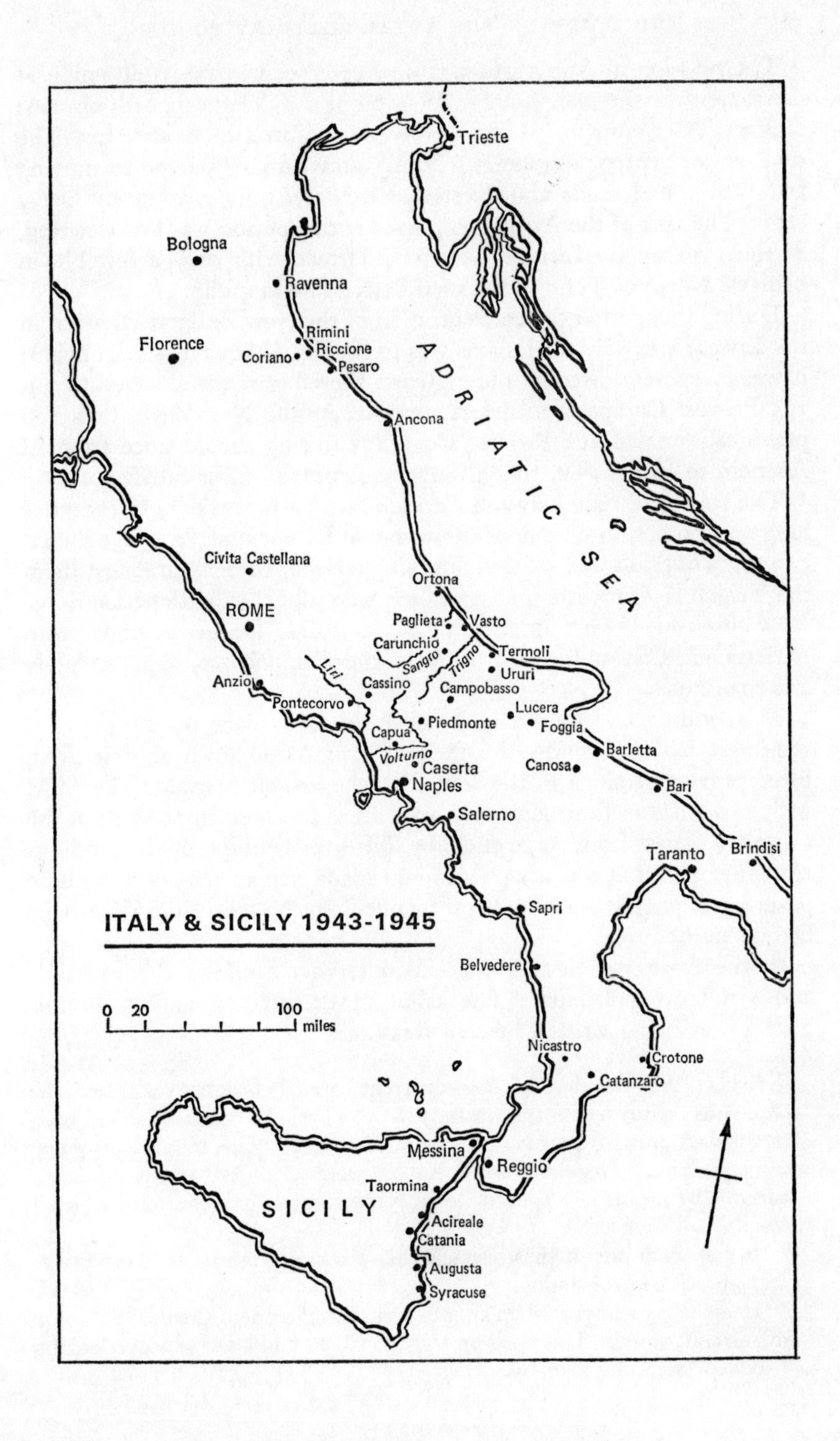
Trieste
Bologna
Ravenna
Florence
Rimini
Coriano
Riccione
Pesaro
ADRIATIC SEA
Ancona
Civita Castellana
Ortona
ROME
Paglieta
Vasto
Carunchio
Sangro
Trigno
Termoli
Ururi
Liri
Anzio
Cassino
Campobasso
Pontecorvo
Lucera
Piedmonte
Foggia
Capua
Barletta
Volturno
Caserta
Canosa
Naples
Bari
Salerno
Brindisi
Taranto
Sapri
ITALY & SICILY 1943-1945
Belvedere
0 20 100
miles
Nicastro
Crotone
Catanzaro
Messina
Reggio
Taormina
SICILY
Acireale
Catania
Augusta
Syracuse

The position in Army area was now eased considerably, although at the same time the plans for the crossing of the Sangro made it obvious that 43 TC Company would shortly be required in Army area. The division and corps companies were by now fully employed in moving traffic over bad roads and diversions rendered much worse by heavy rains. The task of the Army companies at this period was less exacting, as the road up to Termoli was good tarmac with only a few blown bridges. North of Termoli the road deteriorated rapidly.

During this period the concentration of the New Zealand Division in the Lucera area started. Its axis was to be Ururi–Aquaviva–Carunchio; it was to operate directly under Army, therefore it was decided to put 105 Provost Company in direct support. As the New Zealanders had previously known 105 Provost Company during the advance from El Alamein to Enfidaville, this arrangement proved most satisfactory.

The stretch of road between Termoli and Vasto was only thirty miles long and proved to be one of the worst so far encountered; it included two miles of one-way road and nine single Bailey bridges, amongst them the Trigno river crossing, all of which were difficult bottlenecks.

At this time Army provost were responsible for the L of C from Barletta and Canosa forward to Vasto and Campobasso, approximately 210 road miles.

The landing on the Anzio beach-head took place on 22 January, 1944. 1st Division landed on the north of Anzio town at first light, three provost sections in the lead with the assault brigade. The APM with two more sections landed shortly after, followed by the rest of the company. Apart from some shelling and dive-bombing of the landing-craft the operation was unopposed and roads, report centres and traffic posts were quickly organized and manned. In the meantime US troops had taken the town.

In the Anzio beach-head an encounter occurred between a sailor and a military policeman. The sailor never forgot it and when this history was being written he sent this note:

'I believe that the date of the occurrence was February, 1944, and the scene was the town of Anzio, in Italy. At this period a beach-head had been established around Nettuno and conditions were quite rough. Sea-going convoys arriving regularly from Naples were shepherded into the small harbour by means of a special Royal Navy wireless procedure, of which I was a small "cog".

'It was from one of these vessels that I was put ashore to assist in the shore-based control station.

'Imagine my surprise when after experiencing frequent German field-gun and aircraft attacks, I stepped on to dry land to find a very spruce-looking "Redcap" standing near-by.

'In absolute contrast to everyone else, this man was in regulation uniform and freshly shaved. Seeing me he said, "Have you a tin of boot polish to spare, Jack?" Of all the things I had expected to hear in Anzio, a request of this description was most certainly the farthest removed. My admiration for the man persuaded me there and then to search for and find a tin of polish in my kitbag. I hadn't been ashore many hours before I discovered that this "Keep smart" campaign was the watchword of all the "Red-caps" present.

'Two years later I was the 1st Lieutenant of a Fleet Minesweeper and I recall on many occasions using this example to inspire the odd liberty man who failed to pass the routine inspection before going ashore.

'I am now back to my civilian job, a police constable, and I must confess that even here I have found it necessary to quote this incident to a "scruffy" youngster with whom I had "words".'

However, the advance to Rome was not to be. The Germans threw in everything they had to force the attack back into the sea and for four months 1st Division fought and lived in the narrow beach-head, taking everything that the enemy could throw or drop. The functions of provost during this period were not pleasant. Life was only possible underground, but the control of the two roads and many tracks up to the forward positions was of first importance, and in performing these duties the 'Redcap' was much exposed.

There were many provost casualties at the notorious Flyover Bridge and at the various nodal track-junctions. No part of the beach-head was immune from shelling and low-flying attacks by enemy aircraft day and night. Despite the use of smoke to screen activity, the enemy had little difficulty in seeing every move from his outpost in the Alban Hills overlooking our positions.

On 14 February 56th Division arrived and with them the DPM on a visit to see for himself.

16 March was a bleak day for 1st Division Provost Company who had six casualties in the HQ section following an air attack in the small hours. In addition, shelling had set off a large ammunition dump from which flying lumps of metal caused great unpleasantness on the main axis road and was a sticky job to control.

The period 21 November–31 January was a time which saw the Sangro crossed and Ortona captured. The plan provided that after the initial onslaught Corps RE would throw Bailey bridges across the Sangro river by the demolished main road bridge. The Bailey bridge subsequently built proved to be one of the longest ever built in the field. The provost plan was that 5 Corps Provost Company would be responsible for the crossings in the main road bridge area to enable 78th Division Provost Company to concentrate on duties forward of the river, as it was anticipated that proper traffic control would be of the highest importance so long as the crossings were within range of the enemy guns. As far as 8th Indian Division Provost Company was concerned, it was found essential for British sections to handle the division crossings and it was necessary for 5 Corps to assist the division provost with duties well within the division area.

About 28 November 78th Division was relieved by 1st Canadian Division which had been under command 13 Corps in the sector north-west of Campobasso. The Canadians were intended to move in brigade groups via Termoli, stage in the Paglieta area and move from there to the north of the Sangro on the following day. This move started on 30 November. There was heavy rain during the night and the Canadian Brigade Group staying the night at Paglieta took most of the following day to move out of the staging area. The vehicles brought mud on the road in great quantities, which made conditions on this road difficult for several weeks. 78th Division moving back was staged on the side road at Ururi. The change-over was complicated by the Sangro bridges once again being 'out' for a certain period of twenty-four hours. This caused great congestion on the road north of Vasto and had not air cover been complete the consequences might have been serious. Adverse weather continued and it was not until about 20 December that Ortona was entered, nearly a month after the crossing of the Sangro, and fighting went on over Christmas.

February, 1944, found the Army playing a holding and very static rôle for the first time since October, 1942. Operational moves were few; traffic control became a matter of daily routine and during this breathing space plans could be made for the future. The month closed with the news that a vast regrouping of the armies in Italy was about to take place. 8th Army was to take over a new sector west of the Apennines and would assume an offensive rôle in the spring. Early March saw arrangements made for this regrouping.

For provost, it was largely a question of arranging which provost units should go with 8th Army and which should remain. It was decided that 105 and 505 Provost Companies, 43 TC Company and the 8th Army SIB should accompany 8th Army and that 506 Provost and 77 TC Companies should come under command when the Army took over the Cassino sector. It was agreed that 509 Provost and 49 TC Companies should remain on the east coast under No 2 District and 5 Corps respectively.

It was also necessary to replace US Provost by 8th Army provost in the towns and villages and along the roads in an area running from the Volturno River in the south to Cassino in the north bounded on the west by the main Rome road and in the east by the Apennines.

This was by no means a simple undertaking and the matter was further complicated by the fact that for security reasons the use of the Army shield on signboards was prohibited until the actual day of the take-over. No start could therefore be made on the actual marking of routes, report centres or information posts.

As the various routes, Depot area and so on were decided, the boards were painted for erection when the time came. For the short stretch of road north of Capua which was common to 5th and 8th Armies large boards—'No Halting', 'No Double-banking' and such slogans—were prepared with both 5th and 8th Army shields painted in the upper corner. Section tasks had been worked out in detail and sections had moved out to their locations some days in advance. The necessary signboards for the various routes and areas were distributed among the sections ready for erection and all NCOs had thus had time to become acquainted with the varying conditions in the area.

The weather was improving daily. During the preliminary reconnaissance of the new Army area it was obvious that good communications would be required for traffic control and that these would have to be provided by Signals and the advantages of the rapid and reliable communications thus placed at provost disposal were immediately apparent. On the road in the Capua area joint control by US Provost and CMP was maintained—US and British MP side-by-side in the same vehicles on speed traps, checks and road patrols which proved most effective.

The period saw no rapid movement similar to the advance from Reggio. For all ranks CMP throughout the Army it was, however, a great period of activity; as a result many valuable lessons were learned.

From 1 to 10 May final regrouping of the Army prior to the battle continued. During the fortnight prior to the opening of the offensive, Army provost handled on an average eleven thousand vehicles daily on Highway 6 alone. Constant watch by police mobile patrols, the use of loud-speaker apparatus, observation aircraft and first-class police communications made this possible, A ruthless check on 'swanners' was enforced; a number of 'pull-in' areas were established along the main routes into which police signalled suspected vehicles. Offenders were impounded or turned back. Large warning notices in English, Polish, French and Italian were prominently displayed on the principal routes.

Immediately before the battle, 6th (British) Armoured Division moved from Piedmonte into the forward area. The armour was moved at night by a tank track which had been constructed parallel to Highway 6. No lights were permitted on tanks; the track was lit and the armour was escorted by CMP in jeeps.

During the period of heavy tank transporter moves by night which followed, loud-speaker equipment was found to be of the greatest value in passing instructions to tank crews and transporter drivers above the noise of the engines.

At 11 pm on 11 May the offensive opened. By 15 May Canadian Corps was preparing to deploy in the Liri valley on the left of 13 Corps. 1st Canadian Infantry Division was the first to move forward into the valley and was directed on Pontecorvo. On Highway 6 Monte Cassino proved once again a formidable obstacle and it was reduced only after great efforts by the Polish Corps on the right flank. From then onwards the pursuit became very rapid and the chief obstacle was the limitations imposed on road capacity by damage to bridges, craters and major demolitions.

The chief work of provost during this period was the control of heavy road traffic, including some large tank transporter moves. The rapidity of the advance made it necessary for reserve tanks, and in fact whole armoured brigades. to be moved on transporters rather than on their tracks, thus saving both track mileage and also the damage the roads would have suffered.

Rome fell to troops of the US 5th Army on 4 June. Route-marking in a city the size of Rome presented certain difficulties and great credit was due to Lieutenant-Colonel G. C. White, the newly-appointed DPM Rome, and his APM, Major R. A. Whitby, for the excellent traffic and route signing organization which they built up. It was thought at first that there might be considerable traffic blocks in the city but this was not the case, probably on account of the great width of the principal thoroughfares.

The South African Division was the first Commonwealth division to pass through Rome, followed by 78th Division. The pursuit continued rapidly until Civita Castellana was reached, where the bridges over a large gorge had been demolished. Demolitions and breaking weather slowed down the subsequent rate of advance considerably.

By this time preparations were in hand for entry into Florence, which was to be a welfare centre for the Army; but, in point of fact, progress proved to be much slower than had been expected on account of considerably stiffer opposition, many demolitions and rain. The battle for Florence proved a bitterly-contested struggle and it was not until the morning of 4 August that a detachment of Proforce entered South Florence with the South African tanks, established itself, and was operating by 2 pm. At this time the enemy was holding the north bank of the River Arno in strength and German fighting patrols crossed to the south bank nightly.

When the military police entered Florence, 'mob rule' existed. Street fighting flared up in the neighbourhood day and night; unorganized groups of armed partisans picqueted the town. Several civilians were shot and there was persistent sniper fire. It seemed that at any time during the early stages of occupation the partisans could have taken complete control and the military police could have done little to prevent it.

Before the entry into Florence, the decision had been taken to transfer the bulk of British and Canadian forces to the east coast, where the Polish Corps had captured Ancona and thus provided a base for large-scale operations against the eastern portion of the Gothic Line.

The switch was to be executed under conditions of the greatest secrecy and as rapidly as possible so as not to lose the remaining fine campaigning weather. 13 Corps was to pass to command of 5th Army and continue operations in the Florence sector. Little information was available about conditions on the east coast and accordingly an Army reconnaissance party left for Ancona on 6 August.

The heaviest movement was over by 22 August, although considerable transporter and other moves continued for a period of fourteen days or more, and by 24 August the Army Commander, in an address at Jesi, was able to announce that 8th Army, with Polish Corps on the right, Canadian troops in the centre and 5 Corps on the left, was about to attack the Gothic Line positions in the Adriatic sector.

This presented many major problems as, apart from the main coastal road, there were no axes of advance. The coastal road was allotted to the Poles and the Sappers supporting 5 Corps and the Canadians had to create their own axis by bulldozing tracks across country to link up minor roads and lanes and such of these as existed were too narrow for other than one-way use and had numerous craters and blown bridges. Sustained rain was to be dreaded. However, experience gained in the Liri valley enabled a successful job to be done and in a remarkably short time division and corps provost were signing-up these tracks as the advance axes. By 4 September Army provost, who had been deploying up the main coast road behind them, had taken over the main Army axis up to and including Pesaro.

The weather then deteriorated and made progress most difficult. Resistance was stiff, particularly on 5 Corps sector, where Coriano and the neighbouring features were the scene of heavy fighting. The nature of the country forbade any advance on other sectors until this feature was cleared. During this period the Greek Mountain Brigade took over the coastal sector in the Riccione area and were among the first troops into Rimini, having taken part in the hard fighting which took place around the airfield south of the town. Rimini itself was entered on 20 September, nearly a month after the battle had started. As Army road-head No 6 was to be established in the Rimini area, the town was an

Army objective and a detachment of 505 Provost Company entered the town.

It soon became apparent that German resistance remained as stiff as ever and that there was to be no general withdrawal in spite of the fact that the Gothic Line had been overrun in the Adriatic coastal sector. The town of Rimini was considerably damaged and was still within range of enemy shell-fire for some days after its capture. This prevented the immediate establishment of the new roadhead and as a result the work of Army provost during the first few days of occupation was largely anti-looting patrols.

In the spring of 1945 the advance was resumed and had been carried well past Bologna and Ravenna into the valley of the Po when the collapse of Germany in May brought fighting to an end.

The campaign in Italy taught the military police much about the control of bridges, one-way diversions, ferries, timing and routing of convoys, the value of signals and the all-important need for keeping traffic moving all the time.

The operational problems were always severe and testing and the maintenance of close liaison with the US military police was a constant task.

Perhaps no better picture of the military policeman on operational duty in Italy could be drawn than that presented by Fred Majdalany.

Fred Majdalany served in the infantry with 8th Army in Italy and took part in the four battles for Cassino. In 1945 he published *The Monastery* in which, as a participant, he gives a vivid and exciting description of these battles from the 'PBI' viewpoint. In 1957 he followed up with *Cassino*, which narrates the campaign in a fuller and broader way and deals most interestingly with the controversial issues relating to the strategic moves which followed the fall of the Monastery.

It is all the more gratifying to find Mr Majdalany, an infantryman who had no axe to grind for the military police, paying in each book a short but glowing tribute to the work of the Corps in these operations.

This is what he says in *The Monastery:*

> 'At all the tracks, junctions and corners on the way there would be a military policeman. It is a great pity that the popular conception of the "Redcap" is largely derived from the military police in large towns in England, whose duties mainly consist in charging soldiers on leave with minor offences in dress and everyday discipline. It is impossible to praise too highly the work of the "Redcaps", who are a part of every fighting division. Their job in the fighting zones is the vast one of traffic control—whether it be hundreds of vehicles or hundreds of mules.
>
> 'In this instance they used to stand at all the key points from the beginning of the evening until the last mule had passed on the way back shortly

before dawn. Many of these places were plague-spots for shelling. But the "Redcaps" never seemed to mind. They never wore a tin hat; always the familiar red one, and the impeccable white belt and equipment. They developed a tradition of courteous helpfulness which never broke down under the most adverse and dangerous conditions'.

In *Cassino* the author tells of the terrific drive forward, after the fall of the Monastery, to rush the Adolf Hitler Line, round-up the enemy forces and capture Rome. This is his reference to the Corps:

'With 2,000 tanks and 20,000 vehicles surging through the broken Gustav Line, traffic control was for the time being more important than any other military consideration. The congestion was almost awe-inspiring. The most important soldier in the Army at this time was the military policeman struggling to keep the flood of transport moving.'

CHAPTER VII

North-West Europe

On 6 June, 1944, the assault on Europe by 21 Army Group and 12 US Army Group, both under the immediate command of General Sir Bernard Montgomery, began in Normandy.

The principal provost officers in 21 Army Group on D-Day were:

HQ 21 Army Group .	Provost Marshal, Colonel Bassett F. G. Wilson DPM, Lieut-Colonel F. A. Stanley
2nd Army . . .	DPM, Lieut-Colonel F. C. Drake
1st Canadian Army .	DPM, Lieut-Colonel G. Ball
HQ L of C . . .	DPM, Lieut-Colonel J. N. Cheney
1 Corps . . .	APM, Major P. Godfrey-Faussett
8 Corps . . .	APM, Lieut-Colonel P. M. Fitzgerald
12 Corps . . .	APM, Major R. A. Guild
30 Corps . . .	APM, Lieut-Colonel D. W. L. Melville
11 L of C Area . .	APM, Major S. F. Crozier
12 L of C Area . .	APM, Major Peterkin

It is worth noting that the experienced commanders of 8 and 30 Corps, Lieut-General Sir Richard O'Connor and Lieut-General Sir Brian Horrocks, had both given the local ranks of lieutenant-colonel to their APMs.

On D-Day, outside the formation and L of C provost companies, thirty in all, there were fifteen traffic control companies, one signal company, eight vulnerable points companies, five SIB sections and one ports company.

It had been appreciated during the planning stages for the invasion of Europe that additional resources would be needed as the campaign progressed and vigorous steps were being taken by Provost Marshal United Kingdom to raise further ports companies. SIB sections and vulnerable points (overseas) companies. War Office had already promised to release four further traffic control companies after embarkation. One complete provost section, commanded by Lieutenant Hills, served throughout the campaign as personal bodyguard to the C-in-C, Field-Marshal Montgomery.

Throughout the campaign the problems were formidable. At times provost had to contend with appalling congestion, as in the Normandy bridgehead and in the forward areas in Belgium and Holland. On several occasions corps and sometimes four or five divisions at a time were regrouping and army roadheads were stocking against the clock in an acutely restricted area on inadequate and crumbling roads.

In the course of these whirlwind operations the fighting formations were continually moved and shepherded in and out of battle and over minefields and bridges by their own provost companies. They fought their way across the Seine, the Somme, the intricate river and canal system in the Low Countries, the Maas, the Rhine, the Weser and the Elbe, content to leave the subsequent control of the numerous bridges, bottle-necks, roads and defiles in the safe hands of the military police of the higher formations following in their wake.

Field-Marshal Montgomery, in his book *Normandy to the Baltic*, says that in Normandy there were four 'outstanding administrative problems'. Of these, the first arose from bad weather; the remaining three arose from the difficulty of 'expanding the major maintenance installations rapidly from the beaches into the confined area of the bridgehead; from the great traffic congestion within the bridgehead; and from the sudden change from intensive short-range operations to the fast-moving battle up to the Seine and beyond.'

It is an interesting reflection that, of these four major administrative problems, three were problems in which the provost service was of paramount importance.

Among important appointments and upgradings during the campaign, the following must be recorded: an APM (SIB) was added to the staff of PM 21 Army Group, an essential appointment to which Major F. R. Pollard was assigned; a DPM (Paris) (Lieut-Colonel W. H. Diggle) was appointed with an APM and DAPM on his staff; the Provost Marshal 21 Army Group was upgraded to brigadier on 17 March, 1945, and DPMs 21 Army Group, 2nd Army and L of C to colonel and at about the same time APMs Corps Districts (for controlling the corps areas in Germany) were upgraded to DPMs (lieut-colonels). The total provost strength with 21 Army Group grew from 6,648 on D-Day to 10,294 at the end of the war.

Throughout the campaign corps and division provost companies were comparatively little concerned with discipline; they had their normal disciplinary duties within their formations, but their chief work was carrying out their operational traffic control duties. There was a certain amount of looting, and another practice with which they had to deal was the tendency of local inhabitants to make false claims against British troops for looting and damage actually suffered at the hands of the retreating enemy. The cure was for provost or SIB, accompanied by an officer of Claims and Hirings, to enter towns and villages hard on the heels of the forward fighting troops, note the condition of property, etc, and, where necessary, take signed statements from local inhabitants. These statements, often taken under fire, were usually accurate and prevented the later invention of 'second thoughts'.

Owing to a vast circulation of traffic there were throughout the campaign innumerable blocks and jams, most caused by stupidity or disobedience of traffic rules by a single driver; double-banking, overtaking and cutting-in and unnecessary halts without pulling clear of the road were the most common causes. Officers were too often offenders.

The most practical remedy for road blocks was found by 2nd Army. Instead of multiplying road patrols, which were seldom in the right place at the crucial time and often got blocked themselves, pairs of police motor-cyclists were stationed at busy cross-roads and bottlenecks. The instant a block occurred they rode down the road, found and removed the source of the trouble and usually within a minute or two movement began again.

A system of CMP information posts was put into operation from the beginning of the campaign and thereafter steadily developed. The practice was to site the information posts at focal points near an important cross-roads or in a town with as big a 'pull-in' as possible so that enquirers could park clear of the traffic stream. These posts gave information of the locations of HQ, units, installations, drinking water and petrol points, fire service, medical officers, etc, and road information of all kinds. In towns they furnished information on parking facilities, places of entertainment, baths, NAAFI, shopping facilities and so on. Up to 31 March, 1945, 370 military police information posts were opened and manned by CMP, the main ones averaging some 1,000 enquiries per day.

In the early invasion days, 2nd Army, following the custom introduced by 8th Army in North Africa, ordered the whitening of all CMP webbing equipment. This was done to enable military policemen on point duty to be readily distinguished and thereby not only help road users and add to the authority of the military police but also to protect the pointsmen standing in the middle of the whirling traffic. The red bands on steel helmets and MP armlets were, in the Normandy dust and at night, very hard to pick out. The white equipment provided the answer. This change which proved such a success in Italy was equally successful in North-West Europe and it was made the official dress for the whole of the military police and its use by any other troops was prohibited.

Although the superficial relations between the French, Belgian and Dutch population and the liberating armies were pleasant, there were frequent troubles. No sooner were the Germans ejected from their countries in which food, clothing, coal and other bare necessities of life had been progressively dwindling, than the friendly Allied armies poured in, bringing with them thousands of tons of these commodities in enormous dumps in the countryside or passing slowly over the railways in open trucks. For boys aged thirteen or fourteen when the war started, sabotage of the German war machine, pilferage of rations, clothing, cars and accessories, had been a patriotic virtue and an act of heroism. Now young men aged 18, they could hardly be expected to realize overnight that what had been heroic and even encouraged by the British Government on Monday became on Tuesday a crime for which they would be severely punished.

On the whole, the relationship between the British and the United States armies was excellent. Both British and US troops recognized the essential differences in each other's methods and points of view and it was only on rare occasions that such differences produced incidents.

In the provost service disciplinary duties always become more complex and more onerous in a theatre of war than elsewhere. Opportunities for looting multiply; crimes of violence tend to increase; pilfering and racketeering reach a huge scale; absenteeism is enlarged. Provost and SIB become intimately concerned with civil offenders and the checking of crime is essential not only to prevent loss of money to the nation and the lowering of army morale, but also to mitigate the direct menace to the success of operations caused by big losses of stores, equipment and supplies. These losses, although to some extent due to direct theft by civilians, were probably in the main a result of collaboration between a few unscrupulous soldiers and officers and highly qualified civilian thieves and receivers. Apart from 'property' offences, there was little grave crime; cases of murder, rape, assault and looting were few. This type of offence tended to increase during active battle conditions and to die down in more static times.

Army discipline was good. There was little drunkenness, although this may have been partly because of the shortage of liquor in the early days and to its high price later. Serious trouble, however, did arise during the winter from the sale to troops of poisonous liquor produced in illicit stills. With regard to dress and general turnout there was a shaky start in the bridgehead; some of the seasoned veterans from the Desert army felt that their reputation for initiative and toughness and their magnificent fighting qualities needed enhancing, either by wearing strange and gaudy garments or by appearing in a studied state of decay. For a short while some of the other troops of 21 Army Group showed signs of yielding to this seduction; but the phase soon passed, nor did it ever affect the high morale of the troops as a whole.

The numbers of absentees and deserters was at times high. In most cases men were absent because of boredom and family troubles. In previous wars absentees usually gave themselves up after a week or two from shortage of funds; in this campaign, pilfering of army stores and sales to civilians at fantastic prices enabled large numbers of absentees to hide indefinitely. In all 36,366 charges were preferred by the military police during the whole of the campaign up to 31 March, 1945; these included 1,092 for drunkenness and 10,363 for absence.

The invasion started in the small hours of the morning of 6 June, gliders, followed by parachute brigades of 6th Airborne Division, dropping at 2 am astride the Orne, on the east side of which they established a small bridgehead. The assault on the beaches began a few hours later, at 7.25 am, with the landing of 50th Division under 30 Corps on the right and 3rd Canadian Division and 3rd British Division under 1 Corps on the left.

Parachute detachments of 6th Airborne Division Provost Company commanded by Captain Thompson, who was awarded the Military Cross for his work during the first two days, were the first provost to land on the Continent. They were quickly followed by military police of all three wings; many of them were landed with the sea-borne assault troops on the first and second tides of D-Day.

The allotment of provost resources would have been sufficient had the landing gone according to plan; but, owing to the rough sea conditions and the failure of the 'Rhine ferries', only the division companies and some sections of corps provost companies arrived on time: even the Beach companies were not complete. During the first two days there were not enough provost to give adequate control to the assembly areas or the narrow exits from the beaches. On D+1 it was decided to beach the LSTs and do without the 'Rhine ferries'. This produced a far greater flow of traffic than had been planned and stretched the limited provost resources to—and sometimes beyond—their limit. By D+2, however, more provost had landed; and, by D+3, although the volume of traffic was steadily increasing, the routes and circuits within the beach maintenance area were working satisfactorily. By D+5, 11 L of C area, which had arrived on D+1, took command of all beach troops, thus relieving corps of that responsibility.

The bridgehead quickly assumed a shape and size which did not

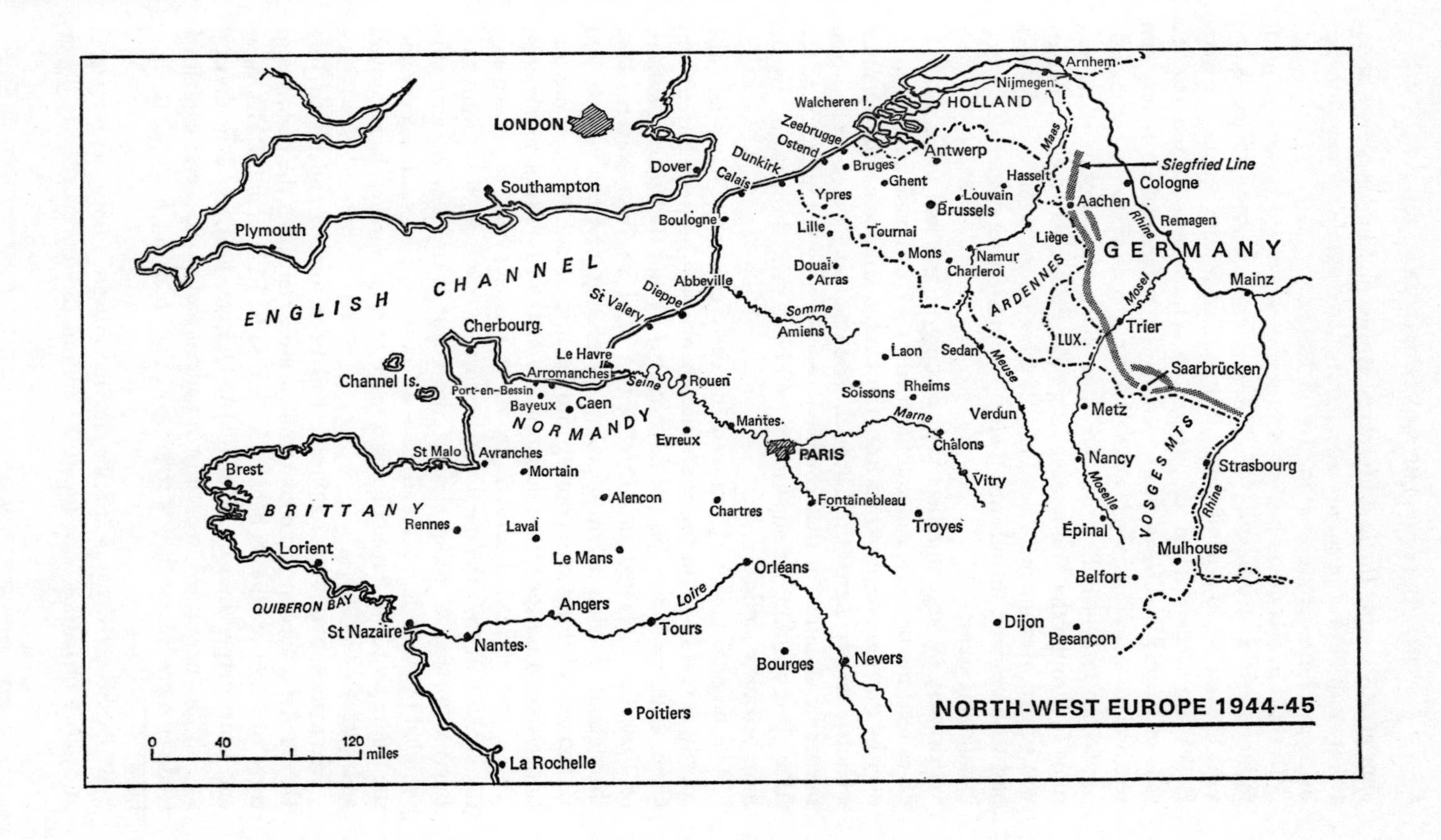
NORTH-WEST EUROPE 1944-45
LONDON
Southampton
Plymouth
Dover
ENGLISH CHANNEL
Channel Is.
Cherbourg
Le Havre
Arromanches
Port-en-Bessin
Bayeux
Caen
NORMANDY
St Malo
Avranches
Mortain
Brest
BRITTANY
Rennes
Laval
Alencon
Le Mans
Lorient
QUIBERON BAY
St Nazaire
Nantes
Angers
Tours
Loire
Orléans
Bourges
Nevers
Poitiers
La Rochelle
Chartres
Evreux
Rouen
Seine
Mantes
PARIS
Fontainebleau
Troyes
Marne
Châlons
Vitry
St Valery
Dieppe
Abbeville
Somme
Amiens
Boulogne
Calais
Dunkirk
Ostend
Zeebrugge
Walcheren I.
HOLLAND
Antwerp
Bruges
Ghent
Ypres
Lille
Tournai
Douai
Arras
Mons
Charleroi
Namur
Brussels
Louvain
Hasselt
Maas
Nijmegen
Arnhem
Siegfried Line
Cologne
Aachen
Liège
Rhine
Remagen
GERMANY
ARDENNES
LUX.
Mosel
Trier
Mainz
Saarbrücken
Laon
Soissons
Rheims
Sedan
Meuse
Verdun
Metz
Nancy
Moselle
Épinal
VOSGES MTS
Strasbourg
Rhine
Mulhouse
Belfort
Dijon
Besançon
0
40
120
miles

alter greatly during the first fifty days. It was, during this period, about twenty miles broad by an average depth of twelve miles; the whole area being much the same size as the Isle of Wight.

But within this minute space, during a period of seven weeks, a great military effort developed. On D-Day alone, 59,900 troops, 8,900 vehicles and 1,900 tons of stores were landed on the beaches; a week later these totals reached 326,000 troops, 54,000 vehicles and 104,000 tons of stores; by D+50 there were in the bridgehead no fewer than 631,000 troops, 153,000 vehicles and 689,000 tons of stores, not including 68,000 tons of bulk petrol. Of these stores a small proportion only came in through the Mulberry during these first weeks; the greater part was landed over the open beaches. All these troops, vehicles and stores had to be moved inland into their appropriate operational depot and installation areas.

Prisoners in large numbers kept coming in and had to be taken to cages near the beaches, run and manned by VP companies, and handed over by them to police escorts from the United Kingdom, who operated a shuttle service across the Channel. The one thing which really saved the traffic situation in that confined beachhead was the fact that the Allies had absolute air superiority. Without that, the position would have become chaotic.

The original plan had assumed the early capture of Caen and the speedy development of the rear maintenance area between Bayeux and Caen. Caen, however, did not fall until 7 July and the adjacent suburb of Vaucelles remained in enemy hands until 20 July. Nevertheless, throughout the first seven weeks a daily average of 3,000 vehicles and 14,000 tons of stores kept pouring into the bridgehead. It was, therefore, impossible to postpone the development of the rear maintenance area. The altered tactical conditions, however, made it necessary to change the layout and shift the main weight north-westwards; this meant that Bayeux, instead of being clear of the depot areas, now became surrounded by main depots on all sides, a feature which greatly aggravated the traffic problem, Bayeux being a maze of bottle-necks, sharp corners and narrow streets.

Meanwhile two army roadheads had been formed and on 20 July HQ 21 Army Group assumed administrative control of the theatre and these two later roadheads became known as RMA East and RMA West and later merged into the final RMA. Despite the Caen difficulty, by 25 July the new RMA was fully organized and stocked and contained reserves more than sufficient to support the break-out from the bridgehead.

While this activity was in full swing the forward troops were engaged in a series of battles. The forward limits of the more southerly depot areas were within three or four miles of the front line and the constant tactical moves and re-grouping of divisions and corps had to be largely carried out in and through the depot areas. The road system which had to support all this movement was scanty, most roads being only lightly surfaced agricultural lanes, with margins which crumbled and disintegrated. Tanks played havoc with these by-ways and 2nd Army swiftly organized a system of cross-country tank-tracks, which were reconnoitred by corps and TC companies with armoured assistance, signed and lamped for night moves. Four hundred minefield lamps per TC company were issued for this purpose and a floating reserve of 3,000 was held by provost for replacements.

Every road in this small bridgehead was full. Provost and 'Q' (M) made a joint air reconnaissance on 10 July shortly after the capture of Caen to observe the road traffic generally and that passing through Caen in particular. Apart from the endless convoys on the roads, it was impossible to detect a single field in the whole area not occupied by troops, vehicles or dumps. The roads, moreover, quickly began to break up and repairs were almost impossible owing to the continuous traffic.

It became vitally necessary to take all possible steps to alleviate the congestion and a number of methods were adopted. One was the speedy construction by sappers of a large circular dirt track around towns, starting at Bayeux. A metalled inner circular road followed, built by connecting suitable sections of existing roads with a few specially constructed connecting links. As soon as these were in use no through traffic was permitted to traverse Bayeux and the situation improved. A similar circular road was constructed to by-pass Caen.

Another important step was the evening-up of the load on the roads by Movement Control orders, which confined operational moves to night and administrative moves to day. Before this was done the policy was to accept all-comers at all times; this resulted in most moves taking place simultaneously during hours of daylight and the roads being nearly empty during the few hours of darkness.

A traffic census taken at a number of the worst points during the height of the congestion showed that at one period in 2nd Army area 305,276 vehicles used the roads in seven days, a daily average of 43,600 vehicles. At the peak 18,836 were counted in one day at the Tierceville cross-roads, an average of one vehicle every four and a half seconds.

By the end of August, 1944, the break-out was complete and the German armies, shattered in the 'Falaise Pocket', were in full retreat; the British, Canadian and American forces were rushing forward in pursuit at great speed; both armies were over the Seine and 30 Corps was actually crossing the Somme. This headlong advance gave rise to new stresses for provost, as divisions shot forward in pursuit of the enemy.

Both armies had to be reinforced with additional TC companies to maintain their swiftly-stretching communications and to control the army roadheads and 'cushions'. During the twelve days between 25 August and 6 September, five new army roadheads and 'cushions' were opened by 1st Canadian Army and three by 2nd Army. The Seine and other river crossings required close traffic control; all the permanent bridges were down and all crossings were on improvised structures. As usual, provost and traffic control reinforcements to both armies had to come from L of C, which at this time could ill spare them as the L of C was continually having to absorb fresh areas of country in order to relieve the two armies from having to look too far over their shoulders.

The capture of Le Havre by 1 Corps produced some difficult PoW problems. The normal 1 Corps cage was already full to its 1,500 capacity and the first Intelligence estimate for PoWs from Le Havre was 5,000. So the APM opened a special cage close to the city and was given a company of Commando troops to run it. A day before the attack the estimate was raised to 7,500 and then to 10,000. And in fact after the capture of the city on 12 September, 11,500 PoWs had to be admitted. This strained resources beyond the limit and at last, on 16 September, the APM arranged with great difficulty the transfer of 6,000 in two convoys to the Army cage. The first 3,000 duly left but in the evening he heard that the Army cage was too full to take them and had returned them! Two German officer PoWs were heard to say that they were sure that the trip to the Army cage and back had been as propaganda to impress the French populace!

After the capture of Brussels and Antwerp there was a short breathing space while armies, corps and divisions curled up their tails, sorted out their resources, overhauled their MT and built up reserves of signing equipment, etc. All the time the L of C was steadily advancing and, in relieving both armies of much territory, was adding greatly to their own burden.

The operation to seize a bridgehead over the Rhine at Arnhem was now to be launched. 1st British Airborne Division and 82nd and 101st US Airborne Divisions, with 30 Corps in charge of ground operations, were responsible for the attempt which started on 17 September, 1944, and which succeeded at Nijmegen and Grave but, after bad weather conditions, failed in spite of much heroism to achieve success at Arnhem. The provost problem which Lieut-Colonel Melville had to tackle was one of great difficulty. 30 Corps moved up with the Guards Armoured Division and 43rd and 52nd Divisions under command; 101st US

Airborne Division came under command later. The control of the operational traffic, including the airborne tail, was the task of 30 Corps Provost.

In the course of this move approximately 20,000 vehicles had to be moved across Holland on a single-axis route, supplemented, in places only, by a subsidiary route; but wherever these two routes joined, as they frequently did, a troublesome bottleneck was produced.

113 Provost Company did some fighting on their own during this action; one detachment at St Oedenrode was in action on 18 September against German snipers, and the following day in action again, together with US airborne troops, repelling a German attempt to break through. In this case an Irish Guards tank which had lost its officer was commanded throughout by Lieutenant Smith of 113 Provost Company. The Guards Armoured Division Provost Company was involved in the fighting around Nijmegen and actually established traffic control over the bridge whilst the action was still in progress. This was, incidentally, another occasion where a section from the traffic control company did splendid work in action; this time in maintaining line communications across the bridge under heavy fire.

A lance-corporal from 113 Provost Company came across a strong party of Germans in a wood near the main road. He reported this to a nearby US unit. The US officer divided his men into two and said, 'You take half and go up one side; I will take half and go up the other'. The military policeman pointed out there was an officer, as well as several sergeants, in his half, but was told by the American officer, 'That's OK, boy; they'll follow you'. After a short bout of woodland fighting the situation was cleared and the policeman returned his 'half' to its rightful owner and went about his duty.

By 9 November German resistance on the island of Walcheren was eliminated and the approaches to the port of Antwerp were opened and cleared, the first convoy actually berthing on 26 November.

Antwerp, however, quickly became the most unhealthy place behind the front line. An incessant stream of V1 and V2 missiles rained upon it; for weeks they came in at the rate of one every half-hour by day and night. The target area was small and much damage and loss of life were caused. As the bombs continued throughout the night no real rest was possible and the whole Antwerp garrison underwent a severe strain. The provost service suffered many casualties. On 27 November a V2 fell at midday just outside the CMP Information Post in the Keyserlei, the main street of Antwerp. NCOs of 244 Provost Company and 602 VP Company were on duty at the post; two were killed—one was never found—and eight were wounded. Many civilians were also hurt, and M. de Potter, the chief of Antwerp police, wrote:

'Belgian civilians and civilian services were most impressed by the kind and efficient organization provided at the incident and the civil police are most grateful for the assistance which the military police gave.'

A special system was instituted for dealing with bomb incidents with the minimum delay. Each of the four traffic control posts took a compass bearing on the smoke rising from bomb incidents and telephoned it immediately to Company HQ who promptly plotted the bearings and located the incident; the special 'incident' squad which was always standing by then went straight to the trouble. Thanks to these arrangements, no main routes in Antwerp were out of use for more than thirty-five minutes; and in each case a diversion was working within fifteen minutes of the incident.

The SIB had more work than they could hope to cope with and more SIB sections were formed to help cope with the burden. The more the advance base, the army roadheads and other dumps and depots grew, the greater became the amount of crime and racketeering. Many civilians were arrested for tapping the petrol pipe-lines and a great many others for improper possession of WD stores. The crossing of the Franco-Belgian frontier was followed by an outbreak of illegal dealings in the currencies of the two countries and also by considerable smuggling of tobacco, cosmetics and liquor.

Soldiers were concerned chiefly in thefts of foodstuffs, petrol, vehicles, cigarettes, clothing and blankets which ultimately found their way into the civilian black market, the blankets often reappearing in the form of ladies' overcoats. On the one hand the local population was suffering from a great scarcity of coal, clothing and food—in fact, all the necessities of life—on the other the British soldier lacked the means to pay the high prices charged for luxury goods such as scent, films, jewellery and watches. These two cravings together had naturally led to racketeering and pilfering.

Major F. R. Pollard, APM SIB, had a task of special difficulty and one which called not only for unassailable integrity and a first-rate technical knowledge of criminal investigation, but for organizing powers and foresight of a high order. It was fortunate for 21 Army Group that he possessed these qualities, as well as an unfailing tact and ability to deal with senior officers.

The provost service and SIB were in daily touch with both French and Belgian civil police and a large number of arrests were made. Unfortunately, civilian convictions failed to have the desired effect because most of the civil prisons were soon filled and fines alone were no deterrent. Many civilians were sentenced to imprisonment and then sent home; having been told by the Judge that as soon as there was a vacancy for them in prison they would be notified!

In Brussels frequent joint checks were held by provost and the civil police or *gendarmerie* and many civilian users of WD petrol and other offenders were caught.

The onset of winter produced new problems and roads were ice-bound when on 16 December the Germans struck hard and unexpectedly at 1st US Army in the Ardennes. Surprise was complete and in conditions of thick mist a partial breakthrough was quickly achieved and the River Meuse crossings were threatened. 1st and 9th US Armies were, for tactical reasons, placed under Field-Marshal Montgomery, who immediately moved 30 British Corps south, to concentrate in the area Louvain-Hasselt and subsequently to operate with 1st US Army, south and east of the Meuse.

The reinforcing 'side-slip' of 30 Corps and the subsequent operations were of especial interest and produced an excellent lesson of what happens at a bottleneck: when formations decide to move without previously notifying either the movement control staff or provost; when movement control puts a greater traffic load on the roads than they can carry: when provost fails to appreciate accurately the probable danger spots and has insufficient resources at those points.

Two brigades, independently and without notification, decided to move simultaneously through Louvain, the busy junction of five important main routes; they, of course, interlocked and for some while there was a colossal traffic jam. The situation was energetically handled by provost and eventually all was sorted out; it was estimated that during the first day of this move 40,000 vehicles were cleared around Louvain by provost of the British and US armies.

By 16 January the German counter-attack had failed. 1st Canadian Army with 30 Corps under command was now able to stage the next operation to expel the Germans from between the Meuse and the Rhine. 30 Corps had been built up to a huge strength of seven divisions, three independent armoured brigades, most of 79th Armoured Division and five Army Groups Royal Artillery; the total strength of 1st Canadian Army being nearly half a million men.

The concentration was complicated and produced a hard traffic control problem for provost, ending with a troublesome move into the Nijmegen bridgehead through the bottleneck of the Grave and Mook bridges. Four TC companies, reinforced by 150 Gunners, were used in this operation, which started on 8 February and was completed by 10 March, by which time 1st Canadian Army had driven the Germans behind the Rhine as far south as Wesel, the good work having been continued with equal success by 9th and 1st US Armies as far up the Rhine as Remagen where a bridge over the river was captured intact by 3 US Corps.

During this operation the traffic conditions in the zone were appalling. The joint effects of melting snow and disintegrating roads, coupled with much organized flooding by the Germans, made all kinds of progress on the roads a nightmare. Many policemen worked up to their waists in water for hours at a stretch. Despite all difficulties, vehicles were kept on the roads and the objectives were attained. The obstacle of the Rhine alone remained to be crossed before our forces could overrun Germany.

It was clear in the very early days of 1945 that the SIB were so busy investigating past crimes that there was a danger of losing the value of these highly trained detectives in tracking down the more serious leakage and vulnerable spots in the army supply machine.

One SIB section was accordingly taken off all routine work, was forbidden to follow up individual cases and was ordered to concentrate on investigating the movement of pilferable stores in transit from the docks to depots and from depots on to the forward areas, whether by road or rail; they were also instructed to recommend steps for tightening up control. Two things stood out in sharp relief. The first was that the check and tally system of the various supply services contained a troublesome gap between the dockside and the depots; mainly because of the need for the quickest possible turn-round of lorries and clearance from the docks. It was decided that this gap must, for operational reasons, be accepted. The second point was the serious amount of pilfering caused by absentees still in the theatre. The hospitality and credulity of civilians made it easy for absentees to go into safe hiding and they became experts in forging false passes and documents. A vigorous attack was, however, made by military police on this problem in February; a large-scale check (organized as a secret operation) was carried out over forty-eight hours; all local leave was stopped, all ranks throughout the whole L of C were confined to their unit lines or billets except men on duty, who were provided with a special duty order. Road checks were operated all over Belgium and north-eastern France; cafés, hotels and suspected areas were raided. Every officer and man in the provost service took part and the civil police co-operated as it gave them an opportunity to find some of their own 'wanted' persons. At the end of forty-eight hours over 450 absentees, many of them long-timers, had been collected.

The final round was now about to begin. 2nd Army was to assault in the area Xanten-Rees, with 9th US Army on their right crossing further south near Rhineberg. 1st Canadian Army on the left were to make feint attacks along the lower reaches of the river; 6th Airborne Division and 82nd and 101st US Airborne Divisions were to drop east of the river to seize tactical points; a considerable naval force was included to man some of the craft required in the actual crossing.

During the week preceding 23 March, the date of the assault on the Rhine, moves by road in 2nd Army area totalled over 32,000 wheeled vehicles, 662 tanks and no less than 4,050 tank transporters; three corps had been concentrated, while over 130,000 tons of stores in addition to ordinary maintenance requirements had been moved into No 10 Army roadhead, formed between the Meuse and the Rhine. In all, 70,000 vehicles moved under strict control in sixteen days.

The assault crossing took place during the night 23–24 March and an elaborate and most carefully signed and controlled scheme was produced to ensure success. This operation sealed the fate of Germany and the advance eastwards then proceeded fast; the Elbe was reached, Hamburg and Kiel occupied, and our troops reached the Danish border and the shores of the Baltic. On 5 May all German armies still opposing 21 Army Group surrendered formally at Lüneburg Heath. The CMP provost detachment which had accompanied the C-in-C's tactical HQ throughout the campaign conducted the German delegation to Field-Marshal Montgomery, who said of the military police: 'The battle of Normandy and the subsequent battles would never have been won but for the work and co-operation of Provost on the traffic routes.'

CHAPTER VIII

Other Theatres

ALTHOUGH these great battles in North Africa and Europe against the German and Italian members of the Axis were the main commitments of the Corps of Military Police, other provost units served in stations all round the world, often in uncomfortable and unglamorous posts. (See Map of the Far East, page 163.)

INDIA

In September, 1939, there were no members of the Corps of Military Police in India. Police duties, which were confined to disciplinary foot patrols in the chief garrison towns, were carried out by regimental and garrison police. But as the war developed it became apparent first that large numbers of new troops would have to be raised and trained and later that India must be put in a state of defence against Japanese invasion and organized as a main base for our own offensive operations in the Far East.

It was not until August, 1942, that the Corps of Military Police (India) (CMP(I)) was formed and many of the personnel were posted, in the case of British and Gurkha other ranks, and transferred, in the case of Indian other ranks, to the Corps. The first static provost unit to be formed in India was the Bombay Provost Unit.

In May, 1941, the first field formation provost unit, comprising one British and one Indian section, was raised for 2nd Armoured Brigade. By July of that year an Indian basic provost unit establishment had been evolved. This allowed for a mixed HQ and a varying number of British and Indian or Gurkha sections.

As the army in India expanded, the need for a fully trained and capable body of military police, on the lines of that existing in the

United Kingdom and Middle East, became apparent. In the first instance, except for the Bombay Provost Unit, all units raised were for formations to be sent to the Middle and Far Eastern theatres for an operational rôle. Later provost units were raised for static and L of C duties in India, in order to maintain the discipline of the greatly increased army in India and to control the movements of troops by road and rail.

One important commitment was the policing of the Assam supply route to Burma from railhead to Dimapur, through Kohima to Imphal and Tiddim. For this purpose additional provost units had to be raised.

When offensive operations against Burma, the Andaman Islands and Malaya were contemplated, beach provost units had to be provided. At the same time the importance of India as a base increased considerably, resulting in a heavy demand for vulnerable points units for the docks at Bombay, Calcutta, and other ports. At the same time a request was sent to the War Office for four companies of military police for normal disciplinary and traffic control duties at Indian ports. This demand was met and their arrival eased the provost situation generally.

The appointment of a Provost Marshal (India), with the rank of brigadier, was sanctioned on 27 February, 1943, but Colonel A. R Forbes, formerly Provost Marshal, Paiforce, was not appointed Provost Marshal in India until July of that year.

The military police in India had a wide measure of responsibility in connection with bounds and price control. Their supervision benefited troops and ensured that hotels, restaurants and cafés, open to them, were maintained up to reasonable standards of cleanliness.

The best example of this was the placing out-of-bounds to all ranks for meals of a hotel in Calcutta. Before the medical service would allow it to be placed in-bounds again the owners had to rebuild the kitchens at a cost of Rs.24,000.

Another important duty was the enforcement of anti-malarial orders. Here again, as a result of provost suggestions, an anti-malarial curfew was introduced in many large towns by varying means, which included mobile patrols displaying large warning notices, sounding of sirens, ringing of bells at railway stations and the display of slides in cinemas.

The smuggling of arms, ammunition and explosives into towns and villages by Indian troops returning from operational and training areas was rife. The civil police became alarmed.

Searches of personnel and baggage were carried out at certain main railway junctions and, at Lahore in particular, recoveries were considerable. On many occasions valuable medical and mechanical transport stores were discovered as well as arms, ammunition and explosives.

A few instances of smuggling large quantities of opium also came to light.

Mechanization of the army in India was very rapid, whereas the standard of driving was low and pedestrians exceedingly unimaginative and careless. The combination of these factors resulted in a high accident rate which caused the concentration of the inadequate provost resources in and around the main towns.

It was not until 1943 that formation commanders in India began to understand and appreciate the organization and functions of provost. Many commanders still retained their conception of the 'Redcap' as he was looked upon in the First World War and it was a long time before they realized that, in this war, it was not possible for them to move their formations without active provost support.

On 1 April, 1945, Brigadier N. C. M. Sykes succeeded Brigadier A. R. Forbes as Provost Marshal, India, and remained until 22 February, 1946, when he handed over to an Indian Army officer, Colonel H. Shuker.

SINGAPORE

The story of Singapore is not so much a story of what provost did but of what it suffered. It is the story of death and disease on the up-country roads and railway, built at the expense of many lives.

18th Division left Great Britain on 30 October, 1941, was at sea when Japan came into the war on 7 December, 1941, and within a few weeks was in Japanese hands almost to a man. Only a handful escaped. Of those for whom there was no escape a remarkable story is in existence. Written in a hand-made, crudely-bound volume on the back of Malayan prison documents by the CQMS of 18th Division Provost Company, this narrative traces the history of the company from its formation in June, 1940, to September, 1944, when liberation was not far away.

The document has little to say of provost activities prior to the surrender, except that the main tasks were dock and town duties, control of traffic to the Nee Soon dump and maintenance of a control point on the Johore Causeway until it was breached on 30 January. But from other sources it is known that as a result of the frequent air raids provost had a difficult task to prevent looting.

After the breaching of the Causeway the beleaguered Singapore garrison experienced almost incessant raids and shelling. The Japanese dropped leaflets calling on Lieut-General Percival to 'give up the meaningless and desperate resistance'. Should he fail to do so, the Imperial Japanese Army Commander added, 'I shall be obliged, though reluctantly through humanitarian considerations, to order my Army to make an annihilatory attack on Singapore.' Five days later, having explained to all ranks the shortage of petrol, food, ammunition and water, Lieut-General Percival surrendered.

18th Division Provost Company, less a small party which escaped, soon found itself imprisoned on Singapore Island.

In the main the narrative is a personal record describing the horrors and infamous treatment suffered by the prisoners, of dysentery, cholera, beri-beri, cerebral malaria and smallpox with no medical aid; of beatings, starvation and other forms of cruelty and of being worked to death. Although the document is worthy of preservation in the Archives, the harrowing story is too familiar to be recorded here and the military police who suffered and died were only a small party of the original 15,200 all ranks who were sent 'up-country' in April, 1943—almost all to their deaths. 18th Division Provost Company itself lost 70 per cent of its strength.

BURMA

The percentage of military police employed in South-East Asia Command was exceedingly small. Total forces were 757,023 of whom only 4,089 were military police; but in April, 1945, there was a general increase in provost sections throughout Allied Land Forces, South-East Asia. Company establishments were increased from two British and four Indian sections to three British and six Indian sections.

The provost service in this theatre developed from these small beginnings for as 14th Army advanced into Burma, its L of C steadily lengthening through Imphal and Kohima and, later when the war ended, into Malaya, new areas and sub-areas were created, all requring provost units and the appropriate officer appointments. In June, 1944, there were only two sub-areas. By August, 1945, there were three areas and eight sub-areas. Apart from normal wastage and replacements for repatriates, strictly operational demands did not greatly increase, though it was realized throughout that provost resources available for operational formations were inadequate.

Provost in India and Burma was an innovation and provost officers frequently found themselves disagreeing with staff officers about the employment of military policemen. This was particularly true of new units. Corps provost were expected to guard corps HQ, act as orderlies and guard and escort PoWs. All this took time to change.

In the Arakan, with the Japanese Army in general retreat, 15 Corps was given the task of seizing the Myebon Peninsula, some thirty miles east of Akyab, by seaborne assault and then at Kangaw to cut the enemy's retreat road. The coast in this vicinity is a maze of uncharted shallow Chuangs reaching the sea through mangrove swamps. In January, 1945, the Navy made a reconnaissance to establish landing sites which was carried out by small boats and frogmen. The sites were finally secured by surprise landings by Commandos. The navigable Chuangs were signed by military police, working in small boats by night, with 'arrows disc-directional' erected on bamboo poles thrust into the river bed for the follow-up landings by the leading brigade of 25th Division. An information post was established on the beachhead with locations of units and routes to all stores areas promptly signed.

Nor was the advance to Meiktila and on to Rangoon all over roads. Many miles of jungle track had to be traversed which virtually put a brigade in single file. Even under these conditions supplies, ammunition and medical stores had to be passed forward to leading troops and ambulances and empty transport returned. One method adopted was for the leading unit to turn its Bren-gun carrier off the track and by spinning on one track clear a passing point every three miles or so. Following units would gradually enlarge the clearing until a sufficient area to harbour fifty vehicles was created which would be manned by two provost NCOs, and eventually was enlarged to 200-vehicle capacity.

By June, 1945, the greater part of Burma had been cleared of the enemy, who however still maintained themselves east of the Sittang River, blocking the way to Malaya, until the eventual Japanese surrender on 14 August, 1945.

Elsewhere, wherever the British Army had operational commitments, however small, the military police were there, carrying out the vital if sometimes routine work of traffic control, security, and crime investigation. From Ceylon to Persia and Iraq, Iceland to Norway, in Gibraltar, Malta, Crete and Greece, in Syria and Lebanon and in Eritrea, South Africa and West Africa provost units, often seriously under strength, tackled with even-tempered efficiency the difficult and frequently unexpected tasks which enabled troops of every arm of the service to operate smoothly and effectively wherever duty called.

PART III

Occupation and Reconstruction

CHAPTER IX

Europe

BRITISH ARMY OF THE RHINE (BAOR)

ON Saturday, 25 August, 1945, 21 Army Group ceased to exist and the remaining forces in North-West Europe became known as the British Army of the Rhine. Some reminder should be made of the past achievements of 21 Army Group. This group of armies fought on the left and northern flank of the allied forces that invaded Normandy in June, 1944. These forces liberated France, Belgium, Holland, Luxemburg and Denmark. They invaded Germany and fought their way half-way across that country, where they joined hands with the Russian armies and thus ended the German war after a struggle which had lasted for over five years.

Since 'VE' Day, 8 May, 1945, when the final surrender of the German forces was accepted, Germany had been divided into American, Russian, French and British Zones of Occupation. The British Zone was roughly the whole of Westphalia and Rhineland, and this was divided into two Corps Districts, administered under HQ BAOR by 1 Corps and 30 Corps. HQ 1 Corps was at Iserlohn, just out of the Ruhr, and HQ 30 Corps was at Osnabrück.

The two APMs, Lieut-Colonel P. Godfrey-Faussett and Lieut-Colonel D. W. L. Melville had been recently upgraded to DPM in recognition of their District responsibilities. These were very considerable and well meriting the extra rank.

This first intermediate period of occupation in 1945 was unique and very interesting and gave provost of all ranks a very full task. Although in theory the new Department of Civil Affairs had taken over the civil administration, there was a great deal that they could not cover. There was every sort of policing—both civil and military—to be done,

hundreds of miles of roads to be signed and controlled, Displaced Persons to be collected, vice and black market to be controlled and normal discipline to be maintained. There was never a dull moment and each day produced a new problem.

Under the control of DPM 1 Corps alone there were no less than 11 APMs and 60 other officers. The Provost force for the Corps District consisted of 6 provost companies—102, 246, Guards Division and 49, 52 and 53 Division Provost Companies, 5 CMP (TC) companies—22, 24, 25, 42 and 101; 2 VP companies, 608 and 613; 3 SIB sections, 72, 87 and 88; 2 Belgian provost companies and 3 companies of German *Feldgendarmerie*—all the latter trained by CMP.

In addition to a great deal of work, there were endless amusements laid on for officers and NCOs and everything, or nearly everything, was free! Although in theory 'fraternization' with the German populace was not allowed, a great deal was winked-at, and friendly relations gradually increased.

Altogether, after nearly six years of war, the summer and autumn of 1945 was a curious and not unhappy interlude, which many British soldiers will never forget. The military policemen who fought through those five years would no doubt be interested to know what happened to those many famous Formations and their provost units with which he served.

As a result of the war much of Europe in 1946 lay in ruins and a period of resettlement and reconstruction followed. Gradually the economic framework of the Continent improved, but, unfortunately, differences of opinion between the governments of countries that had been allies in war became strained in peace. Germany was literally chopped in half and a barrier arose between East and West, followed by a period of cold war. The British Army of the Rhine was reorganized to meet any threats that might develop from the East and in 1951 1 (British) Corps was reborn.

1 (Br) Corps had under command four famous divisions—namely 2nd and 4th Infantry Divisions and 6th and 7th Armoured Divisions. These four divisions developed a new look. The infantry divisions were considerably increased and the armoured divisions reduced. These changes brought them into line with the more modern concepts of war.

1 (Br) Corps Provost Company had been so-named since June, 1951; previously it was 59 Provost Company in Hamburg and was employed on static and dock duties in conjunction with 194 Provost Company. However, the duties of the company changed almost overnight; within a week of moving to Corps they were out in the field on operational exercises, a very rapid change-over from their previous comfort and regular duty periods.

2nd Infantry Division returned from Malaya and joined BAOR in 1947. Its provost company policed an area of great variety and diversity. Flat moorland surrounded the area, while to the east were evergreen-clad mountains and valleys, and to the north the industrial towns provided the smoke, bustle and commotion of the Ruhr. Company headquarters was located near a small textile and market town. Housed in barracks the company lived in luxury and comfort in what may be termed a 'garden' setting. Completely self-contained in one block and possessing its own Sergeants' Mess, Corporals' Mess and NAAFI, the unit enjoyed that exclusiveness which is so necessary for the maintenance of military discipline.

At that time 2nd Infantry Division was the only infantry division in BAOR. All the latest equipment and ideas to combat nuclear warfare were put into operation. Divisional exercises, with the accent on speed and mobility, regularly took the company into the field.

The original 4th Infantry Division was disbanded in the Middle East in 1947. It was re-formed on 1 April, 1956, from 11th Armoured Division, which had been serving in BAOR and was disbanded on that date. The Provost Company was based near one of the oldest monastery towns in Northern Germany.

In company with many other famous formations at the conclusion of the war, there being no further need for the 'punch', nor indeed for an attack at all, 6th Armoured Division was disbanded in 1946.

The succeeding years, however, not bringing the expected peace and plenty in Europe and the increasing demand for British troops in many parts of the world, it became necessary to reform the division in 1951. 6th Armoured Division Provost Company was one of the first units to be ready for service, and in October of that year part of the company moved with the advance parties of the division to BAOR ready to receive the balance of the division when it arrived in February, 1952. In sympathy with tactical re-deployment of formations, the company moved in November, 1954, to an ancient walled town which must be one of the oldest surviving examples of German architecture. There was little time or opportunity for grieving over accommodation problems, however, for in the spring of 1955 the division was selected to fill an experimental rôle and the company was involved in the wealth of exercises and trials that followed.

The company was very busy as, in addition to its operational commitments, it performed static tasks and duties in a very large area of responsibility which included large garrison towns. Apart from normal police duties, the investigation and reporting of traffic accidents at the rate of 800 per year in the divisional area was a guarantee that every NCO was fully employed.

7th Armoured Division (the famous Desert Rats) began its life in the early days of 1940 in the Western Desert of Egypt. It went through all the varying changes of fortune in the desert campaigns, fought its way across Africa and through Italy, and then landed in Northern Europe in June, 1944, and fought its way across France, Belgium, Holland and Germany, 7th Armoured Division Provost Company laying and maintaining the longest division axis in history from Alamein to Berlin.

In writing of the pride and satisfaction that must have been theirs when they played their part in the final Victory Parade in Berlin one can only quote the words spoken by Sir Winston Churchill:

> 'It is not without emotion that I can express to you what I feel about the Desert Rats. Dear Desert Rats! May your glory ever shine, may your laurels never fade, may the memory of this glorious pilgrimage of war

which you have made, from Alamein via the Baltic to Berlin, never die. It is a march unsurpassed through all the story of war, so far as my reading of history leads me to believe. May the fathers long tell the children about this tale, may you all feel that in following your great ancestors you have accomplished something which has done good to the whole world, which has raised the honour of your own country and of which every man has a right to be proud.'

5th Infantry Division Provost Company, one of the most travelled of all units, having served with its division in nineteen different countries in the five years of war, was the first to be involved in beach landings and had become highly specialized in river crossings and was moved up from Italy into Belgium to prepare for the crossing of the Elbe. Events, however, were such that an opposed crossing was not necessary in the fullest sense and, shortly after, all serious fighting ceased.

Problems of a new nature immediately arose; large bodies of enemy troops surrendered in bulk and the entire company was kept busy counting, disarming, searching, directing and transporting. On one day alone 11,000 prisoners passed into the company cage, while sections were concurrently manning subsidiary cages. Soon prisoners were driving themselves to the cages in lorries, fighting vehicles, horse-drawn carts and every type of conveyance.

With the general surrender of all German armed forces in north-west Germany and in Denmark not only did the prisoner situation intensify but a collapse of law and order followed with the breakdown of military control in the former enemy-held areas. Provost immediately moved forward, signing routes, setting up information posts and rounding up loose parties of enemy roaming the countryside or attempting to make their way homeward. For a time all was chaos but long hours of hard work resulted in an organized system. This company finally settled down to its occupational rôle in the Brunswick, Wolfenbuttel, Goslar, Hahnenklee, Göttingen areas.

11th Armoured Division Provost Company, after its wild dash through Belgium and Holland, continued its pursuit heading for the Elbe, through Lüneberg to Lübeck, battling its way not through enemy in opposition but vast drifts of German troops trying to become prisoners. The company then moved on to settle in Schleswig-Holstein for occupational duties.

The Guards Armoured Division Provost Company moved up to Cuxhaven and had to cope with large numbers of sailors who were not so willing to believe the war was over and then moved down to occupy Cologne, Aachen, Euskirchen and Bad Godesberg with company headquarters at Bonn, maintaining a detachment at the Hook of Holland Transit Camp and an Advance Base Section in Belgium.

15th (Scottish) Division Provost Company crossed the Rhine, its leading section crossing with the infantry where it lost two NCOs killed and six wounded, and cleared the way for its traffic against the ever-rolling stream of surrendering enemy, a fitting reversal of the stream of refugees of Dunkirk memory, to arrive at Hammoor, between Lübeck and Hamburg. After the end of hostilities they moved forward temporarily until handing over their area to the Russians, then withdrew to Hanover, where they disbanded on 10 June, 1946.

53rd (Welsh) Division Provost Company reached Hamburg on 3 May and took over the city, which it occupied for a month and was responsible for the initial re-organization.

108 Provost Company, having signed 12 Corps axis forward from Normandy, arrived at Eggestorf on 30 April, where the duty fell to Lieutenant Sharpe to escort the German Commander to 12 Corps Headquarters and back to the centre of Hamburg with the terms of surrender of that city. The company moved into the city on 2 May and settled in the Klein-Flottbek area with headquarters in Hamburg.

109 Provost Company which had its origins in one of the original 1939 TA companies, became 2nd Army Provost Company, under Captain J. Corbett, under command of Lieut-General Sir Miles Dempsey as Army Commander. Hostilities ended for them on Lüneberg Heath with the capitulation of the enemy's North Army Group. The two advance sections of this company were among the first to arrive at Belsen Camp, where they were responsible for its isolation. Special duties were then found, necessitating a move to Berlin, for VIP escorts and security at the Potsdam Conference and then to Minden, where it was re-formed on a Ports basis and seconded to the Control Commission with headquarters at Lübeck and detachments at Berlin, Minden and Bünde.

120 Provost Company was the provost of 21st Army Group and, in addition to founding the first Central Military Police School in North-West Europe, played a big part in resettlement of liberated territory. Two of its sections were, however, operating well in advance with 'R' Force Field Security, a composite force whose main task in conjunction with the Field Security was to seize buildings lately occupied by the enemy, taking into custody any documents or other matter that might have an Intelligence value. In September, 1944, the company took over the policing of Brussels. Almost immediately following liberation a Black Market was organized which grew to enormous proportions. Combating it entailed maintaining a continuous watch on all market places, carrying out constant raids on cafés and other places where the populace congregated, raiding civilian homes where it was reported the occupiers might be in possession of Army property. Petrol checks, to prevent pilfering of any petrol, were organized in conjunction with the

Belgian *Gendarmerie*, samples being taken from the tank and sent for analysis. For a time coal became completely under the control of the Black Market which was only suppressed by issuing permits to drivers of all coal-carrying vehicles and confiscating all loads carried by anyone not in possession of a permit.

Brussels, being on the line of communication, rapidly settled down to 'business as usual' and, the area of operations moving further away, became a principal checkpoint for absentees. Absenteeism reached alarming proportions among forward allied troops necessitating continuous checks on the road approaches, together with organized raids on canteens, cafés and places of entertainment. On one day alone over 100 arrests were made.

Army vehicles fell victim to both absentees anxious to increase the distance from their units and from such concentrated military police activity, and to the Black Market with its thriving trade in tyres, batteries and spare parts; vehicles were quickly broken up, reassembled and disguised. Once more check points were established on main routes or with flying checks descending without warning on unlikely places on alternative routes resulting in the recovery of many hundreds of stolen vehicles.

Venereal disease also became a serious problem, quickly spread by refugees and displaced persons on the move from place to place. An Anti-Vice Squad was formed which, by most strenuous efforts, considerably reduced this form of casualty and held it in check.

In June, 1945, the company moved up to Bad Salzuflen with sections at Bad Oeynhausen, Bielefeld and Herford, where again the suppression of Black Market activity was one of its major duties. At this time they were also very active in the hunting-down and capture of Polish displaced persons who formed into gangs armed with a wide variety of weapons, either improvised, gleaned from the battlefield or stolen, and terrorized the countryside committing rape, murder and robbery with violence.

When the War Crimes Trials opened at Nürnberg a section was posted there for security duties and to find bodyguards for the British judges. Later, volunteers were called for to assist the hangman in the execution of the condemned war criminals.

With forward fighting formations settling down into an occupational rôle, and many specialized units, such as Beach Groups, being disbanded, many well-known operational provost companies lost their formation identities on being merged into static companies for a garrison rôle. Thus elements of 54th Division, 42nd Armoured Division, 102 (1 Corps) Provost Company, and 10 Beach Group merged into 234 Provost Company.

246 Provost Company was formed by the amalgamation of 3rd Independent Provost Company with 640, 641 and 642 Beach Units all of whom had played their parts in landings in Sicily and Italy. Headquarters was at Castellammare with detachments spread over a vast area which included Naples, Torre-Annunziata, Benevento, Pompeii and Auola. Transition from operational to static duties was learned quickly enough with overwhelming experience in Black Market, prostitution and the inevitable spate of crime in which they succeeded in creating an insoluble problem for themselves when their zeal in suppressing the enormous incidence of crime completely saturated the local jails to overflowing.

They eventually moved via Leghorn, Marseilles and Cambrai to settle in Bocholt with detachments at Rees, Goch, Kevelaer, Burgsteinfurt, Rheine and Wesel, and subsequently at Münster and Borken. They were immediately involved with displaced persons of many nationalities, including French, Polish and Russian and the inevitable rape, murder, looting and robbery that marked their presence in the district. The company played an important part in the very serious flooding that occurred in February, 1946, when the River Lippe burst its banks, inundating the countryside. This entailed extensive reconnaissance under hazardous conditions to find and sign diversions and alternative routes in order to supply both the forces' needs and those of the civilian population. In May the company moved to Warendorf to take over from 52nd (Lowland) Division Provost Company.

247 Provost Company was formed of units from the Middle East who had seen service from Alexandria to Tobruk and Tunisia, through Sicily, Cassino and Salerno (as 232 Provost Company) where Provost were used as infantry reinforcements acquitting themselves well under command of Lieutenant A. B. Roberts, RASC, then to re-group in England as 247 Provost Company with Major S. F. Crozier as APM. This company, less two sections diverted via Marseilles (Operation 'Gold Flake') to take the docks there to receive Allied forces arriving from Italy, landed in Normandy on D-Day 6 June, 1944 and the following six days. Moving on through France and earning a congratulatory letter from the C-in-C, they arrived in Menin on VE Day and eventually finished-up in Berlin where they have continued to serve.

104 (3 Corps) Provost Company was the parent of 241 Provost Company and No. 5 Beach Group of 248 Provost Company, which eventually absorbed 240, 242, 243, 245 and 249 Beach Group Companies from Lille, Arras and Ostend. The latter two units formed at Tournai, then passed through Holland pausing at Middelberg, on to the occupation of Berlin and finally to be absorbed in turn by 247 Provost Company.

In the early days of the occupation of Berlin serious crime was very prevalent, murder, rape, robbery with violence and kidnapping were of daily occurrence and the 'Incident Squad', with Russian Military Police attached, were often out dealing with three incidents at a time, involving soldiers of five nations. Three 24-hour duties per week were the rule rather than the exception.

At that time the Four-Power Commission operated smoothly and co-operation made possible the settling down of the city, enabling clearance of devastation to be begun and the city brought back to life. Co-operation between the four Military Police contingents was very good, whether on ceremonial or routine duties such as the daily raising and lowering of the four national flags at the Allied *Kommandantura*, or on active police work in traffic control, crime investigation and military discipline. Russian and German interpreters were attached to all provost detachments and liaison was of the highest order. It was noteworthy that any Russian soldier found in trouble in the British Sector was most severely dealt with by his own Military Police.

The autobahn to the British Zone of Germany was also patrolled with checkpoints manned at both ends—Berlin and Helmstedt, which at that time had recovery posts established half-way. There was also completely free movement between the four Allied Sectors. This fairly happy state of affairs continued until the two states of Germany, East and West, became autonomous and finally disrupted with the 'Berlin Airlift' when the Russians abandoned the Allied *Kommandantura*. This brought to an end the first phase of the occupation of Berlin.

The occupation of Germany continued for over six years. With the passing of time it mellowed and eventually fraternization expanded under the influence of reconstruction until, in September, 1951, the political division of Germany became established with the birth of the Federal Republic as an independent state and a partner in NATO and Western Union, which it joined in May, 1955—ten years after the cease-fire.

The Army of Occupation became the (second) British Army of the Rhine (BAOR) with the new status of an Allied Army stationed in a friendly country to serve mutual interests. The military police rôle changed accordingly and they were henceforth concerned only with the discipline of British troops and liaison and co-operation with the Civil Police as and when necessary. This co-operation was extremely close and affected all incidents when British troops and German civilians were involved. This particularly applied to the Special Investigation Branch.

With BAOR now concerned with training, together with its allies, for its NATO rôle the provost companies became fully engaged in operational training.

This left only 247 Provost Company in Europe still on active service —in Berlin.

BERLIN

The longest period of occupation of enemy territory by British troops is in Berlin and, on that account alone, Berlin is unique as it is in many other ways. It is, perhaps, a classic occupation and will for ever have its own chapter in history. It is also unique in British military history in that never before have Military Police played so important a rôle. The reason for this lies in their organization and training. Infantry are organized by battalions, companies and platoons, the platoon being the smallest unit capable of being deployed. It consists of some thirty-odd men armed with aggressive weapons and is part of a chain of command, support and supply. In Berlin, where an incident of apparent triviality can escalate into a momentous international incident the appearance of armed and organized troops may well be interpreted as a display of force calling for countermeasures.

The requirement, at least in the early stages, is therefore for the smallest possible intervention, to attempt to put things right, to overcome misunderstandings with tact, threatening or provocative action with firmness and, whilst taking such immediate action, to convey an intelligent and accurate report to higher authority. This the Military Police are both organized, trained and equipped to do, and in so doing the incident can be kept down to the scale of a police matter instead of escalating into military action.

Although it has been said that Berlin is unique it is also true that the pattern of occupation follows the overall principles allowing for the nature of the country, its inhabitants and the political relationships. The differences between one occupied city and another are ones of scale and environment. To avoid being repetitive in recounting the background of the many cities occupied, it may perhaps be excusable to take Berlin, both in spite of and because of its uniqueness, as the pattern.

The following account was written in 1957—before the Berlin Wall was erected in 1961—

The 1939–45 war left Berlin a heap of devastated rubble and, following the last stand of Nazidom, the grave of German youth. This ruined capital, which for so many centuries had been a border town on the marches of East and West, was once more over-run from the eastern lands of the Slavs. The nation and country of which it was the capital was divided and it is interesting to note that the dividing line almost approximated to the boundaries known to the Roman Legions and Charlemagne's Teutonic Knights.

At the Yalta Conference in February, 1945 and the Potsdam Conference in July, 1945 the heads of government of the three allies made arrangements for the occupation and control of Germany, leaving the question of its frontiers and, in particular, the Oder/Neisse line for final settlement at a peace conference. It was agreed that Germany should be divided into four zones of occupation, the Military Governors of each of the four countries being supreme in their own zones but responsible for carrying out the international agreement affecting them. Berlin was likewise divided into four sectors of occupation, each under the command of a major-general.

By arrangement between the allies, however, the advance from the west was halted on the Elbe, this facilitating the final advance by the Soviet army to cross the Oder and to take Berlin. Thus it was that Berlin found itself deep in the heart of the Soviet-occupied Zone.

The British, American and French entered Berlin to find the ghost of a city pillaged, starved and its wealth destroyed. The work of relief, clearance and then reconstruction began.

The Allied *Kommandantura* governing the city was soon up against the veto arising out of the conflicting policies, especially currency reform, until, in the Spring of 1948, following the economic recovery of West Germany, now the Federal Republic, with its effect on West Berlin, the Soviets withdrew from the Control Commission and the Allied *Kommandantura* was no longer attended by the Soviet Commandant. An attempt was then made to force the Allied withdrawal from Berlin by an economic blockade, frustrated by the famous Berlin Airlift and the determination of the West Berliners. The result was a city with two economies, two currencies, two ideologies.

The West-East boundary of the city is marked by notice boards with police and customs patrols and picquets and yet there is, in accordance with quadripartite agreement, but sometimes surprising to the visitor, unrestricted movement though intercourse is limited. The Soviet authorities restrict Western residents shopping in the East Sector because of the shortage of consumer goods, while the Western authorities support this attitude to prevent Western currency passing eastwards and weakening the Western economy; whereas shopping in West Berlin is normally beyond the means of the East Berliners.

There is, of course, very little communication between West Berlin and the surrounding countryside which means its food and the bulk of its producer goods must be imported from Federal Germany, a distance of 120 miles, and its products, not consumed at source, must be exported.

The efforts of the West Berliners may be well judged by the fact that West Berlin absorbed an average of 350 refugees from the Soviet Zone daily and yet, since the blockade, unemployment had fallen from about 300,000 to around the 100,000 mark.

The divided city of Berlin is organized into twenty administrative districts, of which twelve are in West Berlin. Its population and area are:

	Population	*Area*
West Sectors	2,200,000	185 sq miles
East Sector	1,200,000	155 sq miles
	3,400,000	340 sq miles

The British Sector, with a population of about 650,000, comprises the districts of:

Tiergarten: The 'St James' of Berlin containing the Grosser Stern (The Memorial to the Franco-Prussian War victory 1870–1871), the old Reichstag Building, the Soviet War Memorial and the Berlin Zoo. The famous thoroughfare comparable to London's 'Mall' renamed '17 Junistrasse' runs up to the Brandenburger Tor and the West-East Sector Boundary. It also includes Moabit, mainly an industrial area intersected by a network of canals.

Charlottenburg: Containing the Kurfürstendamm (comparable to Regent Street), the Kaiser Wilhelm Memorial Church, the Olympic Stadium and Waldbühne open-air theatre, the Funkturm and Exhibition Grounds, the Avus Motor Racing track and the British War Cemetery. This includes the exclusive residential district and the 'West-End'. British Headquarters is in the neighbourhood of the Stadium.

Spandau: Containing the Prison which housed the major War Criminals, the Airport of Gatow and large tracts of the Spandau Forest. Most of the barracks housing the British Garrison and installations are in the Spandau district.

Wilmersdorf: Containing a large residential and commercial district and the greater part of the Grunewald Forest.

Through the British Sector, from north to south, flows the River Havel separating Spandau from the other districts of the Sector. Beyond Spandau is the border of Soviet-occupied East Germany.

The French Sector lies to the north, the American Sector to the south.

The Allied *Kommandantura* is the official governing body of the city representing the Military Occupation. Although the Soviets have not occupied their chair since the Economic Blockade of 1948 they are still, in Western eyes, officially members and their seat is there to be taken whenever they see fit. Technically each power takes the chair for a month, but the only outward sign of Soviet participation is their regular tour of duty at Spandau Prison.

Meanwhile the Western Allies have been constantly occupied with the task of restoring the maximum amount of self-government possible to the city. In 1950 a new constitution set up a city Parliament which elected a Senate and which now has sole responsibility for most of the administration of the West Sectors. The Allies, however, remain responsible for the security and defence of Berlin and in this connection exercise considerable control over the city's Police Forces.

The overall organization of each of the Allied powers follows the same general pattern. In the British Sector the British Commandant, who is also GOC British Troops, heads Military Government with a Foreign Office adviser as Deputy and a staff of Foreign Office advisers and officials concerned with the political, economic and legal aspects of the administration, the rights of the occupying powers and the many varied matters concerned with the daily running of the city and co-ordination with the other Commandants and the City Senate.

As GOC British Troops he has a small military personal staff, which includes the APM (lieut-colonel) and Staff Captain (Provost), and under him is the junior formation: Berlin Independent Brigade. Just as the GOC's military staff is reduced to the minimum, so the Brigade Commander's staff is expanded, approximately to that of a division. Berlin Brigade also contains most of the corps and services associated with a division, including 247 Provost Company and a Special Investigation detachment.

The liaison link between the Commandant and the West Berlin Police is a small unit known as Public Safety under an Inspector-General. The unit is part of British Military Government and staffed by selected British civil police officers. Their duty is to ensure the fulfilment of the Commandant's policy for the security of Berlin by the civil police and to act in a supervisory and guiding capacity to the extent necessary to ensure its efficiency. They also act as the liaison link between the APM and the West Berlin Police.

The West Berlin Police are extremely efficient and effective. They are organized into the branches known to the English system; uniformed branch including traffic, foot, mobile, water, mounted and dog wings, and the 'Kripo' (CID). They make the maximum use of mechanization, radio communications and scientific aids and are a member of Interpol. Many of their officers have visited British, American and French police forces. The one force operates throughout the Western Sectors being organized into three divisions, corresponding to the three Sectors. Each division is responsible to the occupying power of its Sector through its Public Safety unit, while collectively they are administered through their Headquarters and co-ordinated by the West Berlin Senate who are responsible for them to the Allied *Kommandantura*.

Comparable to the British Corps of Royal Military Police and with similar responsibilities, duties and commitments, are the US Army Military Police Corps and the French *Gendarmerie*. Liaison and co-operation between the three forces is of the closest and many duties are performed jointly. Powers of arrest are virtually mutual in that a military offender is initially dealt with by the military police of the Sector in which he commits the offence, irrespective of his nationality, and he is then handed over to his own police unit and reports are forwarded. There is joint participation in exercises, and planning for special events, escorts, etc., are jointly worked out. The overall policy is co-ordinated and mutual assistance prevails at all levels.

The APM, with his Staff Captain, is on the staff of the GOC and therefore in constant and close contact with Military Government political advisers and in many ways is the link between Military Government and Berlin Brigade, who are housed in the same building. For the purposes of liaison it is therefore virtually one HQ. RMP are, however, through the APM, directly under the GOC for operational matters. Housed in separate blocks, but within the same perimeter, are 247 Provost Company and SIB. This lends itself to very tight control and has obvious advantages provided the unit commanders do not forget they are brigade troops and resist a natural inclination to allow command control, as distinct from policy direction, to pass into staff hands.

The duties in Berlin are many and varied. The normal maintenance of military discipline is as important in Berlin as anywhere else, especially when two factors of the utmost importance are realized. The effect of the behaviour of troops on the Berlin citizens is an influential factor in the struggle for the mind and soul of the city; and the world press, as well as three other armies, are constantly criticizing and judging the calibre of the British Army and of Britain by its representatives here, focused under the spotlight. In no other British Army station are military police called upon to live up to the basic elements of the British conception of a police force by example and crime prevention more urgently than in Berlin. The maintenance of discipline has as its corollary the preservation of good relations and this is perhaps the greatest contribution the Royal Military Police have to offer in Berlin: they are truly the guardians of British prestige.

There are three gateways from the west into Berlin: by air, railway and road. By air is not in the normal way the concern of RMP but comes under American control at Tempelhof and RAF control at Gatow. By railway is the responsibility of Movement Control in the normal way, but in addition to routine station patrols 247 Provost Company do pass train control communications through the provost radio net and the provost officer at Helmstedt Autobahn Checkpoint is often involved in liaison with the Soviet authorities over railway matters.

From the RMP point-of-view however Berlin depends for its lifeline on the autobahn. Officially termed the 'Berlin–Helmstedt Autobahn Corridor' it is an international route from the British Army area in West Germany to Berlin. Its use is governed by the Articles of the Potsdam Agreement. It is under the control of the Soviet authorities and used by right of agreement by the Western Allies. Special passes are necessary, supported by military identity cards or passports. Control, from a RMP point of view, consists of the enforcement of regulations which have political and legal significance and the preservation of rights and enforcement of obligations under which the use of the route is agreed. RMP do not patrol the route but are nevertheless responsible for Allied vehicles using it. Speed restrictions are enforced by means of a timed-run schedule from point-to-point. Missing or overdue vehicles are searched-for and broken-down vehicles recovered. The US authorities recover from Berlin and the British from Helmstedt irrespective of nationality, including sponsored civilian cars. Recovery-aid required is notified by a chit system under which the stranded vehicle notifies its trouble to another Allied vehicle who passes it to the Allied checkpoint. Recovery may take five or six hours.

At each end of the corridor are two checkpoints: on the innerside the Soviet and the outer the Allied. Representatives of RMP, US Military Police and French *Gendarmerie* are on permanent duty.

The Berlin checkpoint is manned by NCOs of 247 Provost Company and the Company is responsible for the administration of the post. For duties they come directly under the Staff Captain Provost, Berlin, who is responsible to the APM.

At Helmstedt 247 Provost Company find the Autobahn Control Detachment, approximately a section strong, under the command of a major with a staff-sergeant as 2IC. The major is also a miniature garrison commander, being responsible for the administration of an assortment of military and civilian families and their quarters.

The duties concerned with Autobahn Control are extremely interesting and bring the officers concerned into close liaison with the Soviet officers the other side of the barrier. This is especially so at Helmstedt where, as the Post is in what used to be the British Zone, the Soviets still tend to deal with the British representative on points concerning all travellers irrespective of nationality and he has to be always on call. Interpreters are found from Russian-speaking British other ranks. The OC Helmstedt detachment has one of the most difficult and arduous appointments in the Corps and much indeed can depend on his tact, quick thinking and determination. It is not a job for any but the most reliable and, in proportion, this is equally true of the other ranks.

The nerve-centre, and a most vital one, of RMP in Berlin is the 'control room'. It is housed in 247 Provost Company barracks and is manned 24 hours a day by a duty sergeant and two other NCOs with a German civil police liaison officer.

Its equipment consists of two-way radio-telephone communications, a normal switchboard and a most complicated alarm system protecting the security of British Headquarters in which the presence of intruders is indicated by lights. The radio-telephone net serves the military train communication and the patrol vehicles. The system is such that patrol cars can be received and plugged-in to the ordinary telephone exchange, enabling them to speak directly to the office or residence of any military subscriber. A further modification enables up to six lines to be linked-in simultaneously thus permitting an immediate 'on the spot' conference at higher level while enabling the Patrol Commander to listen directly to the policy governing his instructions and also to advise on the changing or developing situation.

The control room is linked to both checkpoints, border patrols and incident patrols as well as to the American, French and German civil police exchanges, and the brigade command net.

All patrol vehicles and the APM's car are fitted with the two-way telephone apparatus.

There are two zonal Borders to the British Sector: the British–Soviet sector Border in the centre of the city running between the Tiergarten and Unter den Linden, with the Brandenburg Tor as the centrepiece, which is approximately 2¾ miles in length (now, The Wall) and the British Sector–Soviet Zone (East Germany) Border which extends for about 18 miles. Sector Borders march with the French to the north and Americans to the south.

The Border is guarded in the first instance by Customs personnel with dogs, by static civil police posts and mounted mobile patrols and in the second instance by military police in Land Rovers equipped with two-way radio telephones. While refugee traffic and smuggling is the concern of the civil authorities, RMP duties include the maintenance of the border and the preservation of its rights and obligations from the political, legal and military aspects of violation.

247 Provost Company maintains some 250 signs spaced about every

200 yards over the entire length. This creates a never-ceasing task in maintenance for the sign-writing shop which can better be appreciated when it is known that the total number of RMP signs in the city approaches 600.

Patrols are maintained twenty-four hours a day in weather that encompasses extremes of sun and snow. The border-route is divided into about one third built-up, one third open rural and one third forest. Three simultaneous patrols are required working an eight-hour shift, which calls for nine two-man patrols a day plus the supervising senior NCO. Patrols are, of course, armed. Although well-tried drills are put into action in the event of an incident bringing officers into command, it cannot be over-stressed that the lance-corporal on patrol is the individual who takes responsibility for immediate action on becoming aware of an incident. It must be appreciated that his immediate reaction, possibly when faced by armed men, either Soviet soldiers or East German 'Vopos' (*Volkspolizei*) in the early hours of the morning in a mist-shrouded forest with over-sensitive nerves, might have political repercussions. Such incidents cannot be guarded against by Standing Orders and reliance must be placed on the level heads of the junior NCOs. The fact that it is so is the greatest tribute that can be paid to the young NCO of the Corps (in the 1950s nearly all National Servicemen) who are entrusted with the task.

Reference has already been made to the importance of the maintenance of discipline which in Berlin follows the orthodox pattern of mobile and foot patrols, static and mobile checks, anti-vice checks and all the daily routine of a busy provost unit. In addition RMP are responsible for the security of the British HQ in the Olympic Stadium and, in conjunction with American and French military police, the Allied *Kommandantura*. Certain special duties as and when required are also performed at Spandau Prison, in which were detained the major war criminals, and at the Soviet War Memorial. Then again, there are the many escorts to provide for VIPs, perhaps a little more than required at most stations due to the interest value of Berlin and the number of VIPs that are attracted: a semi-official variation of this duty is the provision of guides for conducted tours of the city, especially into the three other Sectors.

Military Police are also called upon to play a very important and public rôle in the support of British national prestige in the city on such occasions as the annual Queen's Birthday Parade, International Exhibitions and Industrial Fairs, British cultural displays and international sporting events. An important aspect of such functions is the carrying out of the arrangements dictated by protocol in this city of four occupying powers, the Berlin civic dignitaries and the numerous national consuls and missions accredited to one or the other. From the RMP point-of-view priorities, timings and courtesies have to be faultless and tact beyond reproach.

An interesting duty that falls exclusively to provost officers is that of visiting the Soviet Army HQ at Karlshorst in the Soviet Sector to take charge of British personnel who have been detained by the Soviet authorities, the situation normally arising after the British soldier has inadvertently crossed over the border into the Soviet Zone.

Military police jurisdiction extends over all families, sponsored visitors, Ministry of Defence British civilian employees and those of associated organizations, including NAAFI, WRVS, YMCA, Salvation Army and others.

Private cars of all these categories of people are registered with and licensed by HQ BAOR and, as such, while having certain privileges and immunities, are under the jurisdiction of RMP who deal with all matters as would the civil police in the United Kingdom.

Berlin is an active service area which under the Army Act extends RMP jurisdiction over most British civilians in the city.

In July, 1951, the British daily newspapers reported an account concerning a Russian private soldier, Sergei Inyankin, who bicycled into the British sector of Berlin seeking political asylum. He stated that he had no wish to return to the conditions awaiting him in the Soviet Union after demobilization. Facilities were extended to the Soviet military authorities to interview Inyankin in the presence of British representatives. Russian officers maintained that Inyankin had been forcibly brought to the British Sector but he denied this and stated that he had come to the British Sector because, while attached to a Russian Guard Company at Gross-Glienicke, he had observed on the other side of the border the British military police, whose turnout and bearing had made such a deep impression on him.

As has been frequently stressed throughout this history, the first objective of police duty, from peacetime duties in the United Kingdom to operational work in foremost battle areas is to set the highest example. That it should win such respect that a foreign soldier should be prepared virtually to stake his life on it is indeed a compliment: '*Exemplo Ducemus*'.

To conclude this account of Berlin it may, perhaps, be forgiven to quote an article, written in late 1952, by the late Richard Dimbleby, that superb observer of the human scene, whose trained journalist's pen could sum up the contemporary atmosphere far better than most:

> 'Were it not that I have just returned to the comparative security of the Army Mess in which I am staying, I could have headed this letter not "Berlin", but "Russian Zone, Germany". An hour ago I was standing at

30 Corporal R. A. Stony CMP supervising a gang of Nagas clearing a road blocked by a landslide in Burma, 1945.

31 The recovery of stolen tyres by SIB in Singapore, 1945. The lorry is already piled high with stolen tentage.

32 Admiral Lord Louis Mountbatten, Supreme Allied Commander South East Asia, arrives to inspect Inter-Service Police HQ, Singapore, on 1 May, 1946 and meets Lt-Colonel H. Salt DPM Inter-Service Police.

33 Lt-General Sir Miles C. Dempsey, C-in-C Allied Land Forces South East Asia, at 123 Section SIB CMP (I) Singapore in March, 1946. He is shown a bottle of confiscated liquor by RSM Porritt CMP; standing behind is Colonel R. A. Leeson MBE PM ALFSEA.

34 *International Patrol, Vienna, October, 1945.*

35 *A mounted detachment of RMP in Vienna, 1946.*

36 Field-Marshal Montgomery (CIGS) visits the RMP Dog Training School at Almaza, Egypt, in November, 1946 accompanied by General Sir Miles Dempsey (C-in-C MELF and later Colonel Commandant RMP 1947–1957) and Colonel D. W. L. Melville (PM MELF).

37 Corporal Lindsay of 245 Provost Company RMP with a Russian female traffic control regulator—Kaiserdammstrasse, Berlin, July, 1945.

38 The War Crimes Trial in Hamburg, 1947 : a female guard from Ravensbruck Concentration Camp receives her sentence flanked by NCOs of ATS Provost.

39 Lance-Corporals Dawson and Gill of 245 Provost Company CMP in Bellevueallee, Berlin, 21 July, 1945 with typical war damage behind them.

40 The first two British soldiers in Berlin—the CMP escort to Major-General Lyne, GOC 7th Armoured Division, on 4 July, 1945.

41 The 'Royal Prefix' Parade on 23 July, 1947 at Inkerman Barracks, Woking. HRH The Duke of Gloucester inspects the MT accompanied by Major-General I. D. Erskine (Provost Marshal) and Lt-Colonel A. R. Forbes (Commandant Depot and Training Establishment RMP).

the Iron Curtain itself, on a windy, snow-covered road called the Heerstrasse, where East and West stand face-to-face.

'The Iron Curtain is not very solid in appearance—and indeed I saw it penetrated without any apparent difficulty by an old lady riding a bicycle—but, nevertheless, it is real enough. Lying across the desolate highway is a red and white pole barrier. It is guarded by three West German Customs men in green uniforms and a solitary German policeman. There is a small wooden hut; otherwise, nothing but a drab farm set back from the road.

'Just beyond this barrier is a black and white military sign at the roadside. It reads "On no account may any person pass this sign. Russian Zone begins here". Twenty feet beyond is another red and white barrier, another hut, another group of restless men. These are the so-called *Volkspolizei* or "People's Police", of the Russian Zone, with a very young Red Army soldier to keep them company.

'From time-to-time a lorry makes its way from West to East or vice versa with much showing of papers and stamping of passes, and an odd pedestrian or two and a cyclist such as the old woman passed through. Otherwise there is silence, heavy and uneasy silence, full of suspicion and curiosity.

'It reminded me very much of the day, twelve years ago, when I stood at one end of the Kehl Bridge over the Rhine at Strasbourg, with a French officer as my guide and looked straight into a machine gun manned by our enemies, the Germans. Manned, but not firing, for there was that same solemn silence. The calm before the storm, perhaps.

'Yet that is not the general view of the men who protect the West Sectors of Berlin, and who are in the closest existing contact with the Russians. The pin-prick, yes . . . to make trouble, to be difficult and petty, to wear our patience thin with the oriental smile, yes . . . that may be the Russian plan, they think. But to go to war, no; not at present, anyway.

'I respect the views of our men on the spot here. They live and work in a supercharged atmosphere, in a city that has made an astonishing recovery from the devastation of our bombing and is full of life and bustle. Yet all round them are the barricades, and beyond them the unknown, the open countryside of mystery and silence, dark at night, invisible by day. They live under continual nervous strain but they show little sign of it.

'Take, for example, the Regimental Sergeant-Major of 247 Provost Company of the Royal Military Police. I will spare him the embarrassment of mentioning his name. He is a stocky, beautifully turned-out man, in faultless battledress, knife-edged trousers and gleaming brown boots. He wears the spotless white belt, revolver holster and gaiters of the Military Police and is known and respected, not only by the British and Allied personnel in Berlin, but the Russians who stand guard all round the city.

'He came with me to the barrier on the Heerstrasse. Together we ducked under it and went on to the Iron Curtain. A man came out from the Red Army post, watched us through field-glasses and went back in. A few moments later a Russian staff car came pelting down the hill from the fort just beyond the frontier line. Five minutes later a small spotter aeroplane bearing the markings of the Red Star came over the treetops and circled round us, watching.

'The RSM took it in his stride. "They're wondering what's up", he said cheerfully. "Very jumpy, they always are. But I think, as a precaution, we won't go any farther down the road. We don't want to start anything." "What would happen if we went on up to their barrier?" I asked. I was measuring the distance—a few feet. "They'd nab you the moment you got there", said the RSM with such certainty that I was glad to turn back and return to the security of the British frontier behind us.

'To him, of course, the incident meant nothing: he has had too many dealings with the Russians, settled too many explosive incidents to be bothered by field-glasses, staff cars and spotter planes. I think it is no exaggeration to say that this determined and courageous man has held the peace of Europe, if not the world, in his hands on more than one occasion.

'It is our policy in Berlin—and a wise one—to leave the men on the spot, the NCOs or warrant officers, perhaps, to settle disputes, if they can, without referring them to higher authority. For it is when higher authority is involved that a border fracas can become a political crisis.

'A good example was the night when the Germans reported that Red Army troops were uprooting part of the frontier wire fence and warning signs, and moving them farther forward—for what purpose no one knew. The RSM took his interpreter and six military police and drove at full speed to the spot. He confronted the Russian officer in command with the agreed map of the Berlin Sectors and pointed out that the frontier was now too far forward. The Russian refused to move the line back. The Sergeant-Major said, "Very well, open fire". The Red Army men were already presenting their sub-machine guns at the police. "All right. If you dare—shoot away", said the RSM, who strode forward and began tearing up the barricade. No shot was fired, the Russians withdrew and an hour later the boundary was back in its proper place.

'They will tell you many such stories in Berlin and every one of them reflects credit on the men—and women too—of the Army and Royal Air Force who garrison this danger-spot of Europe. I see this city today as another Malta and the spirit that held our Mediterranean island secure through all the years of its peril lives again here. It is something of which we should be proud.'

In August, 1961, relations between East and West became further strained. The open city of West Berlin, exhibiting its culture, its reconstruction which made it the most modern city in Europe and too provocative a contrast to East Berlin, its international trade fairs and exhibitions and, above all, the never dwindling flow of refugees from communism to democracy, became too much and the East German authorities sealed off the Berlin border, constructing a permanent concrete wall reinforced with anti-tank barriers and weapon emplacements. Intercourse between the two halves of the divided city then ceased. In 1962 the Russians abolished their office of 'Commandant' Berlin.

The three western powers, however, soldiered on to keep the light of hope burning behind the Iron Curtain, the importance of which was emphasized by the visit of the US President Kennedy in June, 1963 (countered by a visit to East Berlin by General Secretary Khrushchev shortly afterwards) and by Queen Elizabeth II in 1965.

BAOR IN THE SIXTIES

By 1968 BAOR had become the principal training ground of the British Army and RMP had one-third of the Corps serving in Germany; everyone could expect to spend at least one tour in Germany. The British Army of the Rhine is stationed in the former British-occupied Zone, which consists of all West Germany north of a line drawn from the Eifel Mountains in the west, across the Rhine south of Bonn to the East German border east of Kassel.

The British garrisons are generally situated in pleasant country towns, with good shopping centres and a wide range of recreational facilities.

A BAOR Police School was set up at Bielefeld in 1962 to deal with provost continuation training in Germany; this School was transferred to Berlin in 1965 when the Advanced Driver Training Team (ADT) was formed on an experimental basis. This team consisted of Hendon-trained advanced drivers equipped with six Hillman Huskies, which toured BAOR training over 100 advanced driving instructors. Unfortunately the ADT did not receive sufficient support from units or the Treasury and had to be disbanded in April, 1966. However, the six Huskies were retained and, painted white, fitted with blue lights, Martin horns and radios formed the basis of the BAOR Traffic Squads. These Traffic Squads, which included motor-cycles with white fairings, were employed on courtesy patrols and general traffic duties.

4th Division Provost Unit ran several courses to train German traffic law lecturers. Each provost unit then had at least one of these lecturers who toured his 'parish' lecturing to units and schools. Major units in the United Kingdom received visits from these lecturers before they moved to BAOR in order to prepare their drivers for the hazards of continental motoring.

A feature of the campaign to reduce road traffic accidents was the radar speedcheck van which proved to be an effective deterrent against British drivers speeding and, following the Road Safety Act, 1967, in the United Kingdom, the Breathalyser Test was introduced.

The three provost companies, and nine division and brigade provost units in BAOR, were welded firmly to the formations they support in war. The annual training cycle builds up to a climax in October at divisional level.

Throughout the year there is the ever-present problem of policing the garrison towns. Outside barracks the German civil police are nominally the superior authority but they have a healthy respect for the administration of the Army Act and generally allow provost to deal with British servicemen. A good working liaison is vital to the effective policing of these garrisons and the wide spaces between them. A close comradeship between the '*roter und weisser Mützen*' has grown up in many stations.

BAOR had its fair share of crime and perhaps more than its fair share of traffic accidents and associated offences. Most of the incidents sprang from irresponsible motoring, or too much alcohol or both.

In 1964 Stations Radio C.13 were made available to RMP units throughout BAOR. This modern high frequency equipment transformed Provost operational duties overnight. Command of a unit or section in the field through this medium was instantly simplified. A unit or section commander at last discovered mobility. Ranges of 15 kilometres (10 miles) while on the move, using eight-feet rod aerials, became commonplace. By correct siting from static locations and using 16 feet rod aerials, 25 kilometres (16 miles) range on excellent voice communication was easily obtainable by day. Voice communication over a front of 50 kilometres (31 miles) using 16 feet rod aerials and a step-up station was achieved between Soltau Training Area and Hohne Ranges consistently through a two-week exercise and to the delight of NCOs trained as signallers at the Depot, Formation Staff found it necessary to use RMP HF radios in emergency when Royal Signals VHF communications failed.

These radio sets gave excellent control, mobility and flexibility. With the introduction into BAOR in early 1967 of the Pye Cambridge VHF Radio-telephone RMP were launched into a new era of mobile police work. The active policing of a large garrison became a reality.

The mobile patrols were at last able to carry out the functions for which they were always intended. With the outstanding radio-telephone communication provided by this equipment beats were determined by the limit of radio range which varied up to 25 kilometres from base.

The standby no longer stands, he moves. No more does he have to await call-out. With the mobility afforded by Pye he could be directed to an incident from any point within the range of his fixed frequency equipment.

An off-shoot of these radios was that the large control sets permanently installed in duty rooms covered immense ranges control-to-control and it then became possible to switch frequency and speak to a provost unit up to 100 miles away.

A modern addition to the equipment available to provost in BAOR was Telefunken VRG 2 radar speedcheck equipment, which was permanently installed in a Morris police van. This equipment was hired for a six-month trial period in November, 1966, as a result of a directive being received that a determined drive should be made to reduce the high number of traffic accidents and fatalities in BAOR. The cost of third party claims against the Army Department that year was estimated to exceed £400,000 and the number of deaths each year approached 100.

The radar van was deployed throughout the BAOR area and there was no doubt that the use of the equipment had a salutary effect in reducing the incidence of excessive speeding and there is statistical evidence showing that during the same period the number of accidents and fatalities drastically decreased. Over 2,300 offenders were reported during the first eight months.

The trial was considered a success and as a result the radar equipment was purchased locally for the permanent use of RMP in BAOR. This set provided either a photographic record or a graphic card record, or both, of each offender. It did not have to be installed in a vehicle.

Provost in BAOR is rapidly moving into the electronic age and the days of the military policeman checking speed by means of a stopwatch and measured distance, although still a valid operation, will soon become an anachronism. A number of offenders have already been reported for their sixth offence and the reward for such intolerant driving has been a heavy fine and withdrawal of their British Forces Germany (BFG) driving licence for periods of several months by commanding officers.

The use of helicopters for route reconnaissance and for quick transportation to the scene of incidents became a familiar routine.

Several provost units carried out helicopter training with the RAF, learning how to emplane and deplane, load radios and equipment, and undersling motor-cycles. It has been found that with these helicopters, traffic posts can be quickly deployed along a route or patrols ferried from base to deal with traffic accidents and other incidents. In 1965 two Wessex helicopters were used to lift a section and motor-cycles employed on security duties during the Queen's visit.

From time to time military police in BAOR were called upon to carry out patrols of the East–West German border. This interesting and slightly hazardous duty involved 'showing the flag' and occupying certain areas along the border over which possession was in dispute.

A full provost section equipped with arms and ammunition was required to carry out this duty. Patrolling only took place during daylight hours and patrols always included a member of the British Frontier Service (dressed in Naval-type uniform) and of the German *Bundesgrenzschutz*. The barbed wire, watch-towers and minefields, among the pleasant fields and forests provided the grim background to this important task. A week spent patrolling this border brought NCOs face-to-face with the stark realities of divided Germany.

The Headquarters of the British Army of the Rhine is situated in the military township of Rheindahlen, which lies roughly half-way between the Rhine at Düsseldorf and the Dutch border at Roermond.

Until 1964 the policing of this garrison was carried out by a very overworked detachment from 101 Provost Company. However, the steady increase of NATO personnel had expanded the garrison beyond the scope of this detachment and to cope with the work Rheindahlen Garrison Provost Company was formed in January, 1964. It consisted of five sections, including one section of WRAC Provost, with one section permanently detached to the British Advanced Base at Grobbendonk in Belgium. The company had the largest military police 'parish' in the Corps; it included Holland, Belgium, Luxemburg, France and Germany west of the Rhine and north of the Moselle.

The wide variety of duties carried out by the company included ceremonial, tracing and escorting absentees and deserters, provost operational duties as well as the normal duties associated with the policing of a large garrison. NATO anniversaries and visits by VIPs occurred frequently, demanding considerable tact, linguistic ability and 'spit and polish' by those involved. Absentees from BAOR generally made their way back to England by way of Holland, where the alert *Konlikje Maréchaussée* allow very few to slip through their fingers. It has been suggested that the company was a 'static unit'; this was far from the case, there being at least one exercise every month. Garrison police duties ranged from patrolling in the impressive police Zephyrs to the one man bicycle patrol. In November, 1972, the unit's title was re-designated 102 Provost Company.

SHAPE

'Two gold swords, unsheathed, superimposed on a gold scroll, bearing the inscription "*Vigilia Pretium Libertatis*" (Vigilance is the Price of Liberty). Two sprays of olive leaves in gold at the bottom of the scroll indicate the dedication of the NATO Powers to peace, while the swords themselves imply the necessity of armed strength in order to preserve that peace. The position of the swords produce the letter 'A' standing for Allied Powers. Within the scroll and behind the swords twelve silver fronds stem from the olive sprays. These fronds represent the original signatories of the North Atlantic Treaty and produce, by their positions, rays of hope. The whole design is imposed on a shield of dark green, the shield itself representing the crusading nature of the SHAPE mission and its colour signifying the peaceful woods and fields of Europe.'

The letters SHAPE stand for Supreme Headquarters Allied Powers in Europe and the Headquarters itself is the overall senior military formation for the whole of the NATO system in Europe. It was situated about twelve miles west of Paris and flew the flags of fifteen nations; it was housed in a vast one-floored building extending over several acres in a most delightful setting provided by the President of France. The buildings were completed in 1951 and were considered to be the most up-to-date military accommodation possible.

A closely integrated inter-service and international staff controlled an allied command which covered land and ocean areas from the northern top of Norway to the eastern borders of Turkey, and included Northern, Central, Southern and Mediterranean subordinate commands, each of them serving specific needs arising from their respective geographical positions. The whole was commanded by the Supreme Allied Commander, Europe.

It was soon realized that in a headquarters of this type the problem of security was serious. Not only was it necessary to have an efficient pass system but the means of ensuring that unauthorized persons did not gain access to SHAPE was no less important. The high security classification of documents and records used at the headquarters demanded the most stringent arrangements. It was decided, therefore, that such security duties would be best performed by military police, and as a result an American military police company, a company of French *Gendarmerie* and SHAPE Provost Company were charged with that responsibility. All duties were completely integrated and perhaps the solemnity of the daily ceremonies of raising and lowering the flags of the fifteen nations by a combined military police flag party reflected the importance of the rôle played by RMP in their SHAPE tasks.

In May, 1951, the SHAPE Independent Provost Unit was formed under a DAPM/OC, with a WO2, two sergeants, five corporals and twenty-seven lance corporals and joined 520 Military Police Service Company US Army and a contingent of the French *Gendarmerie Nationale* in responsibility for Supreme Headquarters Allied Powers Europe and were situated in St Germain, some ten miles from Paris. Later this became the Paris Echelon Provost Section, Allied Land Forces, Central Europe, whose duties included the security of Atlantic Pact Headquarters.

Early in 1950 a detachment of Eastern Command, of four NCOs, had been maintained for duty at Western Union Headquarters at the Château des Fougères and Cour Henri Quatre at the Palace of Fontainebleau. Their duties included the security of the Château de Courances, the residence of Field-Marshal Montgomery, Chairman of the Commanders-in-Chief Committee, Western Union.

The International Police Organization was part of the SHAPE International Security Force, comprising US MP Corps, French *Gendarmerie*, RMP (both Provost and SIB Wings), Intelligence Corps, Counter-Intelligence and MP CID detachments US Army and representatives of Belgian and Italian military police.

On first arriving for duty in Paris the RMP NCO had, of necessity, to spend considerable time in learning the various types of pass he had to check, becoming acquainted with the orders of the different posts he was called upon to man, and studying the finer arts of what was called 'Shapemanship'. Once he was able to tell the difference between a Turkish brigadier, an Italian warrant officer and the post corporal he took his proper place at SHAPE. He then operated in a labyrinth of passages, in a series of connected buildings constructed in the latest form of contemporary architecture with a unique arrangement whereby the heat came up through the floor and the rain came down through the roof. Life became for him a succession of high-ranking officers of all nationalities with anything below a full colonel a rarity and even an object of suspicion!

Many and varied also were the duties he was called upon to do outside his routine tasks at SHAPE. NCOs from the company have performed security tasks at 'Summit' talks in Geneva, have formed guards of honour at the British Embassy in Paris and were active in most parades and ceremonies involving British installations in France. The State visit of Queen Elizabeth II and the opening of the Bayeux and Dunkirk Memorials were taken in their stride by RMP at SHAPE. The participation of NCOs of the company in the rôle of Colour Party at the annual British Legion procession up the Champs Elysees to the tomb of the Unknown Soldier at the Arc de Triomphe and the re-kindling of the flame became an accepted addition to the Paris scene: it was satisfying indeed to hear the favourable comment on the 'Redcaps' by the British residents in the capital no less than by the Parisians themselves.

Wherever he went in France, whatever tasks he was called upon to do at SHAPE, his immaculate turnout, bearing, tact and good manners were qualities which made the RMP NCO an ambassador himself. All day and every day he was in the sight of senior officers of fifteen nations; commendation was considerable and the regard with which he was held by other nationalities showed that British national prestige at SHAPE was in good hands.

The Treaty which was the origin of the North Atlantic Alliance stipulates that: 'The Nations will contribute to the development of international relations and reinforce their free way of life in assuring a better understanding of the principles on which these ways of life are founded and in developing better conditions to ensure stability and well-being.' The RMP NCO at SHAPE in no small way played his part in its fulfilment.

Operational control of all SHAPE military units was effected by a Provost Marshal (lieutenant-colonel US MP Corps) but the Security Officer SHAPE—a British colonel—was responsible for security.

The great majority of daily duties were security guard and physical security duties. The elaborate system of passes which governed entry and exit into and from restricted areas of SHAPE and the points of entry/exit were controlled by members of the International Police Organization. In the early days, in addition to these more or less static duties, tripartite military police patrols operated in the Paris area and around SHAPE installations. These patrols were later modified—the Allied soldier rarely got himself into any sort of trouble in Paris—and patrols were then used for a variety of tasks, including traffic accidents involving SHAPE vehicles, escorts and other tasks which are familiar to all military policemen.

The normal powers of RMP were not impaired by his being at SHAPE. However for many reasons there was not the same requirement in day-to-day life for exercising those powers. Nevertheless all patrols which operated outside SHAPE installations included a member of the French *Gendarmerie* who had the necessary powers to ensure conformity with French law.

In 1960 SHAPE saw the familiar MP brassard on the rather more shapely arms of WRAC Provost. To the majority of the member nations this was their first real look at a military policewoman. The WRAC detachment which consisted of one staff-sergeant and seven junior NCOs was completely integrated for all duties with the company. To illustrate the esteem in which they were held, it was usual for the visitor to SHAPE to be greeted at the main security desk manned by an international team, including one of the WRAC Provost NCOs. As they did not bear arms they were not required to perform night security duties but were in great demand at ceremonial and other special occasions, particularly at important receptions at the British Embassy in Paris.

Headquarters Allied Forces Central Europe (AFCENT) was located in the Château Cour Henri Quatre, Fontainebleau. Allied Land Forces

Central Europe (ALFCE), of which the Provost Section was a small part, occupied that part of the Château called Ailes des Princes and was a headquarters in the AFCENT complex.

To get things into perspective it is necessary to understand that from 1948 to 1951 the military headquarters of the grouping of nations known as the Western Union was located at Fontainebleau. The post of Commander-in-Chief AFCENT was established in July, 1953. Before that date, from their formation in 1951, the three existing headquarters (Land, Air and Naval Forces, Central Europe) came directly under SHAPE. From 1953 to 1962 there were four headquarters but on 1 July, 1962, the Naval Headquarters was disestablished, the Naval C-in-C's appointment becoming Naval Deputy to the Allied C-in-C.

AFCENT is both international and inter-service and eight nations only were represented at Fontainebleau. The mission of the command concerned itself mainly with the Benelux countries, the Federal Republic of Germany and Metropolitan France.

AFCENT was directly responsible to Supreme Headquarters (SHAPE) in the European Allied Command Organization, in exactly the same way as the other Allied Commands at Kolsas in Norway (AFNORTH), Naples in Italy (AFSOUTH) and Malta (AFMED), and formed the main bulwark opposing the Communist Warsaw Pact countries.

RMP provided, as part of the British Support Element, a section comprising one staff-sergeant, one sergeant and ten corporals. Duties were almost wholly security as in the case of SHAPE Provost Company; however the composition of the Military Police organization was a little different. Detachments were provided by US MP Corps, French *Gendarmerie*, German military police and British RMP and Intelligence Corps. Co-ordinating all provost duties was the Provost Marshal, a French *Gendarmerie* officer.

In 1966 General de Gaulle withdrew his support and France left NATO. SHAPE was required to leave French soil and Belgium offered the necessary facilities and became the new host country. SHAPE settled at Mons, convenient to Brussels, and AFCENT at Brunssum and Maastricht in the Netherlands.

In a remarkably short space of time the new SHAPE complex was established in its new location, RMP playing a big part in the highly complicated move, and became an international village with English as the basic language, overlaid by the native Belgian and undertones of a dozen other European tongues. The vast area of the Headquarters itself was surrounded by satellite housing estates having a population equivalent to a small English town and twenty-five miles of interior road network.

The International police force, of which the RMP contingent was known as 'International Police (British Element) SHAPE', consisted of about two hundred all ranks with military, naval and air provost of Belgium, Canada, Denmark, West Germany, Greece, Italy, Netherlands, Norway, Turkey and USA and to which was attached a detachment of one hundred Belgian *Gendarmerie* in support. With the exception of the *Gendarmerie* who, though their field of co-operation was wide, were particularly concerned with the public roads in the vicinity, all duties were found from a central roster.

Radio-controlled mobile patrols operated within the area twenty-four hours a day, with, in addition to service vehicles, 3,500 private cars to look after, and joint *Gendarmerie* patrols had much to do externally, including coverage of traffic accidents within a specified radius. Foot-patrols manned the international school and shopping-centre approaches and supervised an immense car-parking requirement. A joint UK and USA SIB team operated in their own sphere but fortunately the crime incidence was remarkably low.

International police jurisdiction extended over all members of SHAPE, their families and dependants, though there was, in fact, no codified law specifically applicable to them. The policeman therefore had to rely on his own firmness and tact and the co-operation of commanding officers in dealing with fifteen different nationalities and an indigenous civilian population each accustomed to their own codes, customs and temperaments. The International Police was itself a microcosm. It had exacting standards and that the SHAPE world conformed to them was its own tribute.

AFCENT, in the Netherlands, worked on similar principles with a total strength of 150 International police though some twenty miles separated the detachments at Brunssum and Maastricht.

At both SHAPE and AFCENT the predominant duty was security which followed the same pattern as when in France. Before the move from France RMP administrative responsibility passed from APM Eastern Command to PM BAOR who exercised his control through APM SHAPE and, in the case of AFCENT, through APM Rhine Area at Düsseldorf.

BRITISH TROOPS, AUSTRIA

Russian Armies invaded Austria in the spring of 1945 and captured Vienna on 13 April. The 8th Army, moving up from Italy, followed and its provost company was one of the first British units to enter Klagenfurt, where it was to stay for the next ten years, changing its name to 105 Provost Company. The British took over their zone in accordance with the Four-Power London Agreement of 1945 and Allied Military Government was established.

The Allied High Commission, under the Commanders-in-Chief (in the dual rôles of High Commissioners) took over Austria but following the failure of Treaty talks gradually came to dissolution and the High Commissioners ceased to function as such, occupation becoming a purely zonal affair for all practical purposes.

The Provost organization for British Troops, Austria (BTA) was a DPM and APM with 105 Provost Company and 92 Section SIB. SIB headquarters was at Klagenfurt with detachments at Graz and Villach. A mounted section was also present.

Vienna, under the London Agreement, was divided into five sectors; British, French, American and Russian and the fifth, or '*Innere Stadt*', containing the Parliament, Government offices and more important public buildings, being International. The city itself lay deep in the Russian Occupation Zone of Austria—similar to Berlin.

An inter-Allied Command known at VIAC was set up to govern Vienna Province and the city. Following the failure of the Treaty talks the High Commissioners ceased to function as such and VIAC shrank considerably until it retained only three functional sub-committees: the council of the First District, the joint Restitution Committee and the Provost Marshals' Committee. The decisions taken by the four commanders in Vienna were published by protocols and through this means the work of the military police was governed and had the effect of a quadripartite agreement and order.

Militarily the strengths of the respective forces were unbalanced. The smallest force was the French under the command of a colonel, whose force consisted of a reinforced company of *Chasseurs Alpine* and a company of *Gendarmerie*. The latter were all experienced regular police on long-term engagements under their Provost Marshal of captain's rank. Despite his low rank he was an officer of considerable importance and responsibility as he was the only officer with direct access to the French Ministry of the Interior.

The Americans had a substantial garrison, including three complete military police companies with a lieut-colonel as Provost Marshal, and two majors and a captain on his staff.

The Russian garrison, commanded by a major-general, was by far and away the largest with a lieut-colonel as Provost Marshal and a military police unit consisting mainly of, ostensibly, infantrymen—most of 'Guards' origin, indicating that they were specially selected.

The British contingent consisted of a headquarters, one infantry company and a handful of men from the supporting services and a detachment of 105 Provost Company with an APM (major) and DAPM (captain).

THE INTERNATIONAL PATROL, VIENNA

In August, 1945, at the instigation of the American Provost Marshal for the Vienna area, the 'International Patrol' was formed, a police force comprising members of each of the military police of the occupying powers.

The Standing Orders for the International Patrol included the following:

(1) All patrol members will work at all times in harmony and co-operation, and respect each other in the execution of these orders.
(2) All members of the International Patrol will behave towards all soldiers and civilians alike in such a manner as to reflect credit upon themselves and upon the nation they represent.

This was, perhaps, the outstanding example of its day where military co-operation existed outside the realms of political doctrines and treaties and was, of its kind, unique: a closely-knit body of military policemen working in complete harmony, its sole object the preservation of military discipline and combating crime. This common purpose was perhaps contemporarily the nearest the world achieved to the interpretation of the word 'Allied', where three members were Western Powers and the fourth Russian—the Atlantic Pact and the Cominform working together with the strongest *esprit de corps*. This was to last some ten years and it was a matter of pride that the unique distinction of the only four-powered organization effectively working in the world was a military police one.

The International Patrol operated from Auersberg Palace and later the Palace of Justice; its members wore a metal armband bearing the flags of the four occupying powers and the inscription 'International Military Police Patrol, Vienna' in the relevant languages. Each member of the Patrol also carried a copy of the Patrol orders, numbered and in the three languages, for easy reference between each other. A liaison staff was located at Headquarters with a radio system linking up the patrol cars.

Five patrols operated over the twenty-four hours, one in each of the allied sectors of occupation into which the city was divided and one covering the centre 'International' sector. This patrol took its break for meals at the place appointed in its respective sector. Members of the patrol were thus privileged to get to know their opposite numbers very well and, indeed, co-operation was of a very high standard.

The centre, or International, sector was policed by each power in turn in monthly rotation, while each power was responsible for its own sector. There was, however, complete freedom of access between sectors to soldiers and civilians alike over the whole of the jointly occupied area of the city. Contact was therefore close and frequent. In addition to normal military discipline, military–civilian relationships and high-density unrestricted military traffic, there was the medley of languages, regulations and legal procedures, which could easily have produced chaos. The common denominator was found in the International Patrol. An attempt to capture its spirit and to immortalize it was made in the film *Four-in-a-Jeep*.

Even so, good as relations between military police were, tact, determination and a sense of proportion were the policeman's best weapons, as Major B. F. White, APM Vienna from 1946 to 1950 had reason to know. In August, 1949, a hostile crowd was about to attack a Russian vehicle in which an Austrian was being conveyed against his will. The APM's firm handling of the situation not only freed the Austrian but succeeded in dispersing the crowd and avoiding what might well have become a serious incident. In 1950 firm but tactful action was again necessary to prevent Soviet attempts to snatch the British European Airways omnibus proceeding to and from the British airfield. Such incidents usually followed the day-to-day political climate and it had to be realized and accepted that personal relationships and individual behaviour reflect only what the individual can do in accordance with his official policy. In Vienna Soviet policy was, within certain limits, one of friendliness and co-operation. The Russians, though intensely suspicious, are basically friendly people; consequently a marked degree of reserved cordiality existed amongst patrols. Co-operation was of a high standard and Russian patrols were quick to take action against their own soldiers —often with a severity to which their RMP colleagues were not accustomed.

While the Russians were not allowed to make private visits to the homes of their opposite numbers, their officers were permitted to attend official parties in messes and attend such functions as 'Corps Day'. On such occasions relationships were very good, providing one had sufficient tact not to discuss political or military matters. The 'International Patrol', one likes to think, did perhaps have a wider effect than that confined to police duties in that some at least of the respective nations got to know each other outside the political orbit.

The Occupying Powers withdrew from Austria in September, 1955.

BRITISH ELEMENT TRIESTE FORCE (BETFOR)

Lying at the head of the Adriatic on a narrow coastal strip against a high, rugged and bare background, Trieste is a large port and modern city of ancient origin. The end of the Second World War found the Yugoslav army entering the city on 30 April, 1945 closely followed by the 2nd New Zealand Division of the 8th Army and on 2 May General Freyberg accepted the surrender of the German troops and occupied the dock areas of the city.

Trieste was divided into two zones: Anglo-American and Yugoslav. Modifications followed under the terms of the Italian Peace Treaty, 1947, part being returned to Italy and part passing to Yugoslavia. The remainder became the Free Territory, still in two zones, the British and US forces each maintaining some 5,000 troops in their zone, with Yugoslavia maintaining a similar number in her zone.

The British Element Trieste Force, known as BETFOR, consisted of the reinforced 24th Infantry Brigade, and was policed by 227 Provost Company and 93 Section, SIB.

The Yugoslav zone quickly became sealed-off and the Anglo-Americans were confined to their own area, a coastal strip twenty miles long and of a varying depth up to four miles. The initial policing of the area fell to British and US military police reinforced by other troops attached, in the British case, by Royal Artillery auxiliaries.

An early start was made in raising and training a civil police force which resulted in the establishment of the very efficient and modern Venezia Guilia Police. Responsibility was gradually transferred to them for all civilian affairs, with the British and US military police, who retained jurisdiction over troops, standing by as reinforcements.

This was much needed as riots and disorders were frequent. The majority of citizens were of Italian origin, while a strong minority, plus the rural population, were Slovenes. On top of this explosive populace of some 250,000 was a layer of anti-Tito Slovene refugees. Politics were no concern of the military police but the resulting disturbances were and these came to a head in March, 1952, the fourth anniversary of the proposal by the Western Powers that the Free Territory should be handed over to Italy. The Allied zone suffered most from the disorders due to the fact that, in accordance with democratic principles freedom of speech and expression of opinion were allowed—in fact, encouraged—resulting in a clash of factions that kept the police force constantly busy.

227 Provost Company and 93 Section SIB were centrally situated concentrated under one roof, which eased the administrative and operational problems. Concentration of force at any given spot, swiftly and efficiently, was the key to most operational problems. The company developed an efficient system of patrols linked by radio and were pioneers in the development of control by 'walkie-talkie'.

The military police quickly established a reputation for fair play and firm action and together the British 'Redcaps' and US 'Snowdrops' exercised a moderating influence.

On 26 October, 1954, 227 Provost Company, British Element Trieste Force, stood down and the Anglo-American Zone was handed over to Italy. Throughout the years it was the rôle of the force to support Allied Military Government, first to restore the normal life of the city and surrounding countryside and then to keep the peace until the future of the Territory had been determined and, finally, to ensure a smooth takeover by the new authorities, a pattern familiar to British troops in the post-war years. Provost also grew accustomed to playing a patient but arduous rôle in this process and 227 Provost Company helped to ensure a peaceful and orderly evacuation with all ranks committed to security and traffic control but with one eye looking over their shoulders for possible internal security duties; finally they withdrew and could disband with justifiable pride in their achievements.

This chapter, dealing with the occupation of enemy countries, should properly conclude with the occupation of Japan. That story, however, is a natural link between the re-occupation of Singapore and Hong Kong, the political reorganization of South-East Asia and the Korean War, so, for the sake of continuity, it has been placed within that context.

PART IV

Imperial Policing

CHAPTER X

Minor Stations

THE CARIBBEAN

In the Caribbean Area two sergeants were stationed in Up Park Camp, Jamaica, who were responsible for provost matters throughout the area and, in particular, training and instructing the indigenous Garrison Military Police. The great test of their usefulness came on 17 August, 1951, when a hurricane hit Jamaica and devastated vast areas to disaster magnitude. Telephone, electricity and water supplies failed, roads and communications were blocked and an outbreak of typhus threatened. Military assistance was made available, including provost, one of whose duties was anti-looting patrols, the order being to shoot if necessary; fortunately however necessity did not arise, the threat being sufficient deterrent. The contribution made in reconnaissance, traffic control and maintaining communications was of inestimable value in ensuring the most speedy rescue and relief.

The British garrison, prior to independence, was scattered in infantry company strengths throughout the major islands with a company in British Guiana on the mainland of South America. It eventually became necessary to reinforce British Guiana garrison with the 3rd Parachute Regiment in 1966 and a detachment of 16 Parachute Brigade Provost Unit was stationed there with them.

GIBRALTAR

The early history of the Royal Military Police on the Rock cannot be accurately traced, but there has been a long association with Gibraltar and, until comparatively recent years, horses were kept there by RMP. Recently the Corps has been identified even more closely with the Rock by the presentation to the King's Chapel of an RMP pew from the provost company. The pew bears the Corps badge and is inscribed, '224 GHQ Provost Company'. The establishment latterly consisted of company headquarters, two sections, eight dog handlers, two SIB sergeants and four war dogs.

The provost task can only be adequately described as normal, but ceremonial and escort-riding to the Governor and visiting VIPs figured largely in the day-to-day duties. There was always some important function or important visitor on the Rock and Royal visits were often made. A ceremony which is frequently held, and in which RMP played a major rôle—the DAPM parading with the Governor as one of the officers in attendance—is the ancient ceremony of 'The Keys'. It dates from the Great Siege of Gibraltar in 1779–83 and was inaugurated by Sir George Eliott, Defender of the Fortress, with a view to lessening the risk of the Fortress being captured. The three main city gates were locked after the 6 pm gun had been fired and all aliens had to be out of the Fortress by then. Nowadays it is reduced to a Ceremonial Parade, enjoyed both by resident and visitor.

227 GHQ Provost Company was self-contained and lived in Montagu Bastion Barracks. The living accommodation was, by other standards, some of the best on the Rock.

The DAPM's job could be described as varied. Although on Fortress Headquarters establishment, he commanded the provost company. He also commanded the Gibraltar Security Police—a civil police force about ninety strong which polices the Upper Rock Security Area. In addition the following ex-officio jobs went with his appointment: member Traffic Board, Police Working Committee, Prison Board and Hon. Secretary, Gibraltar Branch of the RSPCA.

With the reduction of the Army and the need to utilize provost resources to the best advantage it was decided to disband 227 GHQ Provost Company in April, 1963, and with it to reduce the total Corps commitment in Gibraltar to one SIB warrant officer although if the need arises extra personnel can always be sent there for special duties.

MALTA

From the end of the Second World War to the grant of independence to Malta in September, 1964, the Corps continued to maintain a presence on the island with both Provost and SIB personnel fully employed with usual provost duties. After independence however, such duties as VIP escorts were a thing of the past and visiting dignitaries were then escorted by a section of the civilian Malta Mounted Police although co-operation with the civil police remained close. Joint patrols with the Royal Navy and with the provost of visiting foreign navies became the principal duty but the large reduction of the Royal Navy was keenly felt and Grand Harbour—once so full of warships of the Mediterranean Fleet—looked empty and forlorn. This was particularly true while the huge dry docks went through a difficult period due to the closing of the Suez Canal and other political problems.

Malta Provost Company and the SIB detachment moved to a splendid barracks at St Francis Ravelin, on the outskirts of the capital, Valletta; the Dog Section remaining at its old location at Fort Mosta in the centre of the island, but the Services rundown in Malta led to a progressive reduction in RMP strength and when the Corps flag was lowered for the last time at 8.30 am on 21 October, 1971, all that remained were one officer and seven NCOs and the last of these flew back to the United Kingdom on 3 November that year. Thus ended the long and honourable association between the George Cross Island and the Royal Military Police.

VIETNAM

In the spring of 1968 the Foreign Office requested the services of provost at the British Embassy, Saigon, and Sergeant Powell and Corporals Fletcher and Levell were posted as the only British troops in Vietnam. Though not actually engaged they saw and heard quite a lot of the fighting during the offensives, when they were confined to their villa for a majority of the time. As the American Embassy was situated on the other side of the street to the British Embassy they witnessed the result of the Tet attack launched against that Embassy, during which our own Embassy lost a large number of windows and suffered a few bullet holes.

Their duties consisted mainly of guarding the front gate of the Embassy, armed with a Browning 9 mm, various internal security tasks, paying frequent visits to the airport to meet the RAF aircraft which brought supplies and medical aid for the British paediatric team and acting as escort to the Diplomatic Courier on his weekly trip to Bangkok with the mail.

CHAPTER XI

Middle East Land Forces and Africa

EGYPT

IN 1939 provost in Middle East Forces (MEF) consisted of small detachments of CMP in Cairo, Alexandria and Moascar, and in addition a company in Palestine which was under direct War Office control. The story of the early years of the Second World War in Egypt are described in Major Crozier's *History of the Corps*, published in 1951, but by the end of 1942 provost manpower had considerably increased but was committed to both Paiforce and MEF which were by then separate Commands under their own respective Provost Marshals, with territorial responsibilities in the following areas: Paiforce: Levant, Jordan, Iraq, Persia and the Persian Gulf: MEF; Palestine, Egypt, Western Desert and East Africa.

It is of interest from a manpower point of view to quote the remarks of Lieut-Colonel T. C. Irvine, DPM 8th Army, who in 1943 said, 'I found my police developed into a force of seventy-three provost officers and 2,047 rank and file'. Although comprehensive manpower figures for the whole of MEF at this time are not known, the figures quoted above in respect of 8th Army give some indication of the provost manpower build-up which took place over a period of some two years.

At the end of 1943 large numbers of operational troops and provost left MEF on the invasion of Italy, which very soon became a separate theatre under its own Provost Marshal. However, provost units in Italy were for some time very largely dependent on MEF for trained reinforcements. When land hostilities ceased in North Africa in May, 1943, provost in MEF were committed to the enormous task of controllIng a very mixed collection of Allied troops in addition to the policing of a country which had contained the main supply depots for the whole of the Middle East during a period of some three years of war. To tackle

this task CMP were organized into the following branches: Provost, ATS Provost, SIB, Mounted Provost and CMP Dog Companies. Locally-enlisted Vulnerable Points (VP) ('Bluecaps') units were also fully employed on docks and store depots security tasks.

In 1947 the withdrawal from Palestine took place and our forces became mainly concentrated in Egypt, where the vast Ordnance Depots, such as Tel-el-Kebir and the various other depots in the Canal Zone continued to exercise the ingenuity of the local 'Clifty Wallahs'.

Provost build-up became substantial. 1st Infantry Division Provost Company moved in from Tripoli to the Canal Zone with particular responsibility for check posts at the swing bridge at El Kantara and at Lake Timsah. 3rd Infantry Division Provost Company, 25 Armoured Brigade Provost Unit and 16th Independent Parachute Brigade Provost Unit also moved in with their formations in an operational rôle. In addition to the field formations were 202 Provost Company, with an

East African detachment with responsibility for Moascar, Ismailia and Port Said, 615 Special Mobile Provost Section (SMPS) and 1 Dog Company and mounted sections at El Kirch, 3 (East African) Provost Company at Fayid, 211 (Mauritian) Provost Company also in the Canal Zone and district provost sections in Tripolitania and Cyrenaica. 2 Section, SIB, was responsible for all the investigations of serious crime within the Canal Zone.

In accordance with the treaty made with Nahas Pasha and ratified in 1936 HQ British Troops Egypt and GHQ MELF moved from Cairo to Moascar and Fayid respectively in 1947 where they were joined by troops withdrawn from Cairo and Alexandria, thus creating a heavy concentration in the Canal Zone.

When General Neguib in 1952 saw fit to implement other terms included in the treaty of 1936 the whole Canal Zone was isolated from the remainder of Egypt and the general build-up of additional provost duties on boundary checks commenced. The peak figure of British troops in Egypt during the years immediately following the abrogation of the treaty is reported as being some 90,000.

Duties in Egypt were among the most difficult of the post-war decade and started unpleasantly enough with the demonstrations in Cairo in February, 1946, followed in March by the Alexandria Riots.

On 4 March, 1946, a large number of students and native labourers gathered in procession in Alexandria as the day was being observed as one of national mourning in memory of the Egyptians killed during the demonstrations in Cairo on 21 February, 1946.

For over two hours crowds of students and labourers moved towards Ramleh Square and a particularly unruly group came via Sharia Said El Awal. On passing the Atlantic Hotel, which was used as Royal Navy offices, and the adjacent annexe, which was occupied as billets and family accommodation by Naval personnel, the mob's attention was drawn to the White Ensign flying over the doorway. This was immediately pulled down by the crowd, who then entered the hotel annexe, took possession of the ground floor and looted it, finally starting a fire in the lift shaft, which took a firm hold. The fire engines were largely ineffective, due to the interference of the crowd, and Egyptian police and military personnel who arrived to quell the crowds quickly lost control of the situation.

In the meantime, a large crowd had gathered on Ramleh Square but nothing serious happened until about quarter past twelve, when the crowd in the square was joined by the mob which had attacked the Atlantic Hotel. About a hundred Egyptian police and a similar number of Egyptian soldiers were present in Ramleh Square, where a small CMP outpost had been built. No action was taken by these Egyptians when, at about 12.45 pm, the crowd started chanting anti-British slogans and throwing stones and bricks at the outpost and at the Cecil Hotel.

The five military policemen manning the outpost were Corporal A. D. Jump, Lance-Corporals H. Ayres, B. Thomas, T. R. Maile and Private A. J. Bailey and when the trouble started they wisely offered no provocation and did not show themselves to the crowd.

After pulling down the military notice nearby and breaking all the windows and shutters with stones and nabouts (iron-shod bamboo staves), some of the mob entered the outpost through the double doors and set fire to books and other inflammable objects. The five military policemen, who had between them three sten guns each with two magazines and containing twenty rounds per gun and two ·380 revolvers each loaded with six rounds, retired to the telephone room and when the natives started to set fire to the barrack room. Lance-Corporal Ayres went to an inner door and fired warning shots over their heads. This had no effect and so single rounds were directed by the defenders and several natives were hit.

At 12.56 pm a Sitrep showed that crowds were still attacking the outpost and missiles and blazing materials were being thrown through the windows. Egyptian soldiers and police took no effective action to restrain the crowds and the last photograph taken of the scene by a nearby resident shows the armed Egyptian police to be some distance from the outpost taking no action whatsoever.

Lance-Corporal Calvert, who was on duty in a CMP wireless truck, tried to reach the outpost but was driven away by the hostile crowd.

The five military policemen in their defensive positions in the telephone room and, within the limits of their now sadly-depleted ammunition, fired occasional shots at the more aggressive members of the mob. One Egyptian officer, with a few policemen, did, at this time, make some sort of effort to placate the mob but failed and quickly faded from the scene.

Corporal Hirst, who was on duty at HQ 202 Provost Company in Kom-el-Dik Barracks, was in telephone communication with the outpost from 12.20 pm until the line finally went dead at 1.45 pm. Some of the messages from the outpost were: 'All of the windows are on fire'; 'Some natives have appeared at the windows'; 'The Army has arrived—one of the boys at the window says that the Egyptians are taking the guns away from the Army and are firing at us, he says that the Egyptian Army are also firing at us'; 'An Egyptian officer has got in the outpost and has told us to stop firing—this we have done'; 'We are running short of ammunition. Only two rounds left'. The last sentence heard from them was: 'They are coming in. I've had it'.

Lance-Corporal Thomas in the CMP wireless truck, managed to get almost to the doors of the outpost at 1.30 pm, where he saw Ayres who shouted, 'We are coming out', but due to the terrific shower of stones from the mob, Thomas had to withdraw temporarily. Ten minutes later the wireless truck returned, but no answer came from within the outpost and it eventually returned to Kom-el-Dik Barracks where the DPM was informed.

Corporal Jump, who later made a successful escape from the outpost, reported that about this time the Egyptian soldiers fired about five volleys but the reason is not known and certainly a little later they had formed up on the west end of Ramleh Square but made no attempt to stop the attack by the mob.

Just before 2 pm CSM Murphy and other military policemen went by truck to attempt a rescue of their comrades but were unable to pass the cordon of Egyptian troops and were told by an Egyptian officer that all the occupants of the outpost had been evacuated. A few minutes later Corporal Jump was shot in the shoulder as he was near a window in the outpost.

At 2 pm three lorryloads of civil police arrived and started to push the crowd back from the outpost and, as their efforts seemed to be meeting with some success, the defenders decided to make a break for it. They broke down the door of the cell into which they had retreated but seeing them at the exit of the burning outpost the crowd broke the police cordon and surged back. An Egyptian police officer then told Corporal Jump to lead his men out and they climbed out through the wash-house window into the street but the mob surged after, found and attacked them. Thomas, Maile and Bailey were thrown to the ground while Ayres ran back into the outpost and picked up a sten magazine. The three men on the ground were being kicked and stoned by the mob and Ayres opened fire on the rioters, temporarily driving them back.

Corporal Jump and Lance-Corporals Thomas and Ayres gained the cover of a nearby restaurant, from which they were ultimately rescued but Lance-Corporal Maile and Private Bailey ran down a narrow street pursued by the rioting natives. Unfortunately another mob of natives was coming towards them and, in answer to the cries of the pursuers this mob struck down the two military policemen. They were stabbed and beaten and killed instantly and their bodies subjected to insult by the crowd in the presence of a detachment of civil police who made no attempt to stop the murders. It seemed as though with the death of the two military policemen, the mob had spent its venom and although there were sporadic demonstrations during the following two or three days, the situation became calmer. Lance-Corporal Maile and Private Bailey were buried with full Military honours on 6 March, 1946, in the

Alexandria Military Cemetery at Hadra. Corporal Jump was subsequently awarded the British Empire Medal for his meritorious service during the Alexandria riots.

THE CANAL ZONE

British troops evacuated Egypt in 1947 and withdrew to the Canal Zone in accordance with the treaty obligations.

In December, 1951, however, extremists raised the cry of 'Unity of the Nile Valley', which implied the annexation of the Sudan and the evacuation of the Canal Zone by British troops. This was followed by anti-European riots, the Ismailia Police Station being shelled and stormed by British troops in January, 1952, and the *coup d'état* by General Mohammed Neguib and the flight of the Wafd leaders in July and the abdication of King Farouk.

Once more British troops in general and RMP in particular were to hold the sticky end of the political stick and during the last three months of 1951 3 and 4 Sections, 203 Provost Company were located in Moascar Garrison and played a major part in the various stages of the cycle of civil disturbances in the Canal Zone.

At the beginning of October, 1951, there was a gradual increase in the number of assaults by extremists on British personnel. A wrong word by a serviceman was sufficient to start a disturbance in which members of both sides were often seriously hurt. During this period it was essential for RMP patrols to be out in strength to prevent clashes and disturbances between service personnel and the local population from daybreak until the last serviceman was clear of the town of Ismailia at night, or, in the case of those who always get lost or miss the last bus, the early hours of morning. These duties were long and arduous and required tact, vigilance and tremendous powers of concentration. In the recreational centre of Ismailia foot patrols were provided for all main thoroughfares and normal policing duties were performed.

On 16 October, 1951, the day after the abrogation of the Anglo-Egyptian Treaty of 1936, three RMP radio jeeps were operating in Ismailia and Arashia. They reported through RMP Control the first signs of a hostile anti-British mob gathering and plotted its subsequent movements. On information obtained from RMP Moascar Control the garrison commander was in a position to decide whether or not the situation warranted the deployment of his infantry. Vehicle stops were brought into action and no service vehicles were allowed to enter the town of Ismailia.

With the failure of the Egyptian civil police to control law and order, it became necessary for the Moascar Garrison infantry battalion to take over their responsibilities. On their arrival in the town RMP Tactical HQ was able to furnish the commanding officer with an overall picture of where and in what strength the rioters were and how they were armed, the location of danger spots, such as the Ismailia Station NAAFI in whose burning buildings were thirty women and children, the location of the families' refuge control centre and the location of burnt and destroyed civilian and service vehicles etc. When the battalion commander received his orders to clear the towns of Ismailia and Arashia of rioters his plan was based on the local topography produced by provost. The situation had now become an operation and the provost rôle was one of refugee control, removing families from private accommodation threatened by the hostile crowds, maintaining traffic control and ensuring that the main traffic routes were open and clear. Patrolling continued, to detect and discover any fresh outbreak of rioting behind the advancing lines of the infantry. By late afternoon law and order had been restored and the town was quiet. The European areas of Ismailia and Arashia had been wired-off and bridge, road and rail blocks had been established to prevent subversive elements from entering the area. The battalion commander asked provost to continue to patrol the town and keep him informed of the strength and armament of the civilian police and of the gathering of crowds, hostile or otherwise, and to report on the general reaction and attitude of the local populace. A radio link was established to RMP Tactical HQ, which was located at the battalion Tactical HQ. Immediate information could be received by Tactical HQ from patrols, fed to the battalion commander and, when necessary, infantry support could be called for to assist any RMP patrol.

During the late afternoon and early evening four hundred auxiliary Egyptian policemen were brought into the Ismailia local district from Cairo. These auxiliaries were quickly issued with arms and sent out on duty. It soon became apparent to the patrols that they were ill-trained and ill-disciplined and in many cases gave the appearance of not knowing which end of the rifle to hold. Disturbing reports became prevalent of the increase in the number of junior constables who were armed with sten machine carbines, which necessitated a closer watch to be maintained by provost on the deployment of the civil police and their activities.

It was decided by the GOC towards the end of October that the civilian police should once again become responsible for law and order in Ismailia. The perimeter wire between the European and Arab quarters was taken over by them and two companies of the garrison battalion were located in suitable accommodation in Ismailia and Arashia. The only troops allowed in the town were RMP patrols and personnel who lived in private accommodation, while infantry and armoured car personnel were confined to their locations, ready to turn out in an emergency. As all troops were now armed, the number of arms snatches increased. Constant watch had to be maintained by RMP patrols for possible arms thieves and to give vigilant cover to those ingenuous service personnel who would shop with all their small children hanging on to them and inundated with parcels, so making them an easy target for determined thugs. The civilian police proved themselves to be quite incapable of stopping these incidents and in many cases assisted the thieves to get away.

The attitude of the civil police towards RMP and other British servicemen became intolerable, with their obscene remarks and gestures and the cocking of their weapons whenever a patrol passed them. It could be seen that their officers had little or no control over them and in one incident an entire squad threw down their arms in the road and marched off without them because an officer had ordered them to carry out an order which was not to their liking. Liaison between the DAPM and the Mamours (District Magistrates) continued, but there was little or no co-operation. The higher officials were courteous and sometimes showed concern but there was very little constructive effort on their part to endeavour to maintain law and order. Relationships between RMP junior ranks and their counterparts were poor and every obstruction was put in their way during local district procedures.

On the night of 17–18 November, 1951, a sleeping policeman was awakened by an infantry patrol; he promptly opened fire and ran into the temporary barracks of the auxiliary police, who immediately turned out and started to fire in all directions. Soon the whole area east of French Square became extremely dangerous because of this uncontrolled fire. RMP patrols had a difficult job endeavouring to localize the firing, putting out vehicle and personnel road-stops and escorting civilian vehicles, which were also fired upon.

The following day, in the early afternoon, an RMP patrol was fired upon at point-blank range by a squad of auxiliary policemen and was fortunate to extract itself with the loss of only a severed radio mast. This incident appeared to be the signal for all Egyptian policemen to get down, adopt firing positions and fire at anyone and everyone who came within their sights. Once again road-stops had to be manned by provost and all Service personnel were prevented from entering the town. Even so, there were a few casualties amongst those personnel who were out walking. Movement of ambulances was made difficult and RMP patrols were called upon to provide escorts. Towards dusk the firing ceased except for a few spasmodic bursts. The Sub-Governor of the Canal Zone was ordered to return and confine his police to their barracks and disarm them. The remainder of the night was spent by

RMP escorting Service personnel and families who had been stranded by the events of the afternoon to their units and homes.

Operation 'Font', the withdrawal of families from Ismailia and Arashia, together with any para-military bodies, Service offices and others located in these areas, took place during the period 20–26 November. The provost commitment was traffic control from the MT control concentration centre to the personnel screening camp and to the Army private furniture depositories. The personnel screening centre was designed to accept husbands, wives, children and their personal baggage. A screening team would inform them of the destination of the family, either a War Department married quarter in one of the garrisons in the Command or Port Said for embarkation to the United Kingdom. The entire operation was a complete success. No incidents were reported by RMP patrols and with the hard work of the troops concerned together with the co-operation of the families, over 600 private quarters were evacuated, in many cases on the edge of the out-of-bounds areas and from narrow, inaccessible streets, and the occupants with their furniture redirected to their final destinations.

On 27 November the towns of Ismailia and Arashia were placed out-of-bounds to all Service personnel. A through route was established from Moascar Garrison to Ferry Point and at each end an RMP check-post was established to prevent and stop unauthorized personnel and vehicles from using the route or entering Ismailia or Arashia. The passage of each vehicle was logged and the opposite checkpost informed by radio of its expected arrival; they in turn cleared it when it passed their post. An RMP patrol covered the route and reported to RMP Control any breakdown, vehicles in the out-of-bounds areas, formation and subsequent movement of hostile crowds and the strength and armament of civilian road blocks.

The GOC decided on 29 November to withdraw all RMP patrols from the town except for the patrol between the two checkposts. So, for the first time in nearly two months the section jeeps, of which there were only three, were allowed to come in for their much-needed maintenance and to be re-painted to cover-up their very honourable battle scars.

During this emergency period many lessons were learnt, the most important, but by no means a new one, was that radio is as essential to RMP as petrol is to vehicles. Without radio, information would have been received too late for the many major decisions that were required and depended entirely upon its use. There was no establishment for radio in a L of C provost company and the sets which were used were an excess issue plus those which it was possible to obtain from Garrison HQ. A radio net was produced and operated by inexperienced NCO operators just before 16 October. This net had ten out-stations manned by RMP personnel and became very efficient. The experience gained during the previous three months operating on patrol, under fire, in among hostile crowds as an infantry link and at RMP Control was invaluable to all NCOs.

Public Address (PA) equipment played an important part in the work of the sections. A PA set was mounted on a Morris Commercial radio van; the interior was converted into a small studio and propaganda broadcasts were given in the heart of the arab town, much to the dismay of the local agitators and civilian police. During 'cordon and search' of villages by the infantry broadcasts were made to direct and inform the villagers of what was expected of them and administrative instructions were broadcast to families on such subjects as food supplies, embarkation dates, bounds and withdrawal information in respect of Operation 'Font'.

The situation in the Canal Zone was unique for, unlike Palestine, there was no friendly or co-operative civil police force. Any military force whose object is to give aid to a civil power in order to maintain law and order, if it is not to enforce martial law must have the assistance of the civil authorities so that the location of extremists can be ascertained and advice given as to the economic, political and religious situations of the area in which the troops have to operate. In Ismailia the nucleus of the original town police force had always tried to do its duty but the introduction by the Minister of the Interior of the police auxiliaries, whose function was to terrorize any would-be rioter into their ranks, had a marked influence on them and each policeman then tried to be more patriotic than the extremist. This situation brought about a wave of ruthless killing and destruction which bordered on a state of anarchy.

The military police added new laurels to the honour of their Corps in this troubled town by their devotion to duty, courage and willingness always to help others. The symbol of the 'Redcap' still stood for law and order in the eyes of British and foreign subjects who remained in Ismailia.

Tel-el-Kebir, although nearest to the populated parts of the Delta, was always the last place to be affected by student demonstrations because it was in effect a 'walled garrison' with no native areas nearer than about a mile. When the trouble started in mid-October, apart from the organization of convoys, Tel-el-Kebir carried on much the same as before except for the gradual loss of labour. Raids on the garrison became less frequent, work slowed down because of shortage of labour and intimidation on a large scale was directed at those who stayed at work. Various attempts were made by talking to the Governor of

Sharkia Province to retain the workers and avoid trouble. These were made fruitless for political reasons, the Governor being between two fires and quite unable to help. At that time the road from Tel-el-Kebir to Moascar was beginning to receive the attention of the thugs—firing at vehicles, wires across the road, and other lethal traps. The Tahag road was then used and, with armed convoys, the interference decreased.

On 24 October it was decided to eject the civil police from their garrison outpost since they were actively spying and intimidating labour to leave the garrison. They were removed to the old checkpost, the RMP having been withdrawn. On 31 October the DAPM saw the Mamour with a view to changing the civil police of Tel-el-Kebir village. While there he was recalled by the garrison commander who ordered him to arrest the police officer of Tel-el-Kebir and a number of constables. This was promptly effected, thus doing the Mamour's job for him.

On the following day RMP took over the policing of Tel-el-Kebir village in an effort to secure the workers against immediate and personal violence. This had some effect but civil police terrorization of families was too strong. The patrol ceased duties on 5 November and the next day a section of 1st Infantry Division Provost Company arrived with 1st Guards Brigade. During all this time movements had been watched and reported and natives were being closely questioned with regard to the situation in the Delta. Much information was thus gained.

On 13 November the brigade moved out on an 'exercise' which many thought might well finish in Cairo. On the 17th they returned, having apparently enjoyed their scheme in the Suez area.

On 16 November a thorough search of Tel-el-Kebir village was ordered. This was done with very little opposition, 125 civil police surrendering with their arms and four officers, including General Ali Raouf the Inspector of Police for Sharkia Province. During this operation RMP played their full part and thoroughly enjoyed the activity after having for so long 'sat down to be shot at'. From then on RMP were the police authority in Tel-el-Kebir village with ten civil police, unarmed, to assist them.

The value to the morale of the garrison of this operation can hardly be over-estimated. Everyone felt that at last the Army was able to take the initiative, having suffered murderous and unprovoked attacks for far too long.

On arrival of 1st Infantry Division Provost Company in October, 1951, duties within the divisional area and in Ismailia started. Owing to the strength of the company at that time, employed staff were also required to carry out these duties. The company was called upon to assist in the evacuation of the Services' families from Arashia. This duty went off without a hitch or incident. Additional checkposts were established at El Kantara Bridge, YMCA Bridge and at Lake Timsah, all of which were manned day and night. It was while performing such duties that many of the younger NCOs came under fire from Egyptian thugs for the first time.

During the evacuation the number of NCOs on duty did not allow for reliefs and it became necessary for food to be transported to the actual pointsmen, the NCOs being fed at their posts. On 2 December some welcome reinforcements in the form of RSM Mooney, Sergeant Brock and Corporal MacAvoy arrived and these were soon followed by Corporal Forder, with nineteen lance-corporals straight from the Depot. On 14 December Sergeant Brock was fired on from ambush while in Ismailia, receiving a gunshot wound in the foot.

While coming back from the Lake Timsah checkposts on 17 December two jeeps from the company were ambushed by Egyptians who hurled a bomb into the leading jeep. Lance-Corporal Blake (a young National-serviceman) with great presence of mind tossed the bomb out of the jeep, which exploded in the roadway between the two jeeps without inflicting any casualties. Immediately both jeeps came under heavy automatic fire. The occupants of the leading jeep were wounded and it slowed down. The other jeep then overtook and managed to reach the safety of the defensive position at the YMCA Bridge, some 300 yards farther on. On arrival at the bridge the occupants of this jeep realized that the other had not followed and was apparently in difficulties so, dropping off Corporal Readings to contact Company HQ, the remaining NCOs, Corporal McAvoy and Lance-Corporals Lindsay and D. Smith, disregarding their personal safety decided to return to give assistance to their comrades in the stricken jeep in spite of the fact that firing was still taking place. On arrival it was observed that all the occupants had been wounded. Without further delay the wounded personnel were transferred to the serviceable jeep by their rescuers and conveyed, while still under fire to the safety of the YMCA Bridge and thence to hospital. Such conduct reflects credit upon the Corps as a whole and is a fine example of the *esprit de corps* in RMP. Most of the personnel involved were National-servicemen.

Lieutenant J. Hampton died as a result of head wounds received in this ambush and Lance-Corporal Chapman was seriously wounded.

The Recce troops of the 4th/7th Royal Dragoon Guards gave close co-operation and ready assistance during this period and they and the company worked closely together in highly successful co-operation.

By now the constant unprovoked attacks were becoming more irritating and on 12 January, 1952, as a result of an armed attack on a WD train, Brigadier Steele decided to teach the village of Tel-el-Kebir a sharp lesson. A considerable force was mounted but was pinned down by determined and fanatical resistance until about 1 pm. They began to move in, being sniped at all the time. Parts of the village were searched, mortars were fired and buildings left burning. The force withdrew at about 5 pm, the natives sniping until the last. Casualties were one killed and three injured. The natives lost three killed and thirty-two prisoners, including seven terrorists who wore a form of uniform for the first time. It was known that many more had been left dead in the village. During that night one terrorist was killed in the garrison and three pilferers also died. The following day the civil police were asked to remove the seven bodies from the mortuary. This they did and afterwards claimed that the bodies had been savaged by dogs before being shot in the garrison. Such was their need for propaganda. It was decided that in future the bodies would be left *in situ*.

512 SMPS was expanded as a result of the redevelopment to become a GHQ section and left the Canal Zone to reinforce Cyprus District and took over Nicosia in time to deal with the troubles in the island over the Christmas period of that year. It would appear that the only two units in the Mediterranean area to remain undisturbed, either through redeployment or internal troubles, were 616 SMPS in Malta and 224 GHQ Company in Gibraltar.

In Egypt during this transitional period the SIB were also fully employed and their primary concern was with WD property. Liaison with the local authorities however often involved them in peculiar cases either because a military investigation led back to civilians or because SIB assistance was sought. The drug traffic was one such example that gave a new flavour to SIB investigations.

A natural barrier in the traffic of drugs was the Suez Canal. Rewards for a successful smuggling operation were enormous and the rewards offered by the authorities for information were also proportionally valuable. In between the two was a floating figure payable as bribes. Human ingenuity on both sides excelled itself in devising new methods of concealment and search, even to the extent of searching camels in caravan with mine detectors to disclose metal containers of drugs the unfortunate animals had been forced to swallow.

From time to time soldiers in the Canal Zone became involved on both sides, sometimes acting in co-operation with the authorities under police instruction, sometimes succumbing to the temptation.

RSM Hudson SIB reported several cases of assistance in combating this trade. One case concerned a petrol tanker which daily crossed the Canal ferry at El Kantara to supply a military unit stationed on the eastern side and, presumably, returned empty. As a result of information received (the time-honoured commencement of almost every police investigation) a NCO was detailed to keep the vehicle under observation. His suspicions aroused, he arranged for the customs officers to stop and search the vehicle. The search was thorough but unproductive. The NCO, however, was not satisfied. He was fortunately of a persistent nature and was prepared to strip the vehicle into component parts if necessary. His opportunity came when the vehicle was waiting for the ferry to load-up and move off and strip it down he did. Inside the 800-gallon-capacity tank, suspended from the lid by a thread and wrapped in a waterproof packet was hashish to the value of £900.

Policemen, according to popular belief, can be spotted a mile off, at least by crooks. True or not it is often desirable to enlist the aid of outside assistance. A particularly well-known contractor was suspected of using his entrée to military camps to contact soldiers. When it was learned that a new contact had been arranged at a RASC camp a RASC sergeant was briefed. In due course he was approached and asked to bring back a parcel from El Kantara, the 'fee'—£20. On his next trip the parcel, which turned out to be two sacks, was collected and delivered. Police however, having been informed by the sergeant of delivery arrangements, were waiting. The sacks contained hashish valued at £16,000.

There were also cases where soldiers were directly involved and in terms of profit, but not ingenuity, one of the outstanding cases was that of an ambulance driver who, when asked by a warrant officer to open his ambulance, said he could not do so as his patient was critically ill and his orders were that he must not be disturbed. The warrant officer did not accept this story and insisted on a search which revealed £80,000 worth of hashish plus £600 in sterling currency notes.

1956 saw the final withdrawal of British troops from Egypt: two British provost companies and 16 Independent Parachute Brigade Provost Unit returned to the United Kingdom, two British provost companies, two non-British provost companies, one SMPS and 2 Section, SIB, disbanded in Egypt and the remaining RMP units deployed to Cyprus in July. The last provost representative to leave Egypt was Lieut-Colonel J. Corbett, APM, BTE.

GHQ MELF moved from the Canal Zone to Cyprus in summer 1956 and the Provost Marshal MELF, Colonel E. D. Rash, together with his staff moved into new brick-built accommodation at Episkopi at the south-western end of the island and the wooden huts in Fayid were at long-last empty.

'He that drinketh the waters of the Nile shall surely return' seemed, at the end of 1956, to be a true prophecy.

CYRENAICA AND TRIPOLITANIA

In 1951, after eight years of British administration which followed the expulsion of the Germans and Italians, Libya became a federal kingdom under King Idris I, hereditary chief of the Senussi. Libya was also elected a member of the Arab League in 1953. The headquarters of Tripoli District was in the town of Tripoli and its boundaries were Cyrenaica on the east and Tunisia on the west. To the south was the Libyan Desert which was used as a British Army training area; it is a barren waste in which only the hardiest human beings and animals can survive and in which boundaries are difficult to define.

Garrison troops in Tripolitania, small in number, were mostly concentrated near Tripoli. Because of treaty obligations they were very rarely seen off-duty in the town wearing uniform and by so doing presented the small provost unit stationed there with a problem which, together with a US MP Corps unit, kept all ranks busy attempting to avoid infringements of the treaty regulations. 10th Armoured Division Provost Company was also in Tripoli. This company, which was raised to full establishment for the Suez crisis in 1956 was finally disbanded in January, 1958. In addition there were two Tripoli District provost sections controlled by a DAPM with a SIB section commanded by an officer. This establishment was soon reduced to a DAPM and one section with a small SIB detachment. British troops finally withdrew from Tripoli by the end of 1967.

Cyrenaica District was commanded by a brigadier whose headquarters were in Benghazi; the District was bounded on the east by Egypt and on the west by Tripolitania, a seaboard distance of some 800 miles. Provost was represented by a DAPM with two sections and a small detachment of SIB. The Provost and SIB detachments had their headquarters in Benghazi and Derna, Tobruk being one of the many places which RMP coast road patrols visited.

Provost in Cyrenaica performed operational duties on exercises in addition to their normal routine discipline patrols. Because of their expert local knowledge provost formed part of the Desert Rescue and Recovery Organization. Also, because of the Libyan Treaty requirements, very careful and close liaison had to be maintained with the local civil police.

In October, 1954, 25th Armoured Brigade moved from Cyrenaica, where they had lived in almost desert conditions at Benghazi, to Tripolitania. Here their provost amalgamated with Tripolitania District Provost Section. A new section was formed in Cyrenaica District with replacements from 203 Provost Company.

1967 saw the final disbandment of Cyrenaica District and with it a further chapter in MELF Corps history closed.

SUEZ 1956

British troops evacuated Cairo and Alexandria in 1947 and, on 15th May, 1948, Egyptian troops invaded Palestine; Israeli troops counter-attacked and invaded Egyptian territory in December. A truce was declared in January, 1949, followed by an Armistice in February.

Colonel Gamal Nasser became premier and virtual dictator in 1956 and the last British troops left Egypt in June, 1956. Egypt took over the defence of the Suez Canal from Britain in November, 1955, and Nasser nationalized the Canal Company in July the following year.

Hostilities broke out again between Israel and Egypt in October and Israel, anticipating an Egyptian invasion, advanced, drove the Egyptians back and once again invaded Egyptian territory and advanced to the Canal. It was therefore necessary for swift action to be taken to stop the fighting and to reopen the Canal to international shipping. Pending action by the United Nations, Britain and France together took steps to achieve this.

The first step was to seize Port Said, which not only controlled the north end of the Canal but was the nearest point on the Canal where Egyptian and Israeli forces would meet.

The military plan to carry this out was Operation 'Musketeer', the spearhead being 3rd Battalion, the Parachute Regiment, of which Captain E. W. T. Mitchell, Officer Commanding 16th Parachute Brigade Provost Unit, gave the following account:

> 'Port Said is situated at the end of a long causeway running north to south through which the Canal passes and is linked to the mainland to the west by a second narrow causeway. This causeway is the only direct land link with the Delta and on this causeway is Port Said airfield.
>
> 'To ensure no reinforcements could reach Port Said after the commencement of the seaborne assault, it was decided to cut off Port Said by dropping an airborne force at two places, one being El Gamil airfield (by the British), west of Port Said, and the other at the waterways south of Port Said (by the French), to seize the bridges: seaborne landings would then take place on the beaches at Port Said and Port Fuad. Twenty-four hours later the British parachute forces, consisting of the 3rd Battalion, the Parachute Regiment and a Tactical Brigade HQ, dropped. Their task was to secure El Gamil airfield, outside Port Said, and to seize the west end of Port Said proper.
>
> 'On the morning of 5 November, 1956, a force of thirty-four aircraft took off from Cyprus carrying 670 officers and men of 16 Independent Parachute Brigade Group. This force was designed to drop directly on the airfield and

carried with it eleven jeeps and trailers containing radio sets and four anti-tank guns to deal with enemy tanks reported in the area of the dropping zone.

'The provost party was very small and consisted of Captain E. W. T. Mitchell, Corporal Taylor and Lance-Corporal Evans. Their task was to assist in the organization and control of the traffic disembarking from the seaborne assault force which was landing directly on the heavily built-up-quayside twenty-four hours later and to sign an axis for the assault follow-up vehicles through the maze of streets of Port Said to the Canal Company road which runs south to Suez. For the signing of the axis paper signs were carried together with 18″ pin stakes.

'The drop took place at 7.15 a.m. On the dropping zone the enemy had placed 40-gallon tar drums as obstacles to a parachuting force and on the north side, on the beach, were two rows of mines. From the time the force jumped they were engaged by small arms fire and as they landed the first bombs and shells landed on the dropping zone (DZ). The force rallied quickly at their RV except for the leading company, which landed so close to perimeter defensive positions that they were committed directly to an assault by their company commander.

'Tactical Brigade HQ established itself against the wall of an outbuilding of the control tower to gain what protection it could from the mortar fire and the shells from Russian SU.100 SP guns which were firing on the DZ. During this bombardment both Captain Mitchell and Corporal Taylor were wounded (not seriously) by mortar fragments.

'There were two pill-boxes sited to cover the airfield and it was fortunate for the force that one was quickly over-run. The second proved much more difficult to subdue. This and slit trenches of a platoon position nearby were cleared by 8.15 a.m. The leading troops were then engaged by snipers from beach chalets on the north side of the road leading to Port Said. These two were cleared by 8.45 a.m.

'Air cover was available the whole time and the airborne force were able to call down aircraft on any target they wished to engage. Strikes were very soon necessary. The first was on a fiercely defended position in a sewage farm just off the airfield perimeter. The enemy were well dug-in and had to be subjected to several air strikes.

'The final strong point of the airfield defences was encountered a few hundred yards further on in a Moslem cemetery surrounded by a thick stone wall. A defensive position had been prepared hidden among and protected by tombstones. This position was alongside the road and blocked the approaches to Port Said. It was held by some thirty Egyptian soldiers who fought most bravely and only after several air strikes and a company attack was this position captured. The Egyptians had fought to the last man.

'The battalion had reached the first block of flats in the residential area of Port Said and Tactical HQ had moved itself forward to the first of the beach chalets from which snipers had been cleared earlier in the day. By late afternoon heavy mortar fire was brought down on the leading company and only lifted when the commander of Port Said garrison asked to discuss surrender terms. The positions, therefore, remained unchanged until the morning when, the terms having been rejected, the assault landings were put in and the advance of 3rd Parachute Battalion continued, this time in an attempt to link-up with 3rd Commando Brigade who had landed on the beaches about a half-mile to the east. During this period two MIG fighters strafed the airfield.

'The link-up was only a matter of time and the main concern of the Parachute Brigade Tactical HQ was to make contact with the French parachute force, who had landed to the south of Port Said, and to prepare for the advance down the Canal road to the south.

'To this end, Captain Mitchell and Corporal Taylor were sent by helicopter over the area of the fighting to French HQ, which was situated at the waterworks south of Port Said to recce a position for Tactical HQ. On arrival they found that far from being a site outside the battle area, the new location was the scene of fierce fighting. Captain Mitchell and Corporal Taylor, having completed the recce, were unable to get back, as had been planned, to bring forward the Main HQ, owing to the heavy fire in Port Said and had, therefore, to remain in the waterworks area until the arrival of the main force that evening.'

Shortly after this a cease-fire was called and fighting ceased.

At the end of the day's fighting casualties were found to be four killed and twenty-five wounded.

Lieut-Colonel L. F. Richards, APM, 2 (Br) Corps then gives his account of the 'Affair':

'It takes some time before the impact of events of national importance makes itself felt on the individual quietly soldiering on Salisbury Plain. The only tangible evidence to hand of a Middle East crisis had been the unusual appearance of a few convoys of sand-coloured vehicles and a little additional bustle and activity at the District Headquarters. The news of the reservist call-up had passed without a great deal of comment and the Canal seemed many, many miles away. It was in this unsuspecting atmosphere of calm and quiet that I suddenly found myself appointed APM to the Suez emergency forces, who had been grouped together under HQ 2 Corps. I had no idea as to what was involved. In Germany I had had the good fortune to see 1 (Br) Corps at work during manœuvres such as "Battle Royal" and I was thankful that Major A. G. Joslin, late APM 1 (Br) Corps, and acknowledged master of the game, was available at the Depot for consultations.

'A visit to the Depot the next day restored my confidence. 22 Corps Provost Company was being formed from the AER under the expert and skilful guidance of the Commandant and staff. Progress was being inspected by the Provost Marshal, who seemed well-satisfied with what was going on. The company commander, Major H. A. Cooper, his officers and senior NCOs were keen and enthusiastic and there were many familiar faces among the junior NCOs—men with whom I had previously served and with whom I was pleased to be serving once again. An hour or so with Major Joslin enabled me to extract the very latest papers on Corps provost complexities and the gaps were filled-in by question and answer.

'With this foundation, having packed overnight, I set forth to report to HQ 2 Corps. Once there I gained contact by letter, telephone and visit with the DAPMs or company commanders of other formations likely to be involved and found that they had very few outstanding problems, which was most encouraging. There was no reason to doubt that they would carry out their tasks according to the traditions of the Corps of Royal Military Police. Their keenness and enthusiasm were great.

'The provost element included Major H. A. Cooper and 22 Corps Provost Company, Majors G. W. Jones and E. G. Lawton with 3rd Infantry Division Provost Company and Captain E. W. T. Mitchell commanding 16th Parachute Brigade Provost Unit. At HQ 2 Corps there was myself and Major B. S. Drewe as DAPM and at HQ 40 Sub-Area, Major E. Robertson. Other units were held in reserve.

'Provost are invariably among the first to arrive in battle and the last to leave and so it was on Operation "Musketeer". On 5 November, the day prior to the seaborne landings at Port Said, 16th Parachute Brigade landed, having been given the task of seizing the airfield and probing towards the town. The initial lift included a small Provost party consisting of Captain Mitchell, Corporal Taylor and Lance-Corporal Evans. The drop took place successfully as planned at 7 am.

'The seaborne assault landings also went according to plan and amongst the early arrivals were Major Lawton and a party of thirteen NCOs of 3rd Infantry Division Provost Company, who were accompanying the advance elements of the division. The advance party itself was under command of Lieutenant Tebbutt and Major Lawton had been briefed for a special task. It is surprising that Major Lawton arrived at the right place at the right time! On flying back to Malta from England he was horrified to observe from the air that both harbours were devoid of shipping—he had missed the boat! However, by a series of co-operative moves by the Royal Navy he caught up with the convoy and ascertained by signal lamp that all was well, finishing the last six miles through a rough sea in an open launch. He arrived at the Casino Palace Quay just in time to observe Lance-Corporal Collins, on point duty, taking swift evasive action from an enemy sniper.

'The Royal Marine Commandos and 6th Battalion the Royal Tank Regiment systematically and effectively dealt with the opposition in Port Said whilst the French forces were operating mainly in Port Fuad. The resistance in Port Said was overcome with minimum loss of life and damage except at points such as Navy House where dogged resistance persisted. It was a great disappointment to those who intended re-occupying the building that Navy House became gutted in the process. Snipers hiding in buildings were a great nuisance and had to be winkled out one by one. The Parachute Brigade and 3rd Division Provost parties got on with their respective tasks, establishing information posts at points of disembarkation, traffic posts on the Raswa bridges with the French, and route signing according to the previously arranged traffic plan. The sinking of the blockade ships had caused a variety of difficulties, the main one being the increase in the length of time before units met up with their equipment and vehicles.

'At this juncture 22 Corps Provost Company was converging on Port Said in no less than seven different ships. I arrived that night with a section of 22 Corps Provost Company, having made the crossing in HMS *Manxman*, a very fast minelayer. My arrival coincided with the advance party of Corps HQ. We were all cussing merrily about the shortage of transport and were making preparations to march on foot to the Canal Company buildings, which was to be our headquarters. We were all very tired and the thought of this party of fairly senior officers, weighed down with suitcases and packs, shuffling along the deserted streets of Port Said at midnight, was more than I could bear. The provost information post directed me to the location of Major Lawton's advance party and lent me a vehicle to get there. I found them in very good heart and not even slightly worried about the sniping which was in progress. Within a minute of arrival food and drink were provided and I gladly accepted the loan of some trucks. It had saved the day. The Corps' advance party was able to proceed with all decorum! Despite the hour the 3rd Division military policemen on duty were alert and smiling, which I thought was a very good omen.

'My early arrival enabled me to secure the Chief Cashier's suite of splendid and palatial offices in the Canal Company building for my own set-up, the SIB and the provost operations room. I lived on the premises—it was much easier than getting dragged out of the Mess night-after-night to attend to various bits of business. I staked a claim for 22 Corps Provost Company by the quayside and close to the headquarters. In the absence of the company it was difficult to retain these premises owing to general shortage. A series of unit commanders disguised thinly as real estate agents, had to be systematically dispensed with almost daily until the main body of the company was flown in from the United Kingdom.

'Our forward troops were dug in at El Cap, some twenty-five miles south of Port Said, and it now appeared that we would proceed no further. The battle was over, but where did we go from there?

'The general cease-fire meant that there would be no further movement forward and that subsequent unloading and disembarkation would be severely restricted to essential stores and administrative units and troops. Provost traffic control problems were thereby greatly diminished but the disciplinary problems vastly increased.

'It was a situation very aptly and adequately described in Chapter XXIII of the *Provost Training in Peace and War* (1950) and the Provost duties carried out during this period were strictly in accordance with the *Manual*—modified very slightly here and there and perhaps with a few unorthodox additions.

'At the peak period we had on the ground the whole of 22 Corps Provost Company and HQ and three sections of 3rd Infantry Division Provost

Company, two of those sections being detached with brigades. 16th Parachute Brigade Provost Unit was amongst the first to leave Port Said and return to base.

'Working with us jointly were the RAF Police under Squadron-Leader Barrett and his very capable Flight-Lieutenant, who gave us great support both in men and, at times, in materials. In charge of the French military police was the DAPM, Commandant Roux, who was acquainted with many of our provost officers, having served alongside the British Army in Vienna. On the Civil Affairs side we had Lieut-Colonel Green and Major Williams as Public Safety Officers, both of whom had served in the Zone previously.

'The order to seal-off the Arab quarter and place it out-of-bounds immediately was a good one and coupled with the imposition of the night curfew was instrumental in maintaining a very successful degree of law and order throughout this exceedingly difficult period.

'Anti-looting and pilfering measures were immediately introduced with great success. Combined patrols, including RAF, French and the Egyptian civil police, were put on the roads immediately transport was available. They scoured the town by day and by night and in addition to their rôle of crime prevention they soon became known to the Egyptians as an impartial body who would carry out errands of mercy during curfew hours. These requests were usually in connection with the requirements of expectant mothers or medical attention as a result of accident or illness.

'CSM V. McMahon and Lance-Corporals C. Baker and D. J. Hilton of 3rd Infantry Division Provost Company distinguished themselves by rescuing several Egyptian women and children from a fiercely-burning tenement. Even the Egyptian crowds could not restrain themselves from clapping and cheering as CSM McMahon appeared through the smoke carrying an ancient grandma in the text-book fireman's lift! All three military policemen were mentioned in a 2 Corps Special Routine Order.

'The out-of-bounds signing of the Arab quarter was a fairly tall order. In all about 400 signs were required and since it was appreciated that wastage by theft would be considerable, it was decided to paint them on the walls and pillars which surround the area. Teams set out during the night firstly to paint the black background—the international sign and the wording to be stencilled on on the following night. We were surprised the next morning to find that many of them bore slogans painted on in very basic English by Egyptians. They read, alternately, "Nasser High", "Eden Low", "Stockwell Low", "Up Nasser", "Up Nasser", "Up Nasser". We agreed heartily with the last exhortation! The general standard of English found in slogan writing was poor.

'The main body of 22 Corps Provost Company arrived by air and had just been told by the company commander how quiet and peaceful things were in Port Said when a near-riot broke out. The astonished NCOs were bundled into vehicles and were at work within minutes of arrival. The arrival of a Norwegian battalion, the first contingent of the United Nations

Emergency Forces, started it off. They arrived at the railway station, where a large crowd of Egyptians had foregathered to greet them. They were due to march through the town to their camp, which was on the northern boundary. The mob became more inflamed and swelled in numbers as time went on. At every cross-roads hundreds more joined in howling slogans and dancing dervishes. I had, at the head of the Norwegian battalion, four Land-Rovers containing crews armed with truncheons, from 22 Corps and 3rd Division Companies, travelling abreast. Ahead of the Land-Rovers, and covered by them, a semi-circular screen of military police on foot cleared the route, giving a perfect demonstration of what can be achieved by minimum force in crowd control. Firmness, good humour and flat hands were the only weapons used.

'Along the route a newspaper correspondent was found in the throes of an epileptic fit and about to be trampled underfoot. He was quickly and without ceremony thrown into the back of a Land-Rover, complete with camera and typewriter, where he was forcibly restrained for the next two hours by four NCOs sitting on him until the party was over. The Norwegian contingent was somewhat taken aback by this mixed reception since it was not at all clear who was on which side! The coolness of the military police in forcing a passage through this mob was an example to all. The Norwegians were delivered to their camp and the military police patrols, joined by reinforcements, then swept the crowds away from the camp towards the Arab quarter, where they were finally dispersed by the Internal Security troops. The only shots fired were by two spectators, not British, who were caught in an isolated vehicle. These shots unfortunately caused the death of two youths who were the only casualties. Many Egyptians themselves appreciated the restraint shown, at times in the face of great provocation, and joined with such shouts as "Military Police very good men, sir—God bless you!" which was undoubtedly encouraging.

'The Royal Navy played a great part in pooling welfare resources, which were very limited, for officers and other ranks alike. Cinema shows, bathing facilities, fresh bread supplies, bottles of blanco and an odd bottle of Scotch here and there, were some examples of their kindly hospitality.

'When it became known that the Egyptians intended blowing up the statue of Ferdinand de Lesseps, which had stood for many years in the entrance to the harbour, much discussion took place at various levels as to how this desecration could be avoided. The most favoured plot was to remove it, but such was its great height and prodigious weight that this scheme was reluctantly abandoned. However, during the last few days my attention one evening was attracted by a small party of men, strangely equipped with ropes, brackets and other gear, about to leave HMS *Tyne* in an open launch. I begged a lift ashore and found that I had walked into yet another plot designed to place the British and French flags in the outstretched hand of de Lesseps as a final tribute. I stayed and watched the performance in the twilight and was impressed with the mountaineering skill and agility of Able Seaman Constable, RN, who did the scaling and flag erection, and Senior Engineer Lieut-Commander Harwood, RN, who organized the expedition. The light was failing fast but there was just sufficient glimmer to take some exclusive photographs!

'The War Office freeze on the build-up at Port Said shut out many administrative units, including the prisoner-of-war cage, which had been formed to deal with prisoners-of-war and civilian detainees. 22 Corps Provost Company was committed to this task, which they handled efficiently under difficult conditions. They were responsible for administration and internal discipline in two detainee centres, guards being provided by the Royal Pioneer Corps, and for internal discipline at the prisoner-of-war cage. They had through their hands approximately ninety prisoners and five hundred detainees who included curfew-breakers, individuals bearing arms against us and other offenders.

'A frequent visitor to these establishments was Dr Thudicum, the Geneva Red Cross representative, who expressed himself well pleased at the procedure and treatment accorded to the inmates. The plan for provost to occupy the Port Said civil prison unfortunately fell through. I visited the building soon after arrival and found it to be in a state of utter squalor. A bomb crater had damaged the sewerage system and the quadrangle was flooded with appalling filth. Released criminals had wrecked the administrative block from end-to-end. Offices which contained records had been set on fire and corpses were still lying around. I learned later that Lieutenant Tebbutt and a small reconnaissance party had also visited the prison on the first assault day and was promptly engaged by two snipers. Having dealt with them and on withdrawing, discreetly, posterior first, Lieutenant Tebbutt nearly had the muddy seat of his trousers blasted off by Lance-Corporal Dooler, who failed to recognize it was part of his superior officer! The prison was no great loss. It was situated next to Shanty Town, from where continuous sniping took place, causing at least two deaths and some injuries.

'Negotiations were started for the exchange of Egyptian prisoners and detainees with the British detainees, who were mainly the Suez contractors' employees from Tel-el-Kebir. The changeover was effected by the United Nations at El Cap. We were very relieved when our party of some four hundred arrived by train, on time and in good heart. They were transferred without delay from the train to a lighter which was to take them to their troopship. As they slowly made their way up the Canal they were received with bands playing and the decks of all ships were lined from stem-to-stern to welcome them. Resounding cheers echoed across the waters. Soon after boarding the *Asturias* they sailed for Cyprus, where arrangements had been made for their immediate air travel to the United Kingdom.

'22 Corps Provost Company was very glad to be able to render some useful assistance to the British subjects who were evacuated from Port Said. Provost arrangements were made by Major Robertson, DAPM, 40 Sub-Area, and included the security of the assembly areas, the marshalling of vehicles and persons, and assistance to aged persons, women and children in embussing and embarkation. The men entered into the spirit of the undertaking.

Their turnout was impeccable, even down to white cotton gloves, and in no time they were to be seen pushing prams, carrying babies and baggage and making themselves useful in many ways. In a letter to Lieut-General Sir Hugh Stockwell, the organizer of the evacuation said: "While I hesitate to pick out any particular body, since they were all so efficient and helpful, I would like to say a special word of praise for the officers and men of the Royal Military Police, of whose helpfulness towards the children and the aged I was myself a witness."

'A great variety of hidden talent in the average provost company has always impressed me a great deal. Whatever one wishes to launch, whether it is a pig and poultry scheme or a cabaret and jazz band set-up, a requirement for horse copers or men to climb poles or go fishing, there are always volunteers and usually some experts among them. I was not, therefore, surprised when Major Cooper produced a fully-trained crew, under Sergeant Pope, to take over the RMP Harbour Patrol launch. The purpose of the patrol was to prevent looting and pilfering by means of water approach to quayside installations, the prevention of theft of small craft, marine stores and fishing gear, enforcement of restrictions as ordered, and the clearance and reporting of floating and submerged hazards and emergency crossing to Port Fuad in connection with crime.

'Due to the high salt water corrosion in Port Said, the electrical apparatus on the launch needed constant attention, and a certain loss of dignity had occasionally to be faced by accepting a tow from the Royal Navy!

'We provided a considerable number of escort parties and guides for the United Nations contingents who arrived in the area. There were "summit" talks as to whether their charter should include joint patrols and reciprocal powers of arrest with the Allies. A provisional negative answer was received and the problem was not properly resolved before we left.

'On 19 December the Corps HQ occupation of the Canal Company building came to a close. Everyone had left and as I was about to leave myself a cigar came into the office through the veranda door, followed by an American civilian who was chewing one end. A deep down-South twang inquired where a chop-suey could be obtained for the Egyptian driver of the cigar who was housed in a glittering Cadillac outside. With due deference to the five dollars' worth of smouldering best Havana leaf I explained the difficulties of operating chop-suey establishments in the prevailing circumstances and the difficulties involved in penetrating the dannert wire perimeters to go in search of food. As an alternative I offered the cigar's owner, who looked a kindly man, the choice of my emergency tinned rations.

'He accepted that it was "mighty kind" of me to make this offer, and I did not hesitate to relieve him of two of the fine cigars from his proffered case. I explained that in the British Army the APM's office was always a sort of stragglers' post where almost anything could be obtained. As the cigar, black Homburg and quizzical smile quietly departed from one door, a posse of bustling UNO officials and others arrived at the other door.

They had lost General Wheeler, the newly-appointed United Nations salvage expert. It was only then that the penny dropped!

'General Stockwell watched the last troops of the Royal Scots and West Yorkshire Regiment embark and chatted to many of them. He also spoke a few words to two NCOs of 3rd Division Provost Company, Corporal Willcox and Lance-Corporal Jay, who were the last RMP NCOs to leave.

'The last company of the West Yorkshire Regiment boarded their LST and the last man to leave Port Said, Brigadier Grimshaw, commanding a brigade, left the quayside in his launch. Two other officers, the APM and the Port Commandant, who had individual plans to be the last to leave, accepted defeat gracefully. At about H minus fifteen it was hinted that it was about time we climbed aboard. We climbed. There was no point in staying and encouraging physical violence at this stage!

'The re-embarkation was completed without casualties. There had been considerable firing from the Arab town from dusk onwards and streams of tracer came overhead in our direction elevated a bit too high to be of any danger. A West Yorkshire platoon received a more effective burst on pulling out of their position, which was dealt with by the United Nations troops.

'The last few days had been a masterpiece of precision and planning. There had been no hurry or bustle. The perimeter had been pulled in day-by-day without serious incident. The embarkation of a very considerable force of men, vehicles and equipment had proceeded smoothly according to the time-table without a single piece of equipment being left behind. The quaysides had never looked cleaner.

'As the last troopships, LSTs and Royal Navy units pulled out of the harbour we were able to relax at last and were thankful it had been accomplished with such dignity. There had been many occasions during this six weeks of occupation when a less disciplined army would have sought vengeance by bloodshed yet despite continuous and at times extreme provocation—officers and men killed by ambush, sniping and bomb-throwing—the British Army observed the highest degree of self-discipline and strictly applied the principle of minimum force.'

CYPRUS

British HQ Middle East Land Forces transferred to Cyprus in 1956. In April, 1955, the EOKA campaign to promote 'Enosis' or union with Greece, which had been the cause of unrest since the Church Plebiscite of 1950, took the form of open terrorism. A State of Emergency was declared in September and Archbishop Makarios was exiled. The Emergency was to last until, as a result of the Anglo-Turko-Greek agreement of February, 1959, Cyprus became an independent republic within the Commonwealth; Makarios becoming President in December and Independence Day being 16 August, 1960. British troops continued to garrison the agreed British bases and later were called in by Makarios to intervene in Greek–Turkish civil disorders until, in 1964, Britain referred the matter to the United Nations, who sent in a Peacekeeping Force.

During the Emergency period RMP deployment was 227 GHQ Provost Company with two sections at Limassol, two at Famagusta, one each at Larnaca, Kyrenia and Government House, Nicosia.

Later this became company HQ with six sections at Nicosia plus one section allotted to Government House, two sections each at Limassol and Famagusta and a section each at Larnaca and Kyrenia. One SMPS was based on Paphos, Cyprus District Provost Unit forming the escort section for the Commander-in-Chief, and 51st Brigade and 16th Parachute Brigade Provost Units were based on Famagusta. In addition there were sections of SIB and WRAC Provost.

Apart from the normal enforcement of discipline in those towns which were in-bounds to troops, provost were very heavily committed to Internal Security duties and the implementation of Emergency Regulations in conjunction with the civil police, of which riot prevention, by means of dispersing unlawful assemblies, became a constant, almost routine, feature of patrol duties. It followed, because RMP patrols were usually the first on the scene, that they became committed if a riot did break out—and, again a natural corollary, were the last to disengage as they were required to patrol the area to ensure dispersal and prevent re-grouping.

A closely allied duty was the constant watch for, and apprehension of, distributors of proscribed literature and the prevention of intimidation of the civilian population by terrorists.

Protection of life (often of pre-selected victims) and of property was considered by those engaged to be the most hazardous duty performed by RMP. A constant watch had to be maintained for gun-runners, movement of explosives and couriers, persons to be apprehended under detention orders and known associates of and sympathizers with EOKA.

In addition were many special duties such as cordon and search operations, security of detention camps and special protective escorts to VIPs.

During the Emergency the civil administration not infrequently broke down and on such occasions, with fear of typhoid epidemics and other dangers, RMP NCOs found themselves either in conjunction with or under the direction of the medical services, responsible for the hygiene and sanitation of considerable areas.

Provost duties were therefore many, varied, long and arduous and often hazardous, with patrols an open target for the sniper or bomb thrower, the searcher a victim to booby-traps and off-duty the possibility of being blown up while having a drink in a café; such was the common round and the following story is selected to illustrate the many incidents because a fair measure of the credit reflects on the work done throughout the Emergency by WRAC Provost, whose duties often took them beyond their routine of looking after members of the Womens' services and married families.

On the list of wanted men were two members of an EOKA mountain group of terrorists named Thoma and Xapolitos, each with a reward of £5,000 on his head. In October, 1956, another member of the same gang, Haritou, was captured during the course of Operation 'Fox-hunter'.

During the course of his interrogation, as a result of his comments on the method by which his group was supplied, he identified the wife of Xapolitos as being responsible for supplying the group with food. This woman lived in Galini and was the mother of four small children.

It was an obvious conclusion that since she supplied the group with food, then she must know the location of the group. Accordingly it was decided to bring her forward for questioning on the matter. The fact that she had four small children to look-after created a problem and it was decided that they should be brought along with their mother so that their welfare should not be endangered. Included in the party were two WRAC Provost NCOs who were present to assist in searching and to look after the children.

Shortly after midnight on the night 29–30 October the party set out for Galini. After a long drive along the mountain roads the two Land-Rovers stopped a short way from Xapolitos' house, which was cordoned-off. The party went in and Xapolitos' wife was found to be in bed and the children asleep.

It was explained to her that she was being arrested on suspicion of supplying food to an EOKA mountain group and that her children would be brought along so that no hardship would befall them. She was asked where her husband was and she said that she had not seen him for several months. She complained bitterly about him in that he never visited her or supported her and she found life extremely difficult with four children to look after and no source of income. The house itself appeared to be well-maintained and well-furnished. It did not indicate the low standard of living she pleaded. She said that she could leave her children with her mother if she was going to be taken away, since she was quite sure that her mother would take care of them and that in any case she would rather not have the added complication of the children while she was under arrest. It was agreed that she be allowed to do this and she left the bedroom to be escorted to her mother's house.

CSM Dempster, in company with Private Thomas, of HQ 16th Independent Parachute Brigade Group, remained in the bedroom, which was later to be searched. CSM Dempster, in process of examining the room, observed what he believed to be a loose floorboard under the bed. He drew the attention of Private Thomas to this and Thomas made a closer examination, covered by CSM Dempster. The floorboard was, in fact, loose and concealed a hide-out built under the bedroom floor. When Thomas removed the board a head appeared and Xapolitos and Thoma burst out and attempted to escape. The CSM and Thomas grappled with them and after a struggle the two men were overcome and taken into custody. This in itself was an achievement, the room being very small.

While this was going on, the wife of Xapolitos, who was in the next room awaiting escort, accompanied by Sergeant Birbeck and Lance-Corporal White, both WRAC Provost, realized that her husband and his companion were discovered and made a whole-hearted effort to get to their assistance and help their escape. Sergeant Birbeck and Lance-Corporal White, thinking and acting very quickly, prevented this with great coolness and efficiency. It was undoubtedly a dangerous situation, nor did they know what dangers may have been present, but they secured their prisoner and kept her under control.

Lieut-Colonel N. E. Huber, APM, Cyprus District in 1956, wrote the following account of provost in the Cyprus Emergency:

'In 1956 terrorism was introduced as a deliberate instrument of policy after Greek agitation for 'Enosis' had been fanned to an artificial heat by the politically-conscious Greek Orthodox Church under its ambitious Archbishop. At that time the military garrison of the island was small and the strength of the Corps a little over one section. The civil police, except for a small number of Colonial Police officers in the highest ranks, was all Cypriot and, particularly in the senior grades, mainly Greek Cypriot. It was not in any way equipped, trained or psychologically prepared to deal with political terrorism, its mentality as a force being essentially rural.

'As the terrorist campaign developed it took two principal forms, the first a rather casual ambushing and murdering of Services personnel by pistol and home-made bomb and secondly the planned and deliberate assassination of Cypriot personalities and officials. This successfully achieved its object of discouraging collaboration with the Government.

'In September, 1955, with the situation rapidly deteriorating, Field-Marshal Sir John Harding was appointed Governor and the military reinforcement of the island's garrison accelerated, including a spectacular increase in RMP resources. At the Governor's request the Cyprus Police were also stiffened by the loan from various United Kingdom forces of substantial numbers in both the uniform and plain clothes branches. Even with these, however, the civil police were not yet able to undertake unaided the maintenance of public order and the suppression of terrorism so that the rôle of the considerable military force now in the island was largely police work.

'There was thus created a wonderful opportunity for the Corps to show what it could do in a situation made-to-measure for soldier-policemen, and this opportunity was seized with both hands and the reputation of the Corps enchanced by the way in which young NCOs competed with the astonishing and onerous range of duties thrust upon them. (These were predominantly National-servicemen at this period.)

'Inevitably, duties which were never thought of when the provost training *Manual* was written now come to be regarded as routine. Of these the principal was the so-called "Anti-Assassin Patrols" carried out daily in the three chief towns, Nicosia, Famagusta and Limassol. Conditions in each varied but, broadly speaking, from early morning until midnight, RMP Land-Rovers each manned by three NCOs and one Cypriot policeman to act as interpreter, equipped with two-way radio, circulated through and round these towns, keeping an eye on things, ready to go instantly to the scene of any trouble. A secondary task was making snap searches at random of the persons and belongings of civilian passers-by in order to increase the hazards of carrying arms and propaganda.

'These patrols were very conspicuous and were becoming at one time rather "Aunt Sallies" for bomb throwers who lurked in alleys, behind walls, trees and bushes and on over-hanging balconies in the narrow streets. These bombs were generally home-made contraptions of lengths of drain-pipe hammered in at one end, stuffed with high explosive, as often as not stolen from the island's many quarries, and fitted with a very short (three or four second) length of fuse which had to be lit an instant before throwing. In the dark, especially, they resembled a lighted cigarette being tossed away. Although some failed to explode a lot of them did go off and the fragmentation of the drain-pipe gave most unpleasant wounds. Nylon armour was fitted to the Land-Rovers to give the best compromise to provide complete freedom for the use of weapons with maximum protection.

'Another unorthodox duty carried out in Famagusta was the "Ambush Patrol". This, in fact, was a sort of counter-ambush, as its object which seems to have been achieved, was to discourage ambushers by lying-up in just those places which careful observation had shown to be their favourites.

'Most of the other duties were more easily recognizable as originating in orthodox provost practice, being variations on the themes of escorts, traffic control and car-parking, searches, PoW cages and action to counter traffic offences, adapted to the unusual circumstances of life in the island.

'Security, as opposed to ceremonial escorts, for senior officers was of course no novelty and there was much to do, but since the attempt on the life of Mr Justice Shaw in broad daylight in one of the main streets of Nicosia, RMP were given the additional task of safeguarding the daily comings and goings of the Chief Justice and his four senior judges by providing escorts and an armed NCO in their cars.

'Some of the problems of traffic control were complicated by the difficult terrain and nearly all by the ever-present need for security. Two examples will suffice. In one large-scale forest fire in the mountains which some 800 troops were helping to fight, the only access to the area in which the troops were working was by a narrow track three miles long, which would just take a one-tonner and which twisted and turned its way up the mountain, solid rock on one side and a sheer drop on the other and not one single place to pass. Radio between top and bottom was, of course, essential and the very strictest control of all movement every minute of the forty-eight hours the operation lasted. It was a weary and begrimed section with smarting eyes which eventually emerged from the pall of smoke which hung all over the area to earn a very grateful letter of thanks from the Commanding Officer of the 1st Battalion The Gordon Highlanders, who had been in command of the operation. As a contrast, traffic control and car-parking for the Governor's reception on the Queen's Birthday, in view of the security demands, took a detail of no less than five officers and thirty-two NCOs.

'Searching was really the basic function of all the Security Forces and, since it is said that the Greeks have been developing hiding both people and things to a fine art for several thousand years, finding anything was never easy. As a Corps, higher authority tends to regard RMP as occupational searchers and in consequence they had to assume responsibility for searching the Cypriot staff at the Central Prison in Nicosia, full to overflowing with bad characters of all kinds, several with high prices on their heads, others under sentence of death. The possibility of escapes, or even a mass breakout, with the assistance of the Cypriot warders was therefore always present and so all the non-British staff at each of the four daily changes of shift and all Cypriot visitors, who included priests, lawyers and doctors, had to be carefully searched by a joint team of RMP and RAF Police under the command and expert guidance of a SIB NCO—a most unpleasant duty. The small WRAC Provost detachment was also much in demand for searching and all its members had visited the mountain villages to lend a hand in the big terrorist hunts by searching women suspects.

'A half-section of 16th Parachute Brigade Provost Unit had been in the island since early in the year and had accompanied the infantry battalions in all their arduous operations in the mountains, their main task being to take over custody of the so-called "hard-core" terrorists as they were flushed from their hide-outs in the caves and crannies of the rugged countryside. These men, many of them pretty desperate characters, had to be held secure in primitive conditions until they could be evacuated from the inaccessible spots in which they were found.

'Not the least of the problems of the island was road safety. The narrow twisting roads were still largely aligned on the goat tracks of centuries ago and were totally unsuitable for the volume of civil and military traffic. Moreover, the military traffic was so often driven by young and inexperienced soldiers, whom either the hot sun or a sense of operational urgency impelled to drive everywhere flat out while the civilian circulated with that light-hearted disregard of elementary road safety so characteristic of the Middle East, the two together making any road journey a nightmare; that this is no illusion was amply proved by the traffic accident statistics. Blitzes against speeding and dangerous driving were always having to be instituted and a special Traffic Section, to work directly under the APM and untouchable even for "ops", had to be created in a determined attempt to cut down the appallingly high accident rate.

'Discipline was far less a problem than might have been thought. Almost every town and village was out-of-bounds so that the troops had very few amenities or opportunities for recreation. Movement both on and off duty was subject to complicated orders which varied from place to place and the number of charges arising from contravention of these orders and/or for being out-of-bounds was fairly high, but other offences were low. Nevertheless, where strong drink is abundant and cheap, where all ranks are armed on and off duty and where a shot in the back or a bomb is always a possibility, the utmost vigilance by provost was required and the relatively small proportion of troops who did break bounds had to be swiftly dealt with and protected from the possibly grave results of their actions. The nightly mobile disciplinary patrols were really necessary and never unexciting.

'Unfortunately all these various duties were not accomplished without casualties which, proportionate to the strength, were higher than those of any other arm. Up to mid-July, 1956, three NCOs had been killed, one officer and one NCO seriously wounded, eight more NCOs admitted to hospital and two officers and fifteen other NCOs slightly hurt, all directly by terrorist action. Of those killed, Lance-Corporals Brian Welsh and Bert Shaw were ambushed on the roads and Lance-Corporal Colin Keightley killed by a bomb thrown over the wall of his billet in Famagusta as he sat in the yard one fine Sunday morning "spud-bashing".

'The morale of these NCOs, most of whom were young National-servicemen, cheerfully working under often dangerous and always arduous conditions for hours long enough to make a Trades Union leader at home blanch and in spite of casualties, never betraying the slightest sign of wanting to get their own back on the local inhabitants by undue toughness, was itself a very great tribute and they were to be commended for their efficiency and cheerful acceptance of the conditions under which they were called upon to perform their duties. The most fitting tribute must surely be to quote the following remarks made by Mr Justice Trainor at the inquest he held on the late Lance-Corporal Welsh:

' "Having heard the evidence at this inquest, I would like to congratulate Lance-Corporals Prosser, Burrows and Smith on their miraculous escape on 21 March, when the bomb was thrown into their truck. It was nothing short of a miracle that saved them from being butchered by the barbarians who threw the bomb. It is tragic that this boy of eighteen years, Brian Welsh, should have been killed. I have had as witnesses in my court on many occasions members of the Royal Military Police and I have always been very impressed by their intelligence and efficiency. They have always struck me as being a body of men well above the average in these characteristics and it is horrible to see that they have suffered heavy casualties, in this case the death of this eighteen-year-old boy.

'"I suppose his murderers would be surprised if their activities were described as barbarous. From the evidence of this case it would appear that this bomb was thrown into the back of the truck and landed in the left-hand corner of the body of it behind the passenger's seat. The deceased was, I have been told, standing at the right-hand side of the truck. The bomb exploded in the left-hand corner. Welsh sustained many injuries but, I think, indicative of the way he met his death were the injuries to his right hand. His right hand was amputated through the carpus and all the tissues in the area showed blackening and charring. My conclusion is that Welsh, seeing the bomb just behind the passenger's seat of the truck, instead of trying to escape from the truck, rushed to the bomb to throw it away, seized it in his right hand as the bomb exploded. I believe that in an heroic attempt to save his companions he met a hero's death. His body absorbed, I imagine, most of the destruction of the bomb and so the other occupants of the car were saved. My finding is that Brian Welsh was on 21 March, 1956, murdered by a person or persons unknown".'

Brigadier G. H. Baker, Chief of Staff to HE The Governor of Cyprus (and one day to become a Field-Marshal and the third Colonel-Commandant of the Corps) added the following to Lieut-Colonel Huber's article:

'I am delighted to take this opportunity of expressing my admiration and thanks to All Ranks of the Royal Military Police in Cyprus for the excellent manner in which they are tackling the many and varied duties they are called upon to perform in fighting what is probably the most difficult type of war—the Internal Security War.

'These duties, so well described in Colonel Huber's article, demand the highest standard of discipline in its widest sense, that is to say not just implicit obedience to orders but also continued alertness, imagination, good temper, stout-heartedness and devotion to duty. The members of the Corps here have shown they possess these qualities to a marked degree and the manner in which they are carrying out their duties is an example to all the three services here in Cyprus.

'I have been privileged to see the Corps in action on many fronts in the last war. To any old sweat who may read this may I just end by saying, "If you could see the younger generation in action here today, you would be proud of them".

20 July, 1956 (Signed) G. H. Baker'.

In 1968 Middle East Land Forces finally closed and the abbreviation MELF, after twenty magnificent years, became a part of British Army history. Its component parts became NEARELF (Near East Land Forces) and, after the withdrawal from Aden, British Troops, Gulf.

NEARELF HQ was in Cyprus at the Treaty Bases and BTG at

Bahrein as a token force with the main duty of preserving the Treaty obligations to the Independent Sheikdoms.

Cyprus District Provost Company became 227 (NEARELF) Provost Company on 31 August, 1967, and on 1 September HQ Cyprus District became HQ NEARELF. The number 227 Provost Company was chosen in honour of its illustrious predecessor, which had seen active service in North Africa, Italy and Trieste and which was disbanded in 1954, re-formed in 1956 for the Emergency in Cyprus and again disbanded in 1960. Phoenix-like, it was re-born in 1967 and could claim direct parentage, and is still (1976) serving on in the Sovereign Bases in Cyprus.

THE UNITED NATIONS MILITARY POLICE FORCE IN CYPRUS

On 27 March, 1964, a United Nations Peacekeeping Force was established in Cyprus, composed of contingents from Austria, Canada, Denmark, Finland, Ireland, Sweden and the United Kingdom. In the exchange of letters constituting an agreement between the United Nations and the Cyprus Government, the Force Commander was obliged to take appropriate action to ensure the maintenance of discipline and good order among members of the Force. By this, the United Nations Military Police organization came into being.

The UNFICYP Provost organization comprised a headquarters and three military police units. These units were the Nicosia Zone Provost Unit, UNFICYP Provost Unit and a Special Investigation Unit.

Nicosia Zone Provost Unit was the largest with a Danish major as officer commanding and a Canadian as second-in-command. The unit was located in Wolseley Barracks just outside the walled city of Nicosia. Duties were similar to those performed by most static military police units. As Nicosia lay in the centre of troop concentrations, thus forming the focal point for personnel on recreation, a majority of the duties dealt with the general discipline of troops and the control of places and areas out of bounds. Duties were performed on a shift system, with some thirteen or fourteen military policemen, drawn from all contingents, working on the basis of twelve hours 'on', twelve hours 'standby' and twelve hours 'off'. One of the tasks peculiar to the Force and carried out by the unit was a patrol of the 'Green line' which was the demarcation zone between the Turkish and Greek sectors of Nicosia city. This patrol consisted of two military policemen and two Greek Cypriot civil policemen with a Land-Rover and provided twenty-four-hour coverage of this strip of no-man's-land. The patrol was designed to protect property in the area, to keep the two communities apart and generally assist in keeping the peace.

The responsibility for traffic control and investigation of traffic accidents devolved upon a ten-man section, headed by a British sergeant. Three patrols, of three men each, worked on the same basic roster as the discipline sections, members of each patrol being taken from different contingents as far as possible, in order to avoid language difficulties when called to the scene of a traffic accident. This section was also responsible for both mobile and static speed checks and traffic control in connection with the movement of large convoys.

The majority of vehicles used by the unit were fitted with 'Motorola' radio, which was very simple to use and very efficient in operation. Under normal conditions the set was effective for a range of up to thirty miles and was not unduly affected by built-up areas or high ground. Should reception be poor, a second frequency was used, transmissions being boosted with the aid of a 100-foot aerial, linked with sets operated by the UNFICYP civilian police.

The UNFICYP Provost Unit, which was located at HQ UNFICYP on the edge of Nicosia airfield, had a Finnish major in command, ably supported by a RSM from the Irish contingent. The basic responsibility of this unit was security of UN HQ and the surrounding camp. The unit also provided escorts for VIPs visiting outlying parts of the island. In addition, liaison with the Greek and Turkish Cypriot police was maintained and military police representatives were frequently present at selected road-blocks, wherever these may have been set up. UNFICYP Provost Unit was fully integrated, including members from all contingents and also the RAF Police.

The Special Investigation Unit (SIU) was comprised of members from all contingents, but the officer commanding, RSM and four of the military staff of nine, were British. The types of enquiry undertaken by this unit were similar to those which are carried out by the SIB throughout the Army. In view of the situation prevailing on the island, losses of arms and ammunition were viewed more seriously than in many other theatres and invariably resulted in court-martial proceedings. An additional responsibility undertaken by SIU was anti-vice duties. This was accepted because unit representatives already had to visit all parts of the island in the normal course of duty, consequently it was more convenient to maintain information in one central agency, especially with regard to the movement of various persons connected with vice and black-market activities.

Overall control of the UNFICYP Military Police lay with the Force Provost Marshal, then Lieut-Colonel Q. E. Lawson, Canadian Provost Corps, who, with his sergeant clerk, constituted the HQ staff. Command of an integrated force of this type was not new to Colonel Lawson;

he having commanded the integrated provost unit of the Commonwealth Division in Korea.

When on duty all military policemen wore the Force armband, which consisted of white letters on a blue ground and the blue beret.

The Corps provided one officer, one warrant officer and thirteen NCOs for service with the UN Force. The tour was for six to nine months, thirty days of which was the qualification period for the UN (Cyprus) Medal.

The problems facing the military policeman on UN duty were sometimes formidable and initially frustrating. He might, for example, have found himself on patrol with a Dane and a Finn and their first contact might have been a Swede. Alternatively, he might have been with a Canadian and an Irishman and had to cover a traffic accident involving an Austrian Field Hospital vehicle and a Greek Cypriot car. Another confusing permutation could be, when accompanied by a Swede, encountering a disturbance involving Turkish/Cypriots and Finns in which some Danes might be trying to explain how it all began. There were indeed any number of possibilities.

Police work in the Force was generally interesting and varied. The policy and implementation of it differed from Corps procedure. Great demand was made upon the initiative of the individual and it was in this respect that RMP training proved its worth.

Although perhaps the RMP contribution to UNFICYP was secondary in relation to numbers and ranks, the Corps representatives were generally self-reliant and in many cases outstanding. Not unnaturally the different system took its toll of a few but the majority not only rose to the challenge of their new way of life but more than surpassed the requirements of it.

ADEN

On 30 November, 1967, the last British troops finally left Aden and, within hours, the new state of the People's Republic of South Yemen came into being amid bloodshed, anarchy and chaos. Rarely has a colonial or protected territory achieved independence with such slender resources and in such an aura of ill-will towards the late Colonial Power.

At first glance the old fortress and port, situated in a commanding position at the approach to the Red Sea, present a sombre appearance to the newcomer. Brown jagged peaks rise from the surrounding desert, pointing out into the Indian Ocean, yet framing a huge natural bay visited by the ships of many nations.

Aden has always been close to history. Legend equates Aden with the Garden of Eden. According to fable Cain, the son of Adam, is buried in the cemetery beside the main pass into Crater and Noah constructed his Ark in the Maala area. The Queen of Sheba's cisterns may be seen to this day.

Invaders came and went through the centuries. It was engulfed by Islam with all Arabia and felt the tread of many conquerors. Then in January, 1839, an expedition was sent against Aden from India consisting of two warships commanded by a Captain Haines. Aden, by this time having deteriorated into a small village, was soon wrested from the Arabs after a short battle with minimal casualties.

In his account of the attack Captain Haines wrote: 'The little village, formerly the great city, of Aden is now reduced to the most exigent conditions of poverty and neglect. In the reign of Constantine this town possessed unrivalled celebrity for its impenetrable fortifications, its flourishing commerce, and the glorious haven it offered to vessels from all quarters of the globe. But how lamentable is the present contrast.' Captain Haines could hardly have known how prophetic his words would sound 128 years later.

Throughout the nineteenth century the Colony and Protectorates of Aden, later to become the controversial Federation of South Arabia, were built up piecemeal through treaties and agreements with the various warring Arab rulers. The port of Aden gradually developed commercially and in the years following the opening of the Suez Canal in 1869 prosperity came to Aden. Finally Aden achieved Colony status in 1937 and its continued future as a free port and bunkering station, in addition to being a vital garrison for British forces, seemed assured. The autocratic, tribal sultanates of the Protectorate were forced into an uneasy federation with Aden and from this British attempt to weld together politically a large part of South Arabia primarily stemmed the initial unrest and discontent that finally resulted in our withdrawal in 1967.

In February, 1957, a detachment of RMP under Sergeant P. Keogh was sent to Aden from Cyprus to assist the RAF Police in dealing with problems arising from the increase in the military garrison in the Aden Protectorate. Provost duties for this detachment were co-ordinated and supervised by the DAPM RAF and naturally there was much joint patrolling. It is believed that, other than during the war years, RMP had not previously been stationed in Aden. The re-appearance of the 'Redcap' there was, therefore, of some interest.

Due to the re-organization of the Middle East, the War Office dealt directly with Aden from 1 April, 1958, and it is of interest to note that the Provost Marshal, MELF, when visiting the detachment, travelled some 1,000 air miles each way from Cyprus to Aden, via Turkey, Iraq and the Persian Gulf.

The upsurge of Afro-Arab nationalism after the Second World War barely touched Aden. There were some indications of industrial unrest and small reactionary political parties appeared, but with little backing from the local populace, who were more concerned with the basic problems of survival in Arabia's uncongenial climate than in the more complex and energetic matters of subversion.

Unimaginative political guidance and a disinclination to act forcefully and firmly against subversive elements, a state of mind that was to bedevil the actions of the British forces to the very end, allowed a gradual growth of nationalist political elements. Rudimentary terrorist training was acquired in the Yemen and Egypt and, by 1964, the dissident organizations considered themselves sufficiently strong to begin overt attacks upon Government and Security forces. As the terrorists became more experienced and sophisticated so a continual build-up of British forces became necessary to counter the threat, and a gradual increase in terrorist attacks continued until 1967.

The year 1967 was the open season for attacks on Security forces, as the following figures will show. During the Emergency a total of 3,850 terrorist attacks were recorded, of which 3,071 occurred in 1967. Casualties inflicted on British troops during the Emergency were fifty-four killed and 620 wounded, of whom forty-two were killed and 318 wounded in 1967. Thus the gruadual increase in dissident activity from 1964 onwards rose sharply during the final months prior to independence, despite an announcement by the British Government in mid-1967 that independence would be granted by the end of the year.

For RMP personnel stationed in Aden during the Emergency the situation proved both interesting and worthwhile. In addition to normal police duties of a disciplinary nature the diversity of provost duties may be illustrated by some examples:

Bounds and curfew patrols in close co-operation with the infantry battalion in the Tawahi area.

Anti-looting patrols in which assistance was rendered to the civil police in the prevention of looting of damaged commercial premises.

Anti-assassin patrols in co-operation with the infantry to endeavour to prevent the frequent and highly-skilled assassination of Europeans in the Tawahi area.

Special escorts were provided continually for senior officers, Queen's Messengers, captured dissidents and British families. Escort NCOs received rigorous training in the handling and use of firearms and in emergency drills. In each escort vehicle it was found expedient to arm the two rear NCOs with rifles as a counter-sniper precaution.

Port security was a particularly hazardous duty carried out by a section on loan from 3rd Division. Their duties included the patrolling of dock areas, searching suspect shipping and persons for illegal arms shipments and the setting-up and guarding of a temporary detainees cage.

Female searching was carried out by a section of WRAC Provost provided as an emergency reinforcement.

Guarding and documentation of captured terrorists was done by provost during 1967 as a set procedure.

From the above it will be realized that provost played an important rôle in the Emergency. On a number of occasions, RMP personnel were subjected to direct terrorist attack and were fortunate in sustaining only one slight casualty. Apart from 24th Infantry Brigade Provost Unit and the RMP Port Security Section, RMP personnel served under HQ Provost and Security Services, a Joint Service unit comprising all three Services.

The last few months in Aden were not without incident. Internal security patrols were intensified, as were escorts, in addition to an increasing number of dissidents to be arrested and guarded.

WRAC Provost accompanied patrols and had a difficult and hazardous duty to perform. On several occasions bomb-throwers and snipers were dressed in women's clothing or, having used their weapons, passed them to women for concealment. Had the suspect in fact been a woman and been searched by men the political strife would have been as nothing compared to the religious uprising that would have followed. Hence the necessity for the immediate availability of WRAC policewomen.

One patrol, on a July evening, was in the vicinity of a grenade attack in Maala and saw the terrorist make-off in a car. They pursued the car to Khormaksar, finally stopped it and arrested the four terrorists, all of whom were armed.

There followed a lull for a time but then terrorist activity again flared up in October when a full-scale gun battle broke out on the 14th in the Crescent, Tawahi, and provost, finding their customary escorts to the ambulance called to the scene, came under fire for the last time in a major incident.

On 30 September RMP withdrew from Steamer Point and, leaving a rear party at Khormaksar as a detachment to supervise the final withdrawal of British Troops Aden, by air, set up their new HQ in Bahrain.

PERSIAN GULF

The geographical features of the Arabian Peninsula vary considerably, from the arid desert of the dreaded Empty Quarter of Saudi Arabia to the lush, wooded hills and cultivation of the southern Oman foothills. The two Gulf stations in which members of RMP were located were the Gulf States of Bahrain and Sharjah.

Bahrain is an independent Arab State consisting of an archipelago of small, low-lying islands situated halfway down the north-east coast of the Arabian Peninsula. The largest island of the group is Bahrain itself, which is joined by a causeway to Muharraq Island. It was on these two islands that British forces were located and the RAF station at Muharraq had become an important staging post on the strategic air link to the Far East.

The narrow northern coastal strip of Bahrain Island is fertile and well-cultivated, rapidly giving way to an inland region of small, undulating hills and numerous dry wadis and rocky cliffs.

Sharjah was an independent State on the Trucial Oman coast, some 300 miles east of Bahrain, fronting on to the Gulf and facing inwards towards the desert and desolate hill country of warlike Arab tribes. It became a member of the United Arab Emirates on 2 December, 1971.

HQ British Forces Gulf was at Bahrain together with the busy RAF station at Muharraq, one infantry battalion and ancillary elements. In Sharjah, in addition to a RAF station, there was a large battalion group.

In addition to purely British forces there were three 'private armies' —the Trucial Oman Scouts, the Sultan's Armed Forces and the Abu Dhabi Defence Force. These forces were British-officered with mostly Arab soldiers and acted in a primarily internal security rôle in Trucial Oman, Oman and Abu Dhabi respectively.

There was also a small British Naval Force whose tasks included patrolling to combat smuggling and the steady influx of illegal immigrants.

The RMP establishment in the Gulf was hardly impressive in numbers but its task and rôle was interesting and unique. The application of local restrictions, frequently beyond comprehension, limited the basic task to detection of crime as scope for effecting the primary object of crime prevention was strictly curtailed.

Under a joint service establishment under the title of HQ Provost and Security Services (Gulf), the unit was commanded by a wing-commander (APM) with a major RMP as DAPM and situated in Bahrain.

The tiny Sharjah detachment existed primarily in an investigational rôle.

The defence cuts of 1968 brought the British presence in the Gulf to an end in 1971 and with it the last remaining station in the Middle East.

WEST AFRICA

RMP in West Africa Command, though few in number, were called upon to cover an extremely large area comprising the Gold Coast,

Sierra Leone, Nigeria and Gambia. There was also a small West African SIB Section under a DAPM.

In this command normal duties ran fairly smoothly apart from the administrative problems imposed by the vast distances. The main and most important duty was the training of local units in preparation for self-government.

In the spring of 1954 a local provost training course was held in West Africa Command and 3 July saw the first passing-out parade of African military policemen from Nigeria, Sierra Leone and Gold Coast who were then posted to Kaduna, Lagos, Freetown and Accra.

On 1 October, 1960, duties in Nigeria were handed over to the Nigerian Military Police and the Royal West African Frontier Force, whose units had distinguished themselves in many campaigns in both World Wars, ceased to exist.

EAST AFRICA

East Africa Command, approximating in area to France and Germany, was policed by 1 Provost Company (EA), 618 SMPS, 3 Dog Company and 5 Section SIB at Nairobi, 2 Provost Company (EA) and 617 SMPS at Mackinnon Road and 624 Provost Section in Mauritius.

RMP companies (EA) were composed of African askari sections with British officers, warrant officers and senior NCOs and a British HQ section.

The first Mauritians in the Corps were trained at the RMP Middle East Depot in 1947. All were English-speaking volunteers. They formed 211 Provost Company (Mauritian) and were stationed in the Canal Zone at Fayid, Suez, Moascar and Tel-el-Kebir, their main duties being traffic control and the discipline of Mauritian troops. They were of particular assistance to SIB when investigating cases involving Creole or French-speaking troops. They were disbanded in July, 1955.

618 SMPS had the honour of providing the first military escort of her reign to Queen Elizabeth II following the news of the death of King George VI being conveyed to her at the Royal Lodge, Sagana, near Nanyuki. A detachment of NCOs had been posted to Nanyuki for security and traffic duties and, on the need for Her Majesty to return home without delay, Sergeant Fettes and Corporal Craddock provided the escort to the airport, while Lance-Corporals Elston, Morton, Heath and Burford provided security and traffic control.

The run-down of East Africa Command, including RMP, commenced in 1951 and by the middle of 1952 the strength of provost units had been considerably reduced when Mau-Mau disturbances began to become a positive menace.

The first RMP unit to become directly involved with Mau-Mau was the independent Dog Section (the then greatly-reduced 3 Dog Company). At the request of the civil police, Command HQ authorized a number of handlers and dogs to be officially loaned to the 'Special Effort Force' of the Kenya Police. In the first four days the dogs with their handlers made ten arrests.

With the increasing menace reinforcements were provided and 39th and 49th Independent Brigade Provost Sections moved in. The Mau-Mau disturbances were declared in Emergency in 1953 and lasted until 1956.

618 SMPS provided all protective escorts to the Commander-in-Chief throughout the Emergency, whenever he made visits to operational areas, and to other visiting VIPs. The escorts were composed of two vehicles commanded by an officer or sergeant, and five NCOs. Vehicles were linked by radio, heavily armed and performed a vital function under very difficult conditions ranging from desert to tropical forest, from intense heat and dust to snow, from sea level at Mombasa to 12,500 feet in the Aberdares and on Mt Kenya.

618 SMPS was also issued with two of the original 4×4 Champs in 1954 for testing under operational conditions. They lasted approximately six months, when the unit went back to Land-Rovers. Although in many ways a comfortable vehicle Champs were not found suitable for provost purposes, especially at high altitudes.

The unit was engaged in numerous anti-Mau-Mau sweeps in and around Nairobi in co-operation with the civil police. Although fired-on a number of times in the operational areas, no escort was ever ambushed and no casualties were recorded.

During Operation 'Anvil' in April, 1954, when Nairobi was completely sealed-off by the Army and civil police and suspected adherents to Mau-Mau were arrested and detained in prison camps, all the route signing was carried out by provost after midnight on 'D' Day. With all the civil police involved in the operation, traffic control in the city had to be taken over by the military police, an event which caused some comment in the city newspapers!

618 SMPS was basically responsible for discipline in Nairobi and Mombasa. Both 39th and 49th Brigade Provost Units gave considerable assistance on numerous occasions in this respect but they were mainly stationed up-country with their brigade headquarters and were themselves responsible for discipline and other provost duties in their own areas.

Nairobi and Mombasa were the main leave centres and at the height of the Emergency during 1953–4 there were anything up to five British and four African battalions together with ancillary units in Kenya at one time. There was also a Lancaster Squadron and many RAF personnel. Some of these troops caused considerable difficulty in the maintenance of discipline in these two cities, especially as the strength of 618 SMPS never exceeded one officer, one sergeant and approximately thirty NCOs and that of the two brigades approximately two sergeants and twenty NCOs, i.e., a total of under sixty all ranks. Despite other commitments, however, the military police remained at all times in control of the situation to which a most important contributing factor was the excellent relationship existing between them, the RAF Police and the Kenya civil police.

With the vast influx of soldiers and airmen and a great increase in the strength of the European civil police, prostitution flourished on a major scale. Control was made more difficult by the proximity of the RAF airfield to, and on occasions the actual stationing of companies of British infantry in, the main brothel areas of Eastleigh. In the main the prostitutes were African with a sprinkling of Europeans and Asians. Conditions in the brothels were appalling and disease control was non-existent. Only intensive patrolling and the raiding of brothels by RMP and RAF Police kept the situation under any sort of control. On many occasions prisoners had to be lodged with the civil police as both Army and RAF cells were full.

The main police problems were desertion, brothels, driving offences, carelessness in leaving weapons in vehicles and the illegal trafficking of ammunition to prostitutes. The use of ammunition as currency was a major cause of SIB investigations with very short shrift for the culprits, especially from their own comrades. To add to these on occasions were lions from the Game Park entering the city, during which provost assisted the Game Department and civil police, language problems with the King's African Rifles askaris and the often wild behaviour off-duty of the locally-recruited Kenya Regiment which was composed in the main of young white Kenya settlers. To counter these difficulties patrols had to be sent out in strength and armed. They had to show initiative, personal courage and toughness and be highly disciplined themselves. It says a great deal for the basic Depot training that all the young National-service NCOs, as well as the seasoned regulars of the military police showed precisely these qualities in many difficult situations.

In Mombasa small RMP detachments covered port duties in connection with troopship movements and provided mobile patrols in the town. Patrols in the old town of Mombasa had to be carried out on foot as the streets were often too narrow to allow a police vehicle to proceed through them.

The last duties of RMP in East Africa were handing over their duties to the local African military police they had trained and supervising the withdrawal of British troops in yet another termination of Imperial Policing duties.

CHAPTER XII

Far East Land Forces

ALFSEA and SEALF

AFTER the fall of Rangoon on 2 May, 1945, the Japanese were driven back over the Sittang river and by August their resistance had ceased in Burma as a cohesive force.

Allied Land Forces South-East Asia Command (ALFSEA) then totalled 910,770 troops composed of men of the British and Indian Armies, East and West African forces, the Burma Army, Indian State forces and the Ceylon Defence Force.

In Burma 12th Army had under command: 4 Indian Corps, 5th, 7th, 17th, 19th and 20th Indian Divisions, 82nd West African Division, 22nd East African Brigade Group and 255th Tank Brigade, together numbering 227,244 all ranks. Also in Burma were an additional 175,000 ALFSEA troops with South Burma District in Rangoon and 505 District in Mandalay. Behind them in Bengal was 404 Area combining 36,500 troops with ALFSEA Reinforcement Centres at Chittagong and Comilla.

Most of 14th Army had been pulled out of Burma to India to reorganize for Operation 'Zipper' to re-enter Malaya and Singapore. 14th Army troops ready to mount this operation included 15 and 34 Indian Corps, 36th British Division, 23rd, 25th and 26th Indian Divisions, 11th East African Division, 50th and 254th Indian Tank Brigades and 5th Parachute Brigade from 6th Airborne Division, together with two Beach Groups; a total of two corps, five infantry divisions, two tank brigades, one parachute brigade with a total strength of 241,163 troops. In reserve were 2nd British Division and 3rd Commando Brigade.

3rd Army was based in Ceylon Army Command and was chiefly composed of 22,000 Ceylon Defence Force, 11,500 West African

non-divisional troops and 3,000 Indian troops, mostly engaged in the build-up of dumps for Operation 'Zipper'.

While this operation was in the process of being mounted the Japanese capitulated—on 14 August, 1945 (VJ-Day).

Operation 'Zipper' in its early stages was carried out as planned with beach landings unopposed at Port Swettenham and Penang under 34 Indian Corps. 15 Indian Corps and 5th Indian Division with 1st Australian Parachute Battalion were switched from beach landings to Singapore where they landed on 8 September.

The sudden capitulation of Japan increased ALFSEA area out of all expectations. It necessitated the occupation of Java, Sumatra, Borneo, Celebes, the outer islands of the East Indies, Siam, French Indo-China, Hong Kong and later Kure, Japan.

The immediate tasks were to accept the surrender of 750,000 Japanese troops in the countries concerned, recover all prisoners of war and civilian internees and administer the civil affairs of the countries concerned. The area involved was two-and-a-quarter million square miles.

In the Netherlands East Indies the Indonesian Independence movement under Dr Soekarno had obtained Japanese arms and Indonesian extremists were forming their BKR (Corps to Preserve Peace). The possession of arms gave the Republican movement a firm foothold to commence activities. The population of the Netherlands East Indies was nearly seventy million.

On 15 October HQ 15 Corps was transferred to Batavia, Java, and 5th Indian Division to Surabaya, followed by 23rd Indian Division and 254th Indian Tank Brigade to Batavia and 26th Indian Division to Sumatra. Clashes between troops and the Indonesians were almost continuous in these countries until the final withdrawal on 30 November, 1946. Our casualties during these fourteen months were over 2,000, including 300 killed and over 600 missing.

20th Indian Division was ordered in September to occupy French Indo-China to accept the surrender of the Japanese. After Division HQ and Sub-Area were established in Saigon fighting between troops and the Annamese population commenced and continued for about three months. The division restored order in areas occupied by them before handing over to French troops early in 1946.

7th Indian Division occupied Siam without any incidents and Borneo, Celebes and the Andaman and Nicobar Islands were occupied by one infantry brigade each while Hong Kong had 150th Indian Infantry Brigade and 3rd Commando Brigade with HQ Land Forces as initial garrison troops.

HQ ALFSEA moved to Singapore in October where provost consisted of a Provost Marshal, one APM and four Indian Army clerks with under command: thirty-four provost companies, three Indian SIB sections, three Gurkha and two British VPP units and two Beach provost units, an effective strength of 4,830.

The Provost Marshal was also ordered to raise a British/Indian division provost company and three British and three Indian sections in Bengal for duty in Japan. These were raised from three sections of 36th British Division Provost Company and by disbanding an Indian L of C provost unit.

With the complete absence of European civil police officers in the countries occupied, provost in early occupation days took on all police work. Later, as Civil Affairs officials were landed they began the re-organization of the local civil police. It was not until 1 April, 1946, that it was found possible to hand over completely to all local governments and in the case of Java provost retained control of the civil police throughout the fourteen months' occupation.

During this period of re-occupation in 1945 there was a fair amount of both Service and civil crime, particularly in Singapore. Investigators of 123 Indian Section SIB were continuously in support of the civil police who at this time had only the Commissioner, his Deputy, Civil Affairs police and seventeen attached British officers on their European staff. Provost staff in Singapore consisted of an APM and DAPM with the newly-formed British six-section provost company and 14th Army Provost Unit of three British and three Indian sections, the 1st Australian Parachute Battalion (for dock police duties) and 123 Indian Section SIB. On 18 January, 1946, the APM's appointment was up-graded to DPM and then an Inter-Service Police HQ was opened in a most imposing-looking hotel in the centre of the brothel area. The Navy cooperated exceptionally well and produced 85 Royal Marines but the RAF gave very little support. With the arrival of 196 Ports Provost Company, CMP availability became 360 all ranks for daily duty at the Inter-Service Police HQ. Jeep radio patrols with twenty-two sets were netted into Inter-Service Police HQ and two CMP launches were also fitted with twenty-two sets to patrol the docks. Strict enforcement of midnight curfew and increased mixed patrols reduced complaints of serious crime. A training establishment was opened in Singapore where new intakes to the Corps were trained.

Brigadier R. A. Leeson was Provost Marshal ALFSEA in 1945 and the theatre was later re-named South-East Asia Land Forces (SEALF). This was a transitional period of re-occupation between the end of hostilities and the period, as yet unforeseen, of civil disturbance and terrorist activity still to come. Brigadier Leeson's report for the year 1946 contained, among other things illustrative of police requirements during re-settlement of a vast but co-operative and friendly area, a summary of offences dealt with by provost. This totalled 62,322 offences, plus 4,975 traffic accidents, of which 490 were fatal—including 159 Service personnel. Extracts from SIB reports showed 1,715 cases investigated, 2,596 arrests and £797,693 worth of property recovered.

In Burma the 17th and 19th Indian Divisions and the 255th Tank Brigade were heavily committed rounding-up Japanese troops and the 82nd West African Division was road-making. The East African Division was preparing to return home and the discipline of this division remained at a very high standard, the very few exceptions being troops stationed in Rangoon and Mandalay where the usual temptations were too plentiful.

HQ British Forces Siam and 7th Indian Division were mostly concentrated in the city of Bangkok. This was a city of two million people where on an average during the occupation nine murders a day were committed. Needless to say the APMs concerned were exceptionally busy men.

In Java the DPM in Batavia acted as Chief Commissioner of Civil Police. Sumatra was covered by 26th Indian Division in Medan. The APM was more fortunate than his DPM in Batavia as the Dutch Commissioner of Police was released by the Indonesians and managed to regain control of the inner perimeter but at no time during the occupation of Medan was more than three-quarters of the city brought under control.

FARELF

On 11 January, 1948, when Brigadier Leeson was succeeded by Colonel P. Godfrey-Faussett as Provost Marshal the Far East appeared to have settled down after the end of hostilities to a period of reconstruction. Demobilization and reduction of Peace Establishments had much reduced the size of the Army and GHQ Far East Land Forces (FARELF) (successors to ALFSEA and SEALF) in Singapore had under command only a handful of infantry battalions and two RA regiments. The RMP contribution was three small provost units spread over the whole theatre, one in Singapore, one in Malaya and one in Hong Kong, 91 Section SIB and a large unit of Ceylon CMP in Singapore and Ceylon, mainly employed on VP duties.

But by June of that year the communists came out into the open and declared their hand. The first area to be hit was Malaya and a State of Emergency was declared. The cold war became guerrilla warfare and communists, mostly of Chinese origin, took to the jungle and waged a war of banditry. The refusal to accord them official recognition led to them being referred to as 'terrorists' and to deal with them the run-down went into reverse and became a steady build-up.

200 Provost Company in Singapore was called upon to cover the whole of Malaya with five widely-spread sections, an impossible task. With the arrival of reinforcements it was able to withdraw into Singapore where it was fully occupied with GHQ FARELF and with the city itself which became the base for troops in Malaya with consequent activity ensuing from the port and from troop movements by both ship and air.

The first reinforcements to arrive, in October, were 2nd Guards

Brigade, bringing with them two RMP sections. Soon followed a provost company headquarters which absorbed the brigade sections, further expanded to become 210 Provost Company comprising six sections based on Kuala Lumpur and taking over responsibility for Malaya District. Early in 1948 17th Gurkha Division began to develop the idea of an integrated British/Gurkha Provost Company and this, all through the year was one of the new Provost Marshal's main problems.

Gurkhas first served in the Military Police as far back as 1941 with the Corps of Military Police (India) (CMP(I)). They continued to serve with CMP(I) in the Middle and Far East throughout the Second World War and afterwards until the partition and independence of India and Pakistan on 15 August, 1947. Then they were divided between the Military Police in the Indian and Pakistan Armies.

On 1 June, 1950, 17th Gurkha Division Provost Company was formed, consisting of four British sections (previously known as 210 Provost Company) and two Gurkha sections which had been under training since 1949 in the State of Johore in South Malaya. In late 1952 it was re-organized into six integrated British/Gurkha sections and soon afterwards one section was allotted to each Gurkha brigade.

On 28 September, 1955, the Gurkha Military Police were constituted as an integral part of the Brigade of Gurkhas, following the pattern set by the Gurkha Engineers, Gurkha Signals and Gurkha Army Service Corps.

In 1959 two brigade provost units were formed for service with 63 and 99 Gurkha Infantry Brigade Groups. This followed the 'Brigade Group' concept then introduced throughout the Army. The decision to reorganize 5 Dog Company into 5 Gurkha Dog Company was taken in 1961 and 48 Gurkha Infantry Brigade Group Provost Unit was formed in July, 1962.

Up to December, 1962, all the training and administration of the Gurkha military policemen was undertaken by 17th Gurkha Division Provost Company, which over the years was a considerable task. However, on 1 January, 1963, Headquarters and Training Establishment, Gurkha Military Police was formed which trained and administered personnel for all Gurkha provost units. But in 1964 Gurkha Military Police were virtually disbanded because of manpower reductions and personnel posted to ERE to serve with 5 Gurkha Dog Company and on 1 January, 1965, the Gurkha Military Police officially ceased to exist, thus bringing to an end a long and honourable partnership with RMP.

Following the end of the Second World War in August, 1945, the duties of the Vulnerable Points Wing in FARELF were carried out by the Ceylon CMP. The Ceylonese returned home by 1949 and were replaced in March, 1948, by locally-enlisted personnel to form the LEP Guard Unit RMP (Singapore) which was later expanded in July, 1950, to form 21 Guard Unit RMP (Singapore) and, in 1951, re-styled The Singapore Guard Regiment RMP. Recruited mainly from Malaya they took over static guard duties at the several large base installations and ceased to be a RMP unit on 25 April, 1955, when the unit was re-designated The Singapore Guard Regiment although the wearing of a red Songkok and a whistle and chain on guard duties continued to be a reminder of their RMP origin.

The Malay Military Police came into being in December, 1950, having been formed as a small unit of two sections of Malay Regiment Military Police. In November, 1954, they became part of the Federal Division Provost Company of six Malay sections with their main responsibility in North Malaya.

SINGAPORE

Before the Second World War Singapore was a vitally important link in the chain of Commonwealth strategy and it became Defence Headquarters Far East. All three Services had their headquarters on the island and as far as the Army was concerned it was the job of Singapore District to store, supply and repair the vast quantities of material required for the Far East.

Singapore, after the Japanese defeat, was re-occupied by the British in September, 1945, and on 1 April, 1946 became a Crown Colony distinct from the Malayan Union which latter became the Federation of Malaya on 1 February, 1948.

From 1945 to 1976 with small gaps only there was a provost company stationed there. It had a variety of titles. First it was 100 Independent Provost Company and later British Provost Company (Singapore). Then in 1949 it became 200 GHQ Provost Company, and at the end of that year took as its title 200 Provost Company. 91 Section, SIB was also based in Singapore and was reinforced in 1949 and maintained detachments at Kuala Lumpur and Taiping in Malaya and in Hong Kong.

The year 1950 found RMP in full force in the Far East. The Provost Marshal and his staff at GHQ FARELF in Singapore with APMs (majors) in Singapore, Kuala Lumpur and Hong Kong and six provost companies deployed in Singapore, Kuala Lumpur, Penang, Taiping, Ipoh, Seremban, Kluang and Johore Bahru in Malaya and in Hong Kong at Victoria and Kowloon.

The undercurrent of communism was flowing but not yet on the surface in Singapore. It expressed itself in the early stages by seizing any opportunity to stir up nationalistic ambitions by provoking the deep racial and religious differences. The population was predominantly Chinese, the members of this community ranging from extreme wealth to extreme poverty, with lesser communities of indigenous Malays, Indians and Eurasians and the expatriate British commercial and Colonial Service elements with their families. Virtually a powder keg waiting for the match.

200 Provost Company, the envy of their comrades in the up-country jungles of Malaya, was not enjoying the smooth run of routine duties as was generally supposed. In fact their duties were in direct contrast. In the Federation of Malaya it was active service out in the open and troops were fully employed in operations, alert and expectant of action.

In Singapore troops were in garrison or on leave with plenty of time to enjoy all that the city had to offer—much of which was out-of-bounds. Drugs, vice and prostitution thrived in the most unhygienic squalor and back-alley robbery and murder were commonplace. This formed the background for the routine RMP patrol.

One such patrol on the afternoon of 11 December, 1950, consisting of Lance-Corporals Andrews and Jacobs, accompanied by Lance-Corporals Mayhew, Higgs and James (the normal patrol doubled because of the danger of riots sparked off by the Bertha Hertzog affair, a Muslim–Christian incident), were travelling in a Land-Rover driven by Jacobs along North Bridge Road towards the Sultan Mosque where a disturbance had been reported. They were closely followed by a covering party in a jeep driven by Lance-Corporal Prest and Lance-Corporal English.

As Lance-Corporal Jacobs overtook a civilian bus he heard cries for help from within the bus. Jacobs stopped his vehicle at once, dismounted and ran to the bus, closely followed by Andrews; inside they saw a woman, either a European or Eurasian, being beaten by an Asian man with a piece of wood about four feet long. The two NCOs entered the bus and Jacobs drew his truncheon, striking the man, causing him to drop his weapon. The man jumped off the bus and fled, pursued by Jacobs who, however, lost him in a hostile crowd. Meanwhile Andrews carried the now unconscious woman out of the bus, forced his way through the crowd and got her into a taxi, taking her to the civil police station.

Two other women who had also been victims of the assault now left the bus, but were instantly attacked by the mob in the street. Seeing these women go down under a crowd of between twenty and thirty Indians and Malays the remaining NCOs, Lance-Corporals Mayhew, Higgs and James, rejoined by Jacobs, charged and drove the attackers back, enabling the women to escape into a side street and take refuge in a shop, while the NCOs held off the mob.

Lance-Corporal Prest, with Lance-Corporal English, drove their jeep to the scene to give assistance. The now infuriated mob attacked the jeep, which was set on fire and had to be abandoned. The courage and initiative of these NCOs undoubtedly saved the three women from serious, almost certainly fatal, injury.

Severe riots broke out again in 1954, following a long series of wild street affairs started by so-called 'students' of Chinese origin. The pattern was invariably the same. The principal agitators, adults, urging on the rioters from windows and doorways—the main body of 'students' chanting slogans and abuse and, in the forefront, a line of children in the ten to fourteen age group, including girls, over whose heads were hurled bricks, petrol bombs and other missiles.

The police were thus severely handicapped; in any determined action the children would have been the first casualties.

This series of riots came to a head and broke out into extreme mass-violence with a bus strike. Europeans became the main target.

All British families were confined to quarters and troops, though standing-by, were confined to barracks. Military Police formed escorts for British children's school buses and organized parties of wives to visit the NAAFI shop until it was considered advisable to confine families to quarters. Many European cars were turned over in the street and set on fire and one European was burnt alive in his car before he could be rescued.

The climax came when a student was shot dead and the students claimed it was by a civil police bullet, though this was denied by the civil police who were supported by the facts of the incident. Two days later the dead student was to be buried and it was feared this might be the signal to launch an all-out attack on the civil police. To avoid provocation it was decided that they would not be seen on duty anywhere near the route from the hospital to the Chinese cemetery some few miles outside the city and all essential patrolling was taken over by military police. It was left to Captain A. V. Lovell-Knight with a lance-corporal driver in a Land-Rover to attend the funeral. There, keeping a respectful distance on a knoll on the outskirts of the cemetery, he was able to report that the body had been interred and the many thousand students and others present were dispersing quietly and, indeed, he was thankful to do so.

Very close liaison existed with the Singapore Police Force and relations with the civil population were excellent. The respect the civilians of all races had for provost was most apparent during the unhappy times of strikes and riots when drivers of civilian cars, needing to pass through an area of strife, would wait and fall-in behind the RMP patrol or escort vehicles.

A new constitution conferring full internal self-government and the new title 'State of Singapore' was introduced on 3 June, 1959. Singapore became a state of Malaysia on 16 September, 1963, on the enlargement of that Federation but left Malaysia and became an independent sovereign state within the Commonwealth on 9 August, 1965.

The last RMP presence in Singapore, 200 Provost Company, continued until final disbandment in March, 1976.

MALAYA

To the student of war, the Emergency in Malaya, which lasted twelve years, must seem very odd, for Command HQ was as large as that normally required by an Army and its two divisions were each responsible for about half of a country which stretches from latitude 1° 20′ N to 7° 58′ N, with a land area of 50,924 square miles, with a mixed population of Chinese, Malays and Indians, all displaying marked differences of racial characteristics and each having their own culture and religious beliefs.

In 1945 Operation 'Zipper' landed 34 Indian Corps on the beaches of Morib, some thirty-five miles south-west of Kuala Lumpur. Then the Liberation Army, who for four long years from their jungle strongholds and hideouts had resisted the might of the Japanese Army, emerged and were welcomed as heroes by all. Unfortunately, after the end of hostilities, the communistic beliefs fostered during the wartime communal life of danger and hardship came to the fore and by 1948 the brave anti-Japanese fighters had disappeared again to the jungle, to wage sheer naked terrorism, murder and brutality throughout the length and breadth of the land.

Provost responsibility in Malaya rested on the shoulders of a APM (major) in Malaya Command HQ at Kuala Lumpur. He had to discipline and control road movement of some 35,000 troops of many differing nationalities, drawn at various times from Britain, Nepal, East Africa, Rhodesia, Fiji, Malaya, Australia and New Zealand. To assist the APM in his task two Staff Captains Provost were provided. One at Taiping operated in the northern half of the country and the other at Seremban in the south. For some of the time both officers also commanded provost units.

The Emergency in Malaya which lasted from June, 1948, to July, 1960, made big demands on RMP but though conditions approached a state of war, the principal provost operational rôle of traffic control was of no great importance. Although the terrorists were definitely and very actively hostile and the troops engaged were on active service, this was not a war against a declared enemy but one of the final episodes of imperial policing.

Although troops of all arms were committed in considerable numbers to operations, they were spread out in small units over wide areas of mountainous jungle and coastal plains frequently broken up by large and wide rivers but virtually no roads. Anti-terrorist operations were therefore mainly conducted on foot without traffic problems.

Provost disciplinary duties of anti-vice, VD and out-of-bounds patrols had their own peculiar problems as elsewhere in addition to normal maintenance of discipline in garrison areas and leave centres.

Although on many occasions provost sections put on jungle kit and went on anti-terrorist operational patrols this was not their rôle but was done partly for the experience and training value and partly as an aid to morale, it being advantageous when dealing with all ranks of other arms to have experienced their operational way of life.

An important operational task for provost was, however, in aid of the civil police and included such duties as clearing squatter areas and bringing outlying family groups or hamlets into the wired-in perimeter of established villages. Road blocks, cordons and searches were carried out constantly in co-operation with the civil police. Invariably, the actual searching was done by the civil police, who were better suited to the task by virtue of their local knowledge, familiarity with the inhabitants and knowledge of the local languages. The Military Police provided the road block and cordon elements for such searches for which they had the mobility, firepower and communication requirements.

A typical operation began with the civil police having information that one or more terrorists had gone to ground in a city or urban area to plot their next activity, in all probability a murder of one or more citizens prominent in the support of law and order or an attack on a bus full of their own people.

Following a secret briefing, the combined civil and military police force went into operation using the local police station as HQ. The normal provost contingent was usually two sections under an officer. A RMP NCO would be left at HQ on the telephone to maintain liaison and communications and also a sub-section as an instantly mobile reserve.

The main party, carrying rolls of dannert (coiled barbed) wire and red traffic lanterns, were constantly on the move. The tactics were to make a sudden cordon round a tight area, set up an immediate road block using half the military police party and a few civil police to carry out the interrogation. All vehicles would be stopped and the identity of all passengers and pedestrians checked. Simultaneously, houses in the immediate vicinity would be searched, the remaining military police forming a swift and silent cordon round the suspect house, to be followed immediately by the civil police who carried out the search.

Usually the occupants were harmless enough and very frightened but terrorists were harboured, sometimes through sympathy, more often through intimidation.

This operation would last perhaps thirty minutes, after which the entire party withdrew and, within minutes, descended on another area in a totally different part of the town.

Several areas having been subjected to this treatment, the patrols stood down for an hour or so while normality returned to the town and then launched the second phase—a cordon and search of selected hotels, cafés and other meeting places.

With each patrol went a medical orderly and a sapper trained in bomb-disposal duties. A cornered terrorist was dangerous and desperate and leakage of police intentions could lead to booby-traps.

This technique was later developed in searching villages for hoarded rice and other foodstuffs intended for terrorists' supplies.

By 1955 only a hard core of terrorists was left. An amnesty offer was made by the Malayan Government and withdrawn in 1956 but gradually terrorism died out. The Federation of Malaya became independent on 31 August, 1957, and on 16 September, 1963, part of Malaysia—comprising Malaya, Singapore, North Borneo and Sarawak. However, Singapore seceded on 9 August, 1965, by mutual agreement.

SARAWAK

In 1963 Indonesia began a policy of aggressive confrontation against Malaysia which was to last until late 1966. Hostile incursions by Indonesian armed forces from their bases in Indonesian Borneo into Federation territory once more saw British troops on the move—and their provost went with them.

99th Gurkha Infantry Brigade's rôle was to prevent any Indonesian incursion across the border into Sarawak from Indonesian Borneo and to assist the Malaysian Government in controlling any internal security situation which might develop as a result of activity on the part of the 'Clandestine Committee Organization' or from Indonesian terrorist activities. The brigade successfully repulsed all attempted hostile incursions within its area and numbers of Indonesian soldiers were regularly killed and wounded by the security forces.

Sarawak comprises a coastal strip 450 miles long and varying from 40 to 120 miles wide, on the north-west coast of Borneo. The brigade area, in fact, covered the entire 1st Administrative District of Sarawak, which extended from the coast to beyond the Batang Sadong. The total population of Sarawak of about 900,000 is made up of Land and Sea Dayaks (or Ibans) and other indigenous races with Chinese, Malays,

Melanaus and Europeans. The main religions are Muslim, Buddhist, Christian and Pagan. The Ibans, renowned for their past head-hunting activities, still live in thriving long-house communities in various parts of the jungle.

99th Gurkha Infantry Brigade Provost Unit was located near brigade HQ in Kuching, the capital city of Sarawak, with a population of about 63,000 people, and situated on the Sungei Sarawak. The strength of the brigade was 5,900 men, making it the largest in the British Army at that time. This high manpower figure, which could have caused a severe disciplinary problem for provost, was balanced by the fact that the majority of the troops were in tactical locations on the border. However Kuching, as the 'Mecca' of Sarawak entertainment seekers, was always a lively and active place, presenting the RMP NCO with interesting and varied duties.

Within Kuching the main provost tasks were curfew enforcement and the checking of numerous out-of-bounds establishments. There were at least eight houses of prostitution from which operated an ever-increasing number of girls, many drawn from outlying kampongs by the prospect of easy financial reward. To combat the resulting spread of disease the unit operated a small anti-vice bureau. All other types of offences were periodically dealt with, especially drunkenness, traffic, absentees and assaults. On occasion more serious offences, normally covered by SIB, were dealt with. Examples included a widespread series of barrack-room larcenies in one of the battalions and the murder of a Royal Navy petty officer. This latter case was fully and successfully investigated before being handed over to the Naval CID in Singapore.

To ensure thorough police coverage of Kuching, combined British and Malaysian mobile patrols were maintained on a twenty-four-hour basis. There was also the closest working co-operation with the local Sarawak Constabulary of the Royal Malaysian Police. The nearest RMP neighbours were 19th Infantry Brigade Group Provost Unit in Sibu, some 160 miles to the north-east.

With regard to the various traffic duties, it was a popular misconception concerning Borneo that as there were so few roads there could not be a traffic problem. While the rivers were the principal means of travel and the Army used RAF helicopters extensively, it must be stressed that considerable troop and heavy equipment moves were made by road. The difficulties encountered in the course of these movements are best illustrated by describing the highway upon which the majority of convoys and heavy equipment travelled. This road was the only one connecting Kuching with the border area and linking the small towns of Serian and Balai Ringin. The branch road to Bau, an important mining centre where gold is extracted, is very similar.

The road was narrow for its entire length with broken, disintegrated verges. It spanned numerous rivers and watercourses by means of narrow bridges, many of single gauge and plank construction. During the monsoon, when heavy flooding occurred, many of these bridges were liable to be swept away. The road was periodically blocked by floods, which rose at an astonishing speed. On these occasions an RMP patrol was maintained until the road was clear for through traffic. The road, passing carefully tended pepper gardens, climbed the hills of the central plain in a series of steep gradients and twisting bends.

On this highway RMP carried out frequent heavy load escorts for unwieldy engineering equipment and also assisted in the reception of units which arrived at Kuching by ship. This task constituted marshalling the vehicles at the reception point and, when necessary, leading the convoy in packets to their various locations. To reduce the number of accidents caused by speeding, traps were regularly laid. A loaded 3-ton vehicle travelling at over thirty miles an hour can be a very real danger on such narrow roads.

The hazard of ambush existed on practically all roads within the brigade area. For this reason all patrols travelled armed and were conversant with ambush drill. VIP escorts were a frequent duty.

At the end of June, 1965, instances of terrorist activity occurred within the brigade area. The 18th Mile Police Station was captured by Indonesian terrorists; the 24th Mile Bazaar bridge was partially blown up and several civilian families were brutally murdered. Road blocks of oil and crude caltrops were placed on the Kuching–Serian road.

Corporals Collins and Bain, while carrying out a heavy-load escort, were involved in these incidents on one occasion; having cleared a road block they were approached by a Chinese civilian who requested assistance. On arrival at the man's house they discovered that his entire family had been shot. Having administered first aid they proceeded to the 18th Mile Police Station for help. On arrival they found the station deserted except for dead and wounded policemen. The NCOs returned to the heavy-load convoy where they received instructions to escort a vehicle to Kuching. On the return journey they discovered that more oil had been poured on to the road on several corners. Arriving safely at brigade HQ they were able to give accurate accounts of the night's events to the brigade Duty Officer.

The result of these incidents was the planning of Operation 'Hammer' by the Sarawak Government in conjunction with the Army and civil police. The purpose of this operation was to evacuate all Chinese civilians between the 13½ and 25th milestones and to move them to various resettlement villages. The aims of the resettlement were as follows:

1. To protect Chinese civilians from indoctrination or physical assault by Indonesians or communist organizations.
2. To facilitate a thorough registration of Chinese within the area.
3. To arrest wanted communists or Indonesian infiltrators discovered within the area.
4. To prevent, in the future, assistance being given to Indonesian and/or communist infiltrators by elements of the civil population.

In the early morning of 6 July the provost unit, after extremely rapid planning and preparation, moved into the area and set up traffic posts and police blocks at the 10th Mile Police Station and at the 13th and 25th milestones, linked by radio on Ferret scout cars of 4th Royal Tank Regiment with the control set in the operational HQ at the 18th Mile Police Station.

By 6.30 am security forces were in their positions surrounding the area. At 6.45 am the troops moved forward and started collecting all the Chinese families and escorting them to their new resettlement villages. Surprise in the operation was achieved and the inhabitants of the area were astounded and bewildered by the swift security forces movements.

The provost rôle was firstly to regulate the flow of official convoys, secondly to ensure that no unauthorized person moved past each traffic post, thirdly to assist the civil police in the forming-up of civilian convoys and, lastly to keep a rigorous watch for wanted persons.

The operation was successfully concluded after six days. The resettlement villages which had been constructed with astonishing speed by various Government departments, were now well organized communities.

On 27 August two grenades were thrown by terrorists in the Open Market at Kuching. The entire provost unit was immediately mobilized and cleared the town of troops. The following evening, a Saturday, the procedure was repeated (described as Operation 'Brussels Ball') after receipt of information warning of further terrorist acts. On Malaysia Day a large home-made bomb (unexploded) was discovered in the Museum Garden, also in Kuching.

With the ending of confrontation with Indonesia in 1966 the last RMP units in Borneo were then withdrawn or disbanded: 99th Gurkha Infantry Brigade Provost Unit returned to Singapore while 51st Gurkha Infantry Brigade Provost Unit in Brunei and Provost Section, Borneo, in Labuan disbanded thus ending three years of arduous and rewarding work for the Corps in an area where previously RMP had never served, at least not as formed units.

HONG KONG

The re-occupation of Hong Kong after the Second World War saw the arrival of the CMP(I) of 26th Indian Division Provost Company. This unit eventually became the British Independent Provost Company, which operated on its own until the Emergency of 1949 when it was joined by 40th Infantry Division Provost Company, which came with its parent formation from the United Kingdom. The new company was stationed at Whitfield Barracks, Kowloon, with a detachment at Tai Lam in the New Territories and became responsible for policing the mainland while the British Independent Provost Company looked after Hong Kong island.

The Nationalist Government of Generalissimo Chiang Kai-shek had collapsed in front of the communist armies and, on the fall of Peking, Mao Tse-tung had proclaimed the Chinese People's Republic on 1 October, 1949. This presented a threat to the Crown Colony of Hong Kong and 40th Infantry Division was formed to reinforce the garrison.

With the reorganization of the garrison in Hong Kong in 1957 both 40th Infantry Division Provost Company and the British Independent Provost Company were disbanded and a new unit, the Hong Kong Provost Company, was formed. The rôle of this company was both interesting and varied. Headquarters and two sections lived in Whitfield Barracks, Kowloon, where they carried out the normal duties of a garrison company. Two sections were stationed in Victoria on Hong Kong island and a fifth section was at Sek Kong in the New Territories acting as the brigade section for 48th Gurkha Infantry Brigade. The SIB detachment Hong Kong was also located in Whitfield Barracks, Kowloon.

In course of time the provost order of battle was expanded to include the Hong Kong Dog Company consisting of a RMP Officer Commanding (major) and RSM and locally-enlisted Hong Kong Chinese dog handlers and a separate provost unit to serve with 48th Gurkha Infantry Brigade, commanded by a captain. At the same time the DAPM at HQ Land Forces Hong Kong was up-graded to APM (lieutenant-colonel).

However, in 1976 this expansion was reversed by the disbandment of 48th Gurkha Infantry Brigade Provost Unit on 31 March and the posting of all personnel in the unit to Hong Kong Provost Company. This was followed by the transfer of Hong Kong Dog Company to the Royal Army Veterinary Corps on 1 September, thus ending, at least for the present, the long line of dog companies in the Corps.

From then on RMP in the Far East was represented by APM HQ Land Forces Hong Kong with Hong Kong Provost Company (now based on the island with a detachment on the mainland) and SIB Hong Kong.

CHAPTER XIII

The Korean War

JAPAN

AT the time of the surrender on 14 August, 1945, of the Japanese forces, British and Indian Army troops were responsible for the overland drive through South-East Asia, while the Americans, for a long period operating through north Burma into China, were concentrating on closing-in on the Japanese mainland from the Pacific. US troops landed in Japan and occupied the country in August, 1945, General McArthur entering Tokyo on 8 September. The Allied Control Council was set up by the Moscow Agreement on 28 December.

The British Commonwealth Occupation Force (BCOF) arrived early in 1946, taking with it an RMP element and units of the Australian, Indian and New Zealand Military Police, the DPM being Lieut-Colonel J. S. Thompson (British Army). One of the first tasks was the establishment of a Military Police Wing at the BCOF Training School, which was attended by members of all contingents. Basic police duties were not part of the curriculum. The purpose was to indoctrinate trained policemen in local regulations, orders and indigenous customs and to know how to deal with problems peculiar to Japan.

Duties were of a similar nature to those in other occupied countries and it is not necessary to re-tell the story of black market, vice and prostitution, stolen WD property and escorts to VIPs—the common round of occupation duties.

The Indian contingent were the first to withdraw, in 1947, followed early in 1948 by United Kingdom troops and the New Zealand contingent in late 1948. The Australian force had originally been 10,000 and had run-down to 3,000 with the intention of withdrawing by 1950.

In July of that year, however, the Australians learnt that their withdrawal home was postponed indefinitely and that the British

Commonwealth was to find contingents under United Nations Command for Korea.

Thus it was that Major A. V. Johnston, Royal Australian Army Provost Corps, having said farewell to the United Kingdom RMP contingent in Japan in 1948, was the first to welcome them back three years later into what was to become British Commonwealth Base Provost Company with bases in Japan and Korea, where the highest degree of co-operation and friendly relations were to become blended into complete integration.

The company came to life as 262 Base Provost Company, formed for duties on the lines of communications and base areas of Korea and Japan, under the command of Captain R. D. L. Caley; with sections transferred from 249 Provost Company it was made up to strength with a company headquarters brought out from the RMP Depot by RSM Footitt. Following the pattern of their parent unit, the company quickly integrated with their provost colleagues from Australia, New Zealand and Canada to become the British Commonwealth Base Provost Company on 15 December, 1951.

The staff and company officers were as follows:

> Major A. W. Johnston (Australian APM) with Lieut-Colonel A. G. Locksley (UK) as DPM, Major Collins and Lieutenant Evans (UK), Lieutenant Slater (Royal Australian Army Provost Corps), Lieutenant Bateman (Canadian Army Provost Corps) later joined by Captain Paterson (Canada) as second-in-command.

The company headquarters was at Kure with sections over a thousand miles apart. One detachment was in Korea based on Pusan with sections on the line-of-communications as far north as Seoul, where it linked up with the division provost company. A special 'Ports' detachment was formed which looked after the security of WD and NAAFI stores loading and unloading at the ports of Kure and Pusan and which found an NCO for duty on every ship carrying stores in transit. This detachment was also equipped with a powerful motor launch to maintain floating patrols in Kure harbour. Troop movement between Japan and Korea was by RAF aircraft and the company justifiably claimed they operated by land, sea and air. In Japan itself sections were established, in addition to Kure, at Hiroshima and Tokyo.

Technical difficulties for the military police arose following the signing of the Peace Treaty with Japan, which presented some acute problems. The Peace Treaty (signed at San Francisco on 8 September, 1951) restored full sovereignty to the Japanese nation—and full authority and jurisdiction to their civil police.

In negotiating the Peace Treaty with Japan reference was made only to US security forces in Japan. The situation therefore arose that Commonwealth troops who were using base facilities in Japan purely as a convenience in support of the Korean theatre of operations, were not classified by the Japanese Diet as security forces and were therefore not protected by the Treaty. It will be recalled that Great Britain had withdrawn her occupational forces in 1948.

The Japanese Government directed that all their judicial and administrative services would proceed against all Commonwealth personnel as though they were independent of the Treaty. Jurisdiction and Customs particularly involved provost. Commonwealth troops were not protected by the Treaty and HQ, British Commonwealth Forces Korea did not recognize the Japanese as authorized to detain and bring to trial Commonwealth personnel.

After six years of Occupation, the Japanese police began to carry out their instructions with considerable vigour and troops were arrested and detained for the most minor offences. Provost policy had to be immediately revised and interim instructions issued.

Negotiations at Embassy level were started with the Japanese and provost were committed to tactful liaison with the civil police on the ground. Politically interested Japanese entered the fray and introduced exaggerated articles into the press with emphasis on discipline and conditions of pay for civilian WD employees.

It is readily understandable that, in a country eager to re-establish its constitutional rights with a resurgence of political ambitions, the local authorities became extremely sensitive and determined to exert their jurisdiction. It followed that this attitude was reflected in the behaviour of the civil police.

Provost policy had, therefore, to be re-adjusted to meet the many problems likely to arise. The immediate and obvious answer was that acme of police training—prevention of crime. This meant intensification of patrols and consequent long and arduous tours of duty, the aim being in the first instance to prevent Commonwealth troops getting into trouble, next to prevent them falling into the hands of the civil police by being on the scene first and, if that failed, to make every endeavour by amicable means to persuade the civil police to surrender the culprit into military custody—no easy problem with the civil police anxious to establish their authority and reputation, and the military police anxious to avoid compromising diplomatic negotiations.

Provost were therefore left to procure the custody of all Commonwealth troops arrested by the civil police as best they could. Their success was a measure of their tact, diplomacy and determination, which was called-for in the highest degree. This story would not be complete without a tribute both to the leadership of the company officers and warrant officers and to the NCOs who quickly established a most amicable co-operation between themselves and their opposite numbers of the Japanese civil police 'on the beat' and it became routine for the military police jeep to be manned by three different members of British Commonwealth Base Provost Company and a Japanese policeman, another example of 'Four in a Jeep'.

When Commonwealth provost had eventually integrated and were performing duties as one unit, liaison between the US and Commonwealth provost services became the outstanding responsibility. Relations between the two services became excellent in all spheres and close understanding and co-operation resulted between Ports police and general-duty companies, corps and division provost and, of outstanding importance, Special Investigation Branches. Exchange of crime information—news-letters, etc—became most effective and produced good results in welding the Korean–Japan provost net together, an important point in a theatre so widely dispersed.

Commonwealth provost representation was obtained on the Korean/American Security Committee, which discussed all military and civil affairs for which US provost had accepted advisory responsibility. Civil police, fire brigades, railways, security measures in towns and rural areas, all came into the Committee's area of responsibility and was most useful in bringing together navy, army and air force representatives of all nations in addition to the civil elements for mutual discussion of their respective problems. This led to many additional tasks for provost.

Earthquakes and typhoons are an ever-present possibility in Japan. Provost were enrolled in a scheme which would assist the civil authorities as well as military, in devastated areas. These responsibilities covered initial reconnaissance, organizing traffic control, anti-looting patrols, signing of diversions, information post duties and assistance with medical evacuation.

The provost service in Japan, where RMP were in part operational base troops and in part on garrison duties in leave and rest centres, settled down to an amicable and harmonious routine with mutual respect and co-operation with the civil authorities. The distance from Kure to Pusan separated them from the Korean theatre of war.

KOREA

27th Infantry Brigade had been in Hong Kong since the summer of 1949, and its training in the hilly country there was to prove very valuable in Korea. Its commander, Brigadier B. A. Coad, received orders on 19 August, 1950, to prepare to take his brigade of two battalions to Korea in five days' time.

An advance party, including the brigade commander, flew to Korea; the main body of the brigade, including one provost section attached from 40th Infantry Division Provost Company left Hong Kong by sea in the aircraft carrier HMS *Unicorn* and the cruiser HMS *Ceylon* on 24 August, the provost section sailing on the former, and disembarked at Pusan.

The whole provost section were volunteers from 40th Infantry Division Provost Company and consisted of Sergeant B. B. Johnson as section commander, two corporals and twelve lance-corporals. At this time no provost officer was immediately available for Korea.

The main body of the brigade disembarked at Pusan on 28 August and it was learned that the brigade was to work under, and be maintained by, the Americans, forming part of the 8th US Army.

The North Koreans had begun a strong offensive on 1 September and by the 5th the situation had become serious. On the latter date 27th Infantry Brigade moved forward on a route marked 'Nottingham' by the provost section and took over a portion of the line on the River Naktong located approximately ten miles south-west of Taegu and occupied defensive positions.

On 15 September US troops attacked in strength in the Taegu area. By 18 September 24th US Division had crossed the River Naktong west of Taegu and was fighting its way north astride the Taegu–Seoul road. As part of these operations 27th Infantry Brigade—under command of 24th US Infantry Division—left its defensive positions and moved north, with the task of crossing the Naktong and advancing on Sangju, a small town about seven miles to the west.

The route forward was signed by Sergeant Johnson and Corporal Turner without incident, although, unfortunately, the first vehicle to pass along the route behind them, belonging to the Brigade HQ Defence Platoon, was blown up on a mine with fatal casualties.

Protected by troops of 24th US Division, the brigade crossed the River Naktong on 21 September. The crossing was made by means of a very insecure footbridge and by ferrying. The battalions suffered a few casualties from shell-fire during the passage of the river but were all over by the early hours of the 22nd and immediately committed to fierce fighting.

On 1 October, 1950, while the brigade was still located in the Sangju area, it was joined by 3rd Battalion Royal Australian Regiment, resulting in 27th Brigade from this date being re-designated 27th British Commonwealth Infantry Brigade.

By the end of September all Korea south of the 38th Parallel had been regained and the General Assembly of the United Nations authorized their forces to pursue the enemy into North Korea. A feature of this

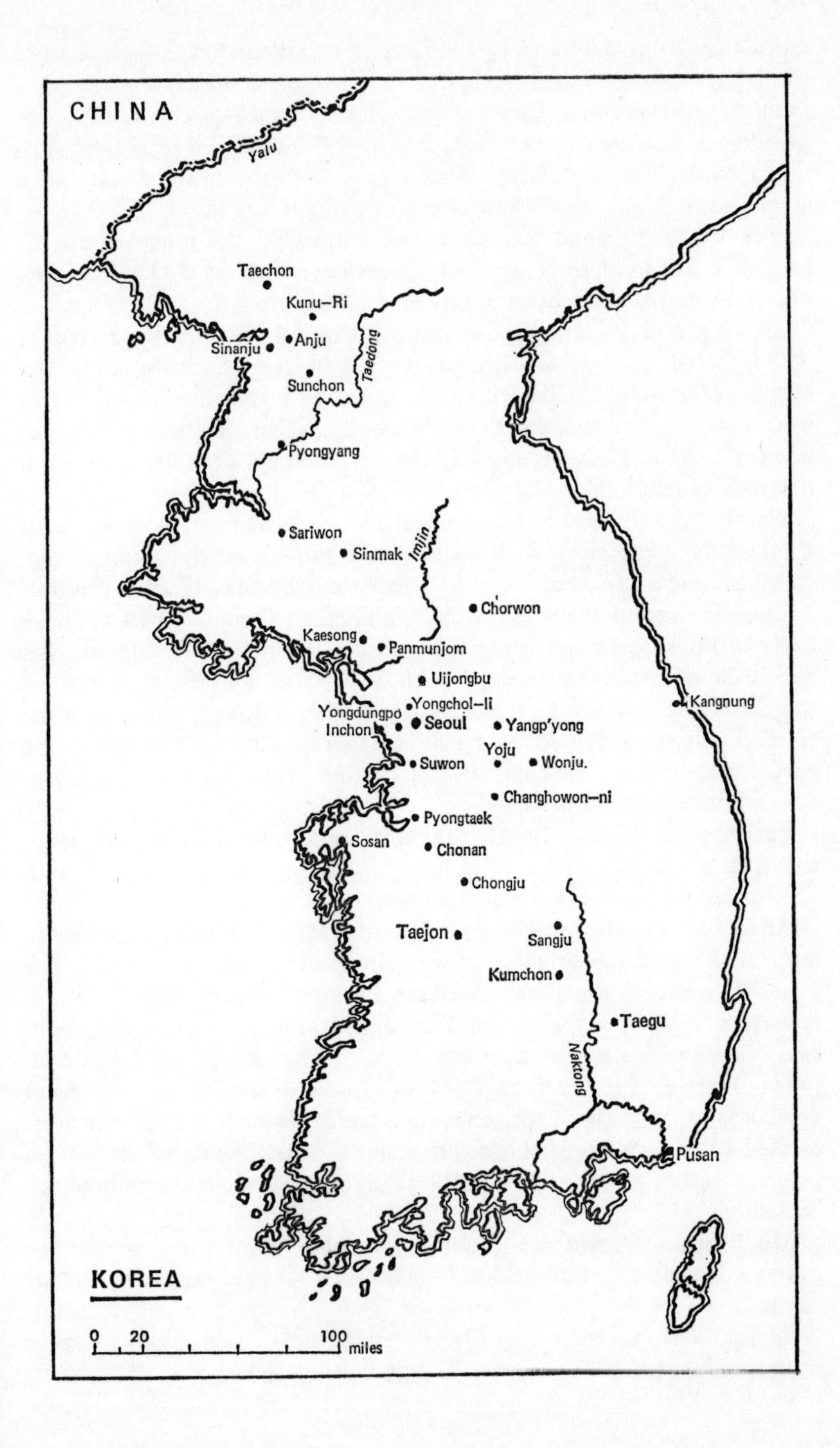

CHINA
Yalu
Taechon
Kunu-Ri
Anju
Sinanju
Taedong
Sunchon
Pyongyang
Sariwon
Sinmak
Imjin
Chorwon
Kaesong
Panmunjom
Uijongbu
Yongchol-li
Yongdungpo
Inchon
Seoul
Yangp'yong
Yoju
Suwon
Wonju.
Changhowon-ni
Pyongtaek
Sosan
Chonan
Chongju
Taejon
Sangju
Kumchon
Taegu
Naktong
Kangnung
Pusan
KOREA
0 20 100 miles

rapid advance was a move by the Commonwealth Brigade from Sangju to Seoul. Provost controlled the move, gathering the various units from their dispersal areas to Taegu airfield. There one British officer and one US officer supervised the emplaning of over 2,000 men who were then flown to deplane at Kimpo. This move was accomplished without a single piece of paper being written and without any hitch.

Provost then signed the route and controlled the move of all the brigade's transport to rejoin with the other troops by 8 October. The order to move had been received by Brigade HQ on 4 October. The brigade then came under command of 1st US Cavalry Division, which it led on its main axis up the Pyongyang–Sariwon road. The advance continued for two days for 34 miles, each battalion leap-frogging in turn to take the vanguard and, brushing aside opposition, to take the town of Sariwon and its North Korean Artillery Training Centre on the 18th at daybreak.

Nearly 3,000 prisoners were taken in this action by the brigade of whom over 1,500 were dealt with by the provost section. Some were wounded and a few were found to be concealing arms and ammunition.

Lance-Corporal Naylor, on the night of 18 October, was taking a party of PoWs back to the 1st US Cavalry Division PoW cage in what had been an abandoned enemy truck of Russian manufacture, when it toppled off the road into a paddy field below. Without any orders the startled prisoners righted the truck and literally lifted it back on to the road by their combined efforts, under the appreciative but watchful eye of Lance-Corporal Naylor.

Early on 20 October South Korean troops entered Pyongyang from the east, to be followed a little later by the leading battalion of 27th Commonwealth Brigade from the west.

After the capture of Pyongyang the forward movement continued and on the 21st the brigade, now again under command of 24th US Division, crossed the River Taedong in spite of considerable enemy resistance at several points, and advanced to the River Chongchun, near Sinanju, during the next few days, a distance of over a hundred miles. During this advance Corporal Edwards and Lance-Corporal Harkness of the provost section were attached to each battalion in turn as the battalions succeeded each other in the lead. The remainder of the provost section signed and controlled the route for the main body of the brigade.

Much improvisation was required to maintain enough material for signs; US ration cartons were often utilized for this purpose to good effect.

Sinanju was entered on 23 October and after a halt of three days a bridge was completed across the Chongchon at Anju and on 28 October, with the bridge manned by the provost section, 27th Commonwealth Brigade crossed and continued its advance.

Sergeant Johnson and Corporal Turner, through a number of unprecedented causes, found themselves signing the main axis some six miles ahead of the Middlesex Regiment, the leading infantry unit of the brigade. They were in the process of placing a 'Nottingham' forward sign at the approach to Pakchon when they suddenly came under fire from close quarters; the two NCOs thereupon made a hasty 'strategic withdrawal'.

3rd Royal Australian Regiment captured Pakchon that night after strong and determined enemy resistance. The rest of the brigade entered the town on 29 October, the provost section being gratified to observe that the signs at the approach to Pakchon placed by the two NCOs were still 'in situ'.

Further ample evidence was seen of the North Korean troops' ability in the art of camouflaging their positions. On 31 October brigade HQ moved to Chongju which the Argyll and Sutherland Highlanders had entered the day previously, the Australians having encountered very heavy opposition east of the town. On arriving at Chongju Lance-Corporal Wood had placed the large 'Nottingham Command Post' sign, indicating the position of brigade HQ, in its correct position and was walking back across the road when he was startled by a sharp report and the sound of splintering wood behind him. An unappreciative enemy had split the newly-placed board in two with an armour-piercing shell from across the river!

At Chongju 27th Commonwealth Brigade went into divisional reserve for the first time for eight weeks, having for two weeks led the advance of 24th US Division to within 40 miles of the Manchurian border.

By the end of October the North Korean army had not only been defeated but almost completely destroyed. At its peak it had numbered about 325,000 men. Of these 145,000 became prisoners of war and about 150,000 were estimated to have been killed by the end of October.

The optimism resulting from success was, however, short lived. It was known that large Chinese forces were concentrated in South Manchuria and the last days of October brought reports from patrols, as well as from the air and from local inhabitants, that strong Chinese forces were converging on Taechon. It was apparent, if reports of their strength were correct, that 27th Commonwealth Brigade would be in a precarious position should the enemy by-pass Taechon and make a drive on Pakchon from the west or north-east.

Meanwhile the most forward elements of the United Nations forces had pushed on and reached positions along the River Yalu, the frontier between North Korea and Manchuria (China).

The Chinese threat soon ended the rest for 27th Commonwealth Brigade and the provost section found itself hard at work controlling many quick moves.

By the end of November the full rigours of winter were being experienced. Even worse than the intense cold, often falling to 44 degrees below freezing point, was the bitter Siberian wind, capable of reaching 120 miles per hour, eventually alleviated by an issue of American windproof clothing.

On 24 November the United Nations began a new advance but at the same time the Chinese renewed their offensive and the second retreat of United Nations forces began which was to continue to a line 50 miles south of the 38th parallel with 27th Commonwealth Brigade in reserve at Kunu-Ri and under command of US 9 Corps. But a steady build-up was in progress—including that of provost.

The section of 40 Infantry Division Provost Company which had landed at Pusan on 28 August, 1950, and was attached to 27th Infantry Brigade was followed on 20 October by Major R. Davenport, as APM, and the Advance Party of HQ British Commonwealth Korean Base which established itself at Taegu. On 3 November Major A. W. Evans, brought HQ 249 GHQ Provost Company and four sections with Captain E. L. Williams as second-in-command, Lieutenants R. D. L. Caley and J. Aspinall and RSM G. S. P. Stead. These were established at Suwon and operational by 8 November.

Also on 3 November CSM Bolting arrived to open an SIB section HQ at Taegu and Sergeant Kearus opened an SIB office with 249 Coy HQ at Suwon, and by 20 December a SIB HQ was set-up by Captain C. Bennett at Pusan.

On the same day that 249 GHQ Provost Company disembarked at Pusan, leading elements of 29th British Infantry Brigade Group from the UK also began to arrive. By 19 November the whole brigade, together with 249 GHQ Provost Company concentrated at Suwon, 18 miles south of Seoul. Late on the 19th the brigade moved to Kaesong, the route being signed and controlled by the Advance Party of 249 GHQ Provost Company. On arrival the brigade came under command of 187th US Airborne Regimental Combat Team.

Major Evans and two sections less one sub-section joined 29th Brigade at Kaesong on the 28th, moving on to Pyongyang the following day.

With the bitter Korean winter now at its height and constant snow falling, the enemy pressed his offensive aided by pockets of enemy resistance and guerrillas operating many miles in the rear of the main battle front. These had been overrun in the swift advance and not swept up. They now came to life with harassing tactics which, added to the weather conditions, caused very considerable hardship and operational difficulties.

Weather conditions also hampered the enemy advance. The already incredibly bad roads, worsened by demolition and bombing, broke up under the snow which materially aided the stout resistance offered by the retreating United Nations forces.

29th Brigade was given the task of forming a bridgehead over the River Taedong and covering the retreat of the American and South Korean troops. 249 GHQ Provost Company was fully committed controlling the four bridges over the river which were besieged by masses of refugees fleeing southwards. In the first five days of December there passed through the bridgehead 1st Republic of Korea (ROK) Division, 1st US Cavalry Division, 25th US Division and the fighting withdrawal of 27th Commonwealth Brigade with, in addition, the phasing through of countless refugees.

Rarely in the history of war was a highly successful pursuit almost immediately followed by so precipitate a withdrawal. In fact, during that first week in December the whole of the United Nations forces were in full retreat before a steady Chinese advance. There was no doubt of the value of the provost organization under these conditions.

27th Commonwealth Brigade, which had moved to Kunu-Ri on 27 November, was ordered to continue the move south on the following morning to Sunchon. Owing to an acute shortage of petrol only essential transport could be used, an order provost were called upon to enforce in a ruthless manner, and the 22-mile march was made on foot.

It is to the credit of the provost section that with 40 degrees of frost most of the time, none of their vehicles sustained a cracked cylinder block, a misfortune that many other vehicle drivers were unable to escape. The section drained off the anti-freeze from their vehicles if they were not being used; the mixture, which was captured and of Russian origin, was then boiled before being poured into the radiators prior to a vehicle moving. The section Land-Rover was always the first to be ticking over and was then used to tow the other vehicles to life.

After passing through 29th Brigade, north of Pyongyang on 4 December, 27th Brigade continued its withdrawal for another 120 miles to just north of the town of Uijongbu, about 15 miles due north of Seoul. The first brief contact occurred on 10 December between RMP personnel of 27th Brigade and 249 GHQ Provost Company with 29th Brigade; Corporal Turner (27th Brigade) meeting Lance-Corporal

14

Carrigan (249 Company) in Kaesong, just south of the 38th Parallel. They had been instructors together at the Depot in Woking in 1948.

Conditions for the time being were peaceful for 27th Brigade in the Uijongbu area but there was little comfort, due to the bitter cold.

By mid-December the United Nations line ran roughly along the 38th Parallel and as the Chinese caught up with the withdrawal, 27th Commonwealth Brigade found themselves once again in the battle zone. Contact was not close, however, and the Commonwealth troops spent a quiet Christmas Day.

Though the section had so far been lucky in having suffered no battle casualties it had fully shared the hazards of war with the brigade. It had been shelled on the River Naktong and had several narrow escapes from enemy road mines and snipers, apart from the fighting withdrawals from Pakchon in which they took their place beside the infantrymen of the Brigade Headquarters Defence Platoon on the roadside, and guerrilla activity was an ever-present hazard to road patrols and traffic posts.

Amongst the section's twelve junior NCOs whose average age was twenty-two-and-a-half, with an average service record of four and a half years, were three National-servicemen. These NCOs all proved their worth and had stood up well to the rigours of a tough and difficult campaign, under extremely severe climatic conditions.

It is good to be able to record that up to this date RMP had not been ordered to form any stragglers' posts; there had been no stragglers.

On New Year's Eve the lull came to an abrupt end; the expected Chinese attack began. By the morning of 1 January, 1951, the situation on the Commonwealth front was precarious.

During the day the provost section resumed its usual duties when accompanying a brigade move, this time routing the brigade back to Seoul where it occupied defensive positions on the night of 3–4 January in and around the town, with the object of covering the retirement of 1st US Cavalry and 24th US Infantry Divisions.

As soon as the US formations had been successfully passed through, the provost section assisted in a further brigade withdrawal, first to Suwon and finally to Changhowon-Ni, 45 miles south-east of Seoul.

During this period 249 GHQ Provost Company had also been active and had settled down well as a unit—if not deployed as sections in positions.

On 5 December 29th Brigade was ordered to withdraw from its covering positions at Pyongyang and move to Sinmak, a road and rail junction some 55 miles to the south. The bulk of the company controlled an early move of the main body of the brigade, a section remaining in Pyongyang until an hour after the 1st Battalion the Gloucestershire Regiment had blown the bridges at 7 am, withdrawing finally with the brigade rearguard.

The dispositions of the provost company by nightfall of 5 December were: No 1 Section with Brigade HQ at Nuchon-ni, No 2 Section manning a TP at Somani; and No 3 Section on refugee control duties, in addition to patrolling the Maintenance Supply Route (MSR).

Within four days a further withdrawal was ordered, some 50 miles to Changdan, and then back to Yongchol-li, just north of Seoul, the provost company being fully engaged in road reconnaissance and route control, No 2 Section in particular having a hectic time manning a traffic post controlling a bridge at Kumchon.

On 14 December Nos 5 and 6 Sections joined the company and on the 15th No 2 Section moved to Seoul for joint duties with 728 US Military Police Company. This liaison was further amplified on the 18th when the Officer Commanding attended a conference with the US Provost Marshal, Seoul, for the purpose of co-ordinating refugee routes and dispersal.

In the first days of January, 1951, it was 249 GHQ Provost Company's turn to experience the enemy's onslaught. With eighteen divisions the Chinese hurled themselves at Seoul, penetrating 1 Corps line on the River Han. 249 Company was ordered back to the Seoul perimeter at Kupabal-li with the task of preparing for the withdrawal through Seoul. By 3 January the enemy had penetrated through to the rear and out-flanked the Royal Ulster Rifles and the Royal Northumberland Fusiliers and 29th Brigade began, at 6.30 pm to withdraw across the Han in the dark with the enemy pressing closely.

Contact was finally broken about midnight and provost were able to report all units clear of the Han; at dawn the bridges were blown. During the whole of this withdrawal the provost company had rendered the maximum assistance to the battle-weary fighting elements of the brigade.

The company signed and controlled all the withdrawal routes from Kupabal-li to Yongdung-po and maintained traffic regulation over the vital river crossings while constantly having to cope with the most difficult, tragic and perhaps most important of all duties falling to provost in the field, the control of refugees. For the first time in the campaign, due to the confused nature of the fighting, stragglers' posts were set up.

By 5 pm on 4 January the company had reached Suwon, 18 miles south of Seoul, together with 29th Brigade; the South Korean capital fell once more into enemy hands by nightfall of the same day.

29th Brigade and 249 Company were only to remain in Suwon for a few hours, for on the following day they were ordered to move south a further 20 miles, brigade HQ establishing itself at Ansong, while Brigade 'A' Echelon, together with the 249 Company, moved to nearby Chonan.

29th Brigade had acquitted itself well in its first serious engagement in Korea. Their losses had been heavy—about 230 killed, wounded and missing in the Royal Ulster Rifles, about fifty in the Royal Northumberland Fusiliers and some twenty (together with the loss of some tanks) in 'Cooper Force'.

So the retreat ended, with 29th British Brigade on the extreme left of the US 8th Army's new line at Pyongtaek near the coast and 27th Commonwealth Brigade some 35 miles inland to the east at Changhowon-Ni. There was to be a brief period of comparative rest for both brigades but the RMP element in Korea was to be kept hard at work in the brigade areas, particularly with the refugee problem.

Morale is very much the direct concern of military police, being reflected in the standard of discipline. They are inversely complementary. It is therefore satisfying to record that discipline throughout the period remained of a high order.

It would be idle to pretend that the retreat had not had an effect on the US 8th Army. In the two British and Commonwealth brigades morale was high but the men were puzzled by the poor military situation. They felt that the Western troops, with their wealth of military experience in the Second World War and equipped with modern weapons, should have been able to stand their ground in face of the Chinese enemy however great their numbers.

Another factor having a bearing on morale at the time was that the retreat was accompanied by confusion and had been unexpected, following a long and swift advance.

The conditions of the retreat made it necessary to destroy immense quantities of stores and equipment which had been brought forward in the wake of the advance. This kind of thing did not unduly depress US troops, backed by immense industrial resources, but to British and Commonwealth troops it was a grievous matter to lose, or abandon, their precious equipment, which might not be replaced for months.

Finally, the difficulty of campaigning in really cold weather over an extended period was bound to have an effect on troops' morale. Apart from the discomforts and hardships, the most irksome and difficult measures were necessary for the preparation of food and to maintain equipment in serviceable condition. Hot water poured into the radiator of a vehicle froze almost at once. Socks had to be changed frequently to prevent frost-bite, and they could not be removed unless the owner was near a fire or had some other means of warming his feet. On British pattern cookers, water took one and a half hours to boil. There were difficulties with weapons owing to lack of a suitable type of oil, which meant that they had to be kept almost dry.

The soldiers were not alone in their troubles; indeed, they fared much better than the unfortunate Korean civilians. Throughout the retreat the troops were face to face with a major refugee problem. As the tide of war flowed south, then north and then south again, the plight of the inhabitants became worse and worse. A high proportion of the population lost their homes and most of their possessions, with little prospect of seeing settled conditions again for a long time to come. The price of being 'liberated' must have seemed very heavy to these unfortunate people. As every soldier knows, a distressed civilian population is in itself conducive to lowering morale.

By early January the United Nations retreat had reached its limit and the line ran from the coast near Pyongtaek, about the 37th Parallel, to near Wonju in Central Korea, and thence to the east coast at Kangnung, some twenty miles south of the 38th Parallel.

In the west there was no contact with the enemy but in the Wonju area the Chinese continued their mass attack. Their attempts to capture the town were foiled by 2nd US Infantry Division and the French Division, who fought with great distinction. The enemy had employed 'human wave' tactics but the enormous casualties inflicted on the attacking hordes eventually brought their offensive down the centre of the peninsula to a halt.

The new army commander, Lieut-General Matthew B. Ridgway apparently was not satisfied with the positions taken up by US 8th Army at the end of its withdrawal and, soon after he assumed command, planned a limited advance to approximately the 38th Parallel.

To implement plans previously made by Major Evans and the US Provost Marshal, Lieutenant J. Aspinall of 249 GHQ Provost Company, together with No 2 Section and 200 infantry to assist him, moved to Pyongtaek on 6 January for the sole purpose of refugee control. It was found necessary on the 8th to reinforce him with No 1 Section also; the refugee flow had reached approximately 2,000 per hour and had become a serious menace to the lines of communication. The main object of this control post was to direct these pathetic streams of frightened humanity into areas less likely to impede the movement of United Nations troops.

On the same day the company sent a 'Recce Party' to Taejon with orders to find a suitable new 'B' Echelon area for 29th Brigade.

The weather at this time was extremely cold, with snow and ice making road movement difficult. On the 12th, 249 Company had its first case of frostbite, needing medical attention. On the same day guerrilla activity near the Brigade 'B' Echelon area intensified, fortunately with no casualties.

During this period 249 Company maintained regular patrols throughout the brigade area and the MSR.

By 7 January, 27th Commonwealth Brigade was properly settled and had taken up its defensive positions around Changhowon-Ni. Contact with the enemy was not close, although constant vigilance was necessary. While the main activity of the infantry was patrolling, the provost section was engaged in routine disciplinary patrol duties and signing the brigade area and the MSR. It was a relief to all in the brigade to be static even for a few days after the previous six months of continuous movement, much of which was in retreat. However, due to the extreme cold (the temperature being usually between 15 to 20 degrees below zero) there was little comfort.

On 22 January 16th Field Regiment Royal New Zealand Artillery joined the brigade as its supporting artillery regiment. The provost section personnel were among the first to greet them into the Commonwealth Brigade; a sub-section consisting of Corporal Turner and Lance-Corporals Leach and Jardine moved south to meet 16th Field Regiment for the purpose of signing the route and escorting them to their operational location.

On 25 January, 1951, the 8th Army offensive began but 27th Commonwealth Brigade did not participate in the initial stages but remained deployed in its present positions. Ichon was entered unopposed by 7th US Cavalry Division on the first day of the offensive.

The enemy counter-attacked 24th US Division, north of Ichon, on 4 February. The attack met with some success and as a precautionary measure the Argyll and Sutherland Highlanders were moved forward that morning to Yoju (12 miles east of Ichon) and HQ 27th Brigade opened up at Chongan-Ni. On arrival in the new area the provost section found themselves controlling a one-way track across paddy-fields to the forward troops. This track was vital for the supply of food and ammunition to the forward troops and for the return passage of wounded or prisoners. There were only four places throughout its length where two vehicles could pass each other so that the section, by the use of their field telephones, strictly co-ordinated the movement of any vehicles travelling in either direction and decided on priorities.

On 18 February 2nd Battalion Princess Patricia's Canadian Light Infantry joined 27th Commonwealth Brigade which now consisted of an Australian battalion, a Canadian battalion, an English battalion, a Scottish battalion, a New Zealand Field Artillery Regiment, an Indian

Field Ambulance and also, under command, the United States 2nd Mortar Battalion, which had rendered magnificent support to the brigades since December, 1950—the whole being commanded by an Englishman, Brigadier B. A. Coad.

The brigade pressed forward day-by-day against little opposition until 27 February, when opposition was encountered on two prominent defensive positions about four miles south of Chipyong-Ni, resulting in fierce fighting by the Australian and Canadian battalions. Enemy resistance in this area was overcome and the methodical advance continued by 1 March. It slowed down considerably, however, the weather being appallingly cold and the line of advance through mountainous country which kept the provost section manning one-way routes with the aid of their field telephones, night and day.

On 1 March some additional South Korean porters joined the Brigade, bringing the total up to about 100 per battalion. It is thought fit to mention these Korean porters for they were to become a feature, and a great help, in solving the problem of supply to the forward troops of most British and Commonwealth units. Indirectly, they were a particular boon to RMP as by their work they greatly relieved congestion on difficult forward supply routes. It was found that with kindly treatment, and good food, they were kept cheerful and efficient. On many occasions they displayed remarkable loyalty to, and affection for, the units to which they were attached.

United Nations forces had made good progress all along the line of advance since their offensive started five weeks earlier, in spite of most stubborn resistance by North Korean forces. By 10 February the enemy had been driven across the River Han south of the capital, leading to the recapture of Inchon, the Kimpo airfield and the south bank of the river. By 14 March he was forced to withdraw from Seoul, the capital. Enemy casualties had been mounting steadily, reaching a peak on 7 March, when the combined casualties for the day were estimated as 21,000.

On 13 March 27th Brigade and its provost section were relieved by the 5th US Cavalry Regiment and concentrated in a river-bed south of Yangp'yong about 15 miles north of Yoju, in 9 Corps reserve. This ended a very strenuous period of operations for the brigade which had lasted for twenty-six days, conducted in bitterly cold weather, against an enemy who merited respect as a tough and skilful fighter.

The provost section recorded that although their task was now a little lighter, they were still unable to get much rest, due to their lack of numbers. Section patrolling and keeping the brigade route and administrative area properly signed was a constant commitment. There were also other duties: Corporal Turner was called upon to investigate a triple murder which had taken place on the night 17–18 March. As a result of preliminary investigation CSM Botting arrived in the brigade area on the 19th and continued the investigation with Corporal Turner. These investigations ultimately resulted in the arrest of seven soldiers who were gravely implicated in the crime.

In the meantime 249 Company was with 29th Brigade in the Pyongtaek–Songwhan area in the left of 8th Army's line.

Company HQ received the warning order for a move on 25 January, made their reconnaissance of the route on the 27th, signed the route on the 30th and then controlled the road and bridges for the actual move of the brigade on the 31st. At the completion of the move on 1 February the provost company established itself close to 29th Brigade HQ, near Osan-Ni about 12 miles further north, where it was learned that Main HQ, British Commonwealth Korean Base (BCKB) was now established in Kure, Japan and that Tac HQ BCKB was to remain at Taegu. Major R. Davenport (APM) and Captain C. Bennett (DAPM, SIB) were both established at the latter. Within the next few days several changes were made within the sub-units of 249 Provost Company. On 4 February the section at Tac HQ BCKB under command of Lieutenant Caley moved from Taegu to Pusan, leaving a sub-section for duties at Tac HQ and FMA at Taegu.

29th Brigade with 249 Provost Company were soon on the move again. The company routed the brigade to Pabalmak on 11 February, where on the following day it relieved the 5th US Cavalry Regiment of 1st US Division. The brigade made contact with the enemy almost at once and for the next ten days it was engaged in hill fighting in conjunction with 24th US Regimental Combat Team.

249 Provost Company assisted the brigade by establishing a PoW cage on the 12th and policing the routes in the brigade area from Suwon to Kungansani and Yongni.

No 1 Section of 249 Provost Company moved to Yongni on the 14th, where they controlled movement over a river crossing, the bridge having been partly blown. No 2 Section was kept busy on the 15th making a reconnaissance and signing supply routes, as the brigade moved north of Yongni on the same day, assisted by the remainder of the available company personnel. The advance continued and on 19 February Tac HQ, with No 2 Section, moved into Kwongjiwoni.

The brigade withdrew to Suwon on the 23rd, once again coming into Corps reserve. The route back to the new concentration area had been reconnoitred and signed by 249 Company on the 22nd. The duty of 29th Brigade was to devise a deception plan to cover the crossing of the River Han by 25th US Division, so was a comparatively quiet period for the company. However, on 7 March they moved to Ichon. 29th

Brigade moved to Yongungpo on the 21st and company HQ was established at Angangni.

On 30 March the brigade came under command of 3rd US Infantry Division and on the following day took over the line of the River Imjin, which was to be the scene of 29th Brigade's epic stand during the battle of 23–25 April. After routing the brigade to its locations in the line, the company was to become a little dispersed, being spread throughout the brigade area with Company Operational HQ and No 1 Section at Tokchong, No 2 Section at 29th Brigade HQ, No 3 Section divided into two sub-sections and located at Uijongbu and Seoul and finally a small representation at Brigade 'B' Echelon area in Seoul.

249 Provost Company was now to play its part with 29th Brigade in preparing for a continuation of the advance, or meeting the expected large-scale Chinese offensive, designed to check the United Nations troops' progress.

On 1 April No 1 Section undertook the task of making a reconnaissance of all routes in the area Tokchong and Passani, having been informed that 249 Provost Company was to be prepared to take over traffic control in these areas from 3rd US Division Military Police in the near future. The administration of the scattered sections and the tasks allotted them were rendered difficult by the terrain.

The main MSR from Seoul to Uijongbu was relatively good but north, all the way to Tokchong, a distance of 12 miles, the road was very narrow and only permitted the movement of one-way traffic and was at paddy-field level for the whole of its length. Use of this part of the route was allotted on a time basis to formations and units, by G4 of 3rd US Division.

The route from Tokchong to Passani was also mostly one-way, but presented the additional difficulty of traversing two mountain passes. No 1 Section laid 8 miles of telephone line along this route on 2 April. With the aid of bulldozers, 'Parking Areas' to hold fifty vehicles each were made, approximately 2 miles apart. An NCO linked by telephone was installed in each area. By this means traffic was called forward both ways, in short hops, with the minimum of delay in each 'Parking Area'.

By 5 April all traffic movement within the brigade area and on the MSR had been co-ordinated and was running smoothly. However, the personnel of the company were beginning to feel the strain imposed on them by continuous duties and lack of sleep. All telephones along the routes, in addition to those at company and section HQ, needed to be manned twenty-four hours daily. No 3 Section had been ordered up to Tokchong on the 4th to permit No 1 Section to move forward on the same day to control forward routes to the battalions.

While most NCOs were employed on traffic control duties in the brigade area and on the MSR, road reconnaissances were being made by RMP parties from the company north of the 38th Parallel and up to the Imjin River.

The main brigade defences lay along the south bank of the river and in some places were as much as 1,000 yards from it. Contact was not close, and infantry patrols were able to penetrate several thousand yards to the north without meeting the enemy. The Imjin in this area was not a very formidable river and at this time of the year it was found possible for infantry to wade across in most places.

On 8 April bridge-crossing sites had been reconnoitred and during the day Corporal Mair and his signing group were winched across the river in their waterproofed jeep. By the afternoon of the same day a bridge capable of carrying jeeps and one-ton trucks had been constructed across the river in the brigade area. A few tanks negotiated the river by fording, the depth of the water being about four feet.

The routes to and across the bridge were lighted by traffic lamps at night by the company and a one-way circuit to the bridge approaches was made and controlled by RMP; this was to become a regular duty. Further RMP reconnaissances were carried out on the 9th with the object of finding more suitable bridge-crossing sites; no more suitable sites were available in the brigade area.

Company HQ (Forward) moved to Pomgamni on the 10th, it being a better location to control duties in the forward areas. On the same day the main brigade supply route was changed, the new route was Seoul–Uijongbu–Tokchong–Tonganch–Omni–Pomgamni–Kahpuri–Ingiam-Dong–38th Parallel–Imjin River Crossing. It was immediately found that the adoption of this new route gave a little relief in provost duties, as it was no longer necessary to control the passes on the Tokchong–Passani road.

Reports were now coming in from patrols, air reconnaissance and civilian sources that considerable parties of Chinese were on the move. In view of these reports all available NCOs of the company spent the 12th digging themselves defensive positions and slit trenches and siting their Bren guns. It was learned on the 14th that small parties of the enemy had infiltrated south of the Imjin, which resulted in a tightening-up of security and an increase in guard duties, particularly at brigade HQ. Mobile twenty-four-hour patrols were maintained throughout the brigade area and MSR with the particular duty of keeping the operational signing in good order.

An innovation occurred for two signing groups of No 2 Section on the 17th. These two groups were detailed to accompany a deep penetration patrol from the Royal Northumberland Fusiliers. The patrol was made in tanks and armoured carriers. One of these RMP parties controlled the fording-place, while the other group proceeded further north with the patrol with the primary object of signing enemy minefields discovered by the Royal Engineers element accompanying the patrol.

The following day No 2 Section changed duties with No 3 Section at Rear Brigade HQ in Seoul. During the Korean campaign it was necessary to keep careful watch on the fair distribution of duties among the sections.

The day after No 2 Section returned to Rear Brigade HQ the PoW cage was completed there and a number of South Korean soldiers were allocated for guard duties at the cage under RMP command. No 2 Section also undertook other duties in the Rear Area, including the laying-out of traffic circuits, signing, the provision of mobile patrols and manning a TP on a twenty-four-hour schedule.

The storm was about to break. The brigade had its usual infantry patrols across the river on the night 21–22 April and these made contact with the enemy much farther south than usual. By 6 am a patrol of the Gloucestershire Regiment was withdrawing in face of the enemy and at 10 am a Royal Northumberland Fusiliers patrol had made contact, the Belgian battalion also making contact by 6 pm. Air reconnaissance in the late afternoon reported that the roads leading south from Pyonggang and Chorwon were crowded with marching troops and vehicles.

By the evening of the 22nd refugees began to appear in large numbers in the brigade area, all moving south and away from the imminent Chinese attack. To meet this threat to the lines of communication, patrols from 249 Provost Company in conjunction with a Civil Affairs officer and some Korean police patrolled the brigade MSR in jeeps. Instructions were given to the refugees through tannoy and loud-hailer equipment carried in the RMP vehicles.

Meanwhile leading elements of the enemy had reached the river by last light and were closely pressing the front-line battalions (Gloucesters, Northumberlands and the Belgian battalion). There was no pause in the enemy advance and just before midnight on the 22nd an attack in strength was made on the entire brigade front in bright moonlight. By dawn on the 23rd the enemy, estimated at battalion strength, was established in Choksong.

It is not the task of this history to record in detail all the fierce engagements fought so gallantly by the fighting units of the brigade during the next few days, but it is necessary to mention those operations which have a direct bearing on the action taken by 249 Provost Company during this period.

It became quickly apparent that this was no local attack with a limited objective, but a full-scale attempt to break the 8th Army front at the point where it turned north, and where, if successful, it would produce far-reaching results by cutting off the troops to the east. 29th Brigade was bearing the brunt of a well-prepared attack in strength. The situation was not improved by the fact that the 1st ROK Division on the left had been driven back several thousand yards, which exposed the brigade's left flank.

Confused fighting continued throughout the 23rd, with the enemy continuing to press his attack in great strength, particularly on the Gloucesters' front. The first attack on the brigade front had been made by 187th Chinese Division, of which it was estimated that not less than one regiment had been directed against the Gloucesters. Later on the 24th a second enemy division was identified on the brigade front.

During the 23rd 249 Provost Company was hard-pressed directing the swollen streams of refugees, controlling the PoW cage (assisted by a Field Security Section of the Intelligence Corps and the ROK guards), placing points-men on all important road junctions and escorting priority columns. In addition to these tasks, RMP NCOs routed and controlled the backward movement of 29th Brigade HQ and certain supporting-arm units for a distance of about five miles.

The stubborn resistance of the brigade had blunted the enemy's attack and although a gap of some four miles existed between the Northumberlands and the Gloucesters at one time during the 24th, by late afternoon of the same day Brigadier T. Brodie was able to move the Belgian battalion to fill the gap, having (with the aid of US tanks) extricated this unit from its location north of the Imjin on the 23rd.

It was learned in the early hours of the 24th that the survivors of 'B' Company, the Gloucesters (now only fifteen strong, some of whom were wounded), together with elements of their anti-tank and mortar platoons, had withdrawn to a feature-point 235, which was to be the scene of the battalion's final stand, subsequently to be known as 'Gloucester Hill'. The remnants of the Gloucesters were completely surrounded and under constant attack. Early in the afternoon a detachment of Filipino tanks tried unsuccessfully to relieve them and in the evening a squadron of Centurion tanks of the 8th Hussars, with American, Puerto Rican and Belgian infantry were also forced back after attempting to fight their way through to their aid.

While these events were taking place on the left flank, the Northumberlands, the Ulster Rifles and the Belgian battalion were all being subjected to almost continuous attack.

Nos 1 and 3 Sections 249 Provost Company were ordered to man routes in the forward area preparatory to the withdrawal of the battalions. By the evening of the 24th these routes were being frequently cut by the enemy, in spite of tanks being used to protect them. The provost section also established stragglers' posts near Brigade HQ during the afternoon of the 24th.

It was realized that the situation was worsening hourly. As night fell on the 24th a tight harbour was formed at Brigade HQ, a small provost HQ with No 2 Section being leaguered there also. Trenches and weapon-pits were dug and manned, and the two Bren guns held by the provost element were sited as part of the all-round defensive fire plan of the HQ. Additional protection was given by the presence of a few tanks from the 8th Hussars. Small groups of the enemy had infiltrated and were operating all round and close to Brigade HQ during the night but no incidents occurred within the HQ perimeter.

Orders for the brigade to withdraw to a position just north of Seoul were issued early on the 25th and by 8 am the leading troops of the brigade began to disengage. Unhappily the Gloucesters were not destined to take part in this withdrawal. All attempts to relieve and replenish their supplies and ammunition had failed; they were five miles away to the west, completely isolated, but continuing in their desperate resistance until almost all of their ammunition was expended. Later in the day a few gallant survivors were to attempt to break through the encircling Chinese in small parties.

Every available officer and NCO of 249 Company was employed from very early on the morning of the 25th assisting the retirement of the battle-weary forward troops down the withdrawal routes, as far as the main US MSR and Uijongbu, Brigade HQ arriving at the latter location by 12.35 pm on the same day.

RMP personnel kept the columns moving, escorted ambulances with urgent cases, picked up walking-wounded in their vehicles and collected and directed stragglers as they came over the hills. By this time most of the foremost routes were under enemy mortar and sometimes small-arms fire. Time and again RMP NCOs returned up the withdrawal routes to perform some urgent task in the furtherance of this most difficult, confused and costly operation but hourly more troops were making their withdrawal, closely pressed by the enemy. Throughout the 25th many members of RMP were in a position, and privileged, to witness the fine work done by 'C' Squadron, 8th Hussars, who were covering the withdrawal.

By the evening, at 7.50 pm, orders were received that the whole brigade was to continue its move south of the River Han, to the area of Yongdungpo. Company HQ (Rear) and No 2 Section were immediately given the task of signing and manning the routes through Seoul and Yongdungpo and to establish an Information Post at the entrance to the latter. Units had been ordered by Brigade HQ to pass details of their movements and locations to this Post as they passed through. At the same time, No 1 Section manned the route Uijongbu–Seoul in addition to supplying personnel to assist No 3 Section who were further north. A stragglers' post was also set up at Uijongbu. No 3 Section supplied a reconnaissance group for Brigade HQ and controlled the route from Pomgamni to Uijongbu. Movement southwards continued all night with every available officer and man of the company doing his utmost to speed the flow of vehicles, personnel, guns and equipment. Prisoners were handed over to an American PoW cage.

The withdrawal continued throughout the 26th, stragglers' posts being still in operation at Uijongbu, Seoul and Yongdungpo. During the day a now-united company HQ moved back to Anyang just south of Yongdungpo, while No 3 Section harboured with Brigade HQ.

When a count was made in the company it was happily found that all ranks were accounted for. All available in 249 Company were now dispatched on road and track reconnaissance through the brigade area.

29th Brigade, now in 1 Corps reserve with the task of denying the Kimpo Peninsula to the enemy, had suffered heavily. More than 25 per cent of its fighting men had become casualties, one battalion (the Gloucesters) having been practically eliminated. Much equipment—including some tanks—had been lost. The stand made by the brigade had, however, completely frustrated the Chinese plan to break the 8th Army front. For three days it had blocked all attempts to cut the road to Seoul and had inflicted casualties on the enemy which had brought his offensive to a halt and resulted in his withdrawal.

In the middle of April, 1951, 27th Brigade, including the Middlesex Regiment and the Argyll and Sutherland Highlanders was relieved by 28th Brigade who disembarked at Inchon on the 24th, accompanied by a half-section of 40 Infantry Division Provost Company under command of Sergeant Myers. This half-section amalgamated with the remaining half-section of 27th Brigade (a half-section under Corporal Turner returning with its brigade HQ to Hong Kong) to form a complete provost section for 28th Brigade.

The hand-over was not to go very smoothly, however, as the Chinese then launched a new offensive against 29th Brigade on the Imjin, some thirty miles to the west, while pressing hard on 27th Brigade front, forcing them to fall back astride the River Kapyong, north of Changchon-Ni, where the actual relief was affected. The enemy broke contact just as suddenly as he had engaged and by the afternoon of the 25th had melted away.

As a result of this battle of the River Kapyong 2nd Battalion, Princess Patricia's Canadian Light Infantry, 3rd Battalion, Royal Australian

Regiment and 'A' Company, 72 US Heavy Tank Battalion became part of 28th Commonwealth Brigade, the Brigade receiving the American Presidential Citation.

27th Brigade had thus fought its last battle in Korea with skill and courage, as indeed it had fought throughout its previous eight months campaigning there. The two British and Commonwealth brigades had played a notable part in defeating the Chinese Communists' spring offensive of 1951.

At the conclusion of this phase of operations RMP in Korea felt that they had dutifully played their part in aiding to the best of their ability their sorely-tried comrades in the United Nations forces.

At midnight 25–26 April 27th Commonwealth Brigade changed its commander and its designation to become 28th Commonwealth Brigade, commanded by Brigadier G. Taylor. On the same day 28th Brigade withdrew further south, being relieved by the 5th US Cavalry Regiment.

249 GHQ Provost Company was making a reconnaissance on 26 April of all the roads and tracks in the Kimpo Peninsula. As a result of these reconnaissances an alternative MSR was signed on the following day by the company. At the same time, No 3 Section moved to Sosa with Main 29th Brigade HQ, while No 2 Section remained at Yongdungpo. Additional signing was found necessary, including a lateral link from Anyang on the main MSR to Pangchongmori. The brigade was, however, fully signed by the 28th, when No 3 Section signed the routes from Brigade HQ to the battalions, No 1 Section to 'A' Echelons and No 2 Section the circuits in the Brigade administrative and 'B' Echelon areas. The company then settled down to a period of static duties.

29th Brigade (with the Belgian battalion and 5th ROK Marine Battalion under command) was to spend the next month on the Kimpo Peninsula under quiet conditions after its heavy losses in the Imjin battle. The fighting elements of the brigade spent their time patrolling, absorbing reinforcements, reorganizing and training. In a very short time units were again battleworthy—including the Gloucesters.

Although 249 Provost Company was also able under these conditions to obtain a limited amount of time for rest and reorganization, nevertheless the new conditions produced new provost duties.

One of the first tasks undertaken in the new area was to establish liaison between RMP and the Civil Affairs officer. Liaison was also made with the civilian police and an agreement made for them to cover points on the brigade MSR to stop the drift of refugees on to this vital route. Information Posts were established throughout the brigade area in addition to the provision of twenty-four-hour mobile patrols.

During the first week in May RMP carried out security patrols in conjunction with Field Security units. It will be appreciated that it was most difficult for Europeans to distinguish the difference in facial features between one Asian and another making it comparatively easy for a North Korean to masquerade as a South Korean.

Due to the unsavoury inducements offered by the native population of Sosa it was placed 'out of bounds' on 3 May and a curfew imposed; RMP patrols were required to enforce both.

Extra work was thrown on the company by the necessity of erecting numerous speed-limit signs. The Inchon–Seoul road seemed to possess a special attraction to speeding Service drivers of all nationalities with the result that by order of higher authority frequent static speed checks were made.

On 8 May General James A. Van Fleet, the 8th Army Commander, presented the 1st Battalion the Gloucestershire Regiment and 'C' Troop, 170th Independent Mortar Battery, Royal Artillery, with an American Presidential Citation as a tribute to their exceptional services during the Imjin battle. The presentation took place at a parade held at 29th Brigade HQ, all RMP personnel on parade wearing white equipment.

During the whole of this static period excellent liaison was maintained between Canadian, American and Belgian military police units. Frequent joint American, British and Belgian patrols were operated.

Considering the abject poverty of the native population it is not surprising to find that Korea was an ideal breeding-ground for black market activities. On 12 May 249 Provost Company was ordered to make a surprise raid on 'black-spots' in Sosa in search of British and Allied supplies; a limited amount of success was achieved. Further raids were made in certain areas of Sosa on the 14th; this time attention was directed against the brothel area and a number of arrests were made. The squalor and filth found in these areas was beyond description; anti-vice patrols were instituted from this date onwards, operating regularly in Sosa and Yongdungpo.

A number of officers and NCOs of 249 Company visited the Canadian Brigade HQ near Suwon on the 20th where they were cordially entertained by the two sections of the Canadian Provost Corps located there. During the spring there had been a considerable increase in the size of the Canadian contingent in Korea by the addition of 25th Canadian Infantry Brigade Group. The Canadian Provost detachment of this brigade group was commanded by Major R. I. Luker, who had been met at the docks at Pusan on 4 May by Major Davenport. This meeting was to be the start of a long and happy association between the Canadian Provost Corps and RMP in Korea, culminating in the fully-integrated Commonwealth Division Provost Company.

At the end of May, 29th Brigade moved to the left sector of its old positions on the Imjin, west of Seoul, where it set about digging, wiring and mining defences.

The routes had been reconnoitred, signed and manned by the company for the move to take place on 23 and 24 May, and was carried out without a hitch. By the evening of the 24th elements of the provost company were located as follows:

Advance Company HQ and No 1 and 3 Sections at Brigade HQ; Rear Company HQ and a part of No 2 Section in the Brigade 'B' Echelon area at Yongdungpo; the remainder of No 2 Section with the Brigade administrative area, responsible for its signing and traffic control.

A busy day was spent on the 25th making liaison with 622 US Military Police Company and the Belgian provost unit in the area; as a result joint disciplinary patrols were instituted. A new brigade MSR, Suwon–Anyang–Yongdungpo–Seoul, was also signed and patrolled.

The company was about to embark on another strenuous period. At 4.30 am on 28 May reconnaissance parties under Lieutenant Aspinall moved off ahead of the main brigade groups to relieve part of 1st US Cavalry Division in the area of Tokchong. A little later in the day No 3 Section moved with the brigade HQ. No 1 Section manned the route north, and No 2 Section controlled the sector south of the River Han. The moves of 'B' Echelons, administrative area personnel and vehicles of 'A' Echelons were controlled by the company on the following day. The whole operation was carried out in torrential rain, which quickly made some of the proposed routes impassable. However, by the evening of the 29th the move was complete. On arrival in the new area immediate liaison was made and assistance offered to the provost section of 28th Brigade who were located to the right flank of 29th Brigade's area.

The heavy rains continued for some days, rendering many roads impassable and necessitating strict 'one-way' control on many others. Control posts connected by telephones were established at several passes in the brigade area. RMP mobile patrols linking 28th Brigade and HQ 1 Corps being a regular duty.

On 2 June the bulk of the newly-arrived 25th Canadian Brigade moved into an area just to the rear of 29th British and 28th Commonwealth brigades, in the vicinity of Tokchong which on the same day became an enlarged advance FMA. The provost commitments were now so heavy that only a small detachment from No 2 Section could be spared to carry out the signing and circuit control within it. Major Evans made a request to the APM BCFK for provost reinforcements.

The Canadian Provost Corps assisted as much as possible by supplying personnel for static points on the local MSR.

As the volume of rain increased so the control of traffic on the vital routes had to be tightened. Bridges in the Commonwealth area were swept away by the floods. The Royal Engineers worked magnificently night and day endeavouring to keep these routes open. Winches were made available at river banks to assist vehicles across. The Sappers also gave great help to RMP mobile patrols by bulldozing 'Passing-Bays', thus allowing jeeps to run against traffic; unfortunately the large engineering vehicles employed themselves made an additional obstacle on the roads, being virtually mobile roadblocks.

By 5 June the company had signed all the roads in the area with 15 mph speed-limit signs; apart from the enforcement of this speed limit, vehicles were required to be spaced at least 100 yards apart, with no overtaking. With effect from 8 June roads were closed to traffic from 1 am to 4 am nightly, to permit RE maintenance.

The liaison existing between RMP and Canadian Provost Corps during this trying period was first-class; by 7 June the MSR and all the main routes linking the Canadian brigade's area with that of the British brigade were jointly controlled.

While the bulk of RMP were heavily committed with traffic control duties, the 'Sign Factory' was working at full pressure, so that by 11 June the route, including the mountain passes, was completely signed from Tokchong to the River Imjin.

In June, 1951, further provost coverage was required and a new unit was brought on to the RMP Order of Battle, designated 262 Base Provost Company, and with the function of policing the lines of communication and base area. Captain Caley, promoted from 249 Provost Company, with three sections, was posted from that unit to form the nucleus, the new Company HQ arriving to take up their station in August at Kure, with sections at Hiroshima, Pusan, Taegu and Tokyo, and detachments with British Advance HQ and British FMA and Docks detachments at Kure and Pusan.

The now depleted 249 Provost Company was faced with extended operational commitments having to take over all static traffic posts from Canadian Provost, that brigade having moved to Chorwon under command 1st US Cavalry Division and in addition patrols had to be found for the main road into Seoul, whose proffered and generally undesirable attractions were beckoning to many 'swanners'.

Provost in Korea rapidly learnt the need for maximum economy in the use of manpower and the development of ingenuity. The company had, through force of circumstances, drastically reduced the number of NCOs who might normally be expected to carry out a specific task. The following are examples of economy in manpower. Bridges across the Imjin River, each at least 100 yards long and in continual use by heavy traffic night and day, were controlled by only two NCOs, two field telephones and two signs marked 'Halt, Await Signals' on each bridge. At the time when the brigade MSR had a six-mile stretch of one-way road it was operated day and night for several months by one corporal and three lance-corporals with three telephones, by the following method: Three TPs were established along its length, the centre one operated by one corporal and one lance-corporal (this centre TP being the control point), one lance-corporal in addition being required at each of the end-points. The traffic was sent from each end and whichever group arrived at the control point first was parked, the other group from the opposite end passing straight through. As soon as the last vehicle passed them the parked group was sent off, the last vehicle in each group being described by use of the telephone to the point the vehicle was approaching. As soon as the last vehicles had passed the two points the whole procedure started again. Later a further two miles was added to this same stretch of road, including a one-way bridge, with only one extra NCO and one telephone being needed for this extra commitment.

The mobile nature of the company rôle brought all officers and NCOs into close contact with both brigade troops and with neighbouring units of the United Nations forces, RSM G. S. P. Stead in particular being a familiar and much-respected figure who seemed always available whenever a quick and accurate provost decision was required.

British and Commonwealth troops in Korea had, up to this time, operated independently, virtually as part of the United States ground forces, although since the arrival of 25th Canadian Brigade early in May a common sentiment and a natural feeling of union had existed between them and the two British and Commonwealth brigades. These three independent brigade groups were now to be integrated into a Commonwealth division, with consequent elevation in prestige and conduct of major operations. Early in June the staff of division HQ started to assemble and organize under Major-General A. J. H. Cassels, the divisional Commander designate, the main body of division HQ having arrived at Pusan towards the end of June.

On 1 July it was assumed that 249 Provost Company was shortly to become absorbed into a new integrated provost company consisting of a HQ and eight sections, two of which were to be formed from 25th Canadian Infantry Brigade Provost Unit. The designation of this new unit was to be 1st Commonwealth Division Provost Company. Preparations were begun immediately to absorb 28th Brigade provost section and also personnel of a new section that had just arrived at Pusan with the main body of HQ 1st Commonwealth Division.

The excellence of the work performed by 249 GHQ Provost Company was recognized by the award of the United States Bronze Star to its Company Commander, Major A. W. Evans, the citation mentioning this officer's 'attention to duty and tireless efforts . . . and most tireless degree of team-work'. This reflected the greatest credit not only on the officer concerned but also on the whole company and was to be the inheritance of the new integrated 1 Commonwealth Division Provost Company about to be formed. Major Evans had also won the Military Medal while serving as a sergeant in the Corps in North-West Europe during the Second World War.

At midday on 28 July, 1951, a short ceremony was held at Main division HQ attended by General James A. Van Fleet, Commander, 8th Army, Lieut-General Sir Horace Robertson, C-in-C, British Commonwealth Forces in Japan, together with other senior Commonwealth and American officers, to mark the formation of 1st Commonwealth Division under the command of Major-General A. J. H. Cassels. General Cassels was later to be Colonel Commandant RMP from 1957 to 1968, succeeding General Sir Miles Dempsey. Here for the first time a Commonwealth Division flag was flown—alongside the flags of Commonwealth countries and that of the United Nations. The Division formed part of 1 US Corps, commanded by Lieut-General J. W. O'Daniel, a stout-hearted American commander—affectionately known to the troops as 'Iron Mike'.

On the same day that 1 Commonwealth Division Provost Company came into being and performed its first duties at the division's inaugural ceremony, Major Evans assumed the appointment of DAPM to the division, while Major Luker, Canadian Provost Corps, took command of the company. Further RMP personnel for the company were supplied as follows:

> HQ and four sections from the disbanded 249 GHQ Provost Company, two sections from Canadian Provost Corps with 25th Canadian Infantry Brigade and Captain E. L. Williams (second-in-command) with Lieutenant J. Aspinall and RSM G. S. P. Stead. A Canadian subaltern was also included in the establishment and an additional two sections were awaited from the United Kingdom.

The division's first major commitment was Operation 'Slam' in which 25th Canadian Brigade was placed under command of 1st US Cavalry Division to hold defensive positions, thus freeing the latter for mobile operations, while the remainder of the Commonwealth Division was to advance with and protect the left flank of the Cavalry Division in a combined crossing of the Imjin and a four-mile advance to the north.

The provost company helped control the columns and the approaches to the river early on 4 August for the leading Commonwealth troops of 28th and 29th Brigades. By 4 pm the objectives, about three miles distant, had been reached, without contact being made with the enemy. However, torrential rain, which caused the Imjin to rise to a depth of twenty feet, prevented the previously-planned withdrawal on the 5th, the troops being cut off north of the river until 6 August, during which time they were supplied by air. The battalions eventually withdrew just before dark on the 6th. 25th Canadian Brigade reverting to division command on the 8th.

Heavy rains during the nights 4–5 and 5–6 August caused extensive damage to all the MSRs and serious blockage at vital points. Every available RMP officer and NCO, with the exception of those engaged on operational duty, was now employed on road intelligence patrols or route control in liaison with Royal Engineers' working parties.

On 13 August traffic control personnel were required to assist in the move of the 2nd Battalion Royal Canadian Regiment, as part of Operation 'Dirk'. This operation was a large-scale raid on an enemy objective, about 7,000 yards north of the river. No bridges being available in the appropriate area, the battalion crossed the Imjin by wading and the use of a ferry crossing, a cessation in the rains during the previous few days making this possible. After inflicting casualties on the enemy, the raiding battalion withdrew to the south bank of the river at dusk on the 15th with the provost company assisting in their return to their unit location.

Between 22 and 24 August Operation 'Claymore' required 25 Canadian Brigade to carry out another raid in force some three to five miles north of the river, for which provost provided normal traffic control duties through the division area and over the river, and stood-by to pass them back on their return.

By the first week in September a new Operation 'Minder' had been planned and provost were required to make the necessary reconnaissances for the Imjin crossings. A preliminary move was Operation 'Pintail' in which 3rd Battalion, Royal Australian Regiment, crossed the Imjin on rafts in order to provide an advance screen to cover the main crossings.

No 2 Section of the provost company accompanied the Australians and provided control at the rafting points. A second crossing point, 'Teal', was then opened and the King's Shropshire Light Infantry and King's Own Scottish Borderers passed over while the Australians held off enemy interference.

The provost company was fully committed in controlling the approach routes, crossing points and dispersal on the north side until 12 September, by which time the division had established itself some 5,000 yards forward of the river with 25th and 29th Brigades firmly on the new line and 28th Brigade in reserve guarding the crossing points which the Royal Engineers promptly bridged. The deployment of the company settled down with No 1 Section with 29th Brigade, No 5 with 28th Brigade, No. 7 ('A' Section Canadian) with 25th Brigade and responsible for the PoW cage, No 2 at 'Pintail', No 6 at 'Teal', No 3 at Main Division HQ and No 4 at Rear Division HQ.

The division was now in the line with forward troops in close contact with frequent patrol clashes and a number of prisoners being passed back to the cage.

During this operation heavy rains caused severe damage to the main MSR forward of 'Teal' and the movement of traffic became extremely difficult; added to this was a new stream of refugees, over 1,500 civilians having to be evacuated from the forward area. This task was accomplished by extensive use of radio—which again stressed the need for provost signal sections in operations.

Then, the new line having been consolidated, Operation 'Commando' was planned, D-Day to be 3 October, by which it was intended to push forward the whole corps front by a further 6,000 to 10,000 yards. Preliminary operational moves began on 28 September with provost committed to round-the-clock control of four river crossings and the sign factory working overtime.

Broadly speaking, the traffic control plan for Operation 'Commando' was to maintain TPs at all important points, the personnel being detailed by company HQ instead of the more usual practice of sections being responsible for any particular unit or formation move. The closest liaison was maintained during this period with the Royal Engineers to ensure up-to-date knowledge of the road development plan.

By the evening of the 28th the bulk of the gunners had been moved across 'Pintail' and Tac HQ 25th Canadian Brigade had moved to new locations north of the Imjin.

The company was fully engaged on 1 October in moving 28th Commonwealth Brigade from reserve. This brigade was to be involved in the first phase of the division attack. The company also assisted in guiding it to an Assembly Area behind the 25th Brigade on 2 October.

By the evening of 2 October the stage was set for the Commonwealth Division's first major attack against the defended position. The relatively quiet period since the division's formation had enabled the company, in conformity with the remainder of the division, to 'settle down' and make good preparations for future operational tasks. It is probably true to say that RMP, together with the Royal Engineers, had been as busy as any arm of the service during the previous few weeks due to the heavy tasks thrown on them by the Korean weather.

At first light on 3 October the Commonwealth Division launched an attack, with 28th Commonwealth Brigade as its spearhead. The provost company during the previous day and night had marked and manned all tracks into the battalion areas in addition to controlling two crossings of the Imjin River, running north–south immediately behind the brigade. Owing to the movement of heavy traffic in supplies and ammunition, all TPs in the division area were now manned continuously.

Prior to the initial assault and throughout the day the division artillery had kept up a continuous heavy bombardment of enemy areas. The company's War Diary makes particular reference to the heavy traffic control commitment required in and around the gun areas and to and from the ammunition points. It is recorded that some 27,000 rounds were fired during the opening phase of this operation.

The closest liaison was still being maintained between the provost company and the Royal Engineers. The roads in the operational area were one-way and their surfaces required almost continual attention from the sappers. Provost made liberal use of radio and telephones in their efforts to bring newly-reconnoitred and marked circuits into use at the earliest possible moment.

Although the night 3–4 October was not hampered by enemy action there was much activity on the supply and main axis routes, again requiring the use of every available RMP officer and NCO. During 4 October 25th Brigade attacked on the left of the division front and made good progress in spite of heavy enemy shelling. One officer and twenty-seven OR PoWs were evacuated by the company during the day. The third day of the attack was one of severe fighting, particularly on 28th Brigade's front; but the advance still continued.

Refugees once again appeared as a special problem for provost. During the 5th the company, together with some Field Security personnel, established Refugee Points at the river crossings where, after screening refugees were evacuated by transport out of the operational area.

PoWs continued to be admitted to the cage, a further twenty-four being handled by RMP on the 5th, together with eight ROK soldiers who were held on the request of Canadian Field Security as a result of investigation into certain black-market activities. During the same day progress was made in establishing a more satisfactory circuit for heavy supply and operational vehicles, a one-way circuit being marked and controlled—north across 'Pintail' and south via the 1st US Cavalry MSR and 'Duckbill'.

The final objective for the division in Operation 'Commando' was captured on the evening of 8 October, following fierce sporadic fighting on the division front and culminating in the successful use of air-strikes on the most stubborn enemy points of resistance. Between the 5th and the evening of the 8th provost had continued in route reconnaissance and signing on the newly-cleared areas. At one period on the 6th No 5 Section supplied pointsmen right up to infantry company positions on a one-way track. RMP assistance was also given on the same day in moving the Royal Norfolk Regiment from Britannia Camp near Uijongbu to relieve the Royal Ulster Rifles who left for Hong Kong on 10 October.

Throughout Operation 'Commando' most RMP personnel were performing tours of duty lasting from twelve to fifteen hours daily, mostly as pointsmen. In spite of the strain imposed traffic continued to move as operationally required and only very temporary disruptions were caused by intermittent enemy shelling.

Following the capture of all its objectives the division immediately set about the task of consolidation. Provost were able to report by 10 October that all routes were running smoothly, in spite of a considerable increase of administrative traffic, even in the forward areas.

The division settled down in defensive positions and prepared for the Korean winter which had now begun. In early November the enemy began harassment with a marked increase in artillery fire, some 10,000 shells falling in the division area in three days, particularly in that of 28th Brigade.

The first heavy fall of snow occurred on the night of 23–24 November, followed on the next night with 16° of frost. The thick ice and heavy snow caused accidents and traffic jams which dislocated the moves of the 3rd Battalion Royal Australian Regiment and 'C' Squadron 8th Hussars. The whole company was engaged attempting to keep traffic moving and hours of duty lengthened from eight to twelve. Radio control was also maintained on 29th Brigade supply route.

The 25th was indeed a particularly busy day for the company. After a brief respite, those off traffic duty were called upon to perform another special duty in the form of a concentrated raid in conjunction with Field Security and Korean National Police on Tokchong necessitated by recent numerous acts of sabotage. In addition to the arrest of large numbers of civilians unable to account for themselves satisfactorily, including prostitutes, a vast amount of WD material was recovered. This put a temporary brake on vice and black-market activity.

Later on the 25th the thaw set in causing even further deterioration on the roads. By this time, however, peace talks were in progress resulting in a sharp decline in battle activity and provost were able to relax slightly after the intense strain of the previous week.

From then until Christmas Day there was little operational activity other than bridging equipment passing forward. The time was spent in consolidating the area, sign maintenance and preparing to receive repatriated prisoners expected as a result of the peace talks. 'Consolidating the area' included a big drive to clear civilians out of the prohibited zones.

Despite severe deterioration in the weather 120 NCOs were able to sit down to Christmas dinner, the senior NCOs taking over normal routine duties.

The respite was, however, short. On the 26th reports came in of many WD vehicles missing, believed 'borrowed' over the Christmas period; heavy snow made the 'Teal' bridge crossing almost impassable and a Centurion tank became bogged down, necessitating the road being closed all night for recovery. This proved a difficult problem and the efforts caused serious road damage as a rescue tank also became stuck and the road was not finally cleared until late on the 30th.

The year closed with special duties at 1st Battalion King's Own Scottish Borderers for the presentation of the Victoria Cross to Private William Speakman.

The first half of the Korean War has been recounted, almost day-by-day, from the War Diary entries over the first eighteen months, mainly because it was the period when provost were part of a purely United Kingdom formation and the emphasis throughout was essentially operational, governed by the ebb and flow of battle.

The second half of the war saw the RMP element as part of fully-integrated Commonwealth companies in 1st Commonwealth Division Provost Company and British Commonwealth Base Provost Company. Just as the first eighteen months also had its routine police duty requirements in back areas, so did the next eighteen months have its operational activity. To recount the whole of both, however, would be repetitive, wearisome reading and unduly lengthy.

The end of 1951 saw the battle settle down on the 38th Parallel, the area becoming static and consolidation taking shape. The emphasis from then was on static police duties.

In January, 1952, the provost picture throughout Korea was as follows:

1st Commonwealth Division was located on the 38th Parallel as part of 1 US Corps. It comprised 25th, 28th and 29th Brigades. Although the division was static the provost company was fully extended. Some of the more important duties were on MSRs, brigade moves and bridge control over one-way river crossings. As time went on and the division continued to remain stationary in the same area, provost responsibilities in the rear division area became a serious problem.

Truce talks at Panmunjom went on month-after-month and it is doubtful if any division provost company had previously been placed in the position of carrying on its operational rôle at the same time being committed to disciplinary duties with all nationalities in the field, under such trying conditions. Only complete reciprocal understanding with 1 US Corps Military Police made control of the situation possible.

262 Base Provost Company, mainly three sections, was committed in L of C areas of two countries, Japan and Korea. Routine duties extended manpower to the full. Seoul, the war-shattered capital of South Korea, contained the FMA, Inchon, 35 miles from Seoul on the west coast of Korea, was the LST Sea Head and Pusan, the nearest port in South Korea to Japan, was the main Sea Head for Commonwealth and American shipping. Kure in Japan contained HQ British Commonwealth Forces Korea (BCFK) and all the main base installations and General Headquarters was located in Tokyo. Each place was in urgent need of Commonwealth provost.

Except between Inchon and Seoul all the towns mentioned in the previous paragraph were so far from one another that eighteen hours by road, rail or sea was required for normal movement between them so the accepted mode of travel within the theatre was by air and sea. Movement of stores and troops, docks duties, pilferage and discipline could not be adequately tackled with the available police manpower.

During the first quarter of 1952 Australian, Canadian and New Zealand provost representation was encouraged by HQ BCFK, the policy of integration was approved but not finally agreed and gradually Canadian, Australian and New Zealand military police in small numbers became available for duties in Korea.

April and May saw military police on the ground in Seoul and Pusan in sufficient numbers to be encouraging. In consequence, increases in recoveries and reported crime became apparent.

The continuance of 1st Commonwealth Division in the same static rôle had caused serious crime to increase, particularly in forward areas. SIB located at Seoul were fully engaged on investigations into crimes committed by all nationalities. Murder, shootings, grievous bodily harm and large-scale stealings were common in Seoul, the FMA and the Rear division area.

Pusan, Sea Head for ammunition and British stores, was a town badly overcrowded with refugees who lived in conditions of the utmost squalor. Drugs, contraband, sexual offences, black-market activities, etc, added their quota of variation to the normal range of crime investigations.

Kure, Japan, was still under the control of BCOF, but the Japanese Peace Treaty signed on 8 September, 1951, became effective on

28 April, 1952, and the establishment of HQ BCFK in Kure, with the changes in policy of the Japanese administration had brought to light a great many matters which called for SIB investigation.

SIB were fully extended and it was eventually decided to move their HQ from Pusan to Kure so that closer liaison could be maintained with the staff and more investigators could be made available in Japan without materially affecting the Pusan and Seoul detachments' manpower.

Assistance from the American PM on all investigations requiring laboratory reports was received. Laboratory facilities available in Tokyo proved to be one of the most up-to-date military establishments of its kind in the world and full use of its staff and branches was promised and thankfully accepted. The co-operation of the Americans in this direction proved invaluable to the Commonwealth provost service.

Because of conditions in the division area it was decided to attach two SIB sergeants to 1st Commonwealth Division Provost Company. Their investigations proved so successful that they were permanently attached.

Although the number of investigations carried out by provost remained constant month-by-month, the incidence of serious crime had gradually decreased during the past eighteen months. The opening of the Military Corrective Establishment at Kure in February, 1952, had considerably assisted in this decrease, by correctly taking out of the Theatre all serious offenders.

The following crime statistics for the eighteen months period January, 1952, to June, 1953, are indicative of the duties performed and work done in the Theatre:

Serious Crime—Cases investigated

Murder	13	Manslaughter	8
Wounding	6	Suicide	8
Indecency	25	Robbery with violence	17
Grievous bodily harm	33	Rape	13
Sodomy	6		
Total cases investigated: 1,500		Individuals arrested or reported: 1,754	

Recovered property: SIB £50,252
Provost £17,070

Total £67,322

Total Provost disciplinary charges: 14,291.

The Commonwealth experiment of fully-integrated companies produced a procedure problem for provost in crime investigations. Common ground on this problem was found and the investigation of serious crime in all Commonwealth components was carried out successfully, irrespective of nationality.

Lessons learned in the Second World War and incorporated in the 1950 RMP Manual, *Provost Training in Peace and War*, had in general proved themselves in Korea. However, climatic extremes there, lack of roads, geographical features and ground conditions, all peculiar to Korea, were hazards difficult to overcome with normally-accepted provost procedures. Improvisation and adaptation were required to meet these circumstances and, of the lessons learned, much was to pass into future standardized methods.

Korea was very badly served with roads. Outside the town areas it was difficult to find a road which would receive a higher grading than Class 3. More often than not in operations no road was available and the Engineers had to make roads over very difficult country indeed. In a country where every available piece of land had been used for the growing of rice and had become natural bog, the Engineers had to tear roads out of the hillsides, or on the plains elevate them above natural ground level by several feet. This unavoidable road building policy set provost several problems.

All traffic had to use the MSRs—there were no alternatives—and rigid control of these routes became necessary. Road surfaces were not metalled in any way and dust clouds were inevitable. Dust became such a menace to daylight driving that orders were issued directing all convoys to use headlights. Torrential rain in the rainy season often gushed down the sides of the hills and wiped out patches of road. Short diversions into 'paddy' were impossible, the only option was to close the road. Meticulous police patrolling was necessary in order to avoid chaos when roads went out of use.

Pilferage of WD and NAAFI stores from docks areas while in transit by rail and sea was not on a large scale but required the constant attention of military police Docks detachments, particularly at Pusan and Kure. Due to pressure of other commitments it was not possible to allot as many men for these duties as desired. However, after considering the amount of cargo handled, the presence of provost in these areas did much to reduce the rate of pilferages in this Theatre to a comparatively small figure.

In 1948 the Supreme Commander Allied Powers (Japan) (SCAP) set out the procedure to be followed in the confiscation, forfeiture and disposal of contraband, i.e., property, including means of transportation or concealment thereof, connected with black-market activities. A Deputy Contraband Property Administrator (DCPA) was appointed in each major formation within Japan to act as SCAP's representative for the forfeiture and disposal of contraband property in his formation area.

Duties of the DCPA devolved on the APM HQ BCOF and were carried out until the Peace Treaty with Japan became effective on 28 April, 1952. It was conservatively estimated that £500,000 worth of contraband property was processed through the APM's office during the period of his appointment as DCPA for the British Commonwealth Forces and Occupation area.

The incidence of venereal disease among British Commonwealth troops had, since their entry into Japan in 1946, been comparatively high. This was due to the high rate of venereal disease among Japanese prostitutes, the apathy shown by Japanese health officials towards its eradication and the comparatively small fee for which servicemen could obtain the services of a prostitute. Military police action to combat the incidence of venereal disease was by formation of anti-vice squads who actively co-operated with Japanese health officials to ensure that all known prostitutes were regularly examined, in accordance with Japanese medical procedure.

As may be expected in a country such as Korea, where food and clothing supplies had been seriously affected by war and in towns such as Pusan where the normal population increased ten-fold due to the influx of refugees from the forward areas, black-market activity was rife. Commodities such as blankets, cigarettes and foodstuffs were eagerly sought by black-market dealers who were often willing to pay US Armed Forces dollar currency for these goods. The greater danger in these illicit dealings was that the serviceman, having once changed his weekly cigarette issue for won (Korean currency), was apt to look farther afield to make money.

Against this background of routine police duties, the war was never far away. Reports of guerrilla activities around Base areas in Korea demanded the utmost vigilance in provost patrols, particularly while on escort duty with VIPs. Several road patrols reported that their vehicles had been fired on.

In June, 1952, a train in the south-west of Korea was ambushed by a party of some fifty guerrillas. Two US servicemen were among the thirty-odd passengers killed as a result of this raid.

With rear areas settled down into almost garrison status it was natural that rest areas should become international and to meet this a detachment of one Australian, two British and two Canadian NCOs was attached to 622 US Military Police Company at 1 US Corps, to carry out combined patrols in the rear areas, with the US Military Police. This combination worked out very well and the PM 1 US Corps was most complimentary on their work. All NCOs were rotated within their own units every two months.

Provost were very busy competing with the rainy season and at one time only one main bridge ('Parker') over the Imjin was left in use. Brigades changed over, one every two months. These reliefs took place at night and consequently it required the maximum of TPs and traffic control right up to the forward positions.

1st Commonwealth Division took over a portion of the 1st US Marine Division's front on the division's left which included the 'Hook' (one of the most fought-over positions in the war). In taking over this frontage it included responsibility for 'Widgeon' bridge, which had been a Marine commitment. This was a floating one-way bridge and required a TP for twenty-four hours daily on the south bank.

'Teal' bridge, which was swept away in the rains, was re-opened three months later as a floating bridge; again this required a TP for twenty-four hours daily at each end as both approaches were steep and dangerous.

The opening of 'Pintail' bridge, a high-level, two-way steel bridge, was a great improvement over the floating bridge of the previous winter and instead of having a TP at each end, as was required for the floating bridge, it was now satisfactory to have one TP on the south end, relieved by the infantry at 6 pm nightly. Provost, however, slept in a tent at the bridge site to deal with emergencies.

The operational work of the company remained constant—brigade moves and re-deployment, battalion reliefs, moves of tank and artillery units and lateral moves of flanking divisions, all required constant manning of TPs, Information Posts and one-way stretches of road.

Dawn patrols of all communication and supply routes were made and reports passed to the Royal Engineers by 7 am daily for immediate remedial action to prevent deterioration. In addition there were the routine disciplinary patrols and the inevitable VIP escorts to provide. Airfield security also became a provost commitment.

Radio communications were essential for movement control and a radio section was established with a control station at company HQ and five jeeps fitted with '63' sets. As a brigade move could take up to four days the provost company built portable huts of light wood framing and waterproof covering which could be placed at all permanent TPs. At night pointsmen worked in pairs both for security and relief in the bitter cold and were equipped with Canadian-pattern luminous traffic sleeves and 'Scotch Lite' traffic signs which reflected vehicle lights. These items both proved invaluable.

Among the worst hazards of what was now a static operational area were old minefields which made diversions almost impossible. All roads had soft shoulders making it impossible to turn—large vehicles and a washed-out section or road-block could bring total standstill of traffic. Everything depended on the dawn road reconnaissance and a clearway for Royal Engineers' vehicles.

The Imjin River was itself a constant source of danger. Enemy agents and infiltrators could float down in rubber boats, to prevent which bridge TPs had to keep constant watch and patrol the base of bridges to prevent sabotage. In winter the Royal Engineers had to blow up the ice to prevent crossings.

In Korea all provost duties were operational and in direct support of war and Commonwealth provost with American and South Korean Military Police combined to keep the Peace. In Japan, where was located HQ BCFK and BCOF with their major staffs and services, provost was in a different position.

Kure was the Base and gateway to the L of C, Hiroshima and Tokyo were leave and rest centres. The rôle here was, therefore, a blend of Base area and garrison duties. This rôle was a difficult one for provost who, as has already been told, through sheer necessity became involved in the political aftermath of the Second World War brought about by the ratification of the Japanese Peace Treaty in April, 1952, which left them in the position of carrying out police duties without authority in a land that accorded them no status.

The fighting ended by an armistice agreement signed by the C-in-C United Nations Forces and by the North Korean army and Chinese People's 'Volunteers' on 27 July, 1953. Thereafter duties reverted to those of a garrison nature in Korea as well as in Japan for a further three years and the RMP contingent, having gradually shrunk in size was finally withdrawn in September, 1956.

BRITISH COMMONWEALTH INTEGRATED PROVOST COMPANIES

One of the outstanding features of the Korean campaign was integration. The campaign itself was the first major United Nations resort to force with the United States playing the major rôle, but contingents of many other countries made their contribution. Within this overall framework were strong elements from the United Kingdom and other Commonwealth countries which were to become welded into the 1st Commonwealth Division as an integrated field-force. It can be fairly said that integration in its fullest achievement was attained in 1st Commonwealth Division Provost Company, comprised of United Kingdom, Canadian and Australian elements and in its sister unit British Commonwealth Base Provost Company, which had also a New Zealand component. The division provost company was a fully-operational unit in the Korean battle area, while British Commonwealth Base Provost Company with its HQ in Kure, Japan, had detachments as already described in both Japan and Korea.

The division company, being operational, probably called for the most closely-knit co-operation where failure could spell disaster and, therefore with the trend towards integrated allied armies in the future, the experience should be recorded.

The company was slightly larger than the then War Establishment of a division provost company.

The DAPM at division HQ was British at the time of this record though, as with the company appointments, future postings did not necessarily follow a national pattern, though the balance of rank structure pro-rata to the overall company size was maintained.

The officer commanding, a major, was Canadian and commanding officer Canadian Element. The second-in-command, a captain, was British and officer commanding the United Kingdom Element. An Australian lieutenant was officer-in-command Australian Element and appointed operations officer. A British lieutenant was MT officer (MTO) and a Canadian second-lieutenant appointed staff-lieutenant.

The United Kingdom Element included the Railway section, HQ section and five sections, a total of 107 all ranks. The Canadian HQ section and two sections totalled forty-three and the Australian section totalled twenty. Attached were a United Kingdom SIB detachment and also an American 'Prisoner of War Interrogation Team' of a captain and six interpreters. Also attached were eight Korean security police and twenty Korean interpreters and employed civilians.

The unit, therefore, brought integration to a peak of fulfilment and quickly developed a strong *esprit de corps*. All operational matters were dealt with by the officer appointed to the relevant function; thus the operations officer was responsible for liaison with 'G' staff, attended all operational briefings and detailed and supervised operational duties. A major difficulty which called for much patience and perseverance was the tendency of staff officers and unit adjutants requiring provost assistance to make direct telephone calls or visits to the officer of their own nationality, but eventually integration was accepted from without the company as well as from within and the division recognized its one Commonwealth provost company.

In normal police duties such as road patrols, traffic checks and vice raids, all ranks were detailed for duty without regard to nationality or to personnel with whom they might be called upon to deal but, nevertheless, certain disciplinary matters were obviously better handled by policemen of the defaulters' own nationality and, if it were not inconvenient to so arrange matters, this was done, though mixed patrols usually provided a standing answer.

With the possibility of inter-allied concerted action becoming ever more likely it may be appropriate to quote the following extracts from the unit's Standing Orders:

'1 Comwell Div Pro Coy is the only integrated unit of its kind in the Allied Forces. Coming, as we do, from all parts of the Commonwealth and springing from various nationalistic strains of which we are all proud, it is very imperative that our first loyalty be to the Unit and that in all dealings we consider our fellow soldiers' viewpoint which through heredity, environment and national pride may be different from our own. Strictly nationalistic problems within the Unit will be dealt with by an officer of that Commonwealth. All officers have the right of direct access to their immediate superior of the Commonwealth concerned but will inform the officer commanding before this right is exercised. All men/other ranks have the right of direct access to their own Commonwealth officer but will observe the normal chain of command through their Section NCO and RSM. To facilitate the handling of troops, MPs will, when possible, deal with troops of their own nationality. However, any breach of Military regulations by any member of the Allied Forces will be dealt with by the MP most readily available. All ranks must know their own Service Law and should be familiar with the differences within the Commonwealth. Reference documents are:

(a) The Army Act (Sections 4–41 and 74)
(b) The National Defence Act (Code of Service Discipline)
(c) The Australian Army Act (Sections 4–41)'

One War Diary was prepared and copies sent to the War Office, UK, the Department of National Defence, Canada, and Army Headquarters, Australia. Separate individual monthly reports were, in addition, submitted through the usual channels to London, Ottawa and Melbourne for the information of the respective Provost Marshals.

On the administrative side, however, there were complications leaving many difficulties to overcome and problems unsolved, albeit met with much inconvenience. The main burden fell on the Quartermaster who was called upon to supervise three separate stores but with jurisdiction limited to his own. He was responsible for the custody and maintenance of all stores and equipment but not for the receipt and issue of two-thirds of them. This problem reached its peak in rations and amenities. For example: a free issue of Canadian beer was for Canadian consumption only. This meant a typical Canadian party could not be held in the canteen but was confined to the Canadian Section tent. The problem was insoluble because an issue of beer for one-third of the personnel could not be distributed to the whole.

In a similar way clothing, equipment and other non-standardized items presented their problems, as also did rations. At the simplest, rations presented an undue strain on unit transport called upon to make daily runs to three separate supply points. On the other hand, given resourceful cooks and a refrigerator, an advantage could be derived from this, the solution being to save Monday's Canadian turkey to match up with Tuesday's Australian chicken and serve on Wednesday with the British steak issue. What other unit on active service could have a menu offering a choice of turkey, chicken or steak!

Complete integration was achieved in the Orderly Room under the Chief Clerk. All clerks dealt with the various forms and returns, understood the differences in staff duties and conduct of correspondence and demands of higher formations, and the Canadian filing system was adopted. Investigation, accident and offence reports were devised to meet the requirements of all nationalities and were standardized.

Transport problems were not so easily solved. Although the MTO had on his staff fitters of other nationalities than his own, the different vehicles called for three different channels of supply and repair and different maintenance schedules. Nor could transport be pooled or transferred between sections as this gave rise to the invidious position of an officer having on his charge a vehicle driven by a soldier over whom he had no power of award.

The integrated system of internal discipline worked well and it is pleasant to think that this was because the experiment was tried out in a military police unit where the incidence of minor crime such as drunkenness, absence and out-of-bounds was rare. Even so there were occasions when a harassed RSM had to prepare for three orderly room cases each to be conducted under different rules of procedure. Each case, though for the same offence, could carry widely-different punishments—each legal and adequate in so far as the individual offender was concerned but not comparable in equity to members of the same unit.

The overall conclusion of this experiment in integration was that a unit can be blended perfectly from command and operational points of view but it cannot be achieved, totally, on the administrative side without much closer standardization between the Allied forces concerned.

Nevertheless, having regard to the fact that the experiment was at unit level, it was a very successful and creditable chapter in Corps history.

CHAPTER XIV

Ulster 1969–1975

'... NEITHER can I, use whatever means I can, restrain them of their evil demeanour. Besides, serving altogether with such kind of companions I am always in danger to have my throat cut amongst them.'

So wrote Barnaby Googe, Queen Elizabeth I's Provost Marshal in Ireland in 1585. As a result he was provided with twelve horsemen to enable him to carry out his duties.

In 1971, Queen Elizabeth II's Assistant Provost Marshal in Ulster, Lieut-Colonel J. F. Thomas, wrote a similar report and as a result the first RMP Regiment was formed.

The assassin's bullet and the planted time-bomb had replaced the knife at the throat, but the 'cause' was the same—the 'troubles' intensified.

By the 1890s military police were established in the garrison towns of Belfast and Cork and at The Curragh and played their part in the post 1914–18 First World War 'troubles' until the independence of the Republic of Ireland (first known as the Irish Free State) on 15 January, 1922. During the Second World War military police were again involved, purely as a precautionary measure, with border patrols and, doubtless more hazardous, sorting out troubles between amorous members of the US Forces and local colleens.

When, in 1967, Confrontation in Borneo came to an end the British Army found itself free of active service commitments for the first time since the end of the Second World War. Young soldiers who thought there was little excitement to be found in a contracting Army with few overseas garrisons had to be constantly reminded by their elders that the only certain thing about the future was its uncertainty. Few would have imagined that within two years the Army would be acting in aid of the civil power within the United Kingdom to deal with sectarian violence and terrorism unparalleled in our recent history.

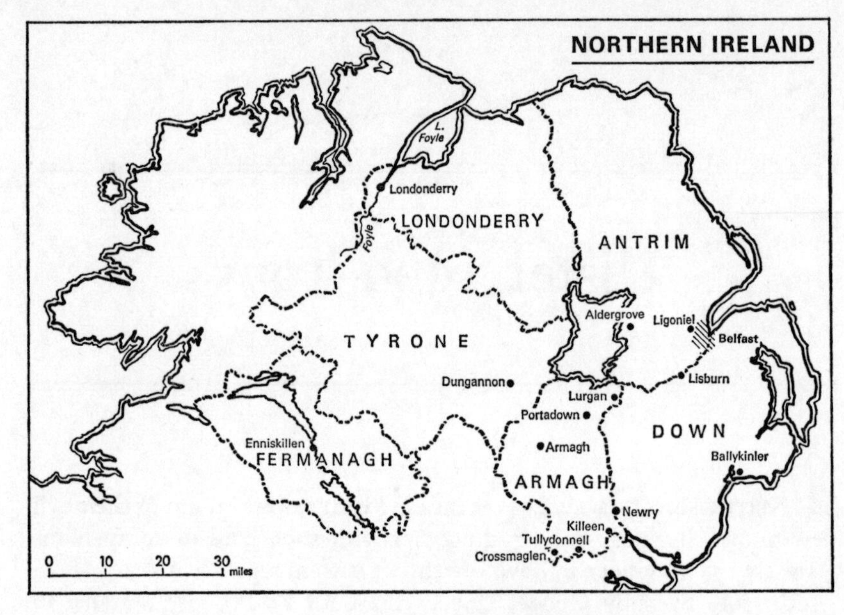

At the height of the campaign the strength of the Regular Army in Northern Ireland reached 22,000 and the RMP contribution grew steadily from a small company of two officers and twenty-nine NCOs in 1969, to two regiments of thirty-five officers and more than 900 soldiers in 1975. The many officers and men of the Corps who saw service in Northern Ireland at this time were to earn more honours and awards than in any other campaign outside the two World Wars. They ranged from a DSO, DCM and four MMs to a long list of Mentions in Despatches as listed in Appendix V.

With its excellent facilities for sport and recreation Northern Ireland was regarded by soldiers as a haven for quiet relaxation after tours of active, and often dangerous, post-war policing in the Near or Far East, and as a welcome break from the pressures of BAOR. Increasing militancy by the Northern Ireland Civil Rights Association in 1968 had little effect on the military community and when Protestant extremists organized counter-rallies and marches which finally led to the violent clash at Burntollet Bridge in January, 1969, soldiers and their families were simply told to avoid getting involved.

Through the spring and early summer violence increased with explosive attacks on public utilities and rioting spread from Londonderry to Belfast. By 14 July, 1969, rioting had become a nightly occurrence and troops were stood-to and moved to the riot areas.

In early August clashes between rival marchers placed so great a strain on the already hard-pressed Royal Ulster Constabulary (RUC) that the Ulster Special Constabulary (the 'B' Specials) had to be called out. Their use in Belfast on 14 August brought the rioting to a climax when Protestant extremists launched repeated attacks on Catholic communities during the night, driving hundreds from their homes.

At this point the RUC could no longer cope with the situation and troops were rushed to the Province to support them. The Hunt Report caused the 'B' Specials to be disbanded, the RUC to be disarmed, put into new dress and to lose their tradition and titles. Troops appeared on the streets in strength. The raising of an Ulster Defence Regiment was announced. Hastily-constructed street barricades that stretched across Belfast between the two rival communities were replaced by the Army with a more substantial Peace Line.

The only RMP unit in Ulster at this time was 173 Provost Company which consisted of two officers, Major J. F. Lindsay and Captain S. G. Edwards, WO2 P. Price, and twenty-eight NCOs organized in three large sections. The company commander held the dual appointment of DAPM HQ Northern Ireland and the company was located near the HQ in Thiepval Barracks, Lisburn, just south of Belfast.

In the weeks that followed the August riots military policemen were in great demand for a variety of tasks, some military and some to relieve the hard-pressed RUC. These included escorts for VIPs, ammunition, Army mail, ambulances and stores, as well as traffic control and many other police duties. The professionalism and impartiality of the 'Red-caps' were quickly appreciated by both sides and when hostile Catholic crowds forced the RUC to abandon traffic points on the Falls and Grosvenor Roads, and Townsend and Divis Streets, their place was taken by unarmed RMP NCOs.

The investigation for the RUC by SIB alone of shop breaking in the 'No-go-land' of the Catholic Falls Road increased this trust and on 9 September the Public Protection Authority was set up for a short time. This small body staffed by RUC, RMP, and WRAC Provost under Captain A. I Purton, WRAC Provost, was based on the RUC police stations at Strandtown, Andersonstown, Springfield Road and Hastings Street with the task of investigating complaints of intimidation.

The need for reinforcement was soon apparent. Sergeant House and six NCOs from 3rd Division Provost Unit were hurriedly flown-in, followed in Londonderry by 24th Infantry Brigade Provost Unit commanded by Captain J. K. Bonell. This unit was strengthened by the temporary attachment of soldiers from the Grenadier Guards, the Queen's Regiment and the Gloucestershire Regiment. RMP posts were established in Belfast at Hastings Street, Springfield Road and Andersonstown and on the edge of the Bogside in Londonderry.

RMP officers and NCOs attended courses of instruction in Northern

Ireland Law and RUC Police Procedures at the RUC Training Depot at Enniskillen in order to be able to give more knowledgeable support to the RUC. At the beginning of October the Director of Operations gave the order that RMP were 'to be used in a civil police rôle to protect life and property, to prevent and detect offences and to preserve public order' and the power of constable was confirmed for most offences except traffic.

On 8th October unarmed RMP foot patrols entered the Catholic 'No-go-land' area of the Falls Road in Belfast: the first uniform police to be seen in this area since the riots in August. On the same day in Londonderry Captain Bonell and Sergeant Swaby went into the Bogside to investigate the accidental death of a drunk. They were the first two representatives of law and order to enter the area since August, and the first to be received without violence for many months. Both events received considerable Press and TV coverage.

A few days later in Belfast when crowds from the Shankill Road marched on the Catholic Unity Flats the Army used CS gas for the first time and sniping broke out. A policeman and two civilians were killed in the exchange of fire that followed, but after this incident Northern Ireland became comparatively quiet again.

The Lord Mayor of Belfast asked for more military policemen for traffic duties, and they were provided.

In January, 1970, 24th Infantry Brigade Provost Unit was replaced by 5th Infantry Brigade Provost Unit, commanded by Captain J. P. Curtin. Soon afterwards Major R. W. T. Love took over from Major Lindsay as OC and DAPM. Before these new arrivals had time to settle in the bombing started again, but now it was aimed at public and private property without regard for the consequences. It added a new dimension to the violence on the streets and though a reward of £5,000, later increased by stages to £50,000, was offered for information leading to the arrest of those responsible, the number and magnitude of incidents continued to increase. The blue flashing light and Martin horn, used extensively by RMP in BAOR, was first used in Ulster by an RMP patrol called to the scene of the explosion that destroyed the statue of the Reverend Hugh Hanna that stood in the centre of Carlisle Circus.

The opening of the marching season in Northern Ireland is heralded by the Easter marches. The Catholics celebrate the Easter Uprising of 1916 and the Protestants follow defiantly with the outing of the Junior Orange Order. On 30 March troops deployed to protect the marching Orange Lodges had their first confrontation with rioting crowds. By the end of the holiday thirty-five soldiers and civil police and forty rioters had been injured, and thirty arrests had been made. On 1 April it was announced that more troops were to be sent to the Province, the

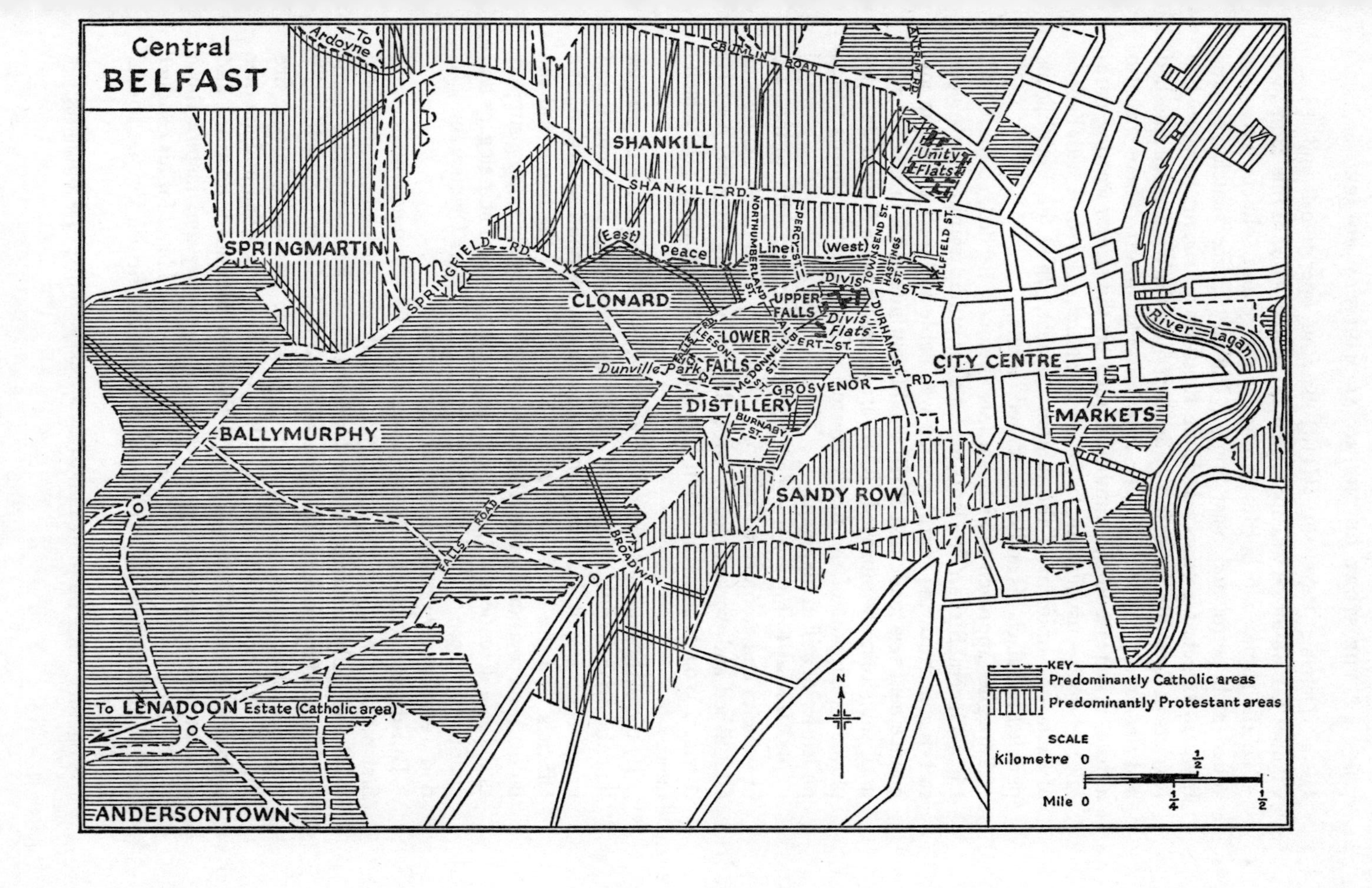
Central
BELFAST
To Ardoyne
CRUMLIN ROAD
ANTRIM RD.
SHANKILL
SHANKILL RD.
Unity Flats
SPRINGMARTIN
SPRINGFIELD RD.
(East) Peace Line (West)
NORTHUMBERLAND ST.
PERCY ST.
TOWNSEND ST.
HASTINGS ST.
MILLFIELD ST.
CLONARD
DIVIS ST.
UPPER FALLS
Divis Flats
LOWER FALLS
ALBERT ST.
DURHAM ST.
LEESON ST.
McDONNELL ST.
Dunville Park
GROSVENOR RD.
DISTILLERY
BURNABY ST.
CITY CENTRE
River Lagan
MARKETS
BALLYMURPHY
SANDY ROW
FALLS ROAD
BROADWAY
To LENADOON Estate (Catholic area)
ANDERSONTOWN
N
KEY
Predominantly Catholic areas
Predominantly Protestant areas
SCALE
Kilometre 0 ½
Mile 0 ¼ ½

Ulster Defence Regiment (UDR) became operational and Lieut-Colonel J. F. Thomas was appointed as the first APM of this campaign.

To the stones and bottles thrown at police and soldiers were now added nail, petrol and blast bombs. Military police vehicles became frequent targets for attacks and one Land-Rover caught between two barriers in Rossville Street in Londonderry had the windscreen smashed and the canopy ripped off. The crew escaped unhurt. There was also a marked increase in the number of men on the streets wearing para-military dress—usually sunglasses, green anoraks and some with badges of rank—the uniform of the militant loyalist, while the Republicans paraded in balaclavas and camouflaged jackets.

A tougher approach to violence was obviously needed, so the GOC, Lieut-General Sir Ian Freeland, gave a clear public warning that anyone carrying or throwing petrol bombs was liable to be shot, and an announcement was made that RMP would continue to act in a police rôle until the situation improved. RMP arrest teams were formed and deployed in support of the newly created infantry snatch squads which pulled in identified hooligans.

173 Provost Company was now six platoons strong with an increase in vehicles and commercial radios. A Company Operations Centre was established and worked closely with HQ 39 Infantry Brigade. An SIB Adviser, Wo 1 Wood, arrived in July to head the growing SIB detachment.

By the early summer it was obvious to even the most sincere optimist that the Irish Republican Army (IRA) had recovered its strength and in spite of a split between those who favoured political action, the Officials, and the break-away group who preferred the bomb and the bullet, the Provisionals, the IRA movement was rapidly gaining support as the sole defenders of the 'Green' (Catholic) areas. Their slogans and graffiti, and those of their Protestant rivals, the Ulster Defence Association were on every street corner and gable wall.

During the week-end 28–29 June, 1970, IRA gunmen made their first major attacks on the security forces in the Ardoyne, Springfield Road and Ballymacarrett. Lance-Corporal G. V. Eastham was a member of a military police patrol ordered into the Ardoyne area to identify and if possible arrest the gunmen. Though he was under intense fire throughout the evening and a civilian near him was killed and another seriously wounded Lance-Corporal Eastham continued, unarmed and without protective clothing, to carry out his duty and inspire those about him. He was only eighteen and a half years old and for his conduct on this and other occasions he was awarded the British Empire Medal for Gallantry.

Together with the now almost customary rioting and bombing the

42 Major R. S. Warman (DAPM BRITCOM S.I. Section) Korea, 1951.

43 Major-General A. J. H. Cassels (first GOC 1st British Commonwealth Division in Korea) being met at Taegu Airfield by Major R. Davenport APM (left) and Major R. I. Luker (right) in July, 1951.

44 Mr Winston Churchill leaves SHAPE HQ with General Dwight D. Eisenhower, Supreme Allied Commander Europe, on 18 December, 1951, and receives a salute from an RMP NCO.

45 Field-Marshal Montgomery, Deputy Supreme Allied Commander Europe, with his RMP escort in 1956.

46 Lance-Corporal Keeling of 227 Provost Company RMP assists a Turkish Cypriot policeman to safety during a riot in Nicosia in December, 1957. For his actions Lance-Corporal Keeling was mentioned in despatches.

47 Two RMP NCOs in Famagusta during 1958 wearing the new Bullet Proof Vests. They were very hot in summer and weighed about 25 lbs. They consisted of sheets of nylon enclosed in a cloth case and provided absolute protection against bomb splinters at 15 yards. ·38" bullets bounced off them and 9 mm Browning bullets ruptured the nylon but did not penetrate.

48 247 Provost Company RMP escort vehicles before the Soviet War Memorial in Berlin, 1956 with the ruins of the Reichstag behind.

49 HM Queen Elizabeth II with HRH The Duke of Edinburgh reviewing troops in the Olympic Stadium in Berlin on 2 June, 1965. Corporal K. Webber, 247 (Berlin) Provost Company, is behind the wheel.

50 Corporal R. Slack RMP assists an injured ammunition expert following a bomb explosion in Kowloon in February, 1968.
51 RMP go back into the 'Green Area' of Londonderry. Corporals Fuller RMP and Jubb RAFP on foot patrol in the Rosemount area in 1974.

52 Dog Handlers Lance-Corporal Harkabahadur Sunwar and Lance-Corporal Manbir Sunwar (Gurkha Military Police) guarding persons involved in the Brunei Insurrection—December, 1962.

53 Sergeant N. Smith BEM RMP separating rioters in the Shankhill Road, Belfast, Summer, 1970. He was subsequently awarded the Military Medal for his bravery.

54 Lt-Colonel B. A. Gait DSO DCM RMP who was awarded the DSO in 1975 for services while commanding the 2nd Regiment RMP in Northern Ireland. This was the first DSO to be won by an RMP officer.

55 Sergeant D. G. Nicklen RMP of 180 Provo Company 2nd Regiment RMP, going on duty at Blairs Yard in Belfast in 1976.

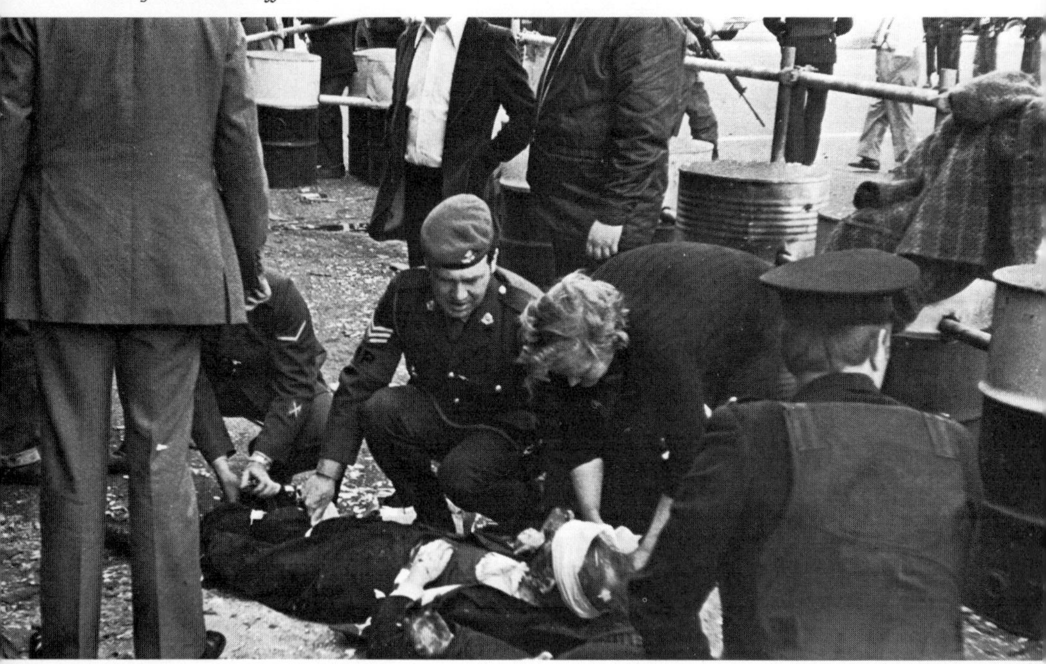

56 A proxy bomb—7.11 pm, 16 July, 1974 at the Sunflower Bar, Corporation St, Belfast. Sergeant Harries, wearing the recently issued scarlet beret, gives first aid to the injured.

week-end toll of death and destruction was five dead, 200 injured, and damage to homes, public houses and business property totalling over £1 million. For their restraint in not returning fire across the densely populated interface in Ballymacarrett the Army received nothing but abuse from both sides. Four days later a successful Army arms search sparked off three days of unprecedented violence in which five civilians died, eighteen soldiers were admitted to hospital with gunshot wounds and 300 people were arrested. The Army clamped down on the area for the next few days and the searching went on. In spite of the rioting over 100 weapons were recovered.

It was during this rioting that Staff Sergeant T. Watt became the first RMP casualty of the campaign when he was hit on the head by a bottle and had six stitches in the wound. The incident occurred at the junction of Roden Street and Grosvenor Road in the Lower Falls area while he was supporting snatch squads of 1st Battalion, The Royal Scots, who presented 173 Provost Company with a commemorative cartoon.

The immediate consequence of these terrible riots and the well-planned attacks on soldiers' lives was the arming of military policemen for their own protection and the issue of toughened plastic windscreens and body panels for Land-Rovers to give protection against the frequent and varied types of missile hurled at military vehicles. These missiles, and shouting abuse and obscenities at the security forces, had become a favourite pastime for young and old alike in many urban areas. Soldiers showed remarkable restraint in the face of this hostility. Their humour never flagged and ditties such as 'Throw well—throw Shell' or 'What's blue and white and burns all right? An Ulsterbus', and endless jokes about the Irish, were frequently heard.

While RMP continued to take on additional tasks concerned with crowd control, it was the Special Powers Act and associated legislation that led to an increased involvement of the Corps in maintaining law and order. The arrest of law breakers, the collection and collation of evidence from soldiers making arrests, the appearance in court of soldier witnesses and their prior briefing on court procedures, soon became regarded as specialized RMP functions. The investigation of complaints made against the Army, and the provision of permanent escorts and bodyguards for VIPs were other tasks given to RMP at this time and these were to grow in importance and frequency.

An RMP Operations Centre was opened in Glenravel Police Station to control more efficiently the many RMP elements now operating in Belfast. In September a joint force of military police and the RUC's Special Patrol Group operated from this centre to prevent rioting on the Shankhill Road between Protestant supporters of Linfield Football Club and the Catholic tenants of Unity Flats. During the fighting that inevitably broke out two Royal Marine Commandos were separated from their patrol and one had his rifle snatched from him. He would almost certainly have been beaten to death by a large mob had not RSM R. H. Poole gone to his rescue. For this act of courage RSM Poole was awarded the MBE for Gallantry. On 16 October the hub of RMP activity in the city was moved to Ardmillan House in Fortwilliam. This large Edwardian house, once a Dr Barnardo's Home, had the space and facilities to accommodate a company group and was to be an RMP base for more than four years.

Londonderry, its majority Catholic population well separated from Protestant Waterside by the River Foyle, enjoyed a slightly more peaceful summer and on 24 July the RUC started to patrol the Bogside again.

On the night of 27 June Corporal J. H. Baseley was in charge of an unarmed patrol in the neighbouring Creggan area when he came upon a crowd surrounding a house on fire. Nobody was attempting to enter the house and on learning that there were people still inside Corporal Baseley doused himself with water and tried to go in the front door. When flames and smoke beat him back he tried again to enter by a bedroom window but an explosion in the house threw him to the ground. Even though his clothes were almost destroyed he draped himself with a wet blanket and got into the house where firemen found him when they arrived. Although in vain, his actions were an example of selfless courage for which he was awarded the British Empire Medal for Gallantry. Yet on 1 October an RMP Land-Rover patrolling from the re-located police post at Bligh's Lane in the Creggan was the target of the first explosive device used against the military in Londonderry when a tin-tack bomb landed only ten yards from the vehicle. Fortunately, neither crew nor vehicle were damaged.

In July HQ 8th Infantry Brigade became the permanent formation responsible for Londonderry City and the north of the Province and asked that their detachment should be re-named 8th Infantry Brigade Provost Detachment, 173 Provost Company, and so it became.

The total strength of the company was now well over 100 and was made up of NCOs from twelve different units. It included eight WRAC Provost girls, and Corporal Ellway made their presence felt when she found three pistols in the clothing of a woman she was searching in Belfast.

A six-month ban on all marches imposed on 23 August undoubtedly contributed to a noticeable lessening of tension and marked reduction in the level of violence. Through the autumn into winter the rival factions attended to their wounds and damaged property, and the Security Forces strengthened and improved the Peace Line and bricked-up hastily abandoned houses. The IRA also took full advantage of the lull to re-group and re-train.

There was little respite for RMP however, and patrols were now deployed into the southern parts of the Province to block roads and search vehicles, including buses, in an effort to stop weapons and explosives reaching the terrorists. More new skills were thus added to the military policeman's rapidly expanding tasks.

Three more platoons arrived in January, 1971, from 3 Division Provost Unit and a few weeks later two more came from England and BAOR. In the subsequent re-organization WO1 Poole moved up, on commissioning, to be company second-in-command and Major B. A. Gait became DAPM.

These were timely reinforcements for on 3 February, once again following a search, this time in the Clonard in Belfast, rioting broke out and there followed a week-long orgy of street battles, bombing, shooting and burning throughout Belfast and in several border towns. Londonderry however remained relatively quiet.

On 6 February the first soldier was shot dead.

Over the next few days bombers struck at the Customs Posts in Newry, Killeen and Tullydonnell. There were nine explosions in Newry alone, but the climax to this spreading campaign of terror came on 9 February when five civilians were killed by a booby trap meant for the Army. The device was a 15 lb mine operated by trip wire laid on a track that led to the Brougher Mountain BBC transmitter in County Fermanagh.

On the night of 28 February the Corps suffered its first fatal casualty from terrorist activity when Lance-Corporal W. G. Jolliffe was killed in Londonderry. He was one of the emergency tour reinforcements from 3 Division Provost Company and died as a result of a petrol bomb attack on his Land-Rover whilst on patrol in the city. Corporal Liddle, the commander of this patrol, chased and caught one of the attackers although he was subjected to a constant barrage of missiles. Many from the Bogside and Creggan communities called on the unit, personally or by telephone, to express sympathy and horror at this tragedy.

Technology translated rapidly into practical equipment was a feature of this campaign, but because of the original concept of military police operations and their customary supporting rôle, RMP were seldom the first to receive new equipment. By March, 1971, however, every officer and NCO was equipped with a steel helmet with visor, a short or long riot shield, and body armour or flak jacket, as it became known. The visor and shields were made from Makrilon, an extremely tough clear plastic, a product of space technology, which was also fashioned into protective plates for vehicles. Twenty-four pieces made a Land-Rover proof against most hand-thrown missiles. The Land-Rovers had military police plates, blue lights, roof-mounted twin spotlights, a wire-cutting metal upright bolted to the side and wire mesh protection on all the windows. These vehicles were formidable weapons and a threat to use them to disperse rioters was a successful tactic employed on several occasions. Later RMP received their first issue of riot guns and rubber bullets although a number of NCOs had used this weapon earlier when dealing with dangerous mobs.

During spring and early summer of 1971 the IRA gave remarkable proof of their daring and their callous disregard for human life. On the night of 11 March three young Royal Highland Fusiliers were lured to a quiet country lane near Ligoniel on the outskirts of Belfast and murdered. When it was revealed that one of them was only seventeen years of age, public concern led to a decision that soldiers under eighteen years of age should not serve in Northern Ireland and as a result several military policemen were returned to their units in England and BAOR.

SIB took the lead in the investigation into this triple murder, Sergeant D. J. Harmon in particular showing great determination and courage in the way in which he conducted his inquiries in extremely hostile areas. This was typical of his conduct in many other investigations into terrorist activities. His determination and skill, often in the face of hostile crowds and sniper fire, resulted in many criminals being successfully prosecuted, and for his work as an investigator he was awarded the Distinguished Conduct Medal, the first awarded to a member of the Corps since the Second World War.

In June, IRA men posing as doctors removed one of their wounded from the Royal Victoria Hospital in Belfast. The Army took immediate steps to ensure the security of wounded soldiers in civilian hospitals, and at the Altnagelvin Hospital in Londonderry this became a RMP responsibility.

By the end of July it was clear that the Province was rapidly moving towards a total collapse of law and order, and the statistics of violence were evidence of this. Since the beginning of the year thirteen soldiers, two policemen and sixteen civilians had been killed. In July, 194 rounds of ammunition had been fired at the Army and this figure was to be exceeded in the first ten days of August. One hundred people had been injured in the 311 explosions that had torn through towns and cities across the Province. Intimidation, hatred and fear were commonplace and terrorists operated in urban and rural areas almost with impunity.

On 12 July, the Battle of the Boyne celebrations, Major B. A. Gait took over command of the company from Major M. H. Rose and very soon after found himself with both the APM and WO 1 Wood SIB in the thick of a religious confrontation on the Newtownards Road in east Belfast. During the stoning and petrol bombing that raged over arrests that had been made from both sides, Major Gait's boots were set alight by a petrol bomb. He was not injured but his brown Bunting boots, a much disliked and compulsory item of dress worn by RMP officers at the time, were ruined.

On 9 August Mr Brian Faulkner, who in March had succeeded Major James Chichester-Clark as the Northern Ireland Prime Minister, announced the re-introduction of internment. The round-up by the Army of known IRA men started early when Operation 'Demetrius' was launched to arrest several hundred men. Many military police platoons were deployed for the next forty-eight hours to assist the RUC.

The anticipated reaction to internment was swift and fierce. Starting with the banging of dustbin lids as an alarm signal in the 'Green' areas it quickly developed into violence in all its customary forms. In the next two days fourteen civilians and five soldiers were killed. Roman Catholics fled south to refugee camps and many Protestants had to flee from their homes.

A ban on all parades was announced on 9 August and though it came late in the marching season it reduced the number of clashes between rival factions. But the IRA, strengthened by a new wave of support among Catholics after the martyrdom of internment, continued their fight with more sophisticated weapons. Bomb attacks in urban and rural areas went on against Customs Houses, police stations and commercial targets and sniping against security forces patrols was stepped-up.

The vulnerability of small RMP patrols to this type of attack was clearly shown in the bomb attack on a mobile patrol, Corporals Ambrose and Spiers and Lance-Corporal Smith, at the junction of the Antrim and New Lodge Roads. None of them was injured but their vehicle was destroyed. A claymore mine ambush of a RMP double patrol led by Staff-Sergeant Love and Sergeant Mills, again miraculously without casualties, was evidence of the variety of weapons available to the terrorists. An isolated attack near the Border when terrorists used a rocket-launcher gave further and ominous proof of the extent of their armoury.

The military response was to increase Border surveillance and to start cratering unapproved crossings. There was a requirement therefore for more troops and three more infantry battalions were ordered to Ulster, bringing the total Army strength to 13,600 soldiers.

The increase in RMP strength was no less dramatic and on 5 November, 1971, the First Regiment of the Corps of Royal Military Police was formed. The first Commanding Officer was Lieut-Colonel J. F. Thomas and 1st Regiment was deployed as follows:

Sub unit	*Location*	*Rôle*
Regimental Headquarters	Lisburn	
174 Provost Company (HQ and three platoons)	Lisburn	OC Lieut J. B. Taylor, who was Police LO to 19 Airportable Brigade. Man PHC Gough Barracks, Armagh. Arrests and Finds.
175 Provost Company (HQ and three platoons)	Lisburn	OC Captain F. W. Chipperfield. Arrests and Finds Teams. Patrol Belfast.
176 Provost Company (HQ and three platoons)	Londonderry	OC Captain R. J. Tilston. Patrolling Creggan and Bogside. Manning Police Post at Bligh's Lane.
177 Provost Company (HQ and three platoons)	Lisburn	OC Captain B. Wood. VIP Escort two platoons. Lisburn Garrison duties—one platoon. Arrest and complaints section. Crime Detachment SIB.

Had the Regiment formed earlier in the year it might well have incorporated in its establishment the section of the RMP Mounted Troop that was sent to Ulster to provide a colourful escort to the Governor for the State Opening of the Stormont Parliament. Before Sergeant Blackley returned to England the detachment saw active service in rural areas checking remote radio installations. These were the first mounted patrols in Northern Ireland for twenty-five years.

Throughout 1971 the Corps in Ulster had been establishing a reputation for efficiency in the face of overwhelming pressure. The paperwork involved in the documentation of 4,000 arrests made by soldiers, and 760 complaints made against the same peacekeepers, was an indication of but two aspects of their work. Yet more was being demanded. Because one of the fundamental skills of a military policeman is to report accurately and concisely, RMP were quickly required to report from the scene of every explosion. Military policemen had now become key figures in every arrest, find, shooting and bombing incident.

1972 started, as had 1970 and 1971, with yet another increase in RMP strength. 179 Provost Company was added to the establishment of the 1st Regiment on 17 January to give direct support to the hard-pressed RUC Divisions in Belfast. The first company commander was Major A. N. Lane of 160 Provost Company, Aldershot. His CSM was WO2 W. G. D. Woodiwiss of 16th Parachute Brigade Provost Unit and the great majority of the NCOs were also on emergency tours from units in England, Scotland and BAOR. HMS *Hartland Point*, moored in Belfast Lough, provided the first cramped home for this company. They were equipped with the first issue of BLMC 1800 saloon cars and these were to figure prominently in future operations.

Violence continued unabated throughout the Province and during the first three months of the year elements of 1st Regiment were employed in Enniskillen, Newry, Armagh and Dungannon. But it was Londonderry that captured the news headlines with Bloody Sunday on 30 January. The recently formed 178 Provost Company (Investigations) played a large part in establishing the facts of this incident. Within hours 150 statements had been recorded from officers and soldiers involved. Counsel for the Army at the subsequent Tribunal, headed by Lord Widgery and appointed to inquire into the incident, concluded that the assistance given by Major J. F. Smith, the DAPM (Liaison), and his team in preparing the Army's case was a major factor in establishing the credibility of the Army's version of the incident.

Then came the first of the much-publicized Provisional IRA Ceasefires. It was only for seventy-two hours and was but a demonstration of disciplined strength in the period leading up to an expected political initiative from Westminster. It ended with a wave of bomb attacks throughout Belfast and Londonderry. On the day after it ended three military policemen were wounded when a car bomb exploded in Lisburn as they were evacuating the surrounding area. Fortunately none of them (Corporal R. Long, Corporal P. Richards and Lance-Corporal G. Smith) was very seriously hurt but they were disappointed to learn that all shrapnel removed by surgeons in this type of campaign is retained for forensic analysis and cannot be kept as souvenirs! The initiative came on 24 March but in an unexpected form—Direct Rule from Westminster. Mr William Whitelaw was appointed to the new and powerful post of Secretary of State for Northern Ireland.

For the next few months serious incidents of every kind became a daily occurrence until on 26 June another Ceasefire was announced. It lasted until 13 July and, though it was far from free of incidents, it did permit RMP patrols to be resumed in many 'Green' areas for the first time as a regular routine since August, 1971. Nevertheless, the existence of 'No-go' areas continued to attract great publicity and criticism.

During this comparatively quiet period the APM's post was upgraded to DPM and Commander Royal Military Police and separated from the CO's post. On 8 July Colonel R. J. Sherville took over this appointment from Lieut-Colonel J. F. Thomas and on 25 July Lieut-Colonel D. A. M. Phipps took over as CO 1st Regiment. A few days later Major T. M. Plewman took over as DAPM (Ops).

Once again the end of the Ceasefire was signalled by an upsurge of violence that reached a climax on 21 July when in one terrible hour nineteen explosions erupted all over Belfast. Nine people died, seventy-seven women and girls and fifty-three men and boys were injured, many maimed for life. This day became known as Bloody Friday.

In July, 1972, there were 104 deaths and 560 people were injured. There were 2,778 shooting incidents. This substantial escalation of terrorism led to an increasing intensity in security forces activity which culminated in the biggest military operation by the British Army since Suez—Operation 'Motorman'. The aim of this operation was to open all 'No-go' areas. Four platoons and six SIB investigators came from Great Britain and BAOR on 26 July to reinforce 1st Regiment. A new company was formed—180 Provost Company—led by Captain I. W. Fulton. When the operation, called 'Carcan' in Londonderry, was launched at 4 am on 31 July the Regiment deployed twenty Arrest and Finds teams and twenty Investigation teams in addition to normal routine duties, and the establishment of a major vehicle check point (VCP) on the motorway leading to Belfast.

Opposition to this enormous display of strength was minimal and by midday the Army had entered and secured even the hardest areas of the Creggan, Bogside, Andersonstown and Ballymurphy. Behind the infantry, often to their surprise, came military policemen in service dress and best red caps. They were met with violence in some areas. A beer barrel was hurled through the windscreen of one RMP vehicle but 'No-go' areas were never to be tolerated again. Thirty arrests were made, and thirty-two weapons with ammunition and 500 lbs of explosives were found in follow-up operations.

Early in 1972 it was realized that the IRA were making explosives from fertilizer (ammonium nitrate) and fuel oil with the nickname ANFO. Less powerful, pound for pound, than commercial explosive it was usually used in car bombs. This type of bomb was to be used by the IRA frequently in the next two years. At the other end of the scale there was an equally significant development in incendiary devices, often extremely simple in construction, and one of these devices placed near a fuel storage tank in the Co-operative store in York Street, Belfast, was responsible for the total destruction of the store.

To counter these increasingly destructive attacks parking restrictions were introduced in cities, towns and villages throughout the Province. Planned and random vehicle checks were made with much greater frequency. In September a start was made on fencing-off parts of Belfast city centre so that every person and vehicle entering these segments, as they were called, could be thoroughly searched. All these measures demanded increased effort and vigilance by the security forces, particularly the police, and the need to search thousands of women who passed through the segment gates each day led to the raising of a new company on 1 September—181 Provost Company WRAC of 1st Regiment. By October there were forty girls, provost and general-duty searchers, in the company and a large part of the city was sealed-off in a surprising but most effective move to counter the bomber. The company grew in numbers and the segment searching extended to the city of Londonderry. It was not unusual for these WRAC girls to search a quarter of a million females in a month.

By November the effect of these and numerous other innovations in tactics and techniques was to be seen in a marked reduction in the level of violence and this lasted until the end of the year. There was an increase in apparently motiveless murders until it became evident that they were both planned and random tit-for-tat sectarian killings. To combat this particular form of violence the Secretary of State announced on 6 December the formation of a joint RMP and RUC unit to be named Task Force after a television programme of the same name. It operated in Belfast with some initial success but during the lull in sectarian murders Task Force was deployed to other duties.

Attacks on soldiers continued and the vulnerability of the wide-ranging RMP patrols was again demonstrated when a Land-Rover driven by Corporal Gregory was ambushed in the Lower Falls and peppered with twenty-three bullet holes. The other two members of the patrol, Corporal Pope and Lance-Corporal McKeown, were wounded. Corporal Pope was medically evacuated but he recovered quickly.

Crimes of violence and against property flourished during this period and NCOs providing direct support to the RUC saw a lot of them. Often they were able to prevent crimes when driving the recently-acquired BLMC saloon cars with dash and skill in high-speed 'cops and robbers' chases. One of the earliest of these incidents was the pursuit and apprehension of a much-wanted criminal by Corporal F. Hembling with Constable Church as navigator. The RUC divisional commander commended them for their action and remarked that he was 'very pleased with the very amicable relations that exist between RMP and RUC, and consider that this incident illustrates the high degree of co-operation that prevails'.

Corporal A. Brodie was involved in the arrest of ten criminals on three different occasions in a period of eight weeks. Three were carrying guns, three were in a stolen car and four were in possession of offensive weapons.

1st Regiment celebrated its first anniversary by moving from Lisburn to the newly-built Alexander Barracks at Aldergrove. The barracks were built for an unaccompanied airportable battalion and consisted of a variety of temporary buildings having an estimated life of ten years. However, it meant 1st Regiment was able to spread a little having endured the confinement of crowded Thiepval Barracks for so long.

In August a section led by Sergeant Vivian moved to Gough Barracks, Armagh, to provide RMP support to 3rd Infantry Brigade, the formation responsible for most of the Border and the southern half of the Province. This section was subsequently increased to a platoon, and was later joined by a large WRAC Provost platoon that became known as 23 WRAC Provost Platoon (Airborne) since they spent so much time travelling by helicopter in response to calls for 'coffee pots' as they were referred to on radio nets.

RMP was fortunate at this point in the campaign in having not only the support of a growing WRAC company but also the services of two Royal Marine policemen and, from 26 October, a detachment of RAF Police. This last detachment was to be built-up to forty-seven in strength and was of enormous help in the build-up to two regiments during the next two years. The co-operation and relationship between the officers and NCOs of RMP and those of the RAF Police were excellent, and when the airmen were withdrawn on 20 December, 1974, the Commander RMP issued a Special Order of the Day in appreciation of their services and presented the Provost Marshal (RAF) with a commemorative plaque with RMP shields from Northern Ireland, 1st and 2nd Regiments RMP and the Special Patrol Group of the RUC.

1972 saw a resurgence of the Ulster Defence Association to demonstrate Protestant dissatisfaction with the security forces' attitude to Catholics 'No-go' areas before Operation 'Motorman'. They were determined to build up their strength and numbers to defend their own areas if, as they believed, it should prove necessary. In November they clashed with the Life Guards in east Belfast and 1st Battalion Parachute Regiment in the Shankhill. There was talk of a Protestant backlash.

Having taken both military and political initiatives in 1972, the British Government was to spend almost the whole of 1973 putting political power back into the hands of an elected Assembly. There was a change of military leaders at the beginning of the year when Lieut-General Sir Harry Tuzo handed over to Lieut-General Sir Frank King as GOC and Major-General P. J. H. Leng relieved Major-General R. C. Ford as Commander Land Forces.

On 22 January, 1973, Task Force was expanded to Londonderry where a platoon and a half of military policemen joined with No 8 Section SPG of the RUC to form a force to operate mostly in the northern half of the Province. This force remained in existence when its

Belfast counterpart was broken-up and it has proved to be the best example of RMP and RUC co-operation. Success came quickly to this part of Task Force and in the first few months of its existence it had smashed a complete IRA unit in Strathfoyle and captured a Protestant extremist wanted for murder in the Republic of Ireland.

Early in the year a pattern began to evolve of terrorist activity shifting from the cities to the Border and back again as the IRA leadership switched their effort to escape the relentless attrition of men and material by the security forces. But bombing spectaculars and attacks on the security forces remained a constant threat everywhere.

On 3 February a major disaster was averted in Belfast when a bomb disposal officer defused a bomb fixed to a petrol tanker in the city centre of Belfast. On that night gunmen in the New Lodge engaged troops who successfully returned fire with the aid of new night-sights. After this the gunmen attacked those who were more vulnerable and in the first half of the year RMP suffered a higher casualty rate than at any other time in the campaign. 176 Provost Company bore the brunt of these attacks in Londonderry when Corporal P. R. Hill was shot in the arm when patrolling the Creggan and three months later Corporal P. Campbell was also shot and wounded while carrying out the same duty. A most cowardly attack was made only a few weeks later when Corporal J. Nylan and Corporal J. Phillips RAF Police were both shot in the back while on foot patrol in the Bogside. In Belfast Corporal Burgess was also shot in the back, and Sergeant McFadean became the first SIB casualty when he received a bad gunshot wound to the arm. All these NCOs recovered, although Corporal Nylan was subsequently discharged from the Army.

As a result of these shootings foot patrols and later the mobile patrols were discontinued in these areas, not however before an unusual idea had been tried to stop the shootings at RMP vehicles. At the suggestion of representatives of the Bogside community two RMP Land-Rovers were painted white and large military police signs were put on the sides as well as the front of the vehicles. This distinguished RMP vehicles from all others but it failed to give them total immunity. Two nights later a patrol was again fired at but in spite of this the roofs of all RMP Land Rovers in Londonderry were painted white for some years.

The Corps' only fatal casualty of the year was Sergeant S. Young, a helicopter pilot, serving with 652 Squadron on a short emergency tour. He and three of his comrades were killed in a booby trap car explosion on 17 May.

In spite of continued bombings and shootings in town and country the Government pressed ahead with political development. On 8 March the Border poll having disposed of the Border issue, proposals for a

Northern Ireland Constitution were published in a White Paper and on 28 June an election was held in the Province on the basis of proportional representation to ensure a political voice for the minority. The seventy-eight newly elected Assembly members were charged with forming a twelve-member Executive before the end of the year. Not only did polls and elections tie down large numbers of military policemen on duties aimed at preventing any interference with the electoral process but, overnight there were seventy-eight more potential targets for terrorists. In routine duties, and in the undignified scuffles that later occurred outside Stormont, military policemen came to know many politicians.

If politically Northern Ireland was taking the first faltering steps on the road back to normality, so too it was hoped were the police, supported by RMP. Commenting in June on the first six months' operation of the joint Task Force the Chief Constable of the RUC said:

> 'The Task Force has certainly achieved impressive results. It has undoubtedly strengthened the overall effort of the security forces in preventing and detecting serious crime. Its stop and search tactics have yielded a considerable arsenal of rifles, revolvers, pistols, ammunition and nearly half a ton of explosive substances in Belfast. In Londonderry, in addition to seizing a large quantity of arms Task Force members have arrested several people including one entire IRA unit. As a result of their operations several people have been charged with murder or attempted murder and with causing explosions. Six men have been charged with armed robbery, thirty-four with riotous behaviour and assault, and many others with various offences. Forty-nine stolen cars have been recovered—inquiries into one case uncovered eleven hidden cars.'

To reinforce this success a RUC CID Support Wing was formed in 178 Provost Company 1st Regiment and eleven SIB NCOs were detached to support the CID throughout the Province.

Another novel task was the searching of HM Prisons. It was performed with increased frequency during 1973 mostly at HMP Maze as the Long Kesh detention camp had been re-titled. On one occasion almost a complete regiment was committed to this task. It proved to be a sight never-to-be-forgotten for those members of the guard regiment on duty as several hundred 'Redcaps' loomed up out of the early morning mist and went by in a seemingly endless procession.

On 1 July 2nd Regiment RMP was formed. After only a year away from Northern Ireland Lieut-Colonel B. A. Gait returned as the regiment's first Commanding Officer. 2nd Regiment was formed by taking 175 and 179 Provost Companies from the now almost unwieldy 1st Regiment and adding a re-formed 180 Provost Company. There was no immediate change of rôle for the two existing companies and, as they were formed, the platoons of 180 Provost Company were deployed to RUC divisions throughout Belfast to give direct permanent support to the RUC as beat and security constables.

On 8 August yet another milestone was to be reached in the successes and progress of 1973 when the Northern Ireland (Emergency Provisions) Act became law. This much-needed legislation was the outcome of a commission headed by Lord Diplock to make the 'administration of justice more effective against terrorism'. It swept away the complex Special Powers Act and other legal confusion and gave wider powers of arrest and search to servicemen. It confirmed the powers of a constable for all service policemen and thus gave military policemen powers of arrest and search greater than ever before. As if to emphasize the need for such strong measures the IRA launched an attack two days later on the Border police post at Crossmaglen using mortars, machine-guns and rocket launchers.

Later in August Mr Edward Heath came to Ulster. He was the first Prime Minister whom 177 Provost Company was to escort during the campaign. During his brief visit he saw several units and told leading politicians that if they did not form an Executive before the end of the year Direct Rule would continue. On 21 November Mr Brian Faulkner led the new Executive to be sworn in at Stormont.

Six days later 2nd Regiment assumed operational responsibility for south and east Belfast, an enormous and largely Protestant area with Stormont in its midst. 2nd Regiment, now complete with three companies each of eight platoons, was deployed as follows:

Tactical HQ	Castlereagh RUC Station.
Ops Centre	Co-located with HQ 39th Infantry Brigade at Lisburn.
Rear HQ	Alexander Barracks, Aldergrove.
175 Provost Company	Ops base—Ardmillan House. Tasks—Arrests and Finds. Patrolling east and south Belfast. OC—Major B. A. Rawlings.
179 Provost Company	Ops base—Musgrave Park RUC Station. Tasks—Joint RMP and RUC Task Force. OC—Major J. R. Standring.
180 Provost Company	Tasks—RUC support. OC—Major J. Graham.

As 2nd Regiment settled down as the first RMP unit to be allocated a tactical area of operational responsibility the leaders of the governments of the United Kingdom, Northern Ireland and Eire met at Sunningdale. They agreed on a Council of Ireland which many Loyalists saw as extending the principle of power-sharing with other parties in

Ulster to power-sharing with the Irish Republic and this they would not accept. On 31 December Direct Rule came to an end but already Ulster's first experiment in consensus politics was doomed.

The General Election in February, 1974, sent the people of Ulster to the polls once more. They were to repeat the exercise many times over the next year and a half. 'Vote early and vote often' became a familiar joke. These polls required a major deployment of the security forces on every occasion. In Belfast 2nd Regiment had three companies of the UDR and a company from the brigade reserve battalion under command to assist in providing security for ballot boxes and polling sations in their area.

But the first crisis of 1974, and the one that provided the recently-arrived Commander RMP, Colonel M. Matthews, with a major problem was the decision of the RUC Police Federation in February to 'go slow'. This was a protest against the coming trial of one of their members before a Diplock Court. This type of Court consists of a judge sitting alone, without a jury, and was recommended by the Diplock Commission to prevent intimidation of witnesses and jury members. It is meant therefore to deal with offences connected with terrorism. The Police Federation objected to its application to police officers and demonstrated their protest by refusing to escort, interview or arrest terrorists or suspected terrorists. For three days RMP carried out these duties throughout the Province. It was an enormous commitment and one that legally could only be carried out by RMP. The greater part of it was concerned with the movement of remand prisoners from gaol to court and back and Captain L. Murray became a familiar figure in Belfast rushing groups of prisoners to and fro between the courts and Crumlin Road gaol.

Over the first few months of the year the organization and deployment of RMP continued to be studied. On 18 February the whole of 174 Provost Company moved to Portadown to provide RMP support to 3 Infantry Brigade. The platoons at Armagh rejoined the company in its Terrapin hut accommodation later in the year. At the same time two platoons from 179 Provost Company were sent to Londonderry to reinforce 176 Provost Company and this became a permanent redeployment.

On 22 April the Belfast Task Force was disbanded and 179 Provost Company now provided the new RMP Mobile Force and a large daily commitment of escorting of prisoners with the RUC. This force came under the very personal direction of the Commander Land Forces who had for a long time wanted such a highly trained and mobile force to move to any part of the Province in a variety of rôles. Brigade commanders bid for its use and for the first few months of its existence it operated in the Border areas to prevent and deter the movement of arms, explosives and wanted men into the Province. In April 2nd Regiment arrested a criminal high on the wanted list in east Belfast and found twenty-one firearms in his hiding place, one of the largest single hauls of the campaign.

The difficulties of 1st Regiment administering both itself and 2nd Regiment were by now apparent and from April to June, when Lieut-Colonel P. W. le S. Herring assumed command of 1st Regiment a reorganization was planned and then approved, which consisted of a new administrative company being formed under Major R. Bird, REME, and a Pay and Documentation Office being set up under Captain R. Kirk, RAPC. A training cell and other changes completed the reorganization.

The task of recalling witnesses to give evidence in civil courts throughout the Province had grown enormously and every month an average of 800 soldiers were being brought back from all over the world. The Courts Witness Section was therefore increased to fifteen and brought under the direction of the DAPM (Legal Affairs) who also controlled the Legal Process Office. Finally, because individual training had been neglected for the more pressing operations a Training Warrant Officer, WO 1 D. M. House, one of the first emergency reinforcements in 1969, was added to Commander RMP's staff to organize all RMP and Theatre individual training.

Through these same months Protestant dissatisfaction with the power-sharing Executive built-up to a climax. To this was added the frustration felt by everybody at the security forces lack of immediate success in countering the terrorists' latest tactic—the proxy bomb. In the middle of May came the long-awaited Protestant backlash, which was in a form as sinister as any amount of violence. A comparatively unknown group, the Ulster Workers Council (UWC), called a strike which quickly spread to every public service. On 12 May the Secretary of State declared a State of Emergency but nothing could break the UWC stranglehold on the Province. Troops were flown in and stood by to man power stations. They were looked after by 1st Regiment while 2nd Regiment kept essential traffic moving by 'talking down' or dismantling scores of barricades thrown-up on every main road. During the next fortnight the UDA began taking over garages and the Army countered by seizing major refineries and selling petrol from a number of soldier-manned garages throughout the Province. The RMP Mobile Force escorted the tankers from the refineries to these garages. During all this the IRA lay low and after a fortnight when scarcely a shot had been fired anywhere in Ulster the Executive fell. Mr Merlyn Rees, Secretary of State for Northern Ireland, prorogued Stormont for four months and the Province was back politically where it had been two years before.

In a year when the civilian and security forces casualty rate fell dramatically the number of RMP wounded was high.

On 5 May Corporal T. F. Lea of 175 Provost Company was blinded and lost his left hand in a booby trap explosion in Belfast, and Corporal Spaughton received minor injuries to his face and chest in the same incident. Corporal Lea was evacuated to St Dunstan's where he was making good progress when on 21 January, 1975, he died suddenly. In Londonderry where 176 Provost Company had once more started 'normal' policing in the Rosemount area three youths shot and wounded Corporal A. C. Dennis and Corporal D. J. W. Perkins. Both NCOs promptly returned fire and the youths fled leaving their weapons behind. Fortunately neither NCO was seriously hurt and these patrols went on. Another two NCOs, Corporals Pearson and Howes of 178 Provost Company were injured in October when a bomb was planted in the Sandes Home canteen in Ballykinler during the crowded morning tea break. Several soldiers were killed. Corporal Howes received superficial injuries but Corporal Pearson had to be evacuated from Ulster with a serious arm wound. Finally, to prove that the risk of stoning was always present, Lance-Corporal Jeffrey of 181 WRAC Provost Company was struck in the face and suffered a broken nose during an incident in Belfast.

The gradual but marked reduction in the level of violence since mid-1972 resulted in a significant reduction in the number of troops stationed in the Province. In Belfast 2nd Regiment was called upon to add the greater part of north Belfast to its already very large area of responsibility. This expansion, to take in some twenty-five square miles with a population of roughly 120,000 people, included one of the largest housing estates in the United Kingdom, and a small but militant Catholic area. 179 Provost Company, commanded now by Captain D. E. Hammond, was given this task. 179 Provost Company set up their base at Ardmillan House, and 175 Provost Company moved their tactical HQ to Tennant Street RUC Station. On 14 November Ardmillan House was vacated after four years as an RMP base when 179 Provost Company moved to Carnmoney Factory, which was well placed in the centre of their operational area. The Operation Room in Thiepval Barracks, set up originally in 1970 to co-ordinate all RMP activity in the Province, was moved to RUC Castlereagh in March to give 2nd Regiment RMP its own Tactical HQ and it was soon clear that an Intelligence Section would have to be added to it. Captain R. T. Gant was 2nd Regiment's first Intelligence Officer and his small section quickly proved its value. In December 2nd Regiment chalked up its 100th weapon recovered and at the time of writing had the highest number of weapons finds of any regiment in the Army.

Hopes that the level of violence would drop throughout 1974 were dashed by continuous proxy bomb attacks in urban areas, cross-border attacks, and occasionally outbursts of street fighting and rioting. Of these and other forms of violence the proxy bomb proved the most difficult to combat. NCOs working with the RUC particularly in the centre of Belfast often dealt with innocent drivers fearful for the safety of their families as well as the enormous task of clearing densely populated streets before the blast, and giving first aid to casualties after it. For work of this sort over a long and trying period Sergeants M. J. Harries and M. J. Gard were Mentioned in Despatches.

Early on the morning of 16 September, IRA gunmen shot and killed a leading Judge and Resident Magistrate at their homes in south and east Belfast. These assassinations triggered-off a wave of inter-sectarian murders that was only brought under control after a major effort by the security forces, a massive publicity campaign, and the detention of extremists from both sides. The Mobile Force was employed on anti-assassination patrols in Belfast and played a major part in the drive to defeat and deter travelling gunmen not only from the normal extremist groupings but also from several new groups whose capacity for senseless killing seemed boundless. The absence of the Mobile Force from the Border areas where it had operated almost continuously through the summer led to 174 Provost Company forming a 'mini' version of its own, using their own cars. This was but one more indication of the demand for this type of military police unit.

For eighteen months, since November, 1973, WO2 J. D. Turnbull of 2nd Regiment produced, almost singlehanded, a Corps magazine for both regiments. In addition he compiled an equally high quality paperback history of the Corps in Northern Ireland, *The Ulster Watchdogs*, largely in his own time. For his efforts he was rewarded by becoming the first recipient of the RMP Northern Ireland 'Tie of Honour' awarded by the Commander RMP for oustanding service—acts of bravery, good police work and performance in operational situations, as well as achievements in administration.

As the security forces took an increasing toll of the successive leaders of the IRA, dissension grew within the ranks of those remaining free and on 10 November a dispute between Officials and Provisionals in north Belfast erupted in Bawnmore, the small Catholic enclave in the area so recently taken over by 2nd Regiment. As night fell the two sides began firing at each other across the estate and an operation was quickly mounted to flush them out using elements of 175 and 179 Provost Companies. After a brief exchange of fire in which one gunman was wounded, six men were arrested, one in possession of an M1 carbine, and charged with offences ranging from attempted murder to illegal possession of firearms. A cordon was placed round the estate and during the next forty-eight hours a total of nine weapons, 353 rounds of ammunition and a quantity of para-military equipment were found in a number of selective searches. Another six men were arrested. For his part in this operation, and for his dynamic and courageous leadership while commanding 2nd Regiment, Lieut-Colonel B. A. Gait, DCM, was awarded the Distinguished Service Order, thus becoming the first RMP officer ever to receive this award.

The strain on the Corps of keeping two regiments in Ulster began to tell during 1974. The most immediate effect of having more than one-third of all RMP NCOs in the Province was the inevitability of them spending four years in every six in Ulster. So the planned build-up was cut back, and almost at the same time the RAF Provost, faced with their own manpower problems, announced that they would be unable to provide any more NCOs to bolster our strength after the end of the year. To offset the effect of these losses forty-four soldiers of other Arms and Services were sent to serve two-year tours in both regiments.

Before the year ended the Secretary of State announced that the people of Northern Ireland would be given the chance to decide their own political future. They would have the opportunity to elect a Convention which would be charged with recommending a form of government for Northern Ireland that would command the support of the majority of the people.

On 16 December the Provisional IRA announced another ceasefire . . .

> 'Old days! The wild geese are flighting,
> Head to the storm as they faced it before!
> For where there are Irish, there's bound to be fighting,
> And when there's no fighting, it's Ireland no more!'
>
> Kipling, 1918.

PART V

Specialist Arms and Formations

CHAPTER XV

Provost with Specialist Arms and Formations

THE Royal Military Police organization has always been flexible. Wings and branches have been formed, some of which still flourish, such as the Special Investigation Branch (SIB); some were raised to meet the need of the moment and then disbanded, such as the Vulnerable Points Wing (VP). Some have been god-fathered to become services in their own right such as the Field Security Sections of the Intelligence Corps and some have become sister services with a common ancestry such as the Military Provost Staff Corps (MPSC).

The following pages outline those wings and branches of the Corps which came into being with the Second World War and are of recent history. These wings and branches are composed of specialist military policemen concentrating on one aspect of police duties.

Policemen in particular rôles are also included in this chapter. It must be emphasized that these are first and foremost military policemen performing normal police duties but who have received such additional training as may be necessary to work with particular formations such as airborne and armour, or in particular rôles such as ports and docks, or with horses or dogs. The policeman in these cases is likely to be posted for a normal tour of duty in any of these rôles subject to him being suitable for the duties involved and having an aptitude for its requirements.

AIRBORNE PROVOST

Early in the Second World War it was decided to create an airborne force. This organization was to encompass all Arms and was to be formed on a completely voluntary basis. There was obviously a requirement for provost and volunteers were called for. The creation of such a force posed many problems and the main aim was to provide a force of highly trained troops capable of being delivered in an assault from the air, either by parachute or by air landing in gliders.

This new rôle of the military policeman necessitated a complete re-examination of tactical thought in respect of the tasks now confronting him. The basic provost duties remained but in addition there was the added complication of delivering the force from the air, complete with equipment and ready to go into action immediately.

The airborne military policeman, both then and now, underwent the same training, for which the same qualifications were required, as any and every other member of an airborne formation. It is not necessary to reiterate these aspects in this history, as they have been amply recorded elsewhere, but to accept the premise that aircraft, helicopter, glider or parachute are a means of delivering a soldier into battle.

Having become a trained parachutist the policeman was now ready to join an airborne provost company. There were two airborne divisions formed during the Second World War; 1st Airborne Division was raised first and was followed by 6th Airborne Division.

On arrival on the ground military policemen were required to revert rapidly to their normal rôle and to be completely self-contained. Their equipment and weapons were carried in a kitbag attached to the leg strap of the parachute harness and lowered on a rope during the parachute descent.

Vehicles and trailers were landed in gliders and the bulk of stores and equipment were delivered in this way. Nevertheless there was a high risk that the glider containing these essential items would not arrive and consequently, to insure against this contingency as far as it was possible to do so, the basic items were duplicated in the kitbags of the NCOs parachuting. Thus, in the event of the glider being lost, or not meeting up with the parachute assault force, the provost elements could operate independently.

In view of the weight and design of much of the provost equipment it was not possible to parachute with it, unless very limited quantities were carried. The weight factor was extremely important and it was not uncommon for NCOs to parachute with kitbags weighing 80 lbs. In order to meet requirements on the ground, lightweight equipment and signs were necessary. In the event, considerable initiative was displayed by members of the Corps who designed and used signs made of stiff paper or card. These, of course, were only of use on a temporary basis and were subsequently replaced on the delivery of normal signing equipment. It should be remembered that the weight of equipment parachuted on the man must be physically carried by the individual after arrival on the dropping zone, and almost invariably there were some miles to be covered on foot before reaching the objective.

Normal provost tasks had to be carried out but, in addition, planning, training and the rehearsal for operations took a considerable time. There were the added commitments of signing routes to airfields and signing within the airfields to dispersal areas. Vehicles and trailers had to be loaded and lashed down ready for installation in gliders.

As the operations came closer the provost task was the sealing and security of camps and airfields and, immediately prior to the operation, the movement of personnel to the airfields which had then to be sealed and secured. In the event of postponement the sealing and security of airfields was vital to the success of operations.

Military policemen were always among the first to land on the dropping zone. Their tasks on arrival were two-fold. Firstly the direction of all personnel arriving on the dropping zone to their correct locations. This was most important in order to effect swift reorganization and to ensure that the dropping zone and objectives were secured quickly.

Secondly, the organization and security of the HQ which was of course of the utmost importance in the subsequent control of operations. Units and specialist groups or HQ were never carried in the same aircraft but were dispersed over several in order to ensure that in the event of the loss of an aircraft a complete element would not be lost. In consequence an aircraft load of troops arriving on a dropping zone would contain personnel having to get to various unit locations. It was the responsibility of the military police to ensure that they did so.

In addition it was invariably the case that there would be enemy resistance and the military police NCO had to be prepared to fight, in common with all other airborne troops to secure the dropping-zone and then to assume responsibility for the custody of prisoners, safety of civilians caught in the zone and appropriation of any useful material. When the dropping zone was secured and the initial assault complete, it was the task of provost to reconnoitre and give guidance in respect of routes off the dropping zone to objectives, and, where applicable, to sign an axis, possibly through villages and towns.

On completion of the operation, when the link-up with ground forces had been effected, provost then were responsible for the withdrawal of the force and the erection and control of harbour areas.

Airborne divisions were not always employed in an airborne rôle but were also used as conventional ground forces. In these cases the airborne provost companies reverted to their usual provost routine.

Both airborne divisions were supported by provost in every operation they undertook during the Second World War. They served in North Africa, Sicily, Italy, France, Holland and Germany. Reference has already been made to the landings of 6th Airborne Division Provost Company astride the River Orne in Normandy on D-Day, 6 June, 1944.

When the Second World War ended both airborne divisions were gradually disbanded until eventually an independent parachute brigade group was all that remained of the two divisions. The figures 1 and 6 which were associated with the 1st and 6th Airborne Divisions were then combined and the new formation was designated 16th Independent Parachute Brigade Group and this formation is served by 16th Parachute Brigade Group Provost Unit.

The gliderborne aspect of airborne forces had been completely discontinued by 1948 and the requirement from then on was for a completely parachute-trained force, although the Glider Pilot Regiment was not formally disbanded until 1957.

16th Parachute Brigade is designed to be able to move anywhere in the world at short notice and, since the end of the Second World War has frequently done so. It has the capability of being dropped by parachute complete with all its vehicles and guns, or being air-landed.

In view of the present-day rôle of airborne forces the military policeman is faced with the problem of the quick move overseas. The provost tasks here range from the security of initial briefings, the control and establishment of Report Centres through which all units pass on the way to airfields, signing of all routes and the dispersal of personnel and freight to locations in the airfields.

Again the military policeman will invariably find himself on the first aircraft, because it is his task to receive the formation on arrival at the new destination. Very little warning is ever given for these moves and, because of weight limitations imposed by air travel the minimum amount of equipment is carried and available.

On all strategic moves overseas since 1945 airborne forces have always moved into areas of unrest. Situations have obviously varied, but for the military policeman it has always been his task to re-establish and support the indigenous police in attempting to restore law and order. It follows that, where the move has been into an area containing no British troops, liaison with the local civil police must be established as a first priority.

Since 1945 members of the Corps have served with 16th Parachute Brigade in Palestine, Egypt, Cyprus, Suez (of which a detailed account appears in Chapter XI) and Jordan and in operational conditions as part of the United Nations Force in Cyprus where they were the first provost unit to wear the blue beret of the United Nations.

BEACH PROVOST

The first lessons in the need for provost on beaches were probably learned in 1940 during the evacuation from Dunkirk where provost played a vital part. Having been driven from the mainland of Europe, from France in 1940 and from Greece in 1941, it then became apparent that any future assault on Europe must necessarily be made over beaches, as ports were unlikely to be available.

Perhaps the first experience of an assault landing over a beach into enemy-occupied territory was by 29th Independent Brigade on 5 May, 1942, on the northern tip of Madagascar. The brigade provost sections were under command of Captain J. Wren and they were immediately supported by 13th and 17th Brigades of 5th Division whose provost sections, led by Sergeants C. Bennett and A. Monk, were under command of Major D. Birrell. Provost carried out their duties of traffic control on the beaches, establishing a PoW cage and signing stores dumps for several days until the capture of Diego Suarez and the opening-up of that port by the Royal Navy.

The next assault landing was Operation 'Torch' carried out in November, 1942, by 1st Army in Algieria. It had been hoped that French forces in Oran and Algiers would not resist an Allied landing and the force was not really equipped for a beach assault. 'B' Group CMP (TC) under Major R. N. Holmes, with Nos 65, 71, 77 and 80 Companies CMP (TC) carried out ports provost duties on the L of C in this operation under the direction of DPM 1st Army, Lieut-Colonel H. V. MacNally.

During late 1942 GHQ Middle East created experimental formations to deal with the landing of large fighting forces into enemy-held territory. These formations were known as 'beach bricks'. No 1 Beach Brick (later No 31) was formed from 7th Battalion Royal Marines for the purpose of maintaining a beach after its capture by an assaulting force during the invasion of an enemy coastline. The factor governing the employment of a highly-trained and battle-experienced Royal Marines battalion in such a task was the necessity to employ the maximum number of infantry in an invasion.

A brick consisted of a basic infantry battalion whose HQ acted as brick HQ, supported by a signal platoon, a medical section and the provost unit. The field company RE of the brick was supported by two infantry companies and a mechanical equipment section. The BMA included a general duties company RASC, detachments from RAOC and REME, a RAF component and an infantry company. Anti-aircraft protection was provided by both a heavy and a light anti-aircraft battery. Thus a beach brick was a sizeable force, capable of working several beaches simultaneously, twenty-four hours a day throughout the period that the beach was in operation and until the capture of one or more ports enabled supplies and reinforcements to be landed on the dockside instead of over the beach.

It is said that if movement ceases, either on the beaches or in the beach maintenance area during an amphibious assault, the whole landing may be jeopardized. To ensure a smooth and even flow of personnel, vehicles, equipment and stores from the beach to the rear maintenance area, a beach provost company was included in the establishment of a beach brigade, as it eventually became known.

The responsibilities of beach provost were briefly:

(a) Traffic control on the beaches and from the beaches to the forward boundaries of the beach brigade area.
(b) The signposting of routes for the various types of traffic: tracked, wheeled, amphibian, supply, medical, formation and internal.
(c) The control, assisted by working parties from the beach group and by unit guides, of traffic through the beach transit areas.
(d) The establishment of traffic posts close to the forward boundary. They also acted as stragglers' posts.
(e) Close liaison with the Royal Engineers in the beach organization in order that switches and diversions to the traffic trace could be implemented swiftly without confusion.
(f) To maintain close and constant touch with formations or other provost on the forward boundaries and flanks.
(g) To assist in the organization and control of the assembly areas should no L of C provost be allocated.

If beach groups operated independently it was usual to allocate them a HQ and four provost sections; an increment HQ being required for a second beach group. The deployment of a beach provost company was usually as follows:

(a) Approximately half of the sections with the beach wings, responsible for the traffic control on the beaches and in the beach transit areas.
(b) The remaining sections responsible for traffic control forward of the beach transit areas and as far inland as the forward boundary of the beach brigade; this was commonly known as the beach maintenance area (BMA).
(c) Company HQ was located near the HQ of the beach brigade with two sections in reserve.

Beach organization embraced the whole process of organizing the beaches and the immediate hinterland in order to land and maintain the assault, follow-up and build-up formations. It was the first link in the chain of supply which connected the fighting troops on enemy territory with their reserves of stores and supplies at the main base area, with its port and base depots. It also contained the necessary organization for the first stages of the reconstitution of the formations and units landed across the beaches into tactical and administrative entities, and for their movement forward from the beaches. A return route had also to be provided for wounded, specialist troops, equipment and prisoners of war in order that they could be evacuated from the beach.

Beach provost equipment was very much the same as in any other provost company, but consideration had to be given to the fact that during the initial stages of the landing the unit was static and in consequence all equipment had to be brought ashore on the NCOs' backs. This naturally necessitated improvisation of traffic control equipment, which had to be of the lightest possible material if the maximum amount of signing equipment was to be brought ashore during this crucial phase of the landing. Any light-weight material such as canvas, tin or hardboard was used. Special improvised carriers for the signs were constructed to fit on a man's back. Large signs, such as 'beach exit' presented no problems as they were made of canvas and could be rolled up between the two posts for easy carriage.

Beach marking lights were issued to beach provost for night marking purposes. They were narrow, oblong metal containers with a suitable spike at one end for sticking in the ground. A small lamp face was provided which could be illuminated by a normal dry electric battery.

The Sicily landing on 10 July, 1943, saw the battle baptism of these new beach bricks. 31 Beach Brick, whose beach provost platoon (as it was called) led by Captain Lennard landed over Red Beach and Amber Beach at 2.45 am on 10 July, saw 51st Highland Division pass over their beaches into Sicily. This brick continued to function as such until 24 August, when it was disbanded. 32 Beach Brick (the original No 2 Brick) was formed in Palestine in March, 1943, based upon the 2nd Battalion Highland Light Infantry. Its provost unit was 640 Independent Provost Company commanded by Captain K. Watson and this brick put 5th Division over the right flank beaches into Sicily. No 33 Brick was formed around 1st Battalion Argyll and Sutherland Highlanders with 641 Independent Provost Company under Captain A. Blackburn.

The next major beach operation was the Salerno landing in Italy on 9 September, 1943, when 35 Beach Brick, based on 18th Battalion Durham Light Infantry with 643 Independent Provost Unit and 37 Beach Brick, based on 2nd Derbyshire Yeomanry with 645 Independent Provost Unit under Captain C. R. A. W. Walker, passed 46th Division over their beach-head. For this operation also, two large beach provost companies (Nos 20 and 21) operated with beach groups; No 20 supporting 78th Division and No 21 supporting 56th Division in Operation 'Avalanche' at Salerno. Soon after the landings these beach provost companies, having completed their beach tasks, reverted to L of C units with Allied Forces HQ in Italy.

The great test of beach landing techniques came with D-Day, 6 June, 1944, in Normandy. Although this story has been told in Major Crozier's *History of the Corps*, published in 1951, an amplification of the beach aspect is here developed to illustrate provost participation.

The length of coastline allotted to the British and Canadian forces of 2nd Army extended from the mouth of the River Orne on the left as they approached, to Port-en-Bessin on the right, and was divided into three beaches to which the code names 'Sword', 'Juno' and 'Gold' were allotted. The beaches were in turn divided into a varying number of sectors.

For the development of the beaches and for the early maintenance of the assault forces, 101 and 102 Beach Sub-Areas were placed in support of 1 Corps and 104 Beach Sub-Area in support of 30 Corps. Each beach sub-area consisted of two beach groups, and for the purpose of L of C control after the initial landings, HQ 11 L of C Area was phased-in early to take over command of the beach sub-areas once the two corps moved forward from the beaches.

The outline plan provided for the maintenance of the British forces over beaches until such time as sufficient ports could be captured and developed.

It was assumed that with the opening of the Seine ports beach maintenance could cease. The British sector contained only the small ports of Port-en-Bessin, Courseulles and Ouistreham, the combined capacity of which, even if captured intact, was considered to be insufficient for our tonnage needs. It thus became necessary to provide the artificial harbour 'Mulberry B', together with its attendant 'Gooseberrys', but it was not anticipated that any appreciable tonnage could be unloaded through 'Mulberry' until D+9. One L of C sub-area HQ was to be landed early with the responsibility for controlling the area of Arromanches where 'Mulberry B' would be constructed as soon as the tactical situation permitted.

In the initial phase of the campaign the organization of military police resources and the distribution of provost units for the initial landings and build-up of the bridgeheads was as follows:

(i) Three division provost companies (each HQ and 6 sections)—Traffic duties for the assault and follow-up brigades.

(ii) Six beach provost companies (each HQ and 4 sections and some additional traffic control sections)—Traffic control and sign-posting of routes in the beach transit and assembly area.

(iii)	Ten vulnerable points (VP) sections	—Construction of cages, guarding of prisoners of war, detention of suspects.
(iv)	Two corps provost companies	—To control area between beaches and forward divisions.

As the position in the bridgehead became consolidated, further provost units were added as below:

(v)	One provost company	—For each assault division.
(vi)	Four provost companies Four traffic control companies One vulnerable points company	—For each army.
(vii)	Seven provost, seven traffic and three vulnerable points companies	—For L of C areas.

This organization and allotment of duties proved suitable and adequate, with the simple exception of the beach provost companies, which found their four sections to be inadequate to cope with the numerous and arduous duties required of them. Moreover, the roughness of the weather interfered with the timed arrival programme, with the result that only parts of any provost unit, except division provost companies, arrived on time.

The weather conditions, which had already caused twenty-four hours' postponement, proved far from ideal for the landings and, though there is no doubt that the conditions led to the assault proving an even bigger surprise to the enemy than had been hoped, the heavy swell which continued on D+1 made off-loading from craft, both of stores and vehicles, a good deal more difficult than had been expected and hindered the organization of the beaches.

The actual landing was achieved according to plan and casualties were very much less than had been estimated. Though resistance was in many places fierce, it was generally less formidable than previous intelligence had anticipated. The general picture was one of heavy fighting along the whole British front with only limited advances being made but these were fortunately just sufficient to give the necessary space for the required administrative layout, albeit very restricted as compared to the area originally planned. In addition to these difficulties, the administrative tasks on the 'Sword' sector were complicated by the fact that the beaches here were observed and under fire from the enemy, and that the Caen–Ouistreham Canal could not therefore be either used or cleared. The canal lock gates at Ouistreham had, by good fortune, been captured intact, although there was constant anxiety as to their safety from enemy artillery.

All the beach sub-areas landed successfully on D-Day. They found that the beaches were not as steep as had been hoped, which meant that, except at high water, all craft and LSTs were beached and that the anchorages for shipping would be necessarily some distance offshore with a consequent increase in the turn-round of craft and DUKWs. Local opposition on and behind the beaches in some cases delayed the start of the administrative schedule as it diverted beach group personnel for 'cleaning-up' operations and taking prisoners.

In November, 1943, a number of beach groups had been formed to serve under beach sub-areas in support of 2nd Army for Operation 'Overlord'. These beach groups contained a HQ provost company, comprising a company HQ and four sections, designed to operate initially as a beach provost company, then later to function as a L of C provost company.

These were:

240 HQ Provost Company, 9 Beach Group
241 HQ Provost Company, 5 Beach Group
242 HQ Provost Company, 7 Beach Group
243 HQ Provost Company, 10 Beach Group
244 HQ Provost Company, 8 Beach Group
246 HQ Provost Company } Never served with beach groups, but
248 HQ Provost Company } were used as L of C provost companies in May, 1945, in 21 Army Group

Some notes on the detailed activities of these beach provost companies together with 245 and 247 HQ Provost Companies which also landed on D-Day are now recorded.

On 6 June, 1944, 240 HQ Provost Company under Captain T. H. Jeffrey landed on 'King' sector area of La Rivière. First flights went in at H+45 mins, all were ashore by H+72 mins and set to work signing beach and main dump areas. By 9 June bigger and better signs was the order of the day and their PoW Cage was handed over to VP Wing, after which anti-looting and espionage duties were then undertaken. By 17 July 'King' and 'Love' sectors closed down and the company under command of L of C moved to Sully near Bayeux and continued as a L of C provost company.

On 6 June 241 HQ Provost Company landed under Captain C. D. G. Pearson, who earned a D-Day MC. The beach section corporals went ashore at H+20 mins. Lieutenant Beard and the beach sections followed 25 minutes later, Lieutenant Jones and the dump sections by H+120 minutes and whole company was ashore by H+5 hours. 'Traffic flowing well by H+8 hours,' says the War Diary, 'but 25% of signs lost going ashore'.

Corporal W. Tweedale and Lance-Corporal G. C. Hilliard were killed in action on the beaches on D-Day and six lance-corporals also were wounded. This was a heavy blow so early but on 7 June 245 Company was ashore and came to assist 241 Company.

245 HQ Provost Company under Captain J. Corbett went in on 6 June and landed at Lion-sur-Mer. On 7–8 June the company HQ was at Ouistreham where the fighting was severe. On that day Lance-Corporals Thompson and E. Schafer were killed by bombs and on 10 June Lance-Corporal Dawson was killed also by a bomb.

By 18 June Captain Corbett had become DAPM 101 Beach Sub-Area and then DAPM 30 Corps on 26 July; Lieutenant W. North became OC company which he took into Caen on 10 July where Lance-Corporal H. Kenny was killed the following day.

242 HQ Provost Company was commanded by Captain H. G. Thornton which landed on D-Day with the loss of one NCO killed. Captain Jeffrey taking over the company on 13 September.

243 HQ Provost Company, under Captain B. E. Durbin landed on 'Jig' sector on D-Day; at this time Major Cook was APM 104 Beach Sub-Area. The company was reinforced by one sergeant and twenty lance-corporals lent by 36 Beach Brick on 10 June.

An indication of beach tasks may be appreciated by the following daily totals of stores landed over 'Jig' Sector alone:

> On 2 July, 1954 tons of stores and 1102 vehicles; on 4 July, 3095 tons and 1022 vehicles; on 5 July, 1643 tons and 1380 vehicles; on 6 July, 1190 tons and 1492 vehicles; on 7 July, 1378 tons and 1166 vehicles and on 8 July, 1804 tons and 1457 vehicles.

During these operations Major S. F. Crozier was APM L of C. On 26 August 4 Beach Group, 8 Beach Group and 102 Beach Sub-Area became 6 L of C Sub-Area.

244 HQ Provost Company, under Captain H. E. Elsmore, landed on D-Day and next day established company HQ at Bernières-sur-Mer under the APM and on 3 July moved to St Aubin-sur-Mer.

Part of 247 HQ Provost Company came ashore on D-Day under Captain E. J. Price, and on 12 June the advance party landed six days late 'due to RN phasing in' preceded on 9 June by the main body at Montfleury but by 12 June they had moved to Arromanches where an escort was provided for Mr Winston Churchill's visit on 21 July.

The story of 14th Army in Burma is one of jungle warfare and air supply in which beach operations played but a minor part, and that at the very end of the Second World War.

There is record of two beach provost units, 94th and 95th Indian Beach Maintenance Provost Units CMP(I) both of which were formed in November, 1944. 94th Indian Beach Maintenance Provost Unit landed at Chittagong on 5 December, 1944, moving south to Akyab in January, 1945, and on 10 February, 1945, to Kyaukpyu at the northern end of Ramree Island, where they took over from 82nd West African Division Provost Company. By 6 May the unit had moved to Rangoon which had been re-occupied on 3 May, but it was not until 9 September, 1945, that they really were engaged activity in a beach rôle when in Malaya they operated 'Charlie' and 'Dog' beaches at Port Swettenham with elements also at Port Dickson on the re-occupation of Malaya after the Japanese surrender, when the landing went in as a tactical operation. This activity continued until 31 October, 1945, when the beaches closed.

95th Indian Beach Maintenance Provost Unit was formed under Captain Mathieson at Bombay on 10 November, 1944. A week later they were on the move; from Bombay to Calcutta by rail, thence by paddle-steamer over the River Ganges to Sumara, another train ride over the River Brahmaputra to Dimapur, on by road to Imphal and Palel, finally reaching Yazayo by air on 30 November. In January, 1945, they again moved forward to Alon and performed provost duties there from the opening of the airhead on 19 Feburary. Airfield duties continued to be a rôle and function of this beach provost unit successively at Myingyan in April, 1945, then at Toungoo, finally culminating at Moulmein in November, 1945, when they reached salt water at last.

In war it had become standard practice to disband beach formations as soon as the beach operation for which they had been assembled was completed. Thus, with the end of the Second World War, all beach provost companies disappeared from the order of battle in the Regular Army.

However, with the re-formation of the Territorial Army in 1947 there appeared 264 (Scottish) Beach Brigade Provost Company TA based at Churchill Barracks, Ayr. This unit continued as a well-recruited and vigorous provost element in the Reserve Army until 264 Beach Brigade was disbanded in 1955. The gap in the Reserve Army order of battle caused by the disappearance of 264 Beach Brigade was filled by the formation of a Port Task Force in the Army Emergency Reserve. Provost support for this took the shape of No 1 Port Task Force Provost Company AER, a category I unit, ready for action at the shortest of notice.

PORTS PROVOST

The supervision of embarkation and disembarkation has always been an important military police function. In peacetime a detachment of military police was stationed either at Southampton or at the garrison town of Portsmouth. The mobilization scheme in 1939 provided two provost officers and seventy military police for duty in ports. Of these, one APM and thirty other ranks were allocated to Southampton and the remainder to other ports.

But the pilfering problems at ports and in transit soon became acute and it was decided to form special Ports provost companies with considerably extended duties and powers. The first of these were formed in 1941; and as sufficient provost sections were not available, authority was given to supplement the deficiency with twenty-five Vulnerable Points (VP) sections. These men were raised gradually and brought the total strength up to sixteen provost and twenty-five VP sections—368 all ranks by February, 1942. An APM (Ports), Major T. G. Ruttledge, was then appointed; on up-grading later to DPM he was promoted lieutenant-colonel. The success of Ports provost owed much to the wide experience and ability of Lieut-Colonel Ruttledge who had served with the provost service with distinction in the First World War and then in Northern Ireland between 1919 and 1922. He was the first provost officer, other than a Provost Marshal, to be appointed CBE.

A SIB section for Ports was formed under Captain J. W. Rignell, with HQ at Liverpool, in January, 1942. A further section was added on 15 November, 1943, and the total strength amounted to 5 officers and 40 other ranks. Owing to the growth of shipping on the north-east coast, a Ports provost company was authorized for service at those ports on 22 January, 1942.

In March, 1942, numbers were allotted to Command and Ports provost companies. This affected the latter as follows: North-East Ports, Bristol Channel Ports, North-West Ports and Scottish Ports Provost Companies became respectively 174 (Ports), 175 (Ports), 176 (Ports) and 177 (Ports) Provost Companies.

The preparation for Operation 'Torch' for the allied invasion of French North Africa in the early autumn of 1942 and the gradual resumption of activity at Southampton led to the formation at that port of 178 and 179 (Ports) Provost Companies. The latter was allotted to Operation 'Torch' and the former remained at Southampton for duty at south coast ports. As preparation for the invasion of north-west Europe grew and the importance of the port of London was recognized, 193 (Ports) Provost Company was formed and allotted to south-east ports. 181 (Ports) Provost Company was raised late in 1942 for duty in

Northern Ireland, but was withdrawn in April, 1943, mobilized and sent towards the end of the year to Italy.

The war establishment of the Ports provost companies on VE-Day was twenty-eight officers and 1,371 other ranks.

Eleven Ports provost companies were raised for service overseas. All but two of these were formed from men belonging to existing UK Ports provost companies. Two companies were formed from surplus sergeants of other units, largely from the Royal Artillery: this was an experiment which proved very successful, the two units in question joining 21 Army Group at the end of 1944. One of these, designated 194 Provost Company CMP (Sergeants) (Ports) policed the docks at Boulogne and Ostend with a detachment at Calais after the capture of those ports by 2nd Canadian Army had materially shortened the lines of communication for 21 Army Group from England. In May, 1945, the unit moved to Hamburg and because of the extensive damage to that port by allied bombing and the large extent of the docks, organized provost water patrols in *Rhoda*, a fast motor-launch and *RMP 2*, a slower but larger diesel-engined craft. These patrols continued after June, 1946, in the re-named 194 Provost Company after the demobilization of the sergeants' companies had ended a unique and successful experiment in the Corps. The distribution of these eleven companies was as follows: two in North Africa (subsequently moving to Italy), three in CMF (Italy), five in 21 Army Group in north-west Europe and (after re-occupation in September, 1945) one company in Singapore.

Throughout the Second World War military convicts and prisoners were sent home and handed over to the Ports provost companies for disposal. The numbers were usually small, only once rising to over 100 in any quarter up to the end of 1944. The following year, however, 1,120 came home. Thanks to good discipline, embarkation duties produced few troubles. Many millions of men were handled at the various ports, mainly without incident. The major task performed by Ports provost was the prevention and detection of pilferage of stores in course of shipment overseas. This crime, prevalent as it has always been in peacetime, grew to alarming proportions during the War.

The Ministry of War Transport set up pilferage committees at many ports and Ports provost officers attended their meetings. At Glasgow for over a year the APM sat as chairman of the port pilferage committee. The number of arrests by military police for pilferage at home ports was as follows: 1942, 796; 1943, 671; 1944, 1,210; 1945, 771. Of these 40 per cent were Merchant Navy personnel, 30 per cent belonged to the Armed Forces and 30 per cent were stevedores. About 32 million tons of military stores were shipped or discharged through UK ports and were given military police protection.

It will be seen that the duties of Ports provost expanded greatly during the Second World War; upon them fell responsibilities for security (not a normal provost function) and for an unrelenting vigilance against sabotage and pilfering of essential war supplies—which, unchecked, would have seriously crippled British war efforts. Overseas, particularly, their duties covered not only the movement of fighting troops but all civilians, civilian vehicles and shipping within the port areas; they undertook the duties of harbour and river police and, together with the SIB, had to search ships, crews, and crews' quarters. They had to learn their powers, the meaning of the various markings on packages and crates, the tricks to which dishonest stevedores might resort to avoid detection, and something, at least, of the construction of ships.

These exacting tasks Port provost performed with a devotion and ability which matched that of the other wings of the Corps. That their efforts were successful in preventing a very great deal of pilferage is evident from the numerous complaints, voiced by commercial undertakings, of the alarming extent of this evil and the enormous losses sustained. No such great losses fell upon the War Department or the Air Ministry.

PROVOST DOGS

The value of animals in peace and war has been recognized for many centuries, such as the famous elephants of Hannibal, the geese used by the Romans to giving warning of an impending attack, and of course the ubiquitous horse used as pack animal and charger.

However, it is only recently that the value of dogs has been fully realized and appreciated, although in England during the Civil War, Prince Rupert was invariably accompanied into battle by his poodle 'Boye', who fought gallantly and on at least one occasion saved the Prince's life and was killed at the Battle of Marston Moor—perhaps the forerunner of the 'Guard Dog'.

In the armies of France, Belgium and Finland dogs were used as pack-dogs and sledge dogs to carry supplies, especially in snow. In the First World War the German Army used them to carry ammunition and mortar bombs to forward positions and to reel out wire between field telephone posts. They were also extensively used as liaison and messenger dogs and as Red Cross dogs to locate and carry first-aid equipment to the wounded.

In the British army the majority of dogs are guard dogs, used to patrol dumps and vulnerable stores under the control of a dog handler. These dogs are trained to detect intruders and, if necessary, to attack and hold them. Others are tracker, patrol, mine detection and messenger dogs.

Tracker dogs and their handlers are trained to follow the trail of a man and were much used after the Second World War in the Emergencies in Cyprus and Malaya. In the former place the handlers were RMP but in the latter infantry battalions provided handlers to work with their own patrols.

Patrol dogs work free in front of their patrols and are used to detect strangers before the patrol reaches them. Their use against ambushes is obvious. Mine and arms detection dogs are able, by some sense not yet explained, to detect hard solid objects, such as mines or caches of arms, under the ground. They then sit down until told to go on. Messenger dogs will carry a message between two points known to them.

Although there is no firm rule, most guard dogs are Alsatians, many trackers are Labrador Retrievers, although Alsatians and Dobermanns are also used. Dobermanns are used for messenger duties and any dog with a good nose may be used for patrols, though perhaps one would expect to see Pointers or Alsatians.

In comparison to continental armies, the British army was slow to adapt the dog to warlike uses. During the First World War they were in limited use, mainly as liaison and messenger dogs. Between the wars little was seen or heard of dogs in the army, although the Royal Engineers maintained a small school at Shoeburyness and trained a few dogs in a very specialized rôle. In 1942 the Royal Army Veterinary Corps (RAVC) took over responsibility and established the first proper Army Dog Training School at Potters Bar.

Before this school was fully established some local progress had been made in the theatres of action. In the BEF a rudimentary 'Guard Dog' unit was formed of Extra-Regimentally Employed (ERE) and medically down-graded personnel with locally-impressed dogs but the unit was disbanded on the evacuation from Dunkirk.

The first major need for dogs became apparent in the Middle East and there the Military Police Dog Training School was opened at Almaza, Cairo, in June, 1942. The idea was originated by Lieut-Colonel C. J. Harper and Lieut-Colonel G. Morgan-Jones, the then officer commanding CMP Base Depot. It was evident that some method of guarding dumps in the Middle East other than posting a sentry on every yard of the perimeter would have to be found, as pilferage had reached such a pitch that the war effort was being very seriously impeded. The CMP war dog proved to be the solution. By December, 1942, some twenty-four dogs had given such a good account of themselves that requests were coming in from right, left and centre for more dogs and yet more dogs.

It is reckoned that a dog saves at least ten sentries; his hearing is far more acute than that of a man, and he has the added advantage of his sense of smell. He is trained to indicate to his handler the presence of strangers and, when released from his lead, invariably gets the would-be thief. When one considers that, between December, 1942, and December, 1944, over 1,000 thieves were caught by war dogs, and many thousands of pounds worth of WD property recovered, the origination of dog sections in the Middle East can justifiably be hailed as a great boost to the war effort. In January, 1943, a war establishment for Dog Sections CMP Middle East was implemented; it consisted of one DAPM, sixty-three NCOs, forty-eight dogs and ten vehicles.

Early in 1943 it had become possible to raise three Dog Companies CMP and these were deployed as No 1 Company in Egypt, No 2 stretched through Palestine to Syria and No 3 in East Africa. These companies became 'Bluecap' units of the Vulnerable Points Wing. After the war, with the disbandment of the VP Wing, dog units were taken over by provost and stayed on in Egypt, the Canal Zone and East Africa Command until 1953 when they were handed over to the RAVC and, in the Middle East, became No 1 Army Guard Dog Unit in the Canal Zone, moving to Benghazi as No 5 Unit with detachments in Tripoli, Derna, Barce and Tobruk. In 1956 a detachment was sent to Cyprus, which was expanded into No 6 Army Guard Dog Unit RAVC.

These dog units remained on the establishment of RAVC until 1 April, 1959, when they reverted to RMP again. At this time RMP Dog Detachments were established at Gibraltar, Malta, Tripoli and Cyprus.

Dogs were extremely successful throughout the Middle East and in the vast areas of base depots in Egypt it would have been impossible to have ensured security of the many miles of perimeter, often through broken, boulder-strewn land impossible even to the jeep, without the co-operation of two branches of the Corps, 605 Mounted Squadron and Provost Dogs. 605 Mounted Squadron patrolled the outer perimeters and the dogs the interior.

In Cyprus, No 6 Guard Dog Unit developed this co-operation to its ultimate, though unofficial, stage. Starting its own Saddle Club with six horses it encouraged riding as a principal unit sport and the logical sequel was a team of three on patrol—man, horse and dog—a formidable combination for any intruder and one that led to remarkable success in the security of the military installations. Mention has been made elsewhere of the success of the use of dogs during the Mau-Mau troubles in East Africa where they more than proved their worth.

In the Far East dogs were not introduced until late in 1948 when No 3 Army Dog Unit was formed by RAVC, its handlers being ERE personnel, and a detachment being sent to Hong Kong in 1950 to become

No 4 Army Guard Dog Unit. In 1958 No 3 Unit became No 5 Unit following the disbandment of the original No 5 in Benghazi. On 1 April, 1962, this Unit became No 5 Gurkha Dog Company manned by personnel from the Gurkha Military Police.

In Germany a Dog Training School was established at Sennelager under RAVC but was not developed on a large scale. It ultimately became a small training cadre assisting training of dogs and handlers for the German Service Organization and the Mixed Service Organization guard dog units and as an overflow cadre for the UK training schools.

As a result of the Hull Committee Report on the future of the Regular Army, the Army Council decided that the responsibility for all army dog units should pass from RAVC to RMP and in April, 1959, provost took over complete responsibility for all army dogs, including purchase, training and operating dogs and training handlers from other units. This was preceded by a short period of one year during which RAVC trained and supplied dogs and handlers found from RMP. New RMP dog companies were formed to be stationed at Gibraltar, Cyprus, Malta, Singapore and Hong Kong. In addition RMP were to be responsible for the supply and training of dogs and training of handlers for 'user units' guarding dumps in over forty different locations in the UK and for the WD Constabulary.

With dog companies becoming part of the permanent RMP establishment, any suitable NCO found himself posted for a tour of duty with dogs as a normal posting following a course at the Training School either as a dog trainer, entailing a four-month course, or as a handler after a fortnight's course. On joining his dog unit, handler and dog were teamed-up for the duration of the handler's tour of duty. After they had got to know each other, and mutual trust and confidence had been established, a keen and efficient combination, essential for the best results, they assumed a duty which saved many man-hours of sentry duty and did the job not only with greater thoroughness but with far greater deterrent effect.

Since the end of the Second World War dogs played their part in most major operations of an internal security and peace-keeping rôle, having carried out patrols and raids too numerous to mention, including jumping from helicopters. Some were killed in action, including one famous dog, who, although suffering from wounds from which he subsequently died, captured the three terrorists he was tracking.

Hong Kong Dog Company, the last RMP dog company in the army, was handed-over to the RAVC on 1 September, 1976, thus reversing the decision made in 1959 and ending, at least for the present, the long association of dogs with the Corps.

MILITARY MOUNTED POLICE

The history of the Military Mounted Police has been recorded in Crozier's *History of the Corps* up to the time of amalgamation with the Military Foot Police in 1926 to form CMP. Though no longer existing as a separate corps, the spirit of the MMP never actually died, having been kept alive by mounted sections in various places from time-to-time, and mounted squadrons existed in the Middle East during the Second World War. Mounted sections were located in Gibraltar and also in Vienna after 1945 as part of British Troops Austria. Of these the most important rôle for the mounted military policeman was in the Middle East where he made a significant contribution to the war effort. Major J. V. J. Bird, officer commanding 605 Squadron Military Mounted Police, wrote as follows:

> 'In early 1943, with the 8th Army's task in the Middle East nearly completed, thousands of pounds worth of supplies were awaiting transit in the bulk supply dumps and wharves. Vehicles, tanks, arms and equipment, besides thousands of prisoners, men and material captured from the enemy, had to be rounded-up and disposed of. This was no easy task for those in command, as the native thieves looted everything they could possibly lay hands on, aided by natives employed in the various static camps, dumps and wharves. Organized gangs looted arms and ammunition with which to protect themselves against security guards while attempting their thefts, and so the conservation of arms and ammunition became a problem.
>
> 'Native villages in and around the Suez Canal areas were invariably transit villages for stolen property. The inhabitants concealed stolen property by every possible means and often hid it by burying it in the desert in and around their quarters. Supply trains were frequently tampered with, bales of stores and clothing and food supplies were dumped off the trains in the vicinity of their homes and along the lonely desert tracks, while their accomplices were waiting to gather the loot under cover of darkness and make good their escape.
>
> 'The task placed on the shoulders of the Provost Marshal was to round up the thieves by the thousand, as their tactics were deterrent to the war effort. It is worth noting here that all dumps, wharves and camps were surrounded by perimeter wires, and security sentries posted, both allied personnel and trusted Ghaffirs; trains had travelling armed guards. Police war dogs, trained in the handling of suspects and attempted thefts, were already employed while the Special Investigation Branch of the CMP was employed in the tracking-down of thieves and the investigation of the numerous thefts. But they could not cope with the time lost in cross-desert tracking to outer villages, where loot was stored. Quite often the thief and his gang escaped as the dogs and the SIB were sighted on their approach. Therefore, the mounted police were considered the solution to the problem by adopting the cavalry tactics of surrounding the villages while the raiding party

went through the village and searched it, preventing the escape of the thieves.'

Thus 605 Squadron Military Mounted Police was started in the Middle East on 1 February, 1943. Formed at CMP Base Depot volunteers were called-for from the various branches of CMP and outside regiments and corps. There was one stumbling block; in the Middle East, still a theatre of war, only low-graded men or A.1 men over thirty-five years of age could be released from front-line units and transit camps. Thus, finding the right type (plus character) for recruiting within the war establishment of five officers and 140 other ranks, made the embodiment progress very slow. Two troops of mounted military police were required immediately for duty at Tel-el-Kebir and Amiriya respectively where thefts were very heavy. A slow trickle of volunteers came in from ex-cavalry or horsed units and stumbling block number two arose. Epizootic Lymphangitis, an epidemic, had broken out in the Horse Transit Depot in Palestine and the issue of the horses was retarded until the quarantine period was completed. Meanwhile the policeman's job of work was being taught to the incoming probationers and the task of erecting stables and camp sites began.

On 14 February, 1943, the first draft of forty-six Sudanese ponies arrived, looking very lean and gruesome from segregation and the journey from Palestine by rail. In this condition and with very heavy rains prevailing only very light exercise could be undertaken for a while, but they were soon put into shape and the men, under intensive training, were fit and ready to fulfil their first posting-out for duty on 18 April, 1943. One detachment of twenty-one ponies and men under command of Lieutenant J. L. Walsh proceeded to Tel-el-Kebir and twenty ponies and men under the command of Lieutenant E. J. Roscoe were sent to Amiriya (Alexandria Area), camp sites having been chosen and stables erected by advance parties. Their job of work started almost immediately. Dawn, midday and evening patrols of the perimeter wires round the dumps, where special attention was paid to exploded trap mines, were begun.

Thieves and suspects were soon being handed over to the SIB with the stolen property in their possession and a notable decrease in pilfering was already prominent in dump-commanders' reports.

In a short while duties such as could only be undertaken comfortably and efficiently by mounted policemen were numerous and made a full-time job. Marshalling natives while they were being searched on leaving static camps and dumps put a stop to riots at the entrance gates, which were previously frequent. Mistrusted Ghaffirs were detected and charged and the passing out of new property from the dumps to the receivers was stopped. Patrols were carried out along the railway tracks and property of great value was recovered before it was handled by the pilferers. Escorts for PoWs were provided, as well as Guards of Honour to important persons visiting the areas, and there were many call-outs to quell native disturbances. Unlicensed hawkers were stopped from selling foodstuffs to troops. Much property of great value was recovered when troop trains were guarded and thieves checked. Thousands of sheep were escorted to WD pens. Many raids on native villages were carried out, in conjunction with the SIB, in search of the pilferer and his loot. Morality patrols were carried out frequently in isolated villages and routes, and a general clean-up of vice areas resulted from these patrols.

So the value of the military mounted police can hardly be exaggerated and demands for their employment from various RAOC and RASC commanders were frequent. These demands were met by the posting of detachments around the Suez Canal area, at El Kirch, Abu Sultan and Geneifa.

Every mounted member was armed with a sword and rifle with one machine-gun to the section. The latter was frequently brought into use against armed gangs and bandits. The mounted police were usefully employed during the Greek mutiny and provided the novelty of Cairo Area mounted escorts to the allied troops' March Past at the King's Birthday Parade, 1944.

In the figures below it must be borne in mind that the mounted police were formed to prevent criminal theft and when assessing the number of arrests and the amount of WD property recovered and converted to war use, it should be assumed that many times their value was prevented from being stolen. Over 9,000 duty patrols were carried out, from which 644 arrests were effected and £8,060 worth of WD property recovered and returned to use. This does not include property of far greater value handed over to the SIB.

The success of 605 Squadron having proved its value, 604 Squadron MMP was later formed in Palestine under Major J. A. Cunard for similar duties there. 604 Squadron was disbanded in 1946 and 605 Squadron in 1948.

The mounted section in Austria also carried on the tradition, keeping the horse active on provost duty, and then in the autumn of 1950 the Military Mounted Police were officially brought back on to Corps establishment when the Provost Marshal (Brigadier L. F. E. Wieler) was authorized to maintain a section, on the strength of 158 Provost Company (Southern Command), its first officer commanding being Captain Richardson and its section NCO, Sergeant E. Scattergood. They re-occupied the original quarters in Stanhope Lines built for the MMP a hundred years earlier.

19

Their duties, though including all normal provost tasks, were specifically to patrol the very extensive WD lands and ranges in the Aldershot area which were open to a surprising range of undesirable activities from theft of Christmas trees to forest fires.

In great demand for ceremonial escorts, they also provide popular display events in which horse and motor-cycle teams, competing in tent-pegging and other gymkhana events, have done much to keep the Corps in the public eye. The first two WRAC Provost joined the Mounted Troop in 1975 and this Troop is now located with 160 Provost Company in Aldershot.

PROVOST SIGNALS

During the Second World War, with the ever-growing commitment of traffic control, the need for signal communications became increasingly apparent. Throughout the greater part, however, field telephones and motor-cycle patrols were the main sources upon which traffic posts and information posts placed reliance.

There were times when for particular operations radio was borrowed from other arms and services, if available, or supplied if the staff could be convinced of priorities from Royal Signals pools. Failing this, provost signals traffic had to be imposed, again subject to priorities often assessed by non-provost-sympathetic controllers, on the most convenient unit or formation network. And just as often the provost motorcyclist got the information through first.

But at an early date it was realized that for control through a long defile or bridge crossing, or enemy-covered land where telephone lines could be damaged, radio was essential to CMP and it must be under their control.

This was recognized in the planning for the Normandy Landing in 1944 and in May, 1944, an army group provost signal company was established and formed for 21 Army Group. It was equipped primarily with the 19 set and came under the jurisdiction of the Provost Marshal at HQ 21 Army Group. Lower formation provost units could ask for its assistance for specified tasks such as 30 Corps' advance to Arnhem in September, 1944, and sections were lent on priorities decided by the provost staff in addition to maintaining an overall skeleton provost linkage.

This system lasted only to the end of the Second World War and following demobilization the army group signal company was scaled-down to a corps provost signal company and allocated to the Territorial Army.

The new style of warfare envisaged for the future and the existing commitments in occupational and imperial policing rôles led to a growing demand for provost-controlled radio networks. Post-war economic difficulties were not conducive to any enlargement of expensive equipment but agreement in principle was reached in 1948 that such was a necessity and a signals training unit was formed at the Depot and Training Establishment RMP in Woking.

The Royal Signals provided an officer to get this new unit started and Captain R. Stewart, Royal Signals, attended the conventional Provost Officers' Course in autumn 1948. In early 1949, 31 Provost Signals Company came into being.

At this time radio equipment was still not normal unit equipment for any provost unit except the Corps Provost Signals Company TA. For training and operations, units in BAOR were dependent on theatre reserves for equipment, though there was a growing number of trained RMP operators. When, in 1953, Captain R. Meakin took over the Depot signals training company, the only change in the situation was the replacement of the 22 set by the 19 set. This was no progress for both were of wartime origin. However, by this time four provost signals companies were in process of forming in the Army Emergency Reserve, and training was given to those National Servicemen destined to form part of these units.

In 1957 Captain A. R. Smith became the Depot signals officer and by this time the case for VHF radio for Home Command companies was approved.

The only equipment readily available was of Anti-Aircraft Command origin. It consisted of a small vehicle radio (B43) linked to large static control receivers/transmitters (C44/R220) sited in each Home Command area. The static control stations were of two types, one of which was a fully automatic relay station. By modification and careful siting it was possible for vehicle patrols and unit HQ to communicate over distances up to approximately 15 miles. It was originally planned to link the system in to the GPO telephone to provide a national network but this was never completed.

The B43 appeared in quantity by 1961 and was replaced in 1965 by a smaller set manufactured by Pye Ltd. This replacement was at the same time adopted by the RAF Police, MOD Constabulary and other service departments. The Corps received fewer of these than of the B43.

During this time units overseas were also being equipped with VHF radio. While Hong Kong, Singapore and Cyprus received the Pye set, Berlin conformed to their garrison equipment policy and had Telefunken sets installed in vehicles. Both types of set provided direct communication between patrols and the control set at unit HQ.

As a result of considerable changes in tactical doctrine during the 'fifties, there was an urgent demand from almost every arm and service for more and better radio in both HF and VHF range. A new range of combat radio was developed to meet this need and provost in BAOR received the C13 (HF) Sets in 1961.

This is a robust and reliable vehicle-borne set, easy to operate and having great flexibility. Voice and key communications are possible over ranges up to 35 miles by day and night. A variety of antennae make greater ranges possible. The operator can be 'remote' from the set up to half a mile and a variety of 'boxes' or harness provides for HF/VHF linking, re-broadcast, remote re-broadcast, amplification and other facilities. Because of cost, then approximately £800 per set, only basic radios were first issued to the Corps.

During the next three years units of the Strategic Reserve received these sets and brigade, division and corps nets were established.

SIGNALS TRAINING

To meet the new requirement for more operators, the Depot Signals Section now under Captain R. A. Lawton increased the number of six-week courses to five a year. The aim, though still to produce an operator of a standard roughly the equivalent to Regimental BIII standards, had to allow for a shortage of trained officers and NCOs in units for supervising operators.

In 1960 tradition was broken and the Depot signals instructors started their training at the Signals Wing, Royal School of Military Engineering, Chatham, instead of at the Signals Wing, School of Infantry, Hythe. Infantry communications were becoming predominantly VHF and the change was an obvious and beneficial move. RMP instructors now received a very thorough fifteen-week grounding up to B1/Regimental instructors standing.

To augment training routine and provide both enjoyable and practical outside work the Depot Signals Section undertook to provide communications for traffic control at the annual Farnborough Air Show, for the annual amateur mixed foursomes golf tournament at Worplesdon and other similar events to give variety to training. By November, 1961, an RMP VHF network was established in all units in the United Kingdom.

By 1964, when Captain A. H. Bushell, having completed the course at Chatham, became the Depot signals officer, the lack of trained officers and senior NCOs in operational units was being keenly felt. By arrangement with the RSME, Chatham, selected NCOs began to attend up-grading courses there and more senior NCOs and warrant officers were drawn into the courses run by the Depot Signals Section.

The C13 Radio Stations were introduced throughout RMP units in

BAOR in 1964 and instantly transformed provost operational duties. The full effect of the exploitation of this radio system, followed in 1967 by the introduction of the Pye Cambridge VHF Radio Telephone, is mentioned on pages 102 and 103.

Signals are now a well-established and integral part of the RMP organization and establishment. Provost communications in any future operations can be relied upon to be immediate and efficient. Horse, motor-cycle, field-telephone, VHF radio, all have played their part; all had their vital contribution to make but modern radio-communication operated by provost personnel has completely revolutionized military police duties.

PART VI

Wings and Branches, Depots and Corps Organization

CHAPTER XVI

The Special Investigation Branch

IT is the duty of the Provost Marshal '. . . to discover the lurking subtleties of treacherous spies, and by learning the true interpretation of men's words, looks, manners, forms and habits of apparel, to be able to turn the insides of their heart outwards and to pull out that little devil of malicious deceit, though he lie hid in never so dark a corner; and truly a better service cannot be done.'

Francis Markham, 1622

Not a bad definition of the art of the detective!

ORIGINS: 1919–1926

The Special Investigation Branch (SIB) had an important rôle in the British Army of the Rhine from 1919 until it was phased out in 1926. The military police HQ, which included SIB, was established in the Excelsior Hotel, Cologne, adjacent to the Cathedral, which was requisitioned to house the various administrative departments of GHQ, following the British Army's declaration of Martial Law.

One officer was in charge of the Branch, which consisted of one WO 2 and some twenty NCOs specially selected from both the mounted and foot sections. A special allowance was paid to personnel employed on SIB duties of £5 for the first year and thereafter £9 per annum. There was a probationary period of one month. Each member carried a special pass bearing his photograph in both uniform and mufti and his credentials in English, French and German. The pass had to be signed afresh each month. A knowledge of German was a most desirable asset and a real hurdle for a volunteer to overcome was learning to use a typewriter—not a very familiar item of equipment to the soldier of 1919.

The Branch had a chief clerk but most documents were retained by the detective who maintained the files of his own cases until they were passed to the Army Prosecution Office.

The Branch was organized into three sections: No 1 dealt with traffic accidents and absentees and deserters, and maintained a two-way liaison on this aspect with Scotland Yard in London. No 2 Section was concerned with German nationals—those employed by the British Army or seeking employment, those the subject of complaints such as over-charging, insulting or assaulting members of the allied Occupation Forces, engaging in quarrels or affrays and being in unlawful possession of arms. Forgery, especially of British Army permits, was a regular subject of investigation.

No 3 Section specialized in anti-vice duties. In the early days this was a very special problem following the order of 'non-fraternization'. Mutinying German troops released a considerable number of detainees from the State Venereal Hospital. Consequently control of prostitution became a major concern and eventually No 3 Section had photographs of over 12,000 women on its records.

Other duties that had to be undertaken varied greatly from investigating German nationals caught smuggling contraband over the border of the Zone of Military Occupation to collecting allied prisoners of war who had been left to their own devices after release from camps or farms where they had been employed. Interrogations of curfew-breakers was a routine duty.

Duties in aid of the Intelligence Office included the arrest of suspects, the giving of evidence in Court in order that the agent or informer need not appear and reports on the local political atmosphere in relation to the Army of Occupation.

Fingerprint equipment, cameras and other aids to investigation were not available and much therefore depended on the goodwill and co-operation of the German civil police. The co-operation was of a high standard; illustrative of which was the case of a soldier of a Scottish regiment suspected of stabbing a German female who died from her wounds.

Fingernail parings and the kilt from the soldier, together with clothing from the girl, were handed over to the German police who arranged for them to be examined at Bonn University. Expert evidence by a professor from the University as to blood-groups brought about a conviction.

One outstanding criminal case of this period involving the SIB was that of a murdered New Zealand soldier. A German national was suspected as the soldier had been seen in the company of a German girl at the time. The German had, however, fled to Unoccupied Germany and thus beyond British jurisdiction. Shortly after the event the New

Zealand contingent returned home and the documents appertaining to the case were destroyed. Twelve months later a fellow-German informed the SIB that the suspect had returned to the Zone. Inquiries at the German State Prosecution Office produced a copy of the report by the New Zealand Provost Marshal. The culprit was apprehended and brought to trial, which necessitated several soldier witnesses being summoned from New Zealand to Cologne.

FORMATION OF SIB: 1939–1940

The advance elements of the British Expeditionary Force landed in France on 9 September, 1939, and from that day stores of every description began to pour into France. To deal with the off-loading of these stores at ports, their formation into dumps and depots, and their subsequent distribution, an ever-growing number of men were needed. The presence of so many attractive stores in often inadequately guarded docks, dumps and depots was accepted by some dishonest soldiers as an invitation to help themselves.

The professional thieves soon established contacts with local receivers, and the French police, already overburdened with work caused by the war, had little time to spare for the affairs of their allies. Then there were many cases of younger soldiers, finding the French drinks attractive and cheap, who over-indulged with the result that there were many reports of assaults, wounding and sexual crimes.

In Rennes, with a civilian population of 125,000, there were approximately 6,000 troops. The crimes recorded between 11 and 28 October, 1939, included a smash and grab raid on a jeweller's shop with watches and jewellery valued at 80,000 francs stolen; four cases of driving away civilian cars (one being the official car of the local French police); one case of housebreaking; two cases of robbery with violence; six cases of larceny; and fifteen other cases of assault, damage and fraud.

In Nantes, where there were 13,000 soldiers (mostly labour companies), the following crimes, alleged to have been committed by British troops, were reported between 30 November, 1939, and 16 December, 1939; one suspicious death of a soldier, three cases of breaking and entering, twenty cases of theft, five cases of car stealing and eight cases of assault. From these statistics recorded in only two cities it will be appreciated how serious the situation was becoming. Nantes, Brest and St Nazaire were suffering particularly badly from shipping thefts, and property which successfully survived the depredations there was being looted while in transit to its destination. Vehicles were arriving in the forward areas stripped of batteries, tool-kits and essential spares, and it appeared that they had been looted by the convoy guards or by the local population when in transit by rail. NAAFI stores suffered very badly.

The French *Gendarmerie*, harassed by overwork, were unable to give much assistance and turned for help to unit commanders who, with the best will in the world, were unable to do much; and the French police, discouraged at finding no one with whom they could collaborate, took little or no action to solve the crimes. The few cases that were successfully concluded from an investigation point of view were handed to officers for disciplinary proceedings but because of the inexperience and lack of knowledge of military law of many of them, many cases were so hopelessly prepared that the Judge Advocate General's Department had no alternative but to recommend that proceedings be dropped.

This, then, was the position when, in late November, 1939, the War Office asked for the help of the Metropolitan Police. The then Commissioner of Police of the Metropolis, Sir Philip Game, ordered Chief Inspector Hatherill to go to France and make an appreciation of the situation. Accompanied by Colonel S. V. Kennedy, Provost Marshal BEF and Detective Constable Nicholls, Chief Inspector Hatherill made a comprehensive tour of France which involved visits to docks, depots and the L of C and to forward areas. Notes were made of specific cases of crime, together with the steps taken by the French police to combat them, and on his return to London Mr Hatherill submitted his report, recommending the formation of an army CID to work in conjunction with the French police.

This was a somewhat radical suggestion; but it was seen that it was necessary and that if such a unit was raised it must come under the control of the Provost Marshal as the officer responsible for the maintenance of discipline in the field. It was therefore natural that such a unit should be a part of the Corps of Military Police, working with and receiving much of its information from them, exactly as in any modern civil police force.

A war establishment was drawn up and entitled: An Investigation Section of the Corps of Military Police, which allowed for one major (APM), one staff lieutenant, six lieutenants (investigating officers), six warrant officers 2 and forty-five sergeants (investigators). In January, 1940, the Commissioner of Police of the Metropolis was asked to release the requisite personnel, but because of the many new duties which the war thrust upon the civil police at first he could only release nineteen detectives of various ranks, all of whom had volunteered on learning of the proposed formation of the section. Of these, seven were granted immediate emergency commissions and the remaining twelve, after attestation, received immediate promotion—six to the rank of Warrant Officer 2 and six to sergeant.

BEF (FRANCE AND BELGIUM): 1940

On 12 February, 1940, the party, under command of their APM, Major C. E. Campion, who had been the detective superintendent in charge of the Criminal Record Office at New Scotland Yard, left for the CMP Depot and Training Establishment at Mytchett, Aldershot, to undergo a short course before embarking for overseas. Fortunately for them certain sections of the Army Act formed part of the training of civil police CID and, so far as law and its application were concerned, it was only necessary for them to 'get down' to King's Regulations, Rules of Procedure and court martial procedure. Structure of the Army, chain of command, channels of communication, foot-drill, small arms instruction and the Army systems of indent, issue and accounting were all duly absorbed in so far as the limited time available allowed and on 28 February, 1940, the section, with its stores, embarked at Southampton, to disembark at Le Havre the next day.

On their arrival in France their small number was increased by one officer, Captain Attfield, also a member of Scotland Yard, who assumed duty as administrative officer to the APM at GHQ. At Le Mans the section divided up, one officer, one warrant officer and one sergeant going to each of certain pre-arranged towns. Lieutenant Dibbens took his two ORs to Brest, Lieutenant Ellis to Nantes, Lieutenant Elliott to Rennes, Lieutenant Hooper to Le Mans, Lieutenant James to Dieppe and Lieutenant West to 1 Corps. Here they were welcomed by the respective APMs of these towns and were given every help and facility to begin their work.

In the provost companies already in France were a number of civil police reservists, recalled to the colours, and some of these were selected for attachment to the detachments of the SIB. These SIB detachments were received with mixed feelings among the various units of the Army. Some commanding officers saw a possible source of interference with their maintenance of discipline within their units, others saw in the Branch the possible precursor of an army Gestapo, but by most they were welcomed. As soon as they started their work it was found an easy matter to dispose of mistrust about their aims and the majority of their successfully completed cases owed much to the co-operation of commanding officers.

Every type of crime was dealt with, from murder downwards, and they soon found that they had not much spare time. Lieutenant Ellis quickly found himself involved in stamping out a large-scale racket in connection with NAAFI stores. Lieutenant Dibbens found so much work in the docks at Brest that he never seemed away from them and Lieutenant Elliott and the others were equally fully occupied in their respective districts.

Then came the invasion of the Low Countries by the enemy and, with the consequent re-grouping of the corps and divisions and their advance, it became impossible to carry out investigations. The enemy's success grew, and finally all SIB personnel found themselves absorbed into provost companies for traffic and refugee control duties.

On the evening of 19 May, 1940, during an enemy air raid on Rear HQ which was then at Boulogne, Major Campion was wounded in the head by bullets from a low-flying aircraft and died the following day from his injuries. As the enemy's advance increased all other SIB finally withdrew to embarkation points and returned safely to the United Kingdom.

THE UNITED KINGDOM: 1940–1975

After the evacuation of France the SIB personnel were not employed on investigation duties and there was much discussion as to whether they would be released from the army to return to their respective police forces. It seemed that the United Kingdom was the one place in the world where SIB was unnecessary in view of the fact that the country was adequately covered by efficient civil police forces. After further discussion, however, it was decided to post the remaining eighteen of the nineteen members who had crossed to France in their original groups of three (one lieutenant, one warrant officer and one sergeant) to the six commands.

At first their help was sought only in cases where continuation of enquiries from a military point of view was required, but gradually, as confidence in the SIB was established and war-time legislation was introduced and laid specific duties and authority on members of the Forces on duty in uniform, more and more enquiries were handed over in their entirety to SIB.

When, as will be shown later, Lieutenant Elliott left Southern Command to take a few men to the Middle East to assist in the formation of SIB there, his place was taken by 2nd Lieutenant Good. It was about this time that enquiries were started in Northern Ireland and Scottish Command into what proved to be the biggest fraud investigated by the Branch up to that date. Interception of a peculiarly-worded signal to Belfast from Scotland led to enquiries into a set of circumstances which revealed large-scale corruption and fraud in connection with conservancy contracts. Lieutenant Ellis and his men in Belfast spent long months carefully building up their case, all the time maintaining close liaison with Lieutenant James who had been posted to Scotland. The enquiries were finally completed and, in conjunction with the Royal Ulster Constabulary and the Scottish police, SIB in both countries arrested some soldiers and civilians. Some civilians, two or three officers and several ORs received heavy sentences before the respective civil and military courts, upwards of £3,000 in cash was recovered and credited to the public and an annual fraud of over £30,000 against the Government was prevented.

Eire's neutrality created a further problem and it was ultimately found necessary to form a special detachment of military police, composed of 'Redcaps' and SIB detectives, to patrol the frontier and deal with crimes committed in that region. Excellent liaison existed with the Garda Siochana and, within the limits possible between a belligerent and a neutral country, every help was given.

Food and petrol rationing regulations were beginning at this time to become more stringent and there was a large increase in cases of theft of rationed commodities. In spite of the addition of a substance which changed the colour of the petrol, there were plenty of people prepared to steal it and plenty of motorists prepared to buy and use it. Many were the subterfuges used to avoid detection. One motor-cyclist, long suspected of improper use of WD petrol, was finally searched by SIB, who found that though the petrol tank of the machine was filled with ordinary petrol, two flat cans of WD petrol were concealed in an anti-gas respirator carried in the 'alert' position and a pipe led therefrom to the carburettor of the machine. Other motorists cut out the petrol pump on their cars and fed the carburettor by gravity from cans of WD petrol concealed under the bonnets of the cars.

In the summer of 1941, after the formation of South-Eastern Command, Lieutenant West, who had recently been transferred there, and his men cleaned-up a very large-scale conspiracy involving the forgery of indents for civilian transport and conspiracy between certain RASC personnel and civilians. After protracted enquiries a suitable crop of courts martial and civil police court proceedings followed and some heavy sentences were awarded to the offenders. A final assessment of the amount involved in these dishonest practices was around £40,000.

It was in May, 1941, that the first big draft of reinforcements assembled at the CMP Depot at Mytchett to go to MEF. After some two months at the Depot they sailed towards the end of July for Suez. Included among them were many who were to achieve field rank and their journeyings and subsequent story is told in the next section of this chapter. Thereafter, up to the end of the war, there was a constant intake into the Branch to meet reinforcement demands from overseas theatres and commands.

The establishment of an SIB section in the early summer of 1941 was one lieutenant, one warrant officer 2, eight sergeants and two corporals, and it so remained until March, 1942, when it was increased by one warrant officer 2 and four sergeants and reduced by two corporals. In August, 1942, a further increase of the war establishment was authorized, allowing an additional officer—a captain—but increasing commitments called for a further review of the war establishment and, in January, 1943, it was again increased (for sections in the UK) to the strength per section at which it remained to the end of the war, i.e., one captain, two lieutenants, one warrant officer I, two warrant officers 2, twenty sergeants and two corporals.

The names of the hundreds of investigators who worked with SIB in the United Kingdom during the war years obviously cannot be mentioned individually but, wherever they may now be, they can congratulate themselves on the fact that they laid the foundation of what is now a permanent branch of the Corps of Royal Military Police—the Special Investigation Branch.

In August, 1945, the SIB units in the United Kingdom, which were then still operating more or less independently within the various commands, were brought under the control of Lieut-Colonel G. A. Hooper, who assumed the appointment of DPM SIB (UK) and who established the first HQ SIB (UK) at Reigate. Later, after a succession of moves, HQ SIB (UK) was established in its present location in Great Scotland Yard, London S.W.1, in late 1954 and Lieut-Colonel Hooper's successors in the appointment to DPM (later re-named APM) SIB (UK) were: Lieut-Colonels H. Purslow, F. H. Elliott, K. G. Thrift, G. Nicholls (later Colonel), A. C. Burcher, C. G. Clymow, W. S. Godden and L. W. Mason.

In addition to his overall control of the investigative rôle of SIB, the APM SIB (UK) was responsible for the training of recruits to the Branch. This was done at the SIB Training Wing (UK) which had a modest beginning in 1942 when it was formed by Captain Ellis and WO1 Wilsdon, who ran short courses primarily designed to test a potential recruit's claim to have knowledge of CID duties. The Training Wing developed and was finally staffed by a captain, a warrant officer I and two staff-sergeants who ran comprehensive primary courses of ten weeks' duration for potential recruits to the Branch and advanced refresher courses for more senior investigators, who received instruction in police photography and regimental fund accounting and were brought up-to-date with current legislation and methods of scenes-of-crime examination. In addition, senior investigators attended Metropolitan Police detective and scenes-of-crime courses.

With the run-down of the Army after the end of the war, the strength of SIB (UK) decreased proportionately until it reached its peacetime establishment of one lieutenant-colonel (APM SIB UK), two majors (DAPMs), three captains, four warrant officers I, six warrant officers 2, thirteen staff-sergeants and twenty sergeants. These were spread throughout the United Kingdom and operated in three well-defined areas, each under the overall control of APM SIB (UK). Despite the decrease in the number of investigators, the demand for their services remained heavy. In 1965, for example, 1,487 investigations were completed during which, in liaison with the civil police, 916 persons, both military and civilian, were arrested and property to the total value of £24,479. 17s. 7d. was recovered. Some of the cases involved investigations into fraud, which entailed investigators being away from their unit for months at a time, while others necessitated investigators travelling abroad in order to conclude their enquiries. These figures, while impressive in themselves, take no account of potential loss prevented by the deterrent effect on would-be offenders and the breaking-up of conspiracies and frauds.

In addition to the cases investigated during 1965 a total of 1,367 enquiries were carried out that year by members of the Branch on behalf of the civil police and other agencies, such as HM Customs and the GPO Investigation Branch. This fact, which in itself constitutes a tribute to SIB, illustrates the confidence placed by the civil authorities concerned in the integrity and ability of the members of SIB in the United Kingdom.

MIDDLE EAST: 1941–1945

With the increase in the number of troops in Egypt and Palestine following the entry of Italy into the war, crime increased proportionately. Conscription had brought into the Army a percentage of soldiers with criminal antecedents or tendencies. Many of these were drafted to the Middle East.

By September, 1940, there was no SIB and, indeed, pitifully few provost in the theatre, but there was an ever-growing incidence of crime which was causing some concern to the staffs of all three services. SIB help was requested and Lieutenant F. H. Elliott was directed to join a draft for Middle East, taking with him a Warrant Officer 2 and four sergeants of the Branch.

On arrival in Egypt they found that a number of soldiers had decided that the delights of Cairo and Alexandria were infinitely preferable to the monotony, discomforts and dangers of the Western Desert and East African campaigns. These deserters combined to form troublesome and dangerous gangs which were to become very familiar to the Branch under the names of 'The Free British Corps' and 'The Dead-End Kids'.

Before the arrival of this section, however, the Provost Marshal, MEF, Colonel F. C. Bryant, selected Captain C. J. Harper to organize a local

SIB force. Captain Harper formed his HQ at Bab-el-Hadid Barracks in Cairo and at first concentrated his efforts in that city and on the Suez Canal. But with the arrival of the section from England new detachments were opened.

Not a day passed without many arrests being made. Most of them were for larceny and many were items of only a few shillings in value. In the docks and on the railways incalculable harm was being done to the war effort by wholesale thieving by the natives. Railway employees marked wagons loaded with attractive stores and failed to seal them properly and thus ensured that the heavily overloaded trains, travelling at little more than walking pace, were looted before arrival at their destination.

In July, 1941, the detachment in Canal North recovered two aircraft engines which had been stolen from a train by being pushed off flat cars, levered into position near some sand dunes and then covered in sand.

In spite of a small, steady flow of recruits to the Branch, its numbers remained woefully inadequate. However, further reinforcements were *en route* from England and on 20 September, 1941, there was much relief to see the arrival at Suez of Lieutenant H. J. Dibbens with half-a-dozen subalterns—Lieutenants K. G. Thrift, R. A. Crocker and G. Nicholls among them.

At the close of 1941 there was one section working in Cairo, one in Alexandria, which performed anything required of them in the Western Desert, one in Canal Area, working from Port Said in the north to Safaga on the Red Sea southwards and to Zagazig and Damanhur in the Delta, one in Palestine with its commitments in the Levant, and small detachments in Cyprus, Sudan and Eritrea.

One of the biggest worries of the SIB remained with them until the last day of the war, in spite of hundreds of arrests and convictions. Most Arabs regard the possession of a firearm as the sign of manhood. The Jews in Palestine were anxious to obtain all the firearms possible and so were numerous other parties in the Middle East, some subversive, some patriotic. Gangs of rifle thieves operated on the troop trains, others entered camps at night. Some gangs concentrated on raiding dumps for arms and ammunition, others relied on the carelessness of soldiers and waited for a rifle to be leaned against a wall and the soldier to turn his back for a moment. The number of thefts of arms of all types and ammunition was appalling and 'The Dead-End Kids' were responsible for many of them. These deserters lived by becoming friendly with soldiers they met, getting themselves invited to a canteen or some place in a unit lines and then taking advantage of any opportunity to steal whatever they could lay their hands on.

Tel-el-Kebir, where there was one of the largest Ordnance depots of the Middle East, remained a problem all through the war. Fullest advantage was taken of the Egyptian Government decree permitting the use of firearms in the protection of WD property and a large number of would-be thieves were shot and killed by SIB as well as by unit guards.

Drug-running was another crime which was beginning to reach alarming proportions. Hashish and opium were the main drugs. These have always been the curse of Egypt, but the Lebanese authorities have always tolerated the growing of the hemp plant and were loath to destroy crops. The Egyptian Government retaliated by training a first-class anti-narcotics organization which co-operated closely with the Palestine Police. By this means the trade had been cut down considerably by the outbreak of war. The answer of the drug-runners was to use WD vehicles and drivers who were immune from search by the Egyptian Police at the frontiers. Profits from the sale of drugs were high and the smugglers were able to offer high rewards to any soldier who was prepared to risk being caught. Numberless cases were successfully dealt with by the SIB, but right up to the end of the war the smugglers always found some soldier who could be corrupted by promise of large rewards for consignments successfully delivered.

With the victory at Alamein and the advance into the desert, it became necessary to extend the Alexandria and Western Desert section. By mid-November, 1942, detachments had been placed at Daba, Mersa Matruh, Sollum and Tobruk. It also became necessary to open detachments in the Delta to intercept the loads of captured enemy stores which were being stolen and brought by camel into the Delta. Ultimately, the Alexandria section advanced to the frontier at Sollum and a new section was formed under Major R. A. Crocker for duties in Libya.

Lieutenant M. E. Good—one of the officers who had arrived in September, 1941—had opened a small detachment in Baghdad. His health suffered and he was transferred to Cyprus, his place being taken by Lieutenant K. G. Thrift, who was to remain there in charge of the destinies of SIB in Persia and Iraq, both during the time that these two countries were included in Middle East Command and when they came under Paiforce.

Thefts continued wholesale on an alarming scale. At the various ports and wharves everything capable of being stolen was fair game for the natives. Much of the unloading of vessels was done by lighters and cases of foodstuffs and other marketable commodities were pushed into the water, later to be retrieved by gangs of thieves who had gone into partnership with 'bum-boatmen'. So high became the incidence of thefts carried out by these water-borne rascals that SIB in port areas were allocated launches and these were operated with a marked degree of success until the end of the war at Suez, Port Said and Alexandria.

Many contracts were entered into between the Army and local contractors for the supply of items which could be produced locally, thereby saving valuable shipping space. There were many abuses and convictions were obtained against soldiers who had succumbed to the temptation to accept a sum of money for merely turning a blind eye to the contractors' deficiency in quantity, quality or both.

A new section had also been formed in Syria and the Lebanon and was very fully occupied. These countries were very poor and the native thieves found a market for all types of WD stores, especially motor vehicles and tyres.

HQ 9th Army had a large number of troops under command to resist any attempt by the enemy to breach the neutrality of Turkey. Airstrips and roads were being built or improved, largely by local contractors under Royal Engineers supervision, and many abuses of specification and quality of materials were uncovered.

One bad case concerned the building of a road which, had the Germans attacked through Turkey, would have been of great importance. The RE officer who was supervising the local contractor received gifts of money and valuable jewellery to pass inferior work on the road. When the offence was brought to light it was found that instead of being a good hardcore-built road it was little more than a strip of tar sprayed on the desert and would scarcely have supported a motor-car, much less tanks and their transporters.

In Alexandria a gang of deserters was making a lucrative business out of stealing motor lorries, driving them to Alexandria docks and, by means of forged gate passes, work tickets and movement orders, loading up with attractive stores and taking them to the Lebanon. Here the goods were sold with the connivance of a member of the Lebanese Chamber of Deputies and the proceeds invested in hashish, which was loaded into four-gallon petrol tins and sealed, then transported to Egypt, where it was sold at an enormous profit. When the ringleaders were finally arrested they were occupying a magnificent villa at Sidi Bishr and possessed a housefull of expensive furniture and two or three cars. Tins of hashish were found buried in the garden and currency notes to the value of several thousand pounds were hidden throughout the villa.

Shortly after the arrests a civilian lorry was seen by SIB carrying mild steel bars of the type used in reinforcing concrete which were unobtainable on the civilian market. It was followed and enquiries showed that large quantities of such steel had been stolen from various RE dumps and sold to civilian contractors for constructing houses. The case became more and more complicated and almost caused an Egyptian Government crisis due to the high social positions of some of the people involved. During the enquiries a large quantity of naval stores was recovered and the total 'bag' of prisoners amounted to over fifty.

During the Cairo conference between Mr Churchill and Mr Roosevelt, held at the Mena House Hotel, SIB were selected to arrange for the security of the perimeter of the building and to escort the principals. Although slightly outside the normal scope of SIB duties, everything went off so well that commendations were received from Army and diplomatic authorities.

MIDDLE EAST AND AFRICA: 1945–1956

At the end of the Second World War SIB units were operating in Iran, Iraq, Syria, Lebanon, Palestine, Egypt, Cyprus, Benghazi, Tripoli, Sudan, Eritrea and Kenya. The rundown in numbers of British troops in the Middle East affected SIB, as it did the remainder of the army and in mid-1946 Paiforce closed down, followed shortly afterwards by the withdrawal of SIB from Syria and Lebanon. Then came the closing down of the SIB units in Iraq in September, 1947, and later in Sudan and Eritrea—although SIB representatives visited the latter country to carry out investigations up to 1949.

In early 1947 the SIB sections in Cairo and Alexandria were moved to the Canal Zone where there was already one section operating and where a SIB Training Wing had been established at the RMP (MEF) Depot at El Ballah.

In 1948 the SIB section in Palestine, which had been operating from Jerusalem with detachments at Haifa and Sarafand, was withdrawn to the Canal Zone from where it was moved to East Africa, eventually being transferred to East Africa Command. SIB strength in the Middle East was then made up of three sections in the Canal Zone operating under the control of Lieut-Colonel G. Nicholls at GHQ MEF, one section in Cyprus and one section based in Tripoli which was responsible for investigations in Tripolitania, Libya and Greece (the responsibility for the latter country having earlier been transferred from CMF to MEF).

In 1951 two of the sections in the Canal Zone were closed down, leaving one section responsible for the whole of SIB work throughout the Zone. The work-load at that time and in the succeeding years was extremely heavy. Attacks by Egyptians on depots and vehicle convoys were frequent and the co-operation which SIB had always enjoyed with the Egyptian Police became almost non-existent. Many cases were dealt with involving losses of arms, accidental shooting and, in addition, SIB had to carry out irksome and time-consuming enquiries of an Internal Security nature. Thefts of WD property from such places as the depots at El Ballah and Geneifa were prevalent and a constant 'war' was waged by SIB against Egyptian thieves who on several occasions attempted to bribe soldiers on guard duty into allowing them to enter the depots to steal property. Numerous false claims and complaints were made against British troops by the civil population, which was then almost entirely hostile, and all had to be investigated by SIB. Added to this, SIB resources were severely strained by the increase in crime among the troops who, concentrated in the Canal Zone, were confined to their camps after normal duty hours.

With the final withdrawal from the Canal Zone SIB left Egypt and moved to Cyprus, where HQ SIB (MELF) was eventually established and was responsible for the control of investigations throughout the whole of the Mediterranean area.

The following years saw much unrest in the Middle East with SIB heavily committed in the various 'trouble-spots'. With the granting of independence to Cyprus, SIB on that island was established in the Sovereign Base Area and a separate SIB unit to cover Malta and Libya was formed under the command of Major L. W. Mason, who controlled detachments in Malta, Tripoli and Benghazi. When a United Nations peace-keeping force was set up in Cyprus, Major Mason was seconded to that force and established a Special Investigation Unit known as SIU UNIFICYP. The SIB contribution to this unit, which was composed of investigators from each of the countries contributing to the force, was one warrant officer I, as warrant officer-in-charge, and one staff sergeant or sergeant. As well as normal SIB duties the unit carried out intelligence and anti-vice duties and in addition to the novelty of wearing the United Nations blue beret the SIB members who served in UNFICYP were awarded the UN Peace Medal which served as a constant reminder of their service with the first truly international investigation unit.

In 1965 Major C. G. Clymow established in Cyprus a combined HQ to control SIB units in Malta, Cyrenaica and Cyprus.

In the meantime SIB units had continued to operate in Africa, but were gradually run-down with the granting of independence to the various countries. With the outbreak of terrorist activities in Kenya and the beginning of the campaign against the Mau-Mau, the small SIB detachment in East Africa was built up to full section strength and Major C. J. Dawson was appointed DAPM (SIB). Investigators worked throughout the Emergency in close liaison with the civil police but, even so, language problems and differing tribal customs made investigation duties often difficult and frustrating—a situation complicated by the difficulties experienced when interviewing witnesses and suspects who had sometimes unwillingly, and under threat of death, participated in oath-taking ceremonies.

The standard of discipline among the troops, however, was of a generally high standard, although several allegations of ill-treatment of suspected terrorists and detainees were investigated. As a result of one such investigation, a British major was convicted by general court martial and sentenced to seven years' imprisonment on charges of causing grievous bodily harm to African civilians who had been in military custody.

At the end of the Emergency the SIB section was reduced in strength but in 1963 opened a small detachment in Swaziland where British troops had been sent at the request of the Government of that country who had found themselves unable to cope with a wave of civil disorders. On the withdrawal of SIB from Kenya and the closing down of East Africa Command in 1965 the control of the Swaziland detachment passed to HQ MELF and then in early 1966 to HQ SIB (UK). The detachment finally closed down in November, 1966.

NORTH AFRICA AND ITALY: 1942–1955

An SIB section landed in Algiers in November, 1942, under the command of Captain W. Heddon. The demands for SIB services were heavy and the need for early expansion soon became evident.

By March, 1943, five sections were operating in North Africa and HQ SIB was formed consisting of one DAPM (Captain Heddon) and five warrant-officers or NCOs.

By June, 1944, Captain Heddon had become the DPM SIB and the number of sections had grown from five to thirteen and was operating throughout North Africa, Sicily and Italy; an average of 2,000 arrests were being made each month. An additional section was formed early in 1945 and used solely to counter the high incidence of theft of WD stores on railways.

The war against theft of WD arms, equipment and stores in Italy involved operations against armed bands of Italians and deserters from the allied armies.

In the different countries in which SIB were employed they had to learn something of the complicated local police systems and, since the occupation of Italy and Sicily, Allied Military Government proclamations, courts, law and procedure. The armies of the Central Mediterranean theatre (CMF) contained a greater variety of races and creeds than any other major theatre in the war. In dealing also with the allied, dominion and colonial troops with their different morals, customs and languages, many new problems called for solution by the police.

Available records show that the total number of cases investigated by SIB during the campaign was 22,809, resulting in the arrest of 38,257 soldiers and civilians. The value of WD property recovered was enormous.

Lieut-Colonel W. Heddon directed SIB affairs with marked success from the beginning to the end of the campaign. Captain H. P. Clarke and Captain W. J. Cooper led operations against Italian gangsters in southern Italy and Captain Archer was responsible for dealing with serious crime in the Rome area, a formidable task which he carried out with success.

In addition to the prevention, detection and investigation of serious crime of all kinds, the SIB were called in at the latter end of 1944 to investigate alleged war crimes and two special sections were raised for this purpose. The scope of these investigations widened rapidly and the operations of these sections covered a distance of 1,100 miles. This sphere of investigation had been allotted to the SIB as there was no other organization capable of undertaking the work. There is no doubt, however, that the assumption of these extra and very heavy responsibilities by the already strained SIB organization seriously affected the efficiency of their work of dealing with serious crime.

At the end of the war the SIB element of CMF was concentrated mainly in central and northern Italy and operated also in Austria, Trieste and on the Yugoslavian border. Heavy demands were made on their services to investigate thefts of WD stores and to combat corruption among those responsible for reconstruction contracts. In addition, the work of tracking down war criminals and collaborators increased in scale. As the allied armies evacuated the Central Mediterranean area, so the number of SIB units and the establishments of the remaining units were decreased and in mid-1947 Major F. Howarth closed down SIB in Italy and two sections of SIB (91 and 93) were transferred to the independent commands of BTA (British Troops Austria) and BETFOR (British Element Trieste Force) respectively. At this time the standard size of a SIB section was one captain, one warrant officer I, one warrant officer 2, one staff-sergeant and twelve sergeants. On the handover of Trieste to the Italians in 1954, 93 Section, then under the command of Captain E. G. Beach, moved to BAOR. When, in 1955, 91 Section was disbanded and SIB withdrew from Austria, nothing then was left of what had been one of the largest and most efficient of the war-time SIB organizations.

INDIA: 1943–1947

The suggestion that SIB should be formed for India received the approval of the War Office in the early autumn of 1943 and by 20 November, 1943, two sections of SIB of the CMP (India) had been formed and were allotted to Eastern Command and Southern Army. Early in 1944 Major J. G. Ellis transferred from Italy and on promotion to lieutenant-colonel became the first DPM SIB India under Brigadier A. R. Forbes. A few members of the Branch were transferred to India from the Middle East and with these and the two sections already raised in India, SIB began to expand until there was a section or detachment in all principal towns and districts.

Records show that during 1944 2,557 cases were investigated, 3,112 arrests were made and property to the value of £786,500 was recovered.

The SIB was highly and efficiently organized. A *Police Gazette*, parallel in every way to that of New Scotland Yard, was circulated to all Indian civil police forces, heads of various services and provost and intelligence sections, British, Indian, and allied, throughout the theatre. The SIB Training Establishment, which was situated within the CMP(I) Training Centre and Depot at Secunderabad, was well established and the chief instructor, in order to facilitate the instruction of SIB personnel in Indian law and police methods, attended and successfully passed the examination of the Police Training College in the United Provinces.

One of the first cases dealt with by SIB India was the discovery of a fraud which involved civilian contractors and a major of the Indian Engineers. Bogus claims for payment (some of which were paid by the Burma Government) were submitted by the civilian contractors and passed by the major who was acting as DCRE. Protracted inquiries by Lieut-Colonel Ellis, Major Beck and RSM Flynn, in conjunction with the civil CID, resulted in sufficient evidence being obtained to arrest the officer and certain civilians. The officer was traced to Imphal, which at that time was besieged by the Japanese and unapproachable except by air. So a special plane was chartered and an officer of the SIB flew over Japanese-held territory into Imphal; the officer was arrested and flown back to India. The civil police arrested twenty-five contractors and £300,000 was recovered for the Government of Burma. Another *cause célèbre* about this time was that of the arrest of an assistant military secretary in GHQ India who, being responsible for postings of all officers of the RIASC, was accepting bribes from officers anxious to avoid overseas service. They received improper postings and the result of this case was that five officers were cashiered and several others received lesser punishments.

After the severe Bombay explosion in April, 1944, when considerable gold bullion was blown up and lost, SIB patiently followed up many rumours and anonymous letters and succeeded after four months in recovering seven bars of gold to the value of Rs 670,000 and these were safely returned to the Reserve Bank of India.

India, throughout its history, has had the reputation of being a country where fraud and corruption are rife and the war seemed to worsen that reputation. A conspiracy at Dum Dum airport led to the arrest of two officers and nineteen others for conspiracies to defraud the Government in connection with forged and fictitious muster rolls for coolie labour. More than six months' investigation revealed a large conversion of Government money. At the same time that this inquiry was proceeding the section was also engaged with the civil police in enquiries into the black market for medical supplies and drugs. Ultimately forty persons were arrested and German and Italian drugs, then practically unobtainable, to the value of Rs 229,000 were recovered.

Cases of dacoity were an ever-present menace to lonely British troops and after a large number of reports of such cases a group of SIB NCOs were struck off other duties specially to deal with them. After weeks of patient observation the time was considered ripe to act and CSM Allen of 117 Section bravely volunteered to act as a decoy. The trap was successful and four dacoits were arrested and later found to have been responsible for twenty-three such cases. Sergeant Clarke of 116 Section was similarly engaged about this time and with some of his comrades finally rounded up nine native armed robbers who had for some time been operating in and around Ranchi.

After the war in Europe ended the majority of the members of SIB in India, who were almost exclusively former civil policemen, opted to return to the UK for premature release so that they could return to their respective police forces. Their work was taken over by SIB-trained Indian personnel and SIB gradually withdrew from India completely before independence was achieved on 15 August, 1947.

FAR EAST: 1945–1975

On VJ Day Major F. R. Pollard moved from India to Singapore to organize SIB enquiries and to report on possible atrocities. Gradually the strength of SIB increased and 91 Section was formed to cover the whole of the area which had been in Japanese occupation. This section, which was much larger than sections operating in Europe, had detachments in Hong Kong and Malaya with its HQ in Singapore. In 1947 Major R. B. Sexton assumed the appointment of APM SIB (FARELF) and Section HQ was established in an ex-Army Nissen hut in Waterloo Street, Singapore, a building which was to become only too familiar to personnel of SIB FARELF during the succeeding years. In addition to carrying out their normal duties the investigators had to learn to cope with periodic invasions of white ants, which threatened to bring the building down about their ears!

The build-up of British troops in Malaya during the communist Emergency brought heavy demands for SIB services and reinforcements were sent from the UK. The investigators soon found themselves heavily committed enquiring into thefts of WD property, losses of arms—many of which found their way into the hands of the terrorists—and many crimes of violence, from murder downward. The detachments in Malaya and Hong Kong were up-graded to section status, each with a captain as OC and Captain T. Sharman was appointed as OC Singapore Section, all working under the central control of DAPM SIB FARELF (then Major R. R. Hughes) who moved his HQ to the offices of the PM FARELF at GHQ.

When British troops were sent from Hong Kong to Korea, two SIB investigators from Malaya accompanied them and were soon followed by other members of the Branch. A section was set up under the command of Major C. Bennett at Taegu with a detachment at Pusan commanded by Captain J. Davidson and another at Seoul under command of a warrant officer 2. An NCO was also stationed at Kure in Japan to carry out investigations among troops at the rest camps in Japan.

In July, 1951, Sergeant D. Kinnear, SIB, was murdered by Filipino troops while attempting to arrest two of their number for rape.

Throughout the early stages of the Korean campaign the SIB investigators who, with their counterparts in the US forces were the only law enforcement agencies functioning in South Korea, worked under the most arduous and trying conditions. They were responsible for all investigations involving Commonwealth and European troops and civilians and their enquiries at times took them into front-line positions where on occasions troops were interviewed while actually engaged on operations against the enemy. They worked in the most adverse weather conditions handicapped by the fact that the protective clothing issued to British troops was not designed to cope with the Korean weather. It was during this period that Major Bennett was mentioned in despatches and WO.2 F. L. Goymer and Sergeant K. L. Williams were awarded the BEM. As the situation eased and the South Korean police authority was re-established the SIB investigators found themselves involved in a pattern of enquiries which had become only too familiar to their colleagues in other active service areas. Murders, accidental shootings and crimes of violence were commonplace and enquiries into thefts of WD arms, ammunition and stores took up more and more of their time.

Space does not permit the mention of individual cases but one particular case illustrates the difficulties encountered by SIB. It concerns a WD vehicle which was stolen and later found, re-painted, in the possession of a South Korean police captain who committed suicide rather than 'lose face' by admitting the theft and returning the vehicle.

At the end of the campaign, SIB withdrew from Korea and the detachment in Japan finally closed in 1956. There was then a gradual run-down of SIB throughout the Far East. In 1963 Malaya Section reverted to detachment status and came under the command of Captain W. J. H. A. Jackson in Singapore. However, that year saw the beginning of the Indonesian confrontation with Malaysia and there was a build-up of Commonwealth troops mainly in East Malaysia (Sabah and Sarawak). At first investigators were flown from Singapore to carry out any enquiries necessary, but later detachments were set up in Brunei and then in Borneo. The investigators operating from Borneo travelled great distances during their enquiries and full advantage was taken of a liaison established with the Army Air Corps to ensure that SIB assistance, when called for, was supplied as speedily and efficiently as possible. The largest number of enquiries dealt with by SIB at this time involved deaths of servicemen or offences involving the discharge or attempted discharge of firearms, but inevitably conditions were such that some soldiers committed offences against the local population, usually as a result of consuming too much of the potent local beer.

One particular case which was widely reported in the British press involved five soldiers who, on returning from a patrol on which one of their comrades had been killed, formed the mistaken opinion that the headman of the village they were using as a base was in league with the Indonesians. They therefore conspired together to kill him and after drawing lots for the 'privilege' one of the soldiers threw a hand-grenade into his hut. Luckily the fuse of the grenade was damp and although it fell on to a bed in which the headman's family was sleeping, it did not explode. As a result of SIB investigations into the incident, the conspirators appeared before a court martial in Singapore and were sentenced to imprisonment.

In May, 1966, the confrontation ended and later that year the Borneo detachment closed down and the investigators concerned returned to Singapore. With the exception of the small detachment in Hong Kong, SIB coverage for the Far East area was provided from Singapore, which was under command of Major B. Thomas as DAPM SIB (FARELF), but here too came closure and from December, 1971, Hong Kong became the only Far East SIB location except for an element in ANZUK Provost Unit which survived in Singapore until 30 September, 1974.

NORTH-WEST EUROPE AND BAOR: 1944–1975

The work of SIB in North-West Europe both during and after the Second World War was so vast that it is not possible to do more than give a brief outline of its activities and some statistics.

The first section to land in 1944 was under command of Lieutenant Fawcett, formerly of the Isle of Wight Constabulary, landing on the Normandy beaches on 8 June (D+2).

It would not be fair to exclude from this history the fact that almost the first case investigated by Lieutenant Fawcett's section involved a military policeman! A member of a provost company was found to have stolen 18,000 francs from a German prisoner committed to his charge for escort. He was tried by court martial and sentenced to eighteen months imprisonment. Almost immediately afterwards SIB discovered that larceny from prisoners-of-war was taking place at one of the PoW camps. A search disclosed that nearly every member of the VP police guard was in possession of articles of property taken from prisoners. The NCOs were court martialled and the private soldiers warned. The case, which received widespread publicity throughout the theatre, had a salutary effect and there was no further case of that nature. It also demonstrated the the military police were not prepared to tolerate any shortcomings in their own ranks.

With 2nd Army HQ was Captain F. R. Pollard and his section. This officer gave service of the highest order throughout the campaign and later became APM SIB at HQ 21 Army Group.

As the theatre of operations and the area of liberated country increased, a ready black market, offering attractive prices for goods, was soon in full swing, but its prosperity was often shortlived thanks to the attentions of the SIB.

To counteract this threat a total of fifteen sections, each section consisting of one captain, one lieutenant, two warrant officers and twelve other ranks per section, were in operation and hundreds of thousands of pounds' worth of Army stores were recovered.

Towards the end of the war the number of crimes involving the sale of military property in the French and Belgian black market became so great that additional SIB sections had to be sent out from England. Even with these reinforcements it was never possible to catch up with arrears of work. SIB officers and NCOs worked to the limit of their endurance but there would have been ample employment for ten times their number.

The following figures compiled for the campaign up to 31 March, 1945, of the North-West Europe theatre of war indicate what they achieved:

Arrests		*Property recovered (value)*	
Military	2,335	War Department	£134,827
Merchant Navy	123	Allied	£18,150
Allied Forces	129	Enemy	£194,834
Civilians	5,288	Civilians	£36,753
Total	7,875 persons	Total	£384,564

The following figures show the total cases reported to and completed by the SIB up to the same date. These figures include both military and civilian offenders; but as in many cases both were involved it is not practicable to separate civil from military crime in these statistics.

	Cases reported	*Cases completed*
Larceny, fraud, etc	1,531	1,222
Looting	152	122
Receiving, etc	3,431	3,395
Breaking offences	110	64
Murder, assault, robbery with violence, etc	141	113
Rape, indecency, etc	112	91
Miscellaneous	927	873
	6,404	5,880

In addition to their ordinary duties detecting crime, SIB personnel were often called upon to undertake extraordinary tasks. Much of the credit for the successful trial and conviction of Kramer, 'The Beast of Belsen', and his subordinates should go to Major F. R. Pollard, Captain A. J. Fox and CSM Liddle of the SIB, who were sent to the concentration camp to select witnesses and take statements of evidence concerning atrocities.

At the end of the war SIB units were withdrawn from France, with the exception of one section which remained at Calais until late 1947 to cover the activities of soldiers engaged in 'trooping' between France and UK, and a two-man detachment in Paris. This detachment was often hopelessly overworked as Paris was a large black-market centre through which passed thousands of pounds' worth of property stolen by displaced persons returning from Germany. The Paris detachment in fact closed in 1948 and thereafter enquiries in France were carried out by members of SIB (UK). However, with the establishment of NATO HQ at Versailles, a SIB NCO was sent to France as part of the establishment of SHAPE Provost Company and eventually moved with SHAPE into Belgium.

With the occupation of Germany SIB units were established

throughout the British Zone. As can be imagined, in the immediate post-war years black-market activity was at its height and SIB investigators worked in close liaison with their American and French counterparts to apprehend the persons responsible. At that time almost all military stores and equipment as well as NAAFI goods such as spirits, cigarettes and coffee, commanded very high prices on the black market and the temptations offered to the poorly-paid servicemen were great. The huge profits that could be made in such transactions attracted, as always, the unscrupulous and dishonest elements and once again SIB investigators found themselves combating organized gangs of thieves and dealing with the inevitable crimes of theft and violence.

At this time the various SIB sections worked directly under their appropriate formation HQ and there was little or no central supervision or co-ordination. However, in February, 1947, Lieut-Colonel K. G. Thrift assumed the appointment of DPM SIB BAOR and established his HQ at Bad Oeynhausen. He had under his control eight sections operating in Hamburg, Hannover, Bielefeld, Berlin, Bad Rothenfelde, Celle, Düsseldorf and Münster, with APMs SIB exercising local control at Hamburg, Hannover, Lübbecke and Düsseldorf.

The following years saw a gradual run-down in SIB strength as the British Army withdrew from areas which had been handed back to the newly-constituted *Bundeswehr*. Space does not permit the details of all the various moves to be given but in 1954, shortly after the arrival of 93 Section from Trieste, HQ SIB BAOR moved to Rheindahlen. At that time the APM SIB (BAOR), Lieut-Colonel F. H. Elliott, had under his command two DAPMs SIB (Major A. C. Burcher at Hannover and Major R. R. Hughes, at Lübbecke) who controlled six sections between them. The number of sections was later reduced to four and so it remained until November, 1964, when, with War Office approval, Lieut-Colonel G. Nicholls disbanded the sections and reorganized SIB (BAOR) on the same lines as SIB (UK). There was then a central HQ SIB (BAOR) at Rheindahlen with twelve detachments stationed throughout Rhine Army from Berlin to Grobbendonk in Belgium.

It would be impossible to detail the numbers of serious crimes dealt with by members of SIB in BAOR during the period since the end of the Second World War. Many of the more 'newsworthy' civil and military offences, such as murder and mutiny, were widely reported in the British press, particularly at times when there was a dearth of other, more interesting, world news. The majority of cases, however, were of little public interest. Throughout, SIB established and maintained the closest liaison with the German civil police forces to whom they have rendered, and from whom they have received, all possible assistance whenever required.

Although the number of SIB investigators has been greatly reduced with the run-down of the Army, and of RMP in particular, the number of cases investigated by individual investigators has remained constant and on occasions has increased. This can be seen from the fact that in 1966—with a total strength of eleven officers and fifty-seven other ranks—SIB BAOR carried out 1,896 investigations of all types during which 1,545 persons, both civilians and military, were either reported or arrested and in which property to the total value of almost £8,000 recovered.

CARIBBEAN AND GIBRALTAR

At various times since the Second World War SIB assistance has been provided when required at places far removed from the normal operational areas. From 1956 to 1961 a detachment operated in the Caribbean area, based in Jamaica. From 1963 the sole representative of the Corps in Gibraltar was a SIB warrant officer, and in August, 1967, Captain S. W. Carrier and Sergeant R. J. Thorpe were flown to British Honduras (now Belize) to investigate the murder of a British serviceman there.

Both during and after the Second World War, in the United Kingdom and overseas, criminals, black marketeers and receivers developed remarkable skill in getting their spoils through the network of checks and guards and disposing of them, and it has been recognized by commanders everywhere that only the ability of the SIB has prevented this type of crime from getting out of hand.

The value of investigation cannot be measured by the value of the goods recovered. Many crimes which were contemplated were never committed because of the deterrent effect of the known presence of detectives in the Army. Many serious crimes adversely affecting discipline and morale, such as murder, rape and arson in which there is no monetary object, are investigated and often several crimes have been exposed simply because a member of the SIB has spotted a small incongruity which might have escaped the notice of a less highly-trained observer.

The investigators of SIB since the formation of the Branch have been about the hardest-worked people in the Army; often nothing but their enthusiasm has kept them going and nothing short of great efficiency could have produced such good results.

Their duties frequently have included the interrogation of senior officers, sometimes as potential offenders. That the SIB have always done this with tact and persistence and without fear or favour is a high tribute to the value and integrity of these fine investigators.

CHAPTER XVII

Wings and Branches

ATS PROVOST

In 1941 the Auxiliary Territorial Service (ATS) was placed under partial Military Law, making auxiliaries liable to Sections 40 and 41 of the Army Act. As a result it was decided in the same year to form an ATS Provost Wing composed of ATS auxiliaries. A call for volunteers met with a good response and courses of instruction in provost duties for selected officers and other ranks began at the CMP Depot at Mytchett in December, 1941.

The first allocation of ATS Provost was made to UK Commands in February, 1942, when fifteen NCOs began duty in London and twelve in Edinburgh. ATS Provost officers were appointed to the Staff as DAPMs (captains) and staff lieutenants.

The immediate effect of the introduction of the ATS Provost Wing was a striking improvement in the discipline and dress of the members of the ATS when out of barracks. The appearance of ATS 'Redcaps' in the streets did not pass without some comment from the general public, but the consensus of opinion was one of admiration for their smart appearance and fine example.

ATS Provost Wing in the United Kingdom experienced a wide variety of duties outside its normal routine, among them escorting German women prisoners-of-war captured in France from south coast ports to their camps, participation in a combined civil police and military raid on the Polish Army camp in Norfolk from where it was suspected that the notorious Polish gaol-breaker, Zobrowski, was receiving assistance. ATS Provost, whose task it was to search the women's quarters, were commended for the part they played in this raid, which resulted in the arrest and subsequent deportation of fifty-six Polish soldiers.

By the end of 1942 the strength of the ATS in the Middle East had reached such proportions that it was decided to form an ATS Provost Wing there. Accordingly, in December of that year, the first party of ATS Provost, consisting of Junior Commander MacDermott, Subaltern Wigmore and Sergeants Franklin, Lewis, Maynard and Dickinson, sailed from the United Kingdom to the Middle East. The first duty of this party on arrival was to recruit and train auxiliaries selected from those already serving there; these were mostly Palestinians and training was carried out at the CMP Depot at Almaza.

In addition to routine street patrols there was the continual search for native ATS absentees. Of the many duties ATS Provost in the Middle East were called upon to perform those of the anti-smuggling patrols were perhaps the most interesting. Large numbers of troops and ATS indulged in smuggling arms, jewellery, cosmetics, wines and spirits and miscellaneous army property from Egypt into Palestine.

On one occasion a member of ATS Provost in Egypt arrested an ATS sergeant suspected of being a member of the Stern gang and successfully escorted her to Jerusalem.

In the wake of BLA in North-West Europe came the first part of ATS Provost of 21 Army Group. This party, under the command of Junior Commander Buckle—later to become APM ATS at HQ BAOR—consisted of CSM Bodel, Sergeants Lewin, Woodhall and Bowles, three corporals and fifteen lance-corporals. They disembarked in France on 11 August, 1944. After a short period of duty at the ATS Port Staging Camp the detachment moved to Brussels and sections were established at Antwerp, Ostend and Calais, with a further section staffing a civilian internment camp at Vilvoorde.

ATS policewomen guarded Mrs Joyce, wife of 'Lord Haw-Haw'. In September, 1945, a section was specially formed to provide guards, court ushers and escorts for women prisoners during the Belsen trials.

ATS Provost on the Continent found themselves saddled with many extraneous duties in addition to their normal routine. Principal among these was the provision of escorts for German women prisoners attending war crime trials from various parts of Europe, guarding prisoners throughout the trials and escorting them to places of execution or internment, searching German women employed at military establishments, participation in brothel raids in conjunction with military police and raids on displaced persons' camps in an effort to suppress the black-market activities of the inmates.

WRAC PROVOST

On the formation of the Women's Royal Army Corps in 1949 HQ 140

Provost Company WRAC was located in London, with sections at Edinburgh, Catterick, Chester and Bulford. The training of the police-women probationers was moved from the Depot and Training Establishment RMP to the WRAC Provost HQ in London.

The main duties of the policewomen were maintaining discipline among women's services, absentee enquiries and assisting service personnel and families when required.

With the gradual reduction in the numbers in the Corps, the provost sections began closing until only the London and Catterick sections remained. The Catterick section was responsible for Northern and Scottish Commands and the three sections in London were responsible for Eastern, Southern and Western Commands.

In 1954 WRAC Provost made history by carrying out the first 'all female' mobile escort to HRH The Princess Royal, then Controller Commandant WRAC, when she visited the WRAC company in Catterick. Since then they have never looked back and have always carried out their own foot and mobile escort duties when the need has arisen. During the earlier days of WRAC Provost ceremonial duties were not often carried out, but as the years went by WRAC were more and more recognized by their male colleagues and it was realized that women could do this job just as well as men.

From 1956 a gradual build-up of WRAC Provost began. In that year the Aldershot section was reopened and in 1962 sections were started in Colchester and Edinburgh.

1961 saw the HQ move to Kensington Barracks in London where they joined London District Provost Company and where the very close liaison was to their mutual benefit.

In 1962 140 Provost Company WRAC was designated HQ and Training Establishment WRAC Provost. The DAPM/WRAC was up-graded to APM/WRAC and the first Quartermaster was commissioned for police duty.

In 1960 the first WRAC Provost were posted to Singapore and later two NCOs were detached for duties in Hong Kong, while in 1961 a WRAC Provost section was opened at HQ SHAPE, the first WRAC other ranks to be posted to this station. This section was later incorporated into the establishment of the SHAPE Provost Company RMP, the first mixed provost company.

In 1963 three NCOs were sent to Aden, mainly to carry out SIB duties.

BAOR

ATS Provost in BAOR in 1949 were then redesignated 145 Provost

Company WRAC. At first the policewomen were located with HQ BAOR but gradually the establishment was increased and WRAC Provost sections were eventually established at Düsseldorf, Bielefeld and Berlin and attached to the local RMP companies for duties.

EGYPT AND CYPRUS

144 Provost Company WRAC had its HQ in Fayid with a section in Cyprus. In Egypt duties were carried out in Fayid, Moascar, Ismailia and Port Said. Duties were normal foot patrols in the garrisons and combined mobile patrols with RMP checking on out-of-bounds areas, ensuring that females were not out after dark unescorted and assistance to SIB in the case of all women's services and families. Families embarking and disembarking from troopships were also assisted.

The section stationed in Cyprus was mainly on the island for the purpose of searching female illegal Jewish immigrants trying to enter Palestine. The searches were carried out at the docks on their arrival at and departure from the island and whenever they left their camps to attend hospital appointments and again on their return. This section was closed and the NCOs returned to Egypt after the partition of Palestine and the inauguration of the state of Israel on 14 May, 1948.

After the abrogation of the Anglo-Egyptian Treaty of 1936 on 15 October, 1951, NCOs manned the radio station and so relieved RMP NCOs for other duties. The senior NCO in charge of the section was awarded the BEM for work carried out during this period. These duties were carried out until all British troops left Egypt.

On the evacuation of British troops from Egypt 144 Provost Company WRAC moved to Cyprus and routine police duties were carried out until the Emergency in 1955 when reinforcements were sent out from the UK. Until the end of the Emergency WRAC Provost were employed on internal security duties on the island working side-by-side with their male RMP colleagues. The rôle of WRAC Provost was a very important one and called for high devotion to duty as personnel had long hours of work and their off-duty periods were very infrequent.

It was quite usual for two NCOs to be attached to a regiment for periods of time varying from four to fourteen days, during which they lived under canvas in the mountains and villages of Cyprus. For two women living so close together with a number of men there were, of course, problems in their day-to-day life. By their cheerfulness, their devotion to duty and awareness of the important job on which they were employed they overcame these inevitable problems. The regiments to which they were attached took the greatest possible care of them and had nothing but praise for their work.

The work of WRAC Provost consisted of searching all Cypriot women who were stopped at road blocks and dealing with welfare problems concerning the women and children. In addition to the daily duties of road blocks, there were of course the duties of house-to-house searching when villages and towns were placed under curfew. In this respect the WRAC job was very important, as no woman favours a number of soldiers entering her house and peeping into the cupboards and under beds, least of all Cypriot women who are of a very excitable nature. Once again WRAC Provost NCOs dealt with the women of the household with great tact, thus allowing the men to carry on with their job of searching uninterrupted. WRAC Provost assistance was also enlisted by medical officers when visiting the sick Cypriot women and children in their villages and towns and their presence was always in demand when a female or child had to be escorted to hospital.

Another task delegated to members of WRAC Provost was carrying out searches in the detention camps on the island. These camps housed Greek Cypriot males who had been caught taking part in some way or another in EOKA activities. The families of detainees were allowed to visit them daily and bring food, etc, to them and WRAC Provost had the responsibility of searching the women, and whatever containers they might be carrying, for bombs, arms or ammunition before they were allowed to enter the camp.

WRAC policewomen are an accepted part of provost and there is no doubt that very many police jobs are well within the capabilities of women and which they now carry out thereby releasing men for more active tasks. WRAC Provost in Northern Ireland is an essential part of 1st Regiment RMP as is described in Chapter XIV. In 1975 the first two WRAC Provost joined the Mounted Troop and led the RMP Display Team (Horses and Motor-cycles) into the Arena at the Royal Tournament, Earls Court.

TRAFFIC CONTROL WING

Traffic control companies came into being in 1940 as a direct outcome of the experience of the BEF in France and Belgium and of conclusions drawn from General Lord Gort's despatches. They were originally formed in July, 1940, under the authority of War Office letter 20/GEN/5878 (AG.1 (c2)) of 4 and 5 July, and comprised thirty-two companies including some hundreds of officers and thousands of men drawn from all arms and regarded as attached and not as transfers to CMP. They were divided into groups, usually of four companies, each company sub-divided into sections.

These traffic control companies were formed on somewhat similar lines to a division provost company, but the rank and file were privates instead of lance-corporals. The sections were seventeen strong instead of sixteen as in a division provost company. One extra subaltern and one extra sergeant were also on the strength, making the total traffic control company strength 123 as compared with a division provost company strength of 115. The transport was mainly buses and charabancs to take sections to their posts along the road.

The personnel were usually recruited from Infantry Training Centres and therefore consisted of men with little or no military background and, of course, no military police training whatever. They were selected by DPMs in each Command. Group and company commanders, CSMs and section sergeants were, whenever possible, individuals with previous military police experience; in most cases the section sergeants were good military police lance-corporals, often men from the Automobile Association, promoted for the purpose, who filled the bill admirably. This initial cadre posted from the CMP provided 500 warrant officers and NCOs.

For the rank and file, who were privates, the only qualifications were that the men should be of good average intelligence and be capable of being trained in map reading and writing reports; they were not at that time required to ride either a motor-cycle or pedal bicycle and there were no special requirements as to character. Both these last points were wisely amended at a later date.

Each CMP (TC) company was allotted by Commands (or by Corps) to a specific area in which they were made responsible for signing, patrolling, facilitating and logging the passage of convoys and furnishing road information on specified military routes. This was a purely static rôle and indeed their function was, at that time, to be little more than human signposts. They were formed as a matter of high priority in July, 1940, but it was not until 10 October that it was decided they should become a new wing of the Corps to be known as CMP (Traffic Control).

Provost officers were, however, given only limited control of this new wing; for while DPMs were responsible for discipline, individual training, administration and supervision of duties, the operational training of traffic control companies, their disposition and tactical use were the direct responsibility of the staff; i.e., of 'Q' (Movements) in Commands, or of a staff officer, usually DAAG, in Corps.

Their duties were to control traffic with the object of facilitating troop movements. The original intention was for them to operate in the United Kingdom, maintaining and operating an organized plan of road control which allocated certain roads for certain uses, particularly during the 'Invasion' period after Dunkirk, i.e., forward-moving and returning troops and supplies, essential services (ambulances, telegraph maintenance vans, etc), civil defence cars and evacuees.

Subsequently they proved themselves invaluable in the control of WD convoys and thereafter operated on lines of communication and in congested base areas overseas. Some of the original thirty-two companies saw active service with 1st Army in North Africa and then with 8th Army and 5th US Army in Italy while many more companies served in North-West Europe with 21 Army Group.

Traffic Control Wing personnel were distinguished by a white band round their steel helmets with a blue diamond flash bearing the letter 'TC'. A story circulated at the time the wing was raised which, though never officially confirmed, was believed to have an element of truth, was to the effect that the demand for men to form the new TC Wing arrived on a ministerial desk at the same time as an order releasing an equivalent number of men from the coal mines. Two problems were solved by simply exchanging the memoranda. Shortly after the new TC Wing went on duty there was much consternation at the alarming casualty rate amongst pointsmen. It was then realized that the short figures of the miners could not be seen over the bonnets of ten-ton lorries!

While the truth of this story cannot be confirmed it is a fact that similar circumstances were the origin of TC Wing wearing the white band on their helmets. The Wing was disbanded at the end of the Second World War but the skill and devotion with which they carried out their duties, bringing distinction to the Corps, has not been forgotten.

VULNERABLE POINTS WING

Vulnerable Points sections (VPs), known as 'Bluecaps' from their blue cap-covers, were raised from older men of low medical category unfit for provost service in late 1940 during the 'Battle of Britain' days, when shortage of man-power was acute. They were also distinguished by a blue diamond flash, but they wore the initials 'VP' and a blue band round their steel helmets.

They were formed under Army Council Instruction 847 in February, 1941, and were designed to carry out purely static guard, patrol, gate and security duties (on the lines of the WD Constabulary) at vulnerable points such as depots, dumps, wireless stations, secret installations, tunnels and bridges.

There were many places of this character throughout the UK which had to be permanently under guard against sabotage, espionage and similar risks; many of them, indeed, contained papers, apparatus and installations of a highly secret nature, which, in the event of the vulnerable points themselves being overrun by an attacking enemy, must without fail either be removed or destroyed.

Vulnerable points were defined as any point at which a blow aimed by the enemy would, if successful, considerably impair the national war effort. They were classified under different headings: VP1s to be held at all costs to the last were rather like a permanent Home Guard post, dug in in a static, all-round defensive position. They were manned by a VP section armed with a formidable array of weapons.

VP2s, the normal VP duty, were operated more in the nature of a flexible guard of a post which, in the event of an invasion, could be dismantled and evacuated, or destroyed if need by. The duties were, therefore, of an anti-sabotage and security nature with disciplinary powers within, and on the approaches to, the post. They carried whistles and truncheons and were armed with automatic rifles and sten-guns.

Several hundred police dogs, together with their handlers, were trained and organized into sections which were allocated to VP companies.

VPs were Command troops and controlled by DPMs at Command HQs assisted by an APM (VP). Companies were commanded by a captain with subalterns according to the size of the company, with a Warrant Officer 2 and CQMS and a small HQ staff. Command DPMs were responsible for their technical training, discipline and supervision and for that part of their administration that was a Corps matter. The allotment of VPs to particular installations was the task of the 'G' Branch of the Command with the technical advice of the DPM. The commanding officers of the installations to which they were attached were responsible for actual working orders and local administration.

The basic unit was the section. No stated number of sections was laid down per company as each detachment had vastly differing requirements. Men of higher age-groups and lower medical category over a minimum height of 5 ft 3 ins were acceptable. Owing to the responsible nature of their duties a character of 'not less than very good' was required. A section strength averaged eight men but again this was flexible, depending on the requirement of the post.

Although VPs were first raised in the UK, they were later used effectively in Egypt, the Middle East, Central Mediterranean and in North-Western Europe. The first to go overseas assumed duties in North Africa by the end of 1942. Many units were raised in overseas theatres by local enlistment for guarding docks, base-areas and various installations in Mauritius, Ceylon, India, Malaya and Singapore.

An assessment of their value may be gathered from the fact that when they assumed duty they took over guard duties from infantry. Infantry, owing to their administrative organization, employed a platoon, its smallest unit, made up of an officer, a sergeant, three corporals and nearly thirty men on each post, whatever its size, and guards were in accordance with infantry requirements—i.e. two-hour spells of duty, each duty being relieved under the supervision of an NCO.

This caused an unacceptable interference in the battle-training of the infantry and was wasteful of manpower. The VPs found they could adequately maintain the same post with a section of six to eight men by doing eight-hour tours of duty as patrols, instead of fixed sentry posts. By the time they had fully taken over their duties in the UK it was estimated that each vulnerable pointsman relieved three or four infantrymen and VPs in fact released many thousand men for combat duty.

This note on the VP Wing should not fail to record the outstanding efforts of 848 VP Section when, on a night in 1942, all ranks, every NCO and man, were commended for gallant conduct and devotion to duty.

At that time Poole Harbour was a base for Royal Navy motor torpedo boats for Channel patrols. High octane fuel was stored in a number of very large concrete tanks, each holding many thousands of gallons. The tanks were located on a hillside behind the harbour towards which the hill sloped with, at the bottom, the MTB anchorage, jetties and ammunition stores containing torpedoes, mines and other explosives.

On this particular night enemy aircraft bombed Poole. A high-explosive bomb penetrated underneath one tank and then blew up, the explosion cracking some of the other tanks, and then down came the incendiary bombs and within seconds an inferno raged.

848 VP Section was responsible for the security of the petrol depot. They realized that to attempt to fight the fire was impossible but saw that petrol spilling from the cracked tanks was flowing downhill towards the MTB base and was igniting. Every man turned out and seizing shovels, began digging. They dug a canal across the path of the petrol to intercept it and by stupendous efforts, kept digging just ahead of the flow until they succeeded in diverting it away from the base whence it could flow harmlessly into the sea, thereby averting a major disaster.

Vulnerable Points Wing was gradually phased out, the various units disbanding as the need for their services ceased. They could find forebears in the 'King's Safeguards' of the seventeenth century (even to the 'Bluecap'!) and in the 'Gods Rejected' in 1914–1918.

FIELD SECURITY WING

Major D. S. Hawker, in an article on the early history of the Intelligence

Corps, published in that Corps' Journal (*The Rose and the Laurel*—December, 1965) refers to a body formed in 1801 under the name of the 'Corps of Guides' and recruited mainly in the south coast counties from gamekeepers and men of similar occupations having an intimate knowledge of the countryside. These men were nominated by their parishes as part of the precautions against the threat of invasion by Napoleon. It is believed that they wore a green uniform but whether or not this may be taken as an historical precedent is an open conjecture but in years to come the Field Security Police first raised as a wing of the Corps of Military Police in 1937, were to wear green cap covers and green was to become the colour of the Intelligence Corps.

The links between the provost service and the Intelligence Corps have always been close. In 1914 the mobilization of the Intelligence Corps included a small section of the Special Branch of the Metropolitan Police and they were referred to as 'Intelligence Police' mainly concerned with the security duties of their corps. After the First World War, in the peacetime establishment, they were redesignated 'Field Security Police' and formed a wing of the Intelligence Corps. In 1937 the CMP Depot at Mytchett was made responsible for the provision and training of other ranks for Field Security duties on mobilization and they were regarded as the Field Security Wing CMP and were so badged on mobilization in September, 1939, under their Commandant, Major Foljambe. The CMP Field Security Wing mobilized at Mytchett presented a truly remarkable collection of men speaking between them almost every known language and representing almost every profession, including lawyers, university professors, journalists and most of them quite out of place in a military camp. But seventy-seven Field Security sections were trained and despatched from Mytchett and from King Alfred's College, Winchester, before, in December, 1940, the wing was transferred to the Intelligence Corps.

CHAPTER XVIII

Depots and Territorials

DEPOTS—ORIGINS

It can almost certainly be said that the Military Police Depot originated when their first permanent home came into being—Stanhope Lines being specially built to house the military police stationed in the cantonment of Aldershot in 1897. Here the Provost Marshal, Major J. L. Emerson, who was also Commandant, had his office and kept the Records.

While the Depot itself moved to Gibraltar Barracks before the outbreak of the First World War in 1914, it is interesting to note that Stanhope Lines remained permanently in provost occupation until the time of its demolition in 1968 when it was occupied by 160 Provost Company, the road on which it stood having by then acquired the official name of 'Provost Road'. This building was replaced by another specially built building on adjacent ground to house all RMP units in Aldershot, including SIB and WRAC Provost and to bring together mounted and airborne, the oldest and youngest in the Corps.

The Depot moved from Gibraltar Barracks in 1920 to Mytchett Hutments, Ash Vale. Chapter II records that the Corps strength in 1926 was 508 all ranks and the Provost Marshal was also Commandant of the Depot and Officer-in-Charge of Records as well. He was assisted by an APM (major) responsible for instruction and by the Quartermaster.

From 1928 until the outbreak of the Second World War, one probationers' course of sixteen, one junior NCOs' refresher course of sixteen and one senior NCOs' refresher course of sixteen men were held at the Depot every six months. The probationers' course lasted six months and the refresher courses one month. The maximum under training at any one time was forty-eight. Probationers had to have at least two years' service, a second-class certificate of education and character of at least 'very good'. The training consisted of foot drill, pistol drill, map reading, police duties, first aid, swimming and life saving.

In 1932 HRH The Duke of Connaught, who always took a keen interest in the Corps ('provost-minded' as we should say today) inspected the Depot and the Aldershot detachment.

In 1937 the Corps was mechanized and all horses withdrawn. Prior to this, probationers for the Military Mounted Police, who were largely from mounted regiments, were trained at the Depot under one squadron sergeant-major and four instructors.

Until 1939 MT training was carried out at Bordon and Woolwich. In those days great emphasis was placed on the 'Best Book' and great pride was taken in having a document worthy of inspection at the end of training.

1939–1946

To understand the importance of the Depot at Mytchett and of the subsidiary Command Depots during the Second World War it is necessary to appreciate three things:

First, the provost service relied on a high and even standard of basic training in reinforcements who, on joining military police units, were at once fully employed under active service conditions in the UK and overseas.

Second, this standard satisfied not only the Corps, but also the rest of the Army, who for many years had looked on the military police to set an example in dress and conduct.

Third, the unique responsibility vested in junior ranks in provost—particularly the lance-corporal. In turn-out and discipline these men had to set an example to all; on duty they had to act, often single-handed, with cool judgement when harassed on traffic routes, and with discretion and determination when enforcing orders or discipline. In all this they had to deal tactfully and incorruptibly with officers and NCOs of every rank.

During the courses, shortened to three months by the exigencies of war and without the means of extensive field training, the Depot was not expected to turn out the finished article; that was the subsequent job of units. The Depot's task was similar to that of a steelworks, which takes in selected and graded raw material, works upon it to eliminate faults and impurities and supplies the manufacturer with well-tempered and high-grade metal from which the finished article may be produced.

The business of the Depot, therefore, was to ensure an exemplary level of drill, turn-out and deportment, a solid knowledge of police powers and duties, report-making and the rules of evidence, first-class motor-cycle riding, the all-important rôle of helpfulness and, finally, that all reinforcements should leave the Depot with the high morale which comes from self-confidence and self-respect.

To produce these results a depot of an unusual character was needed. Alongside good organization and sound instruction it was essential to create an 'atmosphere'. The tone and character of any institution is invariably set from the top. The Corps owed a special debt to the leadership of Lieut-Colonel N. C. M. Sykes, Commandant at Mytchett from January, 1941, to August, 1942, and to the no less solid and vigorous qualities of his successor, Lieut-Colonel E. F. L. Wright, Commandant from August, 1942, to July, 1946. But although much credit for the work of the Depot must go to these two officers, the support they received from a first-class staff must not pass unrecorded. Lieut-Colonel Wright's slogan, aptly reflecting the spirit of helpfulness taught at the Depot was: 'Guide the responsible, check the irresponsible, incarcerate the incorrigible!'

Tribute should also be paid to the work of the Command Depots, who, as will be seen later, acting in relief of Mytchett, successfully copied the example of their parent depot.

At the outbreak of war the Provost Marshal was faced with two problems: recruiting and training. Provision for expansion of the army had already been made but not for the highly-qualified and highly-trained men needed to police it. Immediate steps had, therefore, to be taken to find the right men and to train them.

To meet the first requirement a recruiting officer with the appointment of DAPM (captain) was appointed to obtain recruits on a volunteer basis. His duty was to fill the new training establishments with a steady flow of volunteers; his equipment was an office, a clerk and a motor-car. He had authority to interview every recruiting officer in the country and to employ whatever publicity in the way of poster and newspaper advertising that the Public Relations Branch of the War Office thought proper.

It was soon clear that potential military policemen could be found all over the country. Volunteers poured in but Mytchett Hutments was inadequate to train large numbers as geographically it was badly-placed. It became apparent that duplication was necessary.

Although Mytchett had been the military police training centre since 1920 there was no lecture hall and the probationers had lectures in their own barrack huts. There was no gymnasium and no swimming pool but there was a NAAFI, a fine new building, and about the only place at Mytchett which could accommodate all the probationers at one time. Life for them was strenuous for if the Depot was small it had a proud tradition to maintain. Most of the instructors in the early days were ex-Guardsmen who had joined the civil police and then re-joined from the Reserve; discipline was up to Brigade of Guards standard.

Mytchett received the civilian volunteers who fulfilled the peace-time standards of height, weight and conduct. Many of them were soon commissioned and later achieved distinction as provost officers. A corporal instructor at Mytchett in 1940 was called before the APM of his formation in France in 1944 on a disciplinary matter. To his astonishment he found that this angry field officer was none other than a probationer who had been in his squad at Mytchett.

But another depot had to be found, preferably in the north. It was eventually discovered that at Northallerton, a country town within easy distance of Leeds, York and Newcastle, there was a civilian prison unused since 1922. Forbidding as the building was, with its high walls, its cells and enclosed yards, it possessed all the requirements for an up-to-date, lively training establishment; and so it became. Major N. C. M. Sykes was appointed Commandant of this establishment which was provided with instructors who were all ex-civil policemen and who had served their time with the Brigade of Guards. There was a regular intake and output of fifty men per week.

The north-country men volunteering during these months for provost played their part in the 'build-up' of the Corps—for example, the clerk who compiled the documents was, towards the end of the war, met by his former Commandant, when this ex-corporal had become DPM Ceylon. Many other inmates of the 'prison' at that time gained promotion to high rank. During the period up to January, 1941, the establishment trained between 500 and 530 men.

In January, 1941, a reorganization of Mytchett took place. Major Sykes was appointed Commandant there with the rank of lieutenant-colonel relieving Lieut-Colonel R. T. S. Kitwood, and was himself succeeded at Northallerton by Major Dunkerly. To Mytchett from Northallerton went half-a-dozen key members of the staff, including RSM Baker who afterwards became Chief Instructor at the new post-war Depot at Inkerman Barracks, Woking.

In April, 1941, with the reduction of the intake allowed by the War Office providing insufficient numbers to justify two Depots it was therefore decided to amalgamate them and the Depot at Northallerton then became a military prison.

The trainees at Mytchett during July, 1941, rose to the record number of 1,400. Early in 1942, as no more CID men could be spared for the army, a wing for training selected military policemen in SIB duties was started at the Depot. Major J. G. Ellis, one of the ex-CID officers in the original members of the SIB with the BEF in 1940, was the first officer-in-charge and organized a first-class school which turned out some excellent material.

Early in 1941 small Command Depots were formed to train men for the new Vulnerable Points Wing. These Command Depots soon expanded, first to include Traffic Control Wing recruits, later to train in provost duties selected men transferring from the TC and VP Wings and to run refresher courses for all personnel. They swiftly entered into a healthy rivalry with Mytchett and proved an indispensable addition to the Corps. These Depots were located at Watton-at-Stone and Gatton Park in Eastern Command and at Gosforth, then at Burniston Barracks, Scarborough, in Northern Command and all were closed by the end of 1947.

FROM MYTCHETT TO INKERMAN

Mytchett from July, 1946, was commanded by Lieut-Colonel A. R. Forbes. There were three wings—Police Duties, MT and Depot. Intakes arrived from Infantry Training Centres and the weeding-out of unsuitable material started within twenty-four hours of their arrival. The Commandant, Second-in-Command and Chief Instructor, would walk down the ranks scrutinizing each man closely and those who failed to stand such close inspection were fallen-out on the spot and within a matter of hours returned whence they came. It is surprising how effective this method was and the resultant saving in instructor's time and effort was considerable.

Over and above the intakes were the drafts that were continually arriving in the Depot, either *en route* for some overseas theatre or on their way home for release or posting to a UK company. This constantly-changing population was more often than not far too great for the inadequate accommodation Mytchett could provide. In 1947 came the decision to move the Depot to a more suitable barracks and eventually Inkerman Barracks, Knaphill, Woking was selected. Whether the War Office had overlooked the fact that the Military Provost Staff Corps had been for over seventy years a separate corps, or for what other reason, RMP were once more to make a depot out of a prison.

The buildings had been erected and opened in 1859 as the Knaphill Convict Prison. Invalid convicts were housed in the main block and the buildings opposite were used as a women's prison. The Prison Act of 1877 vested the control and administration of prisons in the Prison Commissioners instead of the local authorities and, as a result, Knaphill became redundant and was taken over by the War Department in 1892 and converted into a barracks by 1895 when it was occupied by the 2nd Battalion the Royal West Surrey Regiment (The Queens).

The barracks were named 'Inkerman' after the famous 'Soldiers' Battle' in the Crimea fought on 5 November, 1854. The Royal West Surrey Regiment moved in in 1895 and thereafter it became a normal garrison barracks being occupied in turn by many line regiments and, in 1939, was allotted to the 1st Canadian Division.

The winter of 1946–1947 had been very severe and when in March 1947 the first survey took place to determine how the various wings of the Depot were to be fitted in, the barracks presented a sorry spectacle. Pipes had burst everywhere, plaster from fallen ceilings lay thick on the ground and every inch of woodwork needed painting.

These then were just some of the problems that faced the Depot staff when it was announced that Mytchett would be vacated in the spring of 1947, that HRH The Duke of Gloucester would visit Inkerman on 23 July, 1947, in order to take the salute at a parade to mark the granting of the Royal prefix to the Corps, and that the Depot would provide men and material for the running of the Aldershot Horse Show, the opening of which would coincide almost exactly with the Duke of Gloucester's visit! Add to this formidable list the task of creating an Officers' Mess with no funds, no silver, no crockery, no linen, no furnishings and above all, no establishment and the picture was complete. It seems incredible that so ambitious a programme could succeed, but succeed it did, although the effort required on the 'Q' side was a severe strain on the harassed Quartermaster.

One more effort must, however, be added to those already described and that was the running of the first Provost Marshal's Study Period. Not only was the training side well organized but prodigies of administrative ingenuity were performed in order to paint, decorate and furnish all the single officers' quarters so as to accommodate not only those attending but a course of fourteen officers as well. At the same time that these problems were being tackled, the main barrack blocks were being redecorated and made habitable while the old prison block was rapidly transformed into the Depot HQ. Only the bare essentials of decoration and maintenance were carried out by the Royal Engineers and their contractors. No outside painting of any kind was even considered and every kind of artifice and cunning had to be employed to bring Inkerman up to the standard demanded by the Provost Marshal!

THE ROYAL PREFIX: INSPECTION BY HRH THE DUKE OF GLOUCESTER

Few of those who witnessed the impressive parade on 23 July, 1947, when HRH The Duke of Gloucester, on behalf of HM King George VI, bestowed the title of Royal on the Corps of Military Police appreciated the exceptional problems already mentioned which faced the Commandant and his staff. Despite the fact that the Corps had only just moved into its new home at Inkerman Barracks the many difficulties were overcome by all ranks with enthusiasm and a determination to make the great day an unqualified success.

The parade consisted of detachments from the Depot, both staff and probationers, all Home Commands, London and Northern Ireland Districts, SIB, BAOR, Northern Command Depot at Scarborough, Ports Provost and, finally, the ATS Provost Company. They were drawn up on the barrack square facing the archway and with the band in the middle behind the parade, the MT drawn up in the rear.

HRH The Duke of Gloucester was received with a Royal Salute and then inspected the parade. Following this he gave a short address. He said:

'I am very pleased to be present today at this parade which the Royal Military Police are holding to celebrate the granting to the Corps of the Royal prefix. Your Corps has great traditions. Some form of provost service has existed for about five hundred years and your actual Corps has been formed since 1855—so will soon be celebrating its centenary. Though it started with only one officer and eighteen men, you have gradually risen with each successive war in strength and importance, until in 1945 you numbered some 36,000. Your responsibilities, too, have greatly increased. Before the late war your duties were only the preservation of discipline and a little traffic control. But during the war the traffic control increased to huge proportions; all forms of civil and military crime became in some theatres your responsibility; you also controlled hundreds of thousands of enemy prisoners-of-war. Protection of ports and stores from thieves and racketeers became your concern as well. Your Special Investigation Branch, both during and since the war, has saved the country millions of pounds in recovered property—£6,000,000 in 1945 and 1946 alone.

'During the war military police took their share in all campaigns and served in every battle area. They became an essential part of every armed formation, without which no Commander could plan or win his battles. They won numerous honours and distinctions, and suffered a sadly large number of casualties. Your Roll of Honour will bear nearly a thousand names of members of the Corps who lost their lives.

'This is a record of which you may all be justly proud, and the King has shown his appreciation, and that of the whole Army, by granting you the distinction of becoming the Corps of Royal Military Police.

'I would like to congratulate you in His Majesty's name on this signal honour.

'But your traditions and honours carry responsibilities. Yours is a standard which must be of the highest and the rest of the Army must be able to look up to your example in discipline, smartness and integrity. I am confident that you will preserve this standard and I wish you and the whole Corps all good fortune for the future.'

After giving three cheers the parade marched past in slow and quick time, followed by a march past of MT. A final Royal Salute brought this spectacular parade to an end.

INKERMAN BARRACKS: 1947–1964

In 1950 training was at its peak. Twelve courses were run concurrently with a constant turn-over of 900 students, with special refresher/promotion courses for junior and senior NCOs, officers' courses and the annual Provost Marshal's Study Period which was attended by officers who could be spared from overseas theatres, officers of the TA and AER and most of those in the UK.

But the accommodation at Inkerman Barracks became saturated and the MT Wing had to move out to Warburg Barracks in Aldershot in August, 1950, when it was re-named 'B' Company. In the next seven years it won many awards in the Army motor-cycling world including the Army team championship, Southern Command and Aldershot District best individual and team championships and many other cups and championships. During 1953 three best individual, twenty first-class and nine second-class awards were won by members of 'B' Company and that November they moved back in Inkerman Barracks.

Three 'B' Company instructors, Captain A. J. Betty, Sergeant V. Monk and Sergeant F. Gamwell represented the Army in the International Six-Days' motor-cycle trial. During the short life of 'B' Company instruction had always been at a very high level and at the end of its life the percentage of probationers passing their driving test was higher than ever before due to the effort of the instructors and the individual methods employed. 'B' Company finally became the MT Section in Courses Wing in 1957 and joined the other specialist parts of the Depot in that wing.

The Depot organization underwent a number of major changes in those years. First, the appointment of Commandant was upgraded to the rank of colonel in July, 1957, with Colonel C. F. Read as the first such officer, and at the same time a new establishment was approved which made sweeping changes. Before that date a probationer, after spending an initial period of training in 'A' Company, moved to 'B' Company for MT training, then to 'C' Company, whence he finally passed out of the Depot via Depot Company for posting. The new establishment provided for two training companies, 'A' and 'B', each receiving intakes and probationers remained throughout their training with the one company until passing out. In addition to 'A' and 'B' Companies was a new Courses Wing commanded by the Chief Instructor, Major R. J. R. Whistler, and consisting of Courses, MT and Signals

Sections. Courses Wing also ran all Provost Officers' courses and took on a further commitment of running Regimental provost courses for outside units. Depot Company carried out the administration of the permanent staff, drafting and releases. In addition, HQ Army Emergency Reserve (AER) and the SIB Training Wing were located in the Depot.

The probationers' training then consisted of sixteen weeks which were divided into seven weeks of basic training, followed by three weeks of MT and six weeks of continuation training and operational exercises. The SIB Training Wing took all squads in sixty-seven periods of military law, criminal law and investigation procedure, in order to improve the lance-corporals' knowledge in these subjects.

In March, 1961, the last National Service intake passed off the square and a fortnight later the first all-regular squad was posted to duty. Prison or not, Inkerman Barracks held pleasant and affectionate memories for countless military policemen who passed beneath the Memorial Arch. It was there that thousands of National Servicemen were trained and sent out at the age of 18 to play a man's part in the post-war world and to add very greatly not only to the respect in which their Corps was held but also to that of their country. Inkerman was also the scene of many post-war landmarks in the history of the Corps, starting with the Inspection by HRH The Duke of Gloucester already described.

For the grant of the Royal prefix the 'Royal Corps of Military Police' would have been perhaps the logical title to adopt in conformity with British Army nomenclature but the initial letters could have been confused with those of the Royal Canadian Mounted Police and the Military Provost Staff Corps already monopolized the word 'Provost' in their title. Many other combinations and variations were considered and a short-list was submitted to HM King George VI by the Provost Marshal, Major-General I. D. Erskine, who had done so much to bring this about.

On 30 September, 1946, the Provost Marshal was informed that the King had approved the title 'The Corps of Royal Military Police', by which title the Corps would henceforth be known, but he preferred, as an abbreviated title, simply 'RMP'. A special Army Order was then published giving effect to the King's decision to take effect from 28 November, 1946.

The Corps of Royal Military Police then took its place in the Army List, eighteenth in the order of seniority and on 13 March, 1947, a very distinguished soldier, General Sir Miles Dempsey, was appointed to be the first Colonel Commandant of the Corps. With more recent alterations to the order of precedence of Regiments and Corps, RMP now ranks sixteenth in the List.

The next requirement for the Corps was a march. Sir Miles Dempsey suggested a tune which he had heard played by the massed bands at the Aldershot Tattoo in 1936 called 'The Watch Tower'. On 2 May, 1949, he took Major-General Erskine (who had originally proposed a Corps march), the then Provost Marshal, Brigadier L. F. E. Wieler, and the DPM, Colonel H. V. McNally, to the Royal Military School of Music at Kneller Hall to hear a special arrangement of this tune played by the Kneller Hall band. Following this it was at once adopted to become the RMP Corps March and notified as such in Army Order No. 137 of 1949. 'The Watch Tower' is an arrangement of an old German march composed by Rudolf Herzer called '*Hoch Heidecksburg!*' and is undoubtedly one of the best regimental marches in the Army.

THE CORONATION: 1953

The Coronation of HM Queen Elizabeth II on 2 June, 1953, was an historic day for RMP. Nearly 1,500 members of the Corps performed public duties and had the privilege of providing both pageantry and service in many ways.

The Mounted Section found two escorts each of a file of four-mounted NCOs to Colonial Rulers. The RMP representation in the marching procession was made up of one major, one captain, one warrant officer 1, one warrant officer 2 (SIB), one staff-sergeant, one sergeant (Provost), one sergeant (SIB), three corporals and six lance-corporals found from the Regular Army and National Servicemen, one captain, one warrant officer, one sergeant, one corporal and two lance-corporals from the Territorial Army and two lance-corporals from the Army Emergency Reserve. The contingent marched in three ranks of eight. London District Provost Company found three officers, one warrant officer 2 and 146 NCOs for normal provost duties in the Coronation camps set up in Hyde Park and elsewhere and for movement control to get the processional contingents to the forming-up points and for service vehicle parking.

The Commissioner of Police for the Metropolis invited the Provost Marshal to provide assistance to the Metropolitan Police in the Coronation area itself. The military police were given two primary tasks: (a) to man, alternately with the civil police all points of entry into or exit from a central ring road, to enforce regulations and direct and assist traffic and (b) to facilitate parking where authorized and prevent it elsewhere. They were also called upon to enforce one-way systems, assist in dispersal and overall to help the general public. To meet this demand a total of 1,072 all ranks were found from the Depot and Training Establishment and HQ AER and from volunteers from TA units. This contingent was known as the 'Coronation 1,000' and was organized as a battalion divided into two companies with an HQ section and thirty motor-cyclists from the Depot MT instructors to act as guides and maintain communications.

Before moving off to London to assume duties the contingent paraded on the playing fields of Inkerman Barracks for inspection by the Provost Marshal, Brigadier R. H. Maxwell. This was probably the greatest number of military police ever on parade together, well over 1,000 in No 1 Dress from the Regular Army, TA and AER being present under the command of Lieut-Colonel E. D. Rash with Major A. V. Lovell-Knight as adjutant and WO 1 G. S. P. Stead as RSM.

FROM WOKING TO CHICHESTER

Inkerman Barracks was 100 years old in 1959 and could no longer provide the standard of accommodation expected in 1960; so once more a new home for the Depot was sought.

The reorganization of the Army and the amalgamation of infantry regiments made the Depot of the Royal Sussex Regiment at Roussillon Barracks, Chichester available and there the Depot moved on 1 March, 1964, under its Commandant, Colonel A. C. Rawlings.

This was no repetition of the move to Inkerman, Virtually a new purpose-designed Depot was created with modern buildings, architect-designed, to meet the needs of the times. The Corps Chapel and Museum were re-established. The officers', sergeants' and other ranks' Messes were housed in purpose-built accommodation, with new well-designed married quarters. Barrack blocks and training rooms provided a perfect home for the Depot and Training Establishment and for Regimental HQ.

There was, however, much preparatory work first to be done and much of the credit for the successful move was due to the two quarter-masters who visited Chichester in 1962 to check earlier plans made for the move and it was as well that they did so, having been led to believe that everything had already been arranged.

The clothing stores at Woking was grossly overcrowded; that being constructed at Chichester was found to be one-fifth the size. A disused RAOC Supply Depot immediately adjacent had been leased to the Ministry of Agriculture! No provision had been made for Signals Wing. Rooms designed as soldiers' bedrooms had been allocated to other purposes, leaving a reversion to double-bunking as the only alternative for sleeping quarters in what was considered to be a model of new barrack accommodation.

The Second-in-Command, Major F. S. Jeffreys, and both quarter-masters then prepared a case based on synopsis scales and arguments to prove that in certain instances these were unrealistic when applied to the many branches of the Depot and Training Establishment RMP. On 13 October, 1962, the three officers attended a conference at the Ministry of Defence where they proved their case and had the satisfaction of having every point conceded, with very few modifications. The battle that was fought and won on that day may not have been appreciated, but the present Corps home at Chichester exists as the result of it. Appropriately, one of the roads in Roussillon Barracks is now named 'Jeffreys Avenue'.

With effect from 1 April, 1968, the Depot and Training Establishment RMP was redesignated 'RMP Training Centre' thus bringing the title into line with those of other training units in the Army.

TERRITORIALS AND RESERVES

In 1938 a CMP Supplementary Reserve was formed into which 850 Automobile Association patrols were enlisted and in the spring of 1939 Territorial Army provost companies were raised with a strength of just over 1,000. These were the first TA units in the Corps and included provost companies for the TA divisions in the Order of Battle and all were mobilized in September, 1939, on the outbreak of war.

After the end of the Second World War there was a considerable interval before the Territorial Army was re-formed but in early 1947 approval was given to the raising of a network of TA provost units throughout the UK. This was followed in 1950 by the re-formation of the Supplementary Reserve, later re-styled the Army Emergency Reserve (AER). Both TA and AER units were formed from volunteers who had seen active service and were built up with A and Z Reservists. National Servicemen who had completed their colour service transferred to these units from 1950 onwards.

TA units were administered through Territorial and Auxiliary Forces Associations and a regular provost officer was included in the establishment of most units for administrative and training purposes as Permanent Staff Officer (PSO). There were corps and division provost companies, independent brigade provost units and certain specialist units, including four armoured, one airborne and one beach provost company, numbering sixteen in all.

The AER was administered separately by HQ AER RMP at Inkerman Barracks, Woking, which consisted of a small regular army cadre for training and administration. The AER included twelve GHQ provost companies, two vulnerable points companies and some SIB sections. The Automobile Association (AA) continued their pre-Second World War close links with the Corps by immediately forming two complete

GHQ provost companies at full strength and many civil policemen re-enlisted to serve with the SIB sections.

Reorganization of the AER took place in 1961, Category II virtually disappearing from the establishment and Category I surviving in a very modest form with only two rear area provost units and one ports task force provost unit administered by the re-named Central Volunteer HQ RMP. Naturally, as was to be expected, the AA were still well represented.

The TA was also very greatly reduced and both TA and AER were amalgamated to become the Territorial and Army Volunteer Reserve (T & AVR). This consisted of 116, 243 Force, 252 Force and 253 Force Provost Companies (with their own TAVR Centres) and 163 and 164 Provost Companies and 83 Detachment SIB administered centrally by Central Volunteer HQ RMP at Chichester. These were left to keep alive the spirit of the generation that volunteered for service in the threatening days of 1939 and of the many thousands of war veterans and National Servicemen who served with pride as RMP Volunteers.

CHAPTER XIX

Regimental Headquarters

DURING the early years of the Corps and through the Second World War, Regimental activities and organizations had been undertaken and co-ordinated by the Provost Marshal's Headquarters with much of the detailed work being carried out by the Depot and Training Establishment. While this had the merit of making use of the existing command structure and of available office facilities it inevitably meant that Regimental activities were added to the existing work-load of officers who were already well occupied with their primary military tasks. Where this proved impossible because of the volume of work involved, as for example in running the Central Benevolent Fund and the Royal Military Police Association, ex-service and civilian staff were engaged and paid for by the funds concerned and housed in offices provided by the Army, first at Steeles Road, Aldershot and then at Inkerman Barracks, Woking. Rising costs and difficulties in the recruitment of suitable staff finally led to the concentration of all Regimental activities into a Regimental Headquarters for the whole Corps staffed by retired Regular officers and this was set up at Woking on 1 April, 1961. The object as set out in the Charter was to provide a Corps Secretariat consisting of retired officers and civilians to handle the domestic affairs of the Corps and so relieve serving officers from these duties. Apart from the later inclusion of Regimental Headquarters to form part of Headquarters Provost Marshal (Army) but still remaining detached at Chichester, this arrangement has been unchanged and has undoubtedly proved workable and in the best interests of the Corps.

The main Regimental activities controlled by or associated with Regimental Headquarters will now be described.

ROYAL MILITARY POLICE ASSOCIATION

The CMP Old Comrades Association had been founded in 1927 and by the outbreak of the Second World War in 1939 had grown to a modest size. This was because the Corps was relatively small and with few exceptions served in small detachments in widely-separated localities making Regimental functions such as Reunions difficult to organize.

In 1939 all the assets were frozen and activities suspended but with the immediate and very large expansion of the Corps in the early years of the war it became evident that an Association was needed to cater for the needs of new members of the Corps particularly when hostilities ceased.

In March, 1941, Lieut-Colonel N. C. M. Sykes, Commandant of the Depot and Training Establishment, formed a new Association under the name of the CMP Old Comrades (War) Association. Its objects were to help members to find employment after discharge or release from the Army, to help them and their families financially if in need and to promote a lasting bond of friendship between past and present members of the Corps. Life membership only was permitted and the subscription was fixed at ten shillings while the Association was administered by the Depot and Training Establishment at Mytchett. At the end of the war membership totalled 6,472 and when this Association was finally incorporated into the RMP Association there were 9,114 members so transferred.

At the end of the Second World War it was decided to form a new and comprehensive Association to take over the assets, responsibilities and membership of the 1927 Association and those of the 1941 (War) Association and also to cater for the greatly-expanded numbers then serving in the Corps. Thus the Royal Military Police Association came into being on 15 June, 1946, and the three main objects of 'Comradeship, Welfare and Employment' together with the fourth aim of support to the Corps in every way possible have since then been the cornerstones of the Association.

A network of branches has been established including Hong Kong and Australia and there are many Representatives to help and advise members all over the United Kingdom and in Australia. A Discount Scheme for members is in operation and also a free Death and Accident Insurance Scheme while an Annual Reunion Dinner and many branch dinners and socials are also organized. The Rules were amended on 14 May, 1966, to admit Women's Royal Army Corps Provost and their predecessors in the Auxiliary Territorial Service Provost as members and at the end of 1976 there were 366 lady Life members. Life membership only is now permitted and there were

17,424 such members at 31 December, 1976, for the Association as a whole.

CENTRAL BENEVOLENT FUND RMP

To meet the inevitable post-war benevolent needs of members of the Corps and of their dependents Major-General J. Seymour Mellor, Provost Marshal of the United Kingdom, inaugurated the CMP Central Benevolent Fund as a Charitable Trust on 31 January, 1944. The Rules approved then have stood the test of time and with the guidance of the Committee provide the framework on which all financial assistance is now granted from the Fund to members and ex-members of the Corps and their dependents if in need of such help.

Massive support for the Fund was provided by units and individuals in the first few years of its existence; £9,370 12s. 9d. in the first six months, £15,619 8s. 8d. by the end of 1944, £24,634 16s. 11d. by the end of 1945 and £32,303 9s. 11d. by 31 December, 1946, a most excellent response indeed from the Corps. Such support has continued over the years and since 1964 the 'Day's Pay Scheme' has provided an increasingly large share of the Fund's income. At the last count 95·51 per cent of the warrant officers and non-commissioned officers of the Corps and all the officers contributed a 'Day's Pay'. This has enabled the Fund to carry out all its benevolent requirements in a time of continuing and inescapable rise in the cost of living and of inflation leading to the erosion of the value of money and consequent financial hardship to the many beneficiaries of the Fund. Total benevolent expenditure is rising each year and in 1976 came to £12,714·48 spread over 193 cases.

Two Holiday Chalets have been purchased by the Fund at Selsey to provide holidays for ex-members of the Corps who are unable to afford them and when not needed for these, inexpensive holidays for serving members and their families. The first Chalet was named 'Silver Jubilee' and opened on 19 July, 1969, and the second (named 'John Mattey' after Major John Mattey, longest-serving member of the Central Benevolent Fund Committee, since 1946) was opened on 31 May, 1972. Both Chalets have been well used since and RMP was the first regiment or corps in the Army to provide such a service.

ROYAL MILITARY POLICE MUSEUM

The Royal Military Police Museum was originally opened at Inkerman Barracks, Woking, and housed in a ground-floor room in the main barrack block. A growing collection of exhibits made this accommodation inadequate and on the move of the Depot and Training

Establishment to Chichester the Museum moved too on 26 February, 1964, to much better premises on the ground-floor of the Keep in Roussillon Barracks. After much preparatory work the Museum was officially opened by the C-in-C Eastern Command, General Sir Roderick McLeod, on 20 May, 1964.

In the years since then much progress has been made; a Museum Library constructed to house the growing accumulation of Corps archives, records, photographs and books; a comprehensive exhibition of firearms, swords, side-arms, flags, trophies, silver, equipment and vehicles built up, and 739 medals donated or bought to form a comprehensive collection.

The Corps Museum is regulated by a Declaration of Trust dated 1 March, 1961, and is registered under the Charities Act 1960.

WAR MEMORIAL

The Corps Memorial Arch to the Second World War had originally been unveiled at Inkerman Barracks, Woking, by General Sir Miles Dempsey, the Colonel Commandant on 17 July, 1949, and dedicated by the Chaplain-General. On moving to Chichester this Arch was incorporated into the RMP Museum as a most impressive entrance and a new War Memorial to the Fallen of all campaigns was then erected in Roussillon Barracks outside the Sandhurst Block in the form of a Portland stone cross with inscribed campaign plaques.

ROYAL MILITARY POLICE JOURNAL

The Royal Military Police Journal was founded in 1950 and is a quarterly publication including news and views from all units of the Corps, both Regular and TAVR, and from the RMP Association and is the accepted means of Regimental communication. It also includes articles of interest to the Corps and ensures that contemporary historical details are recorded for future reference.

CORPS MOTTO

The Corps Motto, '*Exemplo Ducemus*' ('By Example shall we lead') was approved by HM Queen Elizabeth II in September, 1959.

CORPS COMMITTEE

The Corps Committee was formed in 1957 by the Provost Marshal, Brigadier R. H. L. Oulton to control and co-ordinate the policy for all

Corps and Regimental activities. The first meeting was held on 26 March, 1957, and regular meetings have taken place since then. The formation of Regimental Headquarters on 1 April, 1961, was a logical development of this and Regimental activities for the Corps are now organized under one roof at Regimental Headquarters at Chichester within the overall framework of the Corps Committee.

CHAPTER XX

The Corps of Officers

'The Gentleman which should be elected to this place of Provost Marshal would be a man of great judgement and experience in all martial discipline . . . He should be a lover of justice, impartial in his dealings and free from the transportation of passions . . . In brief, he ought to be only the law's servant.'

Francis Markham, 1622

THERE are four outstanding dates in the history of the Corps since 1855 and all have greatly influenced the Corps of today.

The first important date was 13 June, 1855, the date of the circular letter addressed to all Officers Commanding Cavalry Regiments in reply to a letter from the Provost Marshal in which he asked for augmentation of his Provost-men as they were then called. The Provost Marshal, however, in order to distinguish between them and his Prison Provost Staff referred to them as 'policemen'—a new word in the military vocabulary. The letter he received, bearing the date 13 June, 1855, therefore contained the origins of the Corps as we know it today.

The next outstanding date was 1 August, 1877, when the military mounted policemen were transferred from their former regiments' muster and promotion rolls to those of the Corps thus making the Military Mounted Police into a distinct and separate corps within the Army.

The third was 28 November, 1946, when the Corps received the honour of the Royal prefix in acknowledgement of their outstanding record of service in the Second World War having served with distinction in all campaigns and battle areas.

The fourth and most recent important date was 3 March, 1954, being the date on which was authorized the establishment of RMP officers in the Regular Army commissioned directly into the Corps.

Why had not the Corps its own officer element in the past? It seems likely that the real answer lies in the original purpose of the Corps—the purpose for which it was originally established. It was a Corps of experienced NCOs employed solely for the maintenance of discipline, who operated in small detachments and required the minimum of supervision or administration. Such as there was, was well within the military knowledge of any and every officer. The actual performance of duties could well be left to the NCOs and, indeed, none knew that better than they.

The officer's contribution in those days was a part-time job—a small administrative responsibility towards a small handful of NCOs, and carried out in a few spare minutes each day.

With the outbreak of war in 1914 and full mobilization, the officer's job became more onerous. Full-time town-majors and APMs were required and they themselves had to undertake their own disciplinary duties, but still these duties called for no special knowledge; there was still no future for a specialist Regular provost officer.

It was not until the Battle of Neuve Chapelle in 1915 that it began to become apparent that the military police had a rôle beyond that of the maintenance of discipline, for it was in this battle that traffic control proved its value, and the presence of military police on the battlefield became an operational necessity; but as yet the provost officer's rôle had not developed. He was still little more than the company administrator, the military police being directed by the movement staff.

After the First World War and its aftermath, the Corps was reduced again to its disciplinary function and with a total establishment of barely 500 all ranks scattered as garrison police world-wide. There was no rôle for provost officers other than that of the Provost Marshal (who was also Officer-in-Charge of Records and Commandant of the Depot), one APM (major) and the Quartermaster.

No further consideration was given to the officer element until 1933, when in February the War Office arranged a provost exercise which arose out of lessons learnt during the Army manœuvres of 1931, during which it became apparent that the growing mechanization of the Army and the consequent speed of movement necessitated provost being co-ordinated into the organization of field formations and that the work of provost would need an officer's direction. This exercise in 1933 was attended by eighteen officers of other arms who were to be ear-marked for provost appointments on mobilization and who practised their rôle in the manœuvres held in September, 1934, in which traffic control was given great prominence.

Even so, it was not yet appreciated that traffic control was to become more than the actual physical direction of traffic which the name implies.

Provost was not yet concerned in the planning side or in the direction of operational movement.

Therefore, the officer's rôle as yet called for no special qualifications or particular line of thought beyond that which was deemed to be within the normal professional military knowledge of any officer. Traffic control was the duty of the junior NCO, on his point; his direction was by the staff—the provost officer was little more than the company administrator; the APM, deemed to be fully occupied with discipline, was not expected to have much of an opinion on movement. With mobilization in 1939 this was still the position and so it continued until after 1940, when the lessons learnt in the 1940 campaign leading up to Dunkirk and other campaigns began radically to alter ideas.

In the division, and to a less extent at corps level, both in the North African desert and during intensive training at home, the APM at formation HQ and his provost company in the field began to take their place as the trained executives of traffic control. But all the actual traffic control companies, which had been specially raised to deal with the greatly increased administrative traffic problems in the army area and on the lines of communication, still came under the direct command and control of the 'Q' (Movements) staffs.

Then in 1943 was held Exercise 'Spartan'. 'Spartan' was a large-scale exercise of great importance in many ways and its very essence was speed of movement. It taught many important lessons, among which was that between movement planning and traffic control there had to be a link, the functions of which can be described as 'the executive control of operational movement' and the task of the link became threefold. First, to be the eyes of the staff planners, to keep them informed of the state of the roads over which movement is to take place, the capacity of the roads and the progress of movement. Second, to provide co-ordination between the various provost companies concerned in the road move. Third, to relate the deployment and tasks of the military police NCOs engaged on duty to the administration and organization of their units.

It is indeed surprising that these lessons still had to be stated as late as 1943. On the face of it they are fundamental, essential and obvious, but the fact remains that the umpires' report on 'Spartan' disclosed that once a formation was committed to movement, neither the APM, nor the provost company officers, anyway rearwards of division, were concerned with the deployment and duties of the military police who came directly under the control of the 'Q' (Movements) staff.

The link had to be found and it was already there waiting to be used in the APM and the provost company officers. They were undoubtedly the officers who should receive from the staff the movement plan, break it down and deploy provost in the executive control of operational movement. This came about through the publication of a pamphlet known as *The Common Doctrine*, which set out the relationship of the staff, the APM, the military policeman and the road-user and subsequently became the basis for large parts of Training Pamphlet No. 47, *Mechanized Movement bu Road*.

The provost officer's part in the control of operational movement was now established and, as related earlier, is itself the monument to Colonel Bassett F. G. Wilson, then DPM Home Forces and later PM 21 Army Group, whose perception and perseverance brought it about.

The acceptance of this rôle and the provision of the link called upon the provost officer to give considerable study to the problem of movement and of road networks, from which it followed that he became highly skilled in the subject of operational movement and the implementation of the staff's movement plans and the accepted adviser on them to the staff.

With the increase in mechanization, the speed of movement, the ever-increasing weight of traffic and the limited carrying capacity of roads, the degree of skill required became ever greater and was only to be found in experience. That is the answer that the past gives, that the Corps has created for itself a rôle in battle that has become indispensable; to get the right troops to the right place, in the right order, at the right time; that the task can only be carried out by specialists and is based on experience, that it is, in fact, a science.

This was appreciated by most formation commanders during the Second World War and the fact that it was true not only of warfare in Europe but in the desert and jungle too is amply stressed in a report by Major-General Davies, commanding 25th Indian Division who wrote on 1 September, 1943:

> 'On our ability to control our MT and to pass MT up to the battle in the correct priority, on narrow tracks and bottlenecks will depend our entire ability to fight as a division in jungle or close-country warfare.
>
> 'When in contact, therefore, the APM becomes the most important commander of division troops in the entire division. Unless he is fully acquainted with the Commander's intentions and plans, and unless he knows the priority on which the "feeding" of the battle front depends the necessary support of all arms cannot be made available to the troops in contact.
>
> 'In the planning of the battle, therefore, the APM is the Commander's right hand, his function is no longer "A" or "Q" but "G" Ops, and his presence at all planning conferences is essential.'

The answer indicated by the future is that, as in every science, experience must be handed on; that future exponents must be taught the fundamental theories when young, when receptive and with time before them to practise, to develop and to improve, so that when the time comes for the application they are themselves the experts.

The establishment of the corps of officers in RMP therefore means that the contribution that the Corps has to make in battle is highly technical, that it calls for specialist knowledge and the confidence that flows from it beyond that of the normal professional military knowledge of an officer.

All this was appreciated by many during the Second World War but it was not until December, 1951, that a scheme for implementing it began to be worked out by the then DPM War Office, Colonel P. Godfrey-Faussett whose provost experience was unquestionable and whose efforts were then successful in re-grading provost staff officers at formation HQs to their equivalent rank/titles held by 'G', 'A' and 'Q' staff officers and the other services. This was published in Army Council Instruction 903 of 1951. Provost staff appointments were redesignated as follows:

Provost Marshal	brigadier
PM (Head of service, overseas theatre)	colonel
Deputy Provost Marshal (War Office or Army)	colonel
Assistant Provost Marshal (Command or Corps)	lieutenant-colonel
Deputy Assistant Provost Marshal (Division or District)	major
Staff Captain (Provost) and (SIB)	captain

This was a good preparation for the coming struggle to provide the Corps with its own officers and coincided with the appointment of Brigadier R. H. Maxwell as Provost Marshal on 8 January, 1952. His keenness on the project and unremitting work over the next two years brought about the corps of officers with a rank structure offering sufficient career prospects to attract good Regular officers into RMP.

Between 15 May and 28 July, 1954, the first transfers of officers to the Corps in the Regular Army were gazetted. All were then serving with the Corps, many in higher rank than the following substantive ranks:

Majors	34
Captains	98
Lieutenants	30
Second Lieutenant	1
	163

Before this date officers had had the individual option since 1949 of wearing RMP badges and uniform if they so wished and many, in fact.

did so but this was the first gazetting, other than quartermasters, of officers in RMP in the Regular Army, shown as such in the Army List.

A further forty-three officers were transferred to RMP by 15 May, 1955, making 206 in all in the first year.

Officers of the TA and AER and National Service officers had previously been commissioned directly into RMP so no change was involved for them.

The Officers' Mess, Depot and Training Establishment RMP had been authorized to rank as a Corps Mess in 1951 and officers' Mess Dress was authorized in the autumn of 1956.

The first Regular Army officer to be commissioned directly into the Corps from the Royal Military Academy, Sandhurst, was Officer Cadet M. R. Biggs gazetted Second Lieutenant, RMP, on 29 July, 1955. In January, 1962, the first RMP officer, Major P. R. Stock was admitted to the Staff College in open competition and also later became the first provost officer to qualify at the Joint Services Staff College in 1968.

The final seal was put upon the corps of officers on 16 April, 1965, when the first RMP officer, Brigadier R. Davenport, succeeded to the ancient office of Provost Marshal. This precedent has now become accepted as policy and his successors have all been RMP officers.

Not only does this offer a wider career to the provost officer as an individual but, recalling the start made in 1933 in earmarking a small cadre of eighteen officers for provost duties on mobilization, the gradual change of attitude following Exercise 'Spartan' and the recognition accorded since the Second World War, it signified the Corps of Royal Military Police attaining its majority, in itself a fitting conclusion to this history.

In the highly professional Army of today the need for staff-trained provost officers is essential. The military police officer, like his warrant officers and non-commissioned officers, is an individualist by virtue of the nature of his duties, and a specialist. In fast-moving modern battle, insurgency, natural disaster or normal disciplinary duties he is trained to instant reaction using his wide knowledge of military matters, so that not only is he an effective instrument of command but fitted to command. And in his staff rôle he can ensure that the provost service can play an even more efficient rôle in the future and is used to the maximum advantage.

That this is so is the greatest tribute to the officers who have served the Corps so well in the past, including those many distinguished officers who in the appointment of Provost Marshal strove to improve and to help the service they led, and to the loyalty and devotion to duty of the warrant officers and non-commissioned officers of the Corps whose hard work has brought about this development and has been chronicled in this history.

APPENDIX I

COLONELS COMMANDANT CORPS OF ROYAL MILITARY POLICE

General Sir Miles C. Dempsey, GBE, KCB, DSO, MC	13 March, 1947–26 May, 1957
Lieut-General (later General and Field-Marshal) Sir A. James H. Cassels, GCB, KBE, DSO	27 May, 1957–29 February, 1968
General (later Field-Marshal) Sir Geoffrey H. Baker, GCB, CMG, CBE, MC, ADC (GEN)	1 March, 1968–6 March, 1971
Lieut-General (later General) Sir Cecil H. Blacker, GCB, OBE, MC, ADC (GEN)	7 March, 1971–22 July, 1976
Major-General P. J. H. Leng, CB, MBE, MC	23 July, 1976–

APPENDIX II

PROVOST MARSHALS FROM 16th CENTURY TO 1977

England (1511–1707), Great Britain (1707–1800), United Kingdom (1800–1945). United Kingdom and all Overseas Theatres and Commands (21 December, 1945 onwards).

1511 Henry Guylford (or Guildford)
1540 Osborne Itchingham
1544 Thomas Audley
1547 Sir James Wylford
1549 Sir Anthony Kingston
1557 Sir Gyles Poole
1569 Sir George Bowes
1582 Barnaby Googe
1588 Peter Crisp
1589 G. Acres
1589 Humphrey Coningesby
1590 Thomas Nevinson
1595 Sir Thomas Wylford
1597 William Bredyman
1598 Captain John Owen Tudor
1600 George Newcomen (or Newgent)
1643 William Smith
1663 Richard Thompson
1719 John Martyn
1723 Joseph Garton
1726 James Howard
1727 William Heath
1727 John Martyn
1734 John Amyott
1747 Christopher Predham
1796 John Hicks
1829 Death of John Hicks and end of the office of Provost Marshal-General. Provost Marshals were then appointed locally and no records are available until:
1861 Major T. Trout
1881 Captain W. Silk
1885 Major C. Broackes
1894 Major J. L. Emerson
1898 Major J. W. M. Wood, MVO
1910 Major R. J. A. Terry, DSO, MVO
1914 Colonel F. Darling

16 September, 1916–20 July, 1918 — Brigadier-General E. R. Fitzpatrick, CBE, DSO
4 November, 1918–4 November, 1919 — Brigadier-General A. H. C. James, DSO, MVO
5 November, 1919–31 December, 1920 — Brigadier-General H. S. Rogers, CMG, DSO
1 January, 1921–1924 — Colonel H. S. Rogers, CMG, DSO
1924–1928 — Colonel C. V. Edwards, CMG, DSO

1928–1930	Colonel G. T. Brierley, CMG, DSO
1930–1934	Colonel J. de V. Bowles, DSO
19 March, 1934–18 March, 1938	Colonel W. B. Hayley, DSO
19 March, 1938–1 September, 1939	Colonel S. V. Kennedy, MC
2 September, 1939–16 July, 1940	Colonel W. B. Hayley, DSO (Re-employed)
17 July, 1940–25 July, 1943	Brigadier (then Major-General) Sir Percy R. Laurie, KCVO, CBE, DSO
26 July, 1943–30 June, 1945	Major-General J. Seymour Mellor, CBE, MC
1 July, 1945–15 December, 1948	Major-General I. D. Erskine, CB, CBE, DSO (UK only until 21 December, 1945)
16 December, 1948–7 January, 1952	Brigadier L. F. E. Wieler, CB, CBE
8 January, 1952–20 January, 1955	Brigadier R. H. Maxwell, CB, ADC
21 January, 1955–22 January, 1958	Brigadier R. H. L. Oulton, CBE
23 January, 1958–16 December, 1960	Brigadier P. H. Richardson, DSO, OBE
17 December, 1960–9 September, 1962	Brigadier G. F. Upjohn, CBE
10 September, 1962–15 April, 1965	Brigadier C. G. Buttenshaw, DSO, OBE
16 April, 1965–19 March, 1968	Brigadier R. Davenport, OBE, RMP (First RMP officer to be appointed Provost Marshal [Army])
20 March, 1968–13 March, 1971	Brigadier L. F. Richards, CBE, RMP
14 March, 1971–27 March, 1974	Brigadier P. N. Davis, CBE, RMP
28 March, 1974–27 February, 1977	Brigadier D. B. Rendell, CBE MC, ADC, RMP
28 February, 1977–	Brigadier M. Matthews, MBE, RMP

APPENDIX III

PROVOST MARSHALS OVERSEAS

1611 Provost Marshal appointed in Colony of Virginia, America
1678 Thomas Lott, India
1679 Tileman Holt, India
1687 Provost Marshal appointed in St Helena (name unknown)
1703 Wheatley Garthorn, India
1707 Emphraim Goss, India
1727 George Tipping, Gibraltar
1857 Brevet-Major J. W. Carnegie, CB Siege of Lucknow (During the Indian Mutiny)
Appointed under Section 74 of the Army Act in Overseas Theatres.

EGYPT 1885	Lieut-Colonel J. H. Sandwich
SOUTH AFRICAN WAR 1899–1902	Major J. H. G. Byng (Later Field-Marshal Viscount Byng of Vimy)
GREAT WAR 1914–1918 B.E.F. FRANCE AND FLANDERS	
1914–1915	Colonel The Hon. Vesey Bunbury, VC
1915–1918	Brigadier-General W. Horwood
27 October, 1918–4 November, 1919	Brigadier-General H. S. Rogers, CMG, DSO
SECOND WORLD WAR 1939–1945 AND SUBSEQUENTLY:	
B.E.F. FRANCE AND BELGIUM 1939–1940	
2 September, 1939–25 May, 1940	Colonel S. V. Kennedy, MC
21 ARMY GROUP. BLA and BAOR	
(21 AG and BLA)	
22 July, 1943–22 June, 1945	Brigadier Bassett F. G. Wilson, OBE, MC
(BAOR)	
23 June, 1945–25 July, 1946	Brigadier J. N. Cheyney, OBE
26 July, 1946–December, 1946	Colonel L. C. East, DSO, OBE
December, 1946–21 December, 1947	Colonel H. V. McNally, OBE

3 February, 1948–16 July, 1949	Colonel R. A. Leeson, MBE
17 July, 1949–18 December, 1951	Colonel L. C. East, DSO, OBE
(BAOR and NORTHERN ARMY GROUP)	
15 January, 1952–11 February, 1955	Colonel A. H. Gillmore, OBE
12 February, 1955–12 May, 1955 (Temporary)	Lieut-Colonel F. H. Elliott, OBE, RMP
13 May, 1955–28 June, 1957	Colonel C. F. Read, OBE, RMP
(BAOR)	
29 June, 1957–27 August, 1959	Colonel W. A. Bickford, DSO, RMP
28 August, 1959–17 March, 1961	Colonel A. J. P. Ritchie, MBE, RMP
18 March, 1961–15 June, 1964	Colonel G. D. Pillitz, RMP
16 June, 1964–14 June, 1966	Colonel W. P. Ferrier, OBE, RMP
15 June, 1966–21 February, 1968	Colonel L. F. Richards, OBE, RMP
22 February, 1968–2 February, 1971	Colonel (then Brigadier) P. N. Davis, RMP
3 February, 1971–14 February, 1974	Colonel (then Brigadier) D. B. Rendell, MBE, MC, RMP
15 February, 1974–11 February, 1977	Colonel R. J. Sherville, MM, RMP
20 February, 1977–	Colonel P. A. W. G. Durrant, RMP
NEAR AND MIDDLE EAST	
(MEF)	
1940–21 May, 1944	Colonel F. C. Bryant, CMG, DSO, OBE
22 May, 1944–July, 1946	Colonel L. C. East, DSO, OBE
(MELF)	
July, 1946–July, 1947	Colonel D. W. L. Melville, OBE, MC
29 July, 1947–14 October, 1947 (Temporary)	Lieut-Colonel F. H. Elliott
15 October, 1947–16 March, 1949	Colonel G. A. C. Peter, OBE, MC
17 March, 1949–12 March, 1952	Colonel E. N. Everett-Heath
13 March, 1952–27 April, 1954	Colonel H. A. Bateson, OBE
28 April, 1954–1 March, 1957	Colonel E. D. Rash, RMP
2 March, 1957–18 February, 1960	Colonel A. G. Locksley, OBE, RMP
(MELF and NEARELF)	
19 February, 1960–30 September, 1962	Colonel C. F. Read, OBE, RMP (Last PM MELF and first and last PM NEARELF)
FAR EAST	
(DPM SOUTH-EAST ASIA)	
28 October, 1943–13 August, 1944	Lieut-Colonel P. D. J. Waters, MC
(PM SEAC)	
14 August, 1944–22 July, 1945	Colonel P. D. J. Waters, MC
(PM ALFSEA then PM SEALF)	
23 July, 1945–10 January, 1948	Brigadier R. A. Leeson, MBE
(PM FARELF)	
11 January, 1948–27 November, 1950	Colonel P. Godfrey-Faussett, OBE
28 November, 1950–25 July, 1952	Colonel H. V. McNally, OBE
26 July, 1952–21 June, 1954	Colonel T. H. H. Grayson, OBE
22 January, 1954–28 October, 1956	Colonel W. A. Bickford, DSO, RMP

29 October, 1956–5 May, 1959	Colonel A. J. P. Ritchie, MBE, RMP
6 May, 1959–18 April, 1962	Colonel J. F. Astley-Rushton, RMP
19 April, 1962–2 January, 1964	Colonel A. G. Locksley, OBE, RMP
3 January, 1964–15 March, 1965	Colonel R. Davenport, OBE, RMP
16 March, 1965–30 January, 1967	Colonel A. C. Rawlings, MBE, RMP
31 January, 1967–8 July, 1968	Colonel A. G. Joslin, MBE, RMP
8 September, 1968–20 September, 1970	Colonel J. B. Buckmaster, OBE, RMP (Last PM FARELF)

PERSIA AND IRAQ (PAIFORCE)

October, 1942–July, 1943	Colonel A. R. Forbes
July, 1943–1945	Colonel R. E. L. Warburton, MC
1945	Colonel P. V. L. Payne (Last PM PAIFORCE)

INDIA

July, 1943–31 March, 1945	Brigadier A. R. Forbes
1 April, 1945–22 February, 1946	Brigadier N. C. M. Sykes, CBE, MC
1946–1947	Colonel H. Shuker (Indian Army)
1947	Colonel R. M. Davies (Indian Army) (Last PM INDIA)

MEDITERRANEAN THEATRES

(NORTH AFRICA then AFHQ)	
July, 1943 December, 1944	Colonel N. C. M. Sykes, CBE, MC
(AFHQ then CMF)	
December, 1944 June, 1945	Colonel A. R. Rees-Reynolds, CBE
(CMF)	
June, 1945– December, 1946	Colonel H. V. McNally, OBE
December, 1946– 1947	Colonel N. M. Blair, OBE (Last PM CMF)

APPENDIX IV

OTHER SENIOR APPOINTMENTS IN THE UNITED KINGDOM

DEPUTY PROVOST MARSHALS/ASSISTANT ADJUTANTS GENERAL AT THE WAR OFFICE/MINISTRY OF DEFENCE/HQ PROVOST MARSHAL (ARMY)

(DPM to PM) 1941–1943 Colonel P. J. T. Pickthall, MC
1943–1944 Colonel B. D. Armstrong

(DPM (AAG) AG (PM) WAR OFFICE)
19 September, 1944–27 December, 1945 Colonel C. T. O'Callaghan, MC
28 December, 1945–21 December, 1947 Colonel P. Godfrey-Faussett, OBE
22 December, 1947–27 November, 1950 Colonel H. V. McNally, OBE
16 January, 1951–12 May, 1955 Colonel P. Godfrey-Faussett, CBE, RMP

(AAG (PM1)—WAR OFFICE)
13 May, 1955–29 April, 1960 Lieut-Colonel C. Wilkinson, OBE, RMP

(AAG (PM1) (ARMY) MOD)
30 April, 1960–6 November, 1963 Lieut-Colonel R. Davenport, OBE, RMP
7 November, 1963–28 September, 1965 Lieut-Colonel D. F. Salt, RMP

(AAG HQ PM (ARMY))
29 September, 1965–20 July, 1969 Lieut-Colonel A. G. Akerman, RMP
21 July, 1969–16 August, 1970 Lieut-Colonel G. I. Chatham, RMP

(DPM (ARMY)/AAG and Inspector of Training HQ PM (ARMY))
21 September, 1970
19 December, 1973 Lieut-Colonel (then Colonel) M. Matthews, MBE, RMP

20 December, 1973–20 November, 1975	Colonel P. A. W. G. Durrant, RMP
21 November, 1975–	Colonel J. F. Thomas, OBE, RMP

PROVOST MARSHALS UNITED KINGDOM LAND FORCES

1 April, 1972–30 June, 1974	Colonel F. S. Jeffreys, MC, RMP
1 July, 1974–16 November, 1975	Colonel J. F. Thomas, OBE, RMP
19 December, 1975–14 January, 1977	Colonel M. Matthews, MBE, RMP
17 January, 1977–	Colonel P. W. le S. Herring, OBE, RMP

DEPUTY PROVOST MARSHALS AND COMMANDERS RMP NORTHERN IRELAND

8 July, 1972–30 January, 1974	Colonel R. J. Sherville, MM, RMP
31 January, 1974–4 December, 1975	Colonel M. Matthews, MBE, RMP
5 December, 1975–1 December, 1976	Colonel P. A. W. G. Durrant, RMP
7 December, 1976–	Colonel J. Aspinall, RMP

COMMANDANTS DEPOT AND TRAINING ESTABLISHMENT (17 JULY, 1940–31 MARCH, 1968)/RMP TRAINING CENTRE (FROM 1 APRIL, 1968)

17 July, 1940–22 January, 1941	Lieut-Colonel R. T. S. Kitwood
23 January, 1941–18 August, 1942	Lieut-Colonel N. C. M. Sykes, MC
19 August, 1942–30 July, 1946	Lieut-Colonel E. F. L. Wright, OBE
31 July, 1946–6 September, 1948	Lieut-Colonel A. R. Forbes
7 September, 1948–15 January, 1951	Lieut-Colonel T. H. H. Grayson
16 January, 1951–28 February, 1954	Lieut-Colonel A. J. J. Somerville-McAlester, DSO
19 March, 1954–29 April, 1955	Lieut-Colonel C. F. Read, OBE, RMP (First RMP Officer to be appointed Commandant)
30 April, 1955–11 July, 1957	Lieut-Colonel D. V. W. Wakely, MC, RMP
12 July, 1957–15 February, 1960	Colonel C. F. Read, OBE, RMP
11 April, 1960–30 March, 1962	Colonel A. G. Locksley, OBE, RMP
31 March, 1962–4 December, 1963	Colonel J. F. Astley-Rushton, RMP
5 December, 1963–4 March, 1965	Colonel A. C. Rawlings, MBE, RMP
5 March, 1965–18 May, 1966	Colonel L. F. Richards, OBE, RMP
19 May, 1966–5 September, 1968	Colonel D. F. Salt, RMP
6 September, 1968–22 January, 1971	Colonel D. B. Rendell, MBE, MC, RMP
23 January, 1971–22 March, 1973	Colonel A. G. Akerman, RMP (also Inspector of Training)
23 March, 1973–10 May, 1976	Lieut-Colonel J. Aspinall, RMP
16 June, 1976–12 January, 1977	Lieut-Colonel P. W. le S. Herring, OBE, RMP
13 January, 1977–	Lieut-Colonel T. M. Plewman, RMP

APPENDIX V

HONOURS AND AWARDS ROYAL MILITARY POLICE NORTHERN IRELAND – AUGUST, 1969–APRIL, 1976

DSO
Lieut-Colonel B. A. Gait, DCM

OBE
Lieut-Colonel P. W. le S. Herring
Lieut-Colonel J. F. Thomas

MBE
Major R. G. Ding
WO1 J. H. Grandison
WO1 R. H. Poole, BEM (Gallantry)
Major A. H. Le Tissier
WO2 D. R. Williams
WO1 J. S. Wood

DCM
Sergeant D. J. Harmon

MM
Sergeant K. Bridgeman
Staff Sergeant N. Smith, BEM
Lance-Corporal S. J. Warke (WRAC Provost)
Corporal C. G. Williams

QGM
Staff Sergeant J. J. Campbell

BEM
Staff Sergeant J. J. Adamczyk
Staff Sergeant P. G. Allsop
Staff Sergeant R. J. Baldwin
Corporal J. H. Baseley (Gallantry)
Sergeant J. J. Beston
Sergeant J. K. Burton (Gallantry)
Corporal A. Darby-Jones
Lance-Corporal G. V. Eastham (Gallantry)
Staff Sergeant A. Hayton
Staff Sergeant R. Lodge
Corporal J. M. McKinley (Gallantry)
Staff Sergeant P. J. McQuillan
Corporal J. H. Owen
Staff Sergeant N. Smith, MM
Corporal J. R. White
Corporal J. H. Wilson

MENTIONED IN DESPATCHES
Corporal L. N. Barrass
WO1 R. Bend
Captain (QM) F. W. Chipperfield
Staff Sergeant A. Clint
Corporal E. Cox (WRAC Provost)
Corporal G. E. Crossley
Corporal J. Esson
Sergeant C. L. Evans
Corporal J. Evans
Captain R. T. Gant
Sergeant M. J. Gard
Corporal J. Greenoak
Captain D. E. Hammond
Sergeant D. F. Harding
Sergeant M. J. Harries

Captain J. L. Lawson (WRAC Provost)
Corporal R. J. Malt
Sergeant J. McCorkell
Corporal I. A. Mowatt (RAF Police—attached)
Major T. M. Plewman
Major B. A. Rawlings
Squadron Leader J. N. Roberts (RAF Police—attached)
Corporal B. R. Rolf
Private K. Taylor (WRAC Provost)
WO1 R. V. Tilburey
Corporal G. F. Yates

APPENDIX VI

REVISED ORGANIZATION HOME AND ABROAD

	Sergeant-Majors (WO Cl. I)	Regimental Quarter-Master Sergeant (WO Cl. II)	Company Sergeant-Majors (WO Cl. II)	Company Quarter-Master Sergeants	Sergeants	Corporals	Privates (Lance-Corporals)	Totals
HOME								
ALDERSHOT COMMAND								
No 1 Coy	(*a*)1	–	–	1	3	5	29	39
No 2 Coy	–	–	1	–	3	5	29	38
Bordon Section	–	–	–	–	1	1	7	9
Deepcut Section	–	–	–	–	1	1	7	9
EASTERN COMMAND								
Colchester Section	–	–	–	–	1	1	7	9
Shorncliffe Sections	–	–	–	–	1	3	14	18
Dover Section	–	–	–	–	1	1	7	9
Chatham Section	–	–	–	–	1	1	7	9
Woolwich Sections	–	–	–	–	1	3	14	18
NORTHERN COMMAND								
Catterick Company	–	–	1	–	3	5	29	38
SCOTTISH COMMAND								
Edinburgh Section	–	–	–	–	1	1	7	9
SOUTHERN COMMAND								
No 3 Coy, Bulford	–	–	–	1	2	4	22	29
Tidworth Section	–	–	–	–	1	1	7	9
Larkhill Section	–	–	–	–	1	1	7	9
Devonport Section	–	–	–	–	1	1	7	9
Portsmouth Sections	–	–	–	–	2	2	14	18
LONDON DISTRICT								
No 4 Coy	–	–	1	–	2	4	22	29
NORTHERN IRELAND DISTRICT								
Belfast Section	–	–	–	–	1	1	7	9
DEPOT AND SCHOOL OF INSTRUCTION	1	1	1	–	(b)3	4	19	29
Total Home	*2*	*1*	*4*	*2*	*30*	*45*	*262*	*346*

CORPS OF MILITARY POLICE
(1st APRIL, 1936)

		Horses			Vehicles				
Civilians	*Officers*	*Riding*	*Draught*	*Total horses*	*2-seater motor vehicles*	*Motor cycles solo*	*Bicycles pedal*	*Motor Vans*	*G.S. Wagon*
–	(1)	7	–	7	3	18	–	–	–
				(1)					
–	–	7	–	7	3	18	–	–	–
–	–	–	–	–	1	3	–	–	–
–	–	–	–	–	1	3	–	–	–
–	–	–	–	–	1	3	–	–	–
–	–	7	–	7	1	3	–	–	–
–	–	–	–	–	1	3	–	–	–
–	–	–	–	–	1	3	–	–	–
–	–	–	–	–	–	9	–	–	–
–	–	7	–	7	4	21	–	–	–
–	–	–	–	–	1	–	–	–	–
–	–	7	–	7	3	6	–	–	–
–	–	–	–	–	–	3	–	–	–
–	–	–	–	–	–	3	–	–	–
–	–	–	–	–	–	3	–	–	–
–	–	–	–	–	1	6	–	–	–
–	–	–	–	–	–	–	4	–	–
–	–	–	–	–	1	1	–	–	–
–	(1)	9	2	11	1	–	4	–	1
				(1)					
–	(2)	*44*	*2*	*46*	*23*	*106*	*8*	–	*1*
				(2)					

	Sergeant-Majors (WO Cl. I)	Regimental Quarter-Master Sergeant (WO Cl. II)	Company Sergeant-Majors (WO Cl. II)	Company Quarter-Master Sergeants	Sergeants	Corporals	Privates (Lance-Corporals)	Totals
ABROAD								
EGYPT								
Cairo Company	–	–	1	–	3	5	29	38
Abbassia Company	–	–	–	1	1	3	15	20
Moascar Company	–	–	–	1	1	3	15	20
Alexandria Section	–	–	–	–	1	1	7	9
MALTA								
Malta Section	–	–	–	–	1	1	7	9
GIBRALTAR								
Gibraltar Section	–	–	–	–	1	1	7	9
CHINA								
Hong Kong Company	–	–	1	–	1	3	15	20
Shanghai Section	–	–	–	–	1	1	7	9
MALAYA								
Singapore Company	–	–	1	–	1	3	15	20
Total abroad	–	–	*3*	*2*	*11*	*21*	*117*	*154*
TOTAL HOME and ABROAD	2	1	7	4	41	(c) 66	(e) 379	500

(*a*) RSM for Nos 1 and 2 Companies.

(*b*) Includes one orderly room sergeant (may be a staff-sergeant or warrant officer, Cl. 2, according to service).

(*c*) Includes 12 lance-sergeants.

(*d*) Syces. In addition, native servants are allowed for—Sergeants and men's mess, Cairo; men's mess, Abbassia; Section, Alexandria, Section Moascar, on the scale laid down in War Office letters No 60/Abroad/308 (AG1) dated 9 September, 1930.

(*e*) 50 per cent paid lance-corporals.

(*f*) For officers holding the appointment of Assistant Marshal (included in Peace Establishments, Part IV).

Civilians	Officers	Riding	Draught	Total horses	2-seater motor vehicles	Motor cycles solo	Bicycles pedal	Motor Vans	G.S. Wagon
		Horses				Vehicles			
(d)3	(1)	7	–	7 (1)	1	1	–	3	–
–	–	7	–	7	–	–	–	–	–
–	–	7	–	7	–	–	–	–	–
–	–	–	–	–	–	–	–	–	–
–	–	–	–	–	1	1	–	–	–
–	–	–	–	–	–	2	–	–	–
–	–	–	–	–	–	–	–	–	–
–	–	–	–	–	2	–	2	–	–
–	–	–	–	–	1	–	3	–	–
3	(*1*)	*21*	–	*21* (*1*)	*5*	*4*	*5*	*3*	–
3	(*f*) (3)	65	2	67 (3)	28	110	13	3	1

APPENDIX VII

REVISED ORGANIZATION CORPS OF MILITARY POLICE DEPOT AND SCHOOL OF INSTRUCTION (1st APRIL, 1936)

PERSONNEL	*Administrative*	*Instructional*	*Total*
Regimental sergeant-major (WO Class 1)	1	–	1
Regimental quarter-master sgt (WO Class 2)	1	–	1
Company sergeant-major (WO Class 2)	–	1	1
Total warrant officers	2	1	3
Orderly room sergeant *(a)*	1	–	1
Sergeant instructors	–	2	2
Total sergeants	1	2	3
Corporal instructors	–	4	4
Total corporals	–	4	4
Clerks	3	–	3
Storeman	1	–	1
Cooks	2	–	2
Transport driver	1	–	1
Institute and sergeants' mess	1	–	1
Police	2	–	2
Sanitary	1	–	1
Telephone orderlies and post duties	1	–	1
General duties	1	–	1
Stable duties	5	–	5
Q.M. Stores	1	–	1
Total lance-corporals and privates	19	–	19
TOTAL ALL RANKS	22	7	29

Officers' chargers	1(*b*)
Riding horses	9
Draught horses	2
Motor Cars, 2-seater	1
Bicycles	4
Wagons, G.S.	1

(*a*) May be sergeant, staff-sergeant, or WO Class 2 according to service.
(*b*) For APM (extra regimental).

INDEX